Healing Trauma

attachment, mind, body, and brain

The Norton Series on Interpersonal Neurobiology
Daniel J. Siegel, M.D., Series Editor

The field of mental health is in a tremendously exciting period of growth and conceptual reorganization. Independent findings from a variety of scientific endeavors are converging in an interdisciplinary view of the mind and mental well-being. An "interpersonal neurobiology" of human development enables us to understand that the structure and function of the mind and brain are shaped by experiences, especially those involving emotional relationships.

The Norton Series on Interpersonal Neurobiology will provide cutting-edge, multidisciplinary views that further our understanding of the complex neurobiology of the human mind. By drawing on a wide range of traditionally-independent fields of research—such as neurobiology, genetics, memory, attachment, complex systems, anthropology, and evolutionary psychology—these texts will offer mental health professionals a review and synthesis of scientific findings often inaccessible to clinicians. These books aim to advance our understanding of human experience by finding the unity of knowledge, or "consilience," that emerges with the translation of findings from numerous domains of study into a common language and conceptual framework. The series will integrate the best of modern science with the healing art of psychotherapy.

A Norton Professional Book

Healing Trauma

attachment, mind, body, and brain

MARION F. SOLOMON
DANIEL J. SIEGEL
Editors

W. W. Norton & Company
New York • London

For information about permission to reproduce
selections from this book, write to
Permissions, W. W. Norton & Company, Inc.,
500 Fifth Avenue, New York, NY 10110

Production Manager: Leeann Graham
Manufacturing by Haddon Craftsmen, Inc.

Library of Congress Cataloging-in-Publication Data

Healing trauma : attachment, mind, body, and brain / Marion F. Solomon and
Daniel J. Siegel, editors.
          p.   cm.—(The Norton series on interpersonal neurobiology)
"A Norton professional book."
Includes bibliographic references and index.
ISBN 0-393-70396-7
1. Post-traumatic stress disorder—Treatment.   2. Psychic trauma—Treatment.
3. Psychophysiology.   I. Solomon, Marion Fried.   II. Siegel, Daniel J., 1957–
III. Series. [DNLM: 1. Stress Disorders, Post-Traumatic—therapy.
2. Psychophysiology.   3. Psychotherapy—methods. WM 170 H4343 2003]

RC552.P67 .H426   2003
616.85'21'06—dc21   2002038070

W. W. Norton & Company, Inc., 500 Fifth Avenue, New York, N.Y. 10110
                    www.wwnorton.com

W. W. Norton & Company Ltd., Castle House, 75/76 Wells St., London W1T 3QT

                3   4   5   6   7   8   9   0

To Matthew,
whose love gives meaning to
"earned secure attachment"

— M. F. S.

To Caroline,
my in-house healer

— D. J. S.

Table of Contents

List of Contributors

Kelley Yost Abrams, Ph.D., completed her doctorate in developmental psychology at the University of California, Berkeley (2000), and is currently Principal Research Psychologist and Evaluation Specialist for Through the Looking Glass, a non-profit organization serving families with disability. Her dissertation research investigated frightened, threatening, and dissociative parental behavior and disorganized infant attachment. She is a certified coder in several methods for assessing attachment, and has conducted international trainings in attachment theory and its research methodologies.

Diana Fosha, Ph.D., is Associate Clinical Professor at The Derner Institute of Advanced Psychological Studies, Adelphi University, New York and Director of Training of IESA (International Experiential Short-Term Dynamic Psychotherapy Association). She is also the author of *The Transforming Power of Affect: A Model for Accelerated Change*, the developer of AEDP (Accelerated Experiential-Dynamic Psychotherapy) and maintains a private practice in New York.

Erik Hesse, Ph.D., is Director of the Social Development Project at University of California, Berkeley, and Adjunct Scientist at Leiden University, the Netherlands.

Mary Main, Ph.D., is Professor of Psychology at the University of California, Berkeley.

Louise Maxfield is a doctoral candidate at Lakehead University, Thunder Bay, Ontario. An experienced clinician, she has taught hundreds of workshops on the treatment of abuse and trauma, and has published numerous articles and book chapters.

Robert J. Neborsky, M.D., is in the private practice of psychiatry in Del Mar, California. He serves as a Clinical Professor of Psychiatry at UCSD School of Medicine. He is also Medical Director of Lifespan Learning Institute and the recipient of the 2002 Distinguished Psychiatrist Award from UCLA School of Medicine.

Anne Rifkin, M.A., is a doctoral candidate in psychology (cognition, brain, and behavior) at the University of California, Berkeley. Her research interests include attachment across species and within families, and how attachment relates to emotional, physiological, and cognitive development. Her dissertation study focuses on frontal and hippocampal functioning as related to HPA axis responses to stress.

Allan N. Schore, Ph.D., is on the clinical faculty of the University of California at Los Angeles Medical School. He is the author of *Affect Regulation and the Origin of the Self*, as well as numerous articles and chapters in various disciplines. He is the editor of the Special Issue of the *Infant Mental Health Journal*, "Contributions from the Decade of the Brain to Infant Mental Health," is on the editorial board of the journal *Neuropsychoanalysis*, and has written the Foreward to the reissue of John Bowlby's volume *Attachment*. He has been in private psychotherapy practice for over three decades and currently resides in Northridge, CA.

Francine Shapiro, Ph.D., is a Senior Research Fellow at the Mental Research Institute and founder and President Emeritus of the EMDR Humanitarian Assistance Programs. She is a recipient of the International Sigmund Freud Award for Psychotherapy of the City of Vienna and the Distinguished Scientific Achievement in Psychology Award of the California Psychological Association.

Daniel J. Siegel, M.D., is an associate clinical Professor on the faculty of the Foundation for Psychocultural Research-UCLA Center for Culture, Brain, and Development. He is a practicing child, adolescent, and adult psychiatrist, the author of *The Developing Mind*, coauthor of *Parenting from the Inside Out*, and series editor for the Norton Series on Interpersonal Neurobiology.

Marion F. Solomon, Ph.D., is founder of the Lifespan Learning Institute in Los Angeles, dedicated to advanced training and research in psychotherapy; Senior Extension Faculty at UCLA, Department of Humanities, Sciences and Social Sciences. She is author of *Narcissism and Intimacy* and *Lean on Me: The Power of Positive Dependency in Intimate Relationships*, as well as co-Author of *Short Term Therapy For Long Term Change*. She resides in Los Angeles, CA.

Bessel A. van der Kolk, M.D., is Medical director of the Trauma Center of the Human Resource Institute Brookline, MA. He is the author of *Traumatic Stress: The Effects of Overwhelming Experience on Mind, Body, and Society.*

Introduction

Daniel J. Siegel
Marion F. Solomon

Born out of the excitement of a convergence of ideas and passions, this book provides a synthesis of the work of researchers, clinicians, and theoreticians who are leaders in the field of trauma, attachment, and psychotherapy. As we move into the third millennium, the field of mental health is in an exciting position to bring together diverse ideas. Drawn from a range of disciplines—neurobiology, developmental psychology, traumatology, and systems theory—these ideas illuminate our understanding of human experience. The convergent perspective resulting from this interdisciplinary outlook provides the clinician with a new view on the origins of trauma and brings into focus innovative approaches to the healing process.

The contributors to this volume gathered initially for a conference in which the energy and enthusiasm of the speakers and participants alike were electrifying. The spirit in which ideas were shared and the eagerness with which the participants from varied disciplines sought to find common ground are woven into these pages. Our hope is to use the materials made available from different disciplines and construct a foundation for clinicians upon which they can build on their practice of healing those who have experienced trauma. The contributors emphasize the ways in which the social environment (including relationships in childhood, adulthood, and the treatment milieu) changes aspects of the structure of the brain and, ultimately, alters the mind. Various chapters translate complex brain phenomena into readily understandable models that have immediate applicability for clinical practice. These approaches incorporate the intricate and powerful ways in which biology and environment continuously interact to shape perception and behavior. A new paradigm for treatment is made possible by these integrative ideas.

This book examines the following crucial issues: 1) how life experiences influence the maturation of the brain *and* mind in achieving mental health; 2) the central role of emotion in the functioning of healthy minds, brains, and relationships; 3) the importance of the body in influencing the nature of the mind and subjective experience; and 4) the impact of both positive and traumatic experiences on the development of coherent functioning, interpersonal relatedness, and the emergence of mental disturbance.

Recent analyses of responses to trauma reveal that adults exposed to overwhelming events might have both acute and long-lasting effects. Though individuals may go on to have a number of psychological and somatic sequelae of trauma including depression and anxiety, the minority (around 15%) will develop the full syndrome of posttraumatic stress disorder (PTSD) (Yehuda, 2002). Shalev (in press) has described PTSD as a "disorder of recovery" in which the initial response to trauma continues and evolves into a disabling condition. Specific factors—i.e., adverse early childhood experiences including emotional abuse as well as posttrauma situations such as depression and loss of social supports—might be conditions associated with impaired recovery. Studies confirm earlier findings that terror and dissociation at the time of and immediately following a traumatic event are also robust risk factors for developing PTSD (Charles Marmar, unpublished data from studies of the aftermath of the September 11, 2001 terrorist attacks in New York on first responders).

Basic science studies on the generation as well as extinction of fear responses can further help to understand some possible mechanisms of both PTSD and its treatment. The limbic structure of the brain, the amygdala, has been shown to enable the encoding of fear. Studies of a higher cortical part of the brain, the medial aspect of the prefrontal cortex, revealed that prefrontal circuits are involved in the extinction of fear (Milad & Quirk, 2002). Though performed in rodents, these initial studies suggest that the prefrontal cortex might be essential in the new learning required to modulate the effects of the initial acquisition of a fear response. In other words, acute trauma might lead to an amygdala response of fear, but the majority of individuals (85%) will go on to "recover" from this acute learning phase via the possible involvement of the prefrontal cortex.

We can propose that those that go on to develop PTSD, and other prolonged conditions following experiences of helplessness and terror, might be those that are not able to harness the new learning carried out via the prefrontal regions. As we will see in the chapters ahead, the prefrontal cortex integrates the social, emotional, bodily, and autobiographical aspects of an individual's life. The identified risk factors of early adverse life experiences, peritraumatic dysregulation (in the form of hyperarousal or dissociation), and posttraumatic social support difficulties can each be linked to the self-regulatory role of the prefrontal cortex.

Why would these pre-, peri- and post-event factors be associated with risk for long-term negative outcomes after exposure to trauma? When combined with the emerging view of how early adverse experiences may alter the genetically influenced development of brain structure and function (Meaney 2001; Suomi, in press), we can conceptualize how the experientially sculpted prefrontal cortex can serve as the mediator of risk following trauma. Early adverse experiences might impair the ability of the prefrontal cortex to respond to new overwhelming events via balanced self-regulation. The capacity to modulate deeper emotional responses of the amygdala, to maintain social networks of support, and to find new "meaning" from horrific events are each under the influence of prefrontal circuitry. In this manner, understanding early experience, self-regulation, and the ongoing impact of relationships on neural and mental function can help us understand both the origin of risk following trauma and the necessary ingredients for prevention and intervention.

The first four chapters of this book offer explorations of the possible developmental origins of the risk factors for developing long-term sequalae of trauma. The second four chapters build on this developmental and descriptive framework by examining detailed approaches to treatment. By providing an overview of both the development and treatment of trauma, this book offers a broad framework for understanding both the genesis and the treatment of difficulties following traumatic experiences.

In the first chapter, Daniel Siegel considers the mind as a process that regulates the flow of energy and information in order to create a conceptual foundation for mental health and mental disturbance. Trauma impacts the self by impairing the integrative capacities of the mind that are themselves ultimately created by processes of neural integration. From this perspective, developmental trauma can impair the acquisition of self-regulation, created by a process that is dependent upon integration for its adaptive functioning. Acute trauma may create impairments in the integration of sensory, emotional, bodily, and perceptual implicit memory encoding into the contextually woven explicit forms of semantic or autobiographical memory. With impaired integration (resulting from trauma), the mind becomes restricted in its capacity to respond flexibly. Such restrictions might be revealed in nonintegrated memory processes as well as in impairments to self-regulation.

Why is the process of integration important? Drawing on complexity theory may provide some answers. When combined with differentiation, integration allows for the achievement of the most complex states. Systems that are able to move toward maximal complexity are thought to allow the most stable, flexible, and adaptive states to occur. Trauma, however, blocks the capacity of the mind to adapt by inhibiting the process of integration. When we delve more deeply into the regions of the brain that enable neural integration to occur, we can examine the role of such areas as the hippocampus, prefrontal regions, anterior cingulate, corpus callosum, and cerebellum. Future studies that address these regions of the brain and their function may reveal the ways in which trauma specifically impacts the brain's capacity to create stable, flexible, and adaptive states of mind.

Examining the layers of integrative processes including those at the level of neurons, mental processes, and interpersonal relationships, can help us focus on the "health" of the systems in which our lives are lived. Trauma can impair integration at each and every one of these levels. The different psychotherapeutic strategies described in this book may achieve their positive effects by entering this complex system at a variety of entry points. Each strategy can facilitate a cascade of interdependent integrative processes up and down the mutually reinforcing levels and relations that constitute the self.

The importance of viewing the cascading processes of trauma across the dimension of time is revealed in the second chapter. In Chapter Two Eric Hesse, Mary Main, Kelly Yost Abrams, and Anne Rifkin, provide a fascinating, in-depth view of "second generation" effects of trauma. This view enables us to envision the process of interpersonal integration as it occurs from one generation to the next. As minds become integrated within attachment relationships, impairments to balanced forms of self-regulation can be transmitted from one individual to another. Main and Hesse have already offered important research that helps us to understand how the relationship between parent and child is influenced by the parent's mental processes. These mental processes are revealed in the semi-structured narrative discourse elicited by the Adult Attachment Interview. The contributions of Main and Hesse, plainly evident in this comprehensive and thought-provoking chapter, reveal the intricate and profound ways in which the attachment paradigm can contribute to our insights into how familial experiences impact the development of our minds.

Chapter Two provides an overview and in-depth discussion in such a way that the clinician unfamiliar with this exciting field of study can gain a basic understanding of the crucial research findings and then move into the clinically useful details of mental processes illuminated by the AAI. The interview is unique in its capacity to assess the unresolved aspect of an individual's present state of mind. A history of trauma or of loss does not, by itself, predict negative effects. Rather, the finding of a lack of resolution is the crucial component in determing the likelihood of negative effects. Children raised by non-maltreating parents who themselves have unresolved loss or trauma provide these children with specific kinds of interactions. These interactions are likely to create a state of alarm that is a "biological paradox"—the attachment system becomes activated by the emotions of terror and drives the child to seek proximity to the very person who has induced the state of terror. Unresolved parental states can produce sudden shifts in parental expressions that are frightening and disturbingly confusing to the child. In Chapter Two the authors carefully note an extremely useful way for the practitioner to clarify the conditions that do, and those that do not, cause disorganization in the child. Noting the evolutionary origins of our attachment system and the biological roots of our survival mechanisms, Hesse, Main, Abrams, and Rifkin offer a new synthesis of material that can help us in our clinical understanding of developmental trauma.

Chapter Three, by Allan Schore, builds on the framework of development and trauma by leading us into the depths of the neural circuitry at the core of the crucial integrative process of self-regulation. As the flow of information and energy in the brain creates the mind, the regulation of this flow is central to how the self develops. Schore's important contributions to our understanding of self-regulation and its impairment by traumatic attachments—upon which he draws in this chapter—have provided us with a view into the complex mechanisms of our social and emotional brains in their healthly and disorderly states.

Addressing the circuits of the prefrontal region, Schore synthesizes the findings from a variety of disciplines and reveals how this integrative neural area balances the two branches of the autonomic nervous system. (Each of these branches has its regulatory endpoint in the right orbitofrontal region.) The sympathetic branch of the autonomic nervous system acts as an "accelerator," while the parasympathetic branch serves as the "brake." The regulatory "clutch" of the orbitofrontal cortex can develop well with secure attachments, but develops poorly with insecure (especially disorganized), attachments. Schore postulates that, under certain conditions, parent-child relationships founded in rejection produce underarousal of the autonomic nervous system and predispose the child to develop an antisocial personality. In contrast, abusive parenting may lead to excessive arousal and a predisposition on the part of the child to both disorganization and borderline personality disorder. Understanding the possible ways in which interpersonal relationships early in life may impact the development of the neural pathways involved in self-regulation can greatly help us in our clinical understanding of the effect of trauma on personality organization.

Extending this theme, Bessel van der Kolk offers a broad overview of the history and phenomenology of Post Traumatic Stress Disorder. Van der Kolk's work has helped us to appreciate the wisdom of our past luminaries, such as Janet and Freud. His research has also provided important new insights into our current understanding of the ways in which trauma can impact the brain. PTSD can present in one-time experiences, but, more often, those who seek help have had chronic exposure to overwhelming events or traumatic attachments that create complex PTSD.

In Chapter Four, van der Kolk reports on his explorations into the activity of the brain of subjects during the reading of a script recounting the theme of their personal trauma. These findings suggest that the ability to speak (via left hemisphere Broca's area activity) is shutdown during a flashback. At the same time, the non-verbal right hemisphere's visual cortex becomes activated. This finding parallels van der kolk's impression, drawn from his clinical work, that a disconnection arises that impairs the ability to create a verbal narrative during the flooding of unresolved traumatic memories. Chapter Four explores the notion, suggested over one hundred years ago by Janet, that post-traumatic states are fundamentally impairments in the integration of the self.

In Chapter Five, Francine Shapiro and Louise Maxfield offer an overview of Eye Movement Desensitization and Reprocessing (EMDR), a powerful and important treatment for individuals with various forms of trauma. EMDR is a form of therapy that can be integrated with a wide range of approaches to healing. EMDR addresses comprehensively the dysfunctional aftermath of both major and minor traumas that have impacted the individual by creating symptoms and impediments to flexibility and the freedom to feel the joy of life.

The chapter introduces the stages involved in EMDR treatment and explores its application to cases involving traumatic experiences as well as suboptimal attachment relationships. In protocols that encourage the individual to focus on emotional and somatic representations while at the same time considering word-based thoughts about the self (both negative and then preferred positive cognitions), EMDR facilitates an effective accelerated information processing of both traumatic, and reparative positive experiences. This empirically supported therapy likely facilitates a form of simultaneous activation and associative process that efficiently promotes multiple layers of representational integration. In this way, this chapter furthers the overall theme we are proposing for this book – effective therapy for trauma involves the facilitation of neural integration.

Diana Fosha, in Chapter Six, provides an in-depth view of the central role of emotion in both the adaptation to trauma and in the process of healing. In the first part of the chapter, accelerated experiential-dynamic psychotherapy

(AEDP) is described. In this form of therapy the therapist explores affective experience and utilizes intense emotional transactions between patient/client and therapist to alter rigid adaptations to past traumatic events. The approach involves the key elements of the dyadic regulation of affective states, the experience and expression of emotion, the empathic reflection of self, somatic focusing, and reflections on the experience of transformation in a meta-cognitive process that join client with therapist.

The AEDP approach to treatment that Fosha describes involves the synthesis of a number of processes, including the interpersonal regulation of emotion, within the three phases of attunement, disruption, and repair. In the second part of this chapter, there is a detailed recounting two therapy sessions that illustrate some of the real life, moment-to-moment emotional transactions found in the therapeutic process. These interactions can reveal the ways in which emotion is fundamentally a process of integration. In this manner, the emotion-activating process can be seen to involve the internal integration of bodily/emotional/language-based processes with the interpersonal integration of emotional states. This rich integration occurs within the authentic communication featured in the therapeutic relationship. Changes in the trauma-induced impairments to integrative functioning—both internal and interpersonal—are at the heart of the emotional process that distinguishes this approach to healing.

In Chapter Seven, Robert Neborsky offers his synthesis of the work done in the short-term intensive dynamic psychotherapy model as it pertains to the attachment framework. At the core of this approach is the patient/client experience of genuine feelings from the past in the present moment. Layers of defense might have been constructed based on suboptimal attachment experiences characterized by a range of feelings embedded in what Neborsky calls a "primitive aggressive self-organization." This hypothesized mental structure is comprised of a complex mixture of feelings and defenses that have formed in response to earlier experiences of an insecure attachment. These processes are the target of the therapist's interventions.

Neborsky offers case examples that illustrate the role of the "central dynamic sequence" in which feelings are explored and defenses revealed as pressure is applied encouraging the patient to experience genuine, core emotions. In Neborsky's words, this process makes it possible that "dissociated feeling states can be rapidly experienced, processed, and integrated." What is the form of integration that this approach facilitates? One can propose that the focus on defense mechanisms, outlined in this chapter, highlights the ways in which suboptimal attachment experiences have produced adaptations that are actually the "dis-integration" of innate, authentic core (pre-conscious) experiencing from secondary, externally adaptive (conscious) processes and responses. For example, adaptation to suboptimal attachment experiences enables the child to *not* consciously feel the longing for closeness that might become unbearable in sustained family environments of rejection and emotional neglect. Later in life, such effective adaptations to suboptimal attachment relationships become restrictive processes that impair future responses to stress and inhibit the readiness to enter into authentic ways of being (with oneself and within intimate relationships with others). The treatment process, focusing as it does on defenses, would then enable not only traumatic memories and their somatic and affective components to become integrated into the larger authentic, spontaneous processes of self. They would also permit the self to become free to engage in direct, life-affirming, open relationships with others. Releasing the disintegrative grasp of rigid defenses frees the self to become integrated in memory, emotion, and interpersonal connections.

The final chapter of the book directly explores the nature of interpersonal relationships. In Chapter Eight, Marion Solomon provides an overview of an attachment-oriented approach to couples therapy. Building on the concepts of the prior chapters, Solomon constructs a model of the therapeutic experience that focuses on the processes of connection, disruption, and repair. Research on relationships—including attachment, romantic, and therapeutic—suggests the inevitability of disruption in the contingent communication that integrates people within these relationships. The key to a healthy relationship is the capacity to remain emotionally accessible during the repair and reconnection that needs to occur to maintain the vitality of the interpersonal connections. Suboptimal attachments—including those that lead to organized and disorganized forms of insecure attachment—can produce disturbances in the capacity for healthy intimacy. Re-enactments of earlier small and large *t* traumatic experiences within the relationship can create repeating patterns of dysfunctional communication. Such developmental histories challenge the couple and therapist alike to discover new ways to find and then liberate rewarding interpersonal connections.

Harnessing the power of this paradigm, Solomon suggests that therapists can help transform maladaptive patterns from earlier insecure attachments by focusing couples on the nature of the defensive processes that block effective repair. At the core of this approach is facilitating the attitude that people are "doing the best they can," but that prior efforts to survive have left each member of the pair with a defensive system that blocks authentic relatedness and inhibits each person's capacity to bounce back after disruptions. Seeing such disruptions as an opportunity to deepen intimacy and enhance self-understanding can promote a more adaptive and flexible way of being within intimate relationships. With disconnection, two people become "dis-integrated" in their sense of joining. With repair interpersonal integration is restored. An openness to deepening layers of integration between two people, and within each individual, can create a renewed sense of vitality and enhance the journey of life.

The contributors to this book draw upon decades of clinical experience in the effort to deepen our understanding of trauma and its treatment. By focusing on the many layers of reality that compose our lives, the authors aim to integrate the latest scientific findings of attachment, mind, body and brain so as to further define the therapeutic relationship and the healing process. Trauma is painful. Attachment trauma is tragic, creating impediments to our capacity to adapt and connect to others. Healing professionals are challenged to bear witness to this pain and join together in the mission to help people heal unresolved trauma and achieve lives that are not only free from symptoms but filled with a new sense of vitality and hope. It is *our* hope that these chapters will offer you new ideas and approaches that will help you in the important and sacred task of helping others heal.

References

Meaney, M. J. (2001). Maternal care, gene expression, and the transmission of individual differences in stress reactivity across generations. *Annual Review of Neuroscience, 24,* 1161–1192.

Milad, M. R., & Quirk, G. J. (2002). Neurons in medial prefrontal cortex signal memory for fear extinction. *Nature, 420*(7),70–74.

Shalev, A. (in press). Treating survivors in the acute aftermath of traumatic events. In R. Yehuda (Ed.), *Psychological trauma,* Washington, DC: American Psychiatric Press.

Suomi, S. J. (in press). How gene-environment interactions can shape the development of socioemotional regulation in rhesus monkeys. In B. S. Zuckerman & A. F. Lieberman (Eds.), *Socioemotional regulation: Dimensions, developmental trends, and influences.* Skillman, NJ: Johnson & Johnson.

Yehuda, R. (2002). Post-traumatic stress disorder. *New England Journal of Medicine, 346*(2), 108–114.

1

An Interpersonal Neurobiology of Psychotherapy: The Developing Mind and the Resolution of Trauma

Daniel J. Siegel

Overview: Interpersonal Neurobiology

The field of mental health is in a tremendously exciting period. Recent findings from cognitive neuroscience have revealed some new insights into how mental processes emerge from the activity of the brain. Independent advances in the science of development, especially longitudinal studies in the field of attachment, shed new light on how early experiences influence such fundamental processes as memory, emotion, and the regulation of behavior. The often isolated fields of neurobiology and attachment have a fascinating set of convergent findings relevant to the understanding of trauma. Examination of these and other areas of research can offer us new ways of understanding how the developing mind is shaped by the interaction of interpersonal experience and neurobiological processes in the creation of the human mind. This approach has been described as "interpersonal neurobiology" in earlier writings (Siegel, 1999, 2001a) and will serve as the conceptual foundation for this chapter.

By drawing on a wide array of independent branches of science from neurobiology to attachment, we can deepen our understanding of human experience and the art of psychotherapy. An extensive interdisciplinary approach can draw on findings from a wide range of isolated academic disciplines to find the convergence of perspectives. Such a consilience (Wilson, 1998) or unity of

1

knowledge helps us to remain grounded in the "objective" empirical findings of science as we focus on the equally real aspect of the "subjective" mental lives of our patient/clients. Such a broadened view can enable practitioners to gain new insights into their own work and also to propose some new possibilities that expand their therapeutic potentials and point to new directions for the future. Our efforts to enhance and understand mental health can be greatly nurtured by a scientifically grounded interdisciplinary focus on the mind, the brain, and human relationships.

As relationships are created by the communication patterns between people, one can envision that psychotherapy allows two minds to join each other as they share in the flow of energy and information between them. This joining process may feel exhilarating, but how does it promote change and healing? How do we incorporate the ideas about relationships and development into our modern understanding of brain and mind? How can we move as psychotherapists between the intersubjective nature of interpersonal communication and the ways in which mental processes emerge from patterns of neural firing? Let us take this seeming conceptual leap and build a practical bridge that is founded in science and can deeply inform our understanding of subjective life and human development across the lifespan. Here are some ideas that serve as building blocks.

The location of firing within the brain determines the nature of the emerging mental process. The particular activation determines the nature of the representation. For example, visualizing the Eiffel Tower in your mind may involve activation of areas of the occipital cortex, in the back of the brain. Visualizing the Grand Canyon may involve similar areas, but a distinct neural net profile of activation. What we don't yet know is exactly how neural firing patterns create the subjective experience of mental processes and representations. The brain functions as an associational organ, making functional links among various representations and processes. In this manner, when recalling the Eiffel Tower, you may first see the tower in your mind's eye, then sense the smell of baguettes, feel a romantic urge, and then recall actually being there with your lover. These can all be triggered by the linguistic representation of "Eiffel Tower" with the subsequent cascade of multirepresentational associational linkages. This is the foundation for memory and imagination.

New neural connections in response to experience can be made across the lifespan. As new synapses are formed in response to experience, we create the foundation for memory. In this way experience, memory, and development are overlapping processes. Recent findings from neuroscience also suggest that new neurons growing in integrating regions of the brain may also continue to emerge across the lifespan. How experience, especially that of psychotherapy,

may continue to create new neural connections and perhaps il
of new integrative neurons is yet to be determined. We will b
process of neural integration as the fundamental manner in
creates functional linkages by making neural connections acr
gions. These pathways of neural integration are the same pathways that help
with self-regulation. As we'll see, when we think about how to help a traumatized individual to heal, we may be focusing directly on how the therapeutic
interpersonal experience enables integrative fibers to actually grow and thus
enable new abilities to be attained. We will have to await the empirical research to prove it, but this is the central hypothesis for the view described in
this chapter.

We will examine how traumatic experiences influence the development
of the brain and the mind and how these experiences and the adaptations
to them can create clinical difficulties. Then, we will offer an approach to
psychotherapy that is based on an interpersonal neurobiological understanding
of development, mental health, and the power of relationships to nurture and
to heal the mind.

Mental Health and Complex Systems

The human mind is a complex system. In order to deepen our understanding
of the mind's response to trauma and how the healing process can occur, it is
helpful to examine the nature of complexity and its potential relationships to
mental well-being.

The nonlinear dynamics of complex systems, revealed in the mathemati-
cally derived probability perspective of chaos theory or complexity theory,
can help us to understand how systems capable of chaotic behavior organize
themselves over time. The application of complexity theory to mental processes is an exciting adventure into consilience and a deepening of our ability
to understand such processes as self-regulation, states of mind, and interpersonal relationships. Complexity theory offers several conceptual foundations
that can serve as guide posts to creating a working definition of mental health
(Siegel, 1999, 2001a).

A complex system is defined as one that is open, multilayered, and capable
of chaotic behavior. The behavior of the component parts of a complex system
can be described by assessing their emergent states as they change across time.
These states involve the activation or position of the component parts (water
molecule position in clouds, neuronal activation profiles for brains, and the
flow of energy and information for minds). The *nonlinear* dynamics of complex

systems describe the ways in which small changes in initial input to the system can lead to large and unpredictable outputs. A dynamic (complex) system can thus be observed and its short-term states anticipated, but in the long run the emergence of overall states cannot be exactly predicted. The human mind, and indeed pairs of minds and communities of minds, meet these criteria for complex systems (Cicchetti & Rogosch 1987; Fogel et al., 1998; Boldrini et al., 1998).

Here are some salient principles of complexity theory that are relevant to psychotherapy and mental health:

1. Complex systems have a *self-organizational process* that emerges out of the nature of the properties of their component parts;
2. The flow of states of the system has *recursive features*, both internal and external, that reinforce the flow in a particular direction;
3. Both internal and external *constraints*, or features, determine the course of change or trajectory of the system over time;
4. Self-organizational processes tend to move the system toward *maximal complexity*;
5. The ability to create maximally complex states offers the *most stable, flexible, and adaptive states* to emerge. Complexity is a state of the system that flows between sameness, rigidity, order, and predictability on the one hand and change, randomness, chaos, and unpredictability on the other;
6. Complexity is achieved by the *balancing of the two fundamental processes of differentiation and integration*; and
7. The inability of the system to move toward complexity can be seen as a form of *"stress" to the system*.

One exciting idea that emerges from the application of complexity theory to mental processes is this: Systems that are able to move toward maximal complexity are healthy systems. They are the most stable, adaptive, and flexible. What a wonderfully concise definition of well-being! Mental health can thus be defined as a self-organizational process that enables the system—be it a person, relationship, family, school, community, or society—to continually move toward maximal complexity.

The brain appears to be naturally driven, by both genetic information and the impact of experience, to differentiate its circuitry. Such a process enables the brain to achieve an unfathomable variety of cognitive processes. Some have estimated that the number of firing patterns within the human brain is an astonishing ten times ten one million times (ten to the millionth power)! Of course these are human brains that are making this estimation, so they are a bit biased. Nevertheless, even the fact that we can reflect on our own mental processes is quite amazing. We now believe that complex mental processes emerge from neuronal firing patterns that are profoundly influenced by synaptic connections created by our inheritance and our experiential history. One aspect of brain development is the specialization of function of component parts that we have called differentiation. The other important aspect of development is the bringing of these parts together into a functional whole in the process called integration.

The complex web of interconnected neurons in the brain and the rest of the body become functionally linked through neural integration, which enables the differentiated circuits of the brain to become part of a coherent information processing system. Complex mental processes thus depend upon widely distributed regions of the brain to be linked together into a functional whole. Memory is one such process: The association of neuronal firing from distributed areas of the brain is the essence of memory. We learn by how our neurons create functional linkages in the moment of initial learning that then influence the likelihood of these neurons firing together in the future. This view is called "Hebb's Hypothesis" and is named after the psychologist physician, Donald Hebb, who described the phenomenon over fifty years ago summarized as "neurons which fire together, wire together." Memory is based on this process of integration. Learning requires that we create linkages to alter the nature of our future neuronal firing patterns.

These dynamic processes create a flow that moves toward complexity by balancing the differentiation (specialization) of components with the integration (bringing together as a functional whole) of components of the system. In experiential terms, complexity flows between boredom and anxiety. Optimal flow runs right down the middle and is experienced as a kind of harmony. When a system does not move toward complexity, it can be seen as "stressed." Such deviations move the system to either side of complexity: rigidity (monotony) on the one side, chaos (cacophony) on the other. A stressed system does not function optimally, oscillating to either side of complexity. This is the hallmark of unresolved posttraumatic conditions. We can apply these ideas to optimal learning experiences. Learning environments which bombard an individual with information that cannot be processed effectively produce stress in that they overwhelm the system and lead to chaos and uncertainty. Experiences that are under-stimulating create stress in that they are filled with excessive sameness and predictability and do not enable the system of the student's mind to move toward complexity. In effective psychotherapy, the therapist offers the client a relationship foundation and specific experiences that help to promote complexity during the session and eventually to have the ability to self-organize and move toward complexity outside the sessions.

Sailing the C's of Psychotherapy

What happens in psychotherapy from an interpersonal neurobiology perspective? The following sections will offer a scientifically informed conceptual foundation for how therapeutic relationships can be seen to promote healing by enabling the self-organizational processes of the mind to move toward complexity. These ideas are derived from empirical research into the interconnections among mind, brain, human relationships, and developmental processes. As each individual is unique, so too is each therapeutic relationship uniquely created by the therapist and patient/client. Each contributes to the mutually created relational world that becomes the cornerstone of the emerging states of each person. In this way, the shared and mutually coconstructed subjective experiences become the lived moments that emerge as the complex system of the therapeutic relationship unfolds. Attachment research has objectively demonstrated the crucial importance of the parent's focus on the child's subjective experience for the development of the child's well-being. Adult attachment studies further suggest that the parents' own subjective internal coherence, or how they have come to "make sense" of their lives, is the most robust predictor of their child's development of security of attachment to them. These research findings highlight the central importance of internal and interpersonal subjective states in the emergence of well-being.

To describe the process of human development within therapy, we can explore the "C's" of psychotherapy that can serve to organize and communicate the essential experiential elements of an interpersonal neurobiology of psychotherapy. The dozen C's are: connection, compassion, contingency, cohesion, continuity, coherence, clarity, co-construction, complexity, consciousness, creativity, and community. Rather than explore each element in great detail here, let me briefly offer a narrative describing each of these aspects of psychotherapy and how they are related to each other. A more complete discussion of this framework will be found in another text (Siegel, 2002).

As a patient/client enters the process of therapy with the psychotherapist, a *connection* begins to become established within the interpersonal relationship that emerges. As the therapist shows *compassion* for the patient's here-and-now subjective experience as well as the unfolding of past-present-future "mental time travel" of autonoetic (self-knowing) consciousness, *contingent* communication becomes an integral part of the unfolding relationship. Contingency involves the ability of one person to perceive, make sense of, and respond to the signals of the other person in a timely fashion. Such a form of communication creates a sense of communion, of joining, in the attuned, resonating pair of minds. A sense of trust begins to infuse this growing connection and the patient may experience a sense of *cohesion* in the present. Over time, the *continuity* that is created from these contingent connections, and the repair of their inevitable ruptures, enables the patient to experience a sense of *coherence* across the various states of mind unfolding in therapy with an emerging sense of *clarity* of the self and other.

The *co-construction* of shared experiences, often taking the form of nonverbal communication as well as the co-creation of stories woven into therapeutic dialogues, deepens the sense of clarity and communion. The *complexity* achieved by such joining is experienced both individually in the form of multiple layers of neural integration, as well as interpersonally as vital forms of dyadic resonance. Resonance involves the mutual influence of each person on the other and entails the sense of being present in each other's minds even during separations. Present throughout the therapy, but heightened as these dyadic states and interhemispheric integration emerge, *consciousness* of the self-as-experienced begins to deepen. Both the here-and-now awareness of the self and a past-present-future autonoetic form of consciousness expand in their focus.

The flow of the patient's mind toward maximal complexity enables the self to achieve the most stable, flexible, and adaptive states. Healing is achieved as overwhelming events and suboptimal developmental experiences, encoded in various forms of memory, become freed from their restrictive or chaotic patterns. Information in the mind becomes more spontaneously flowing, enabling an enriching sense of discovery and connection. The energy released from such an emerging flow is vitalizing. Often such therapeutic progress is associated with the emergence of *creativity* as new combinations of representational processes become possible, imagination is enhanced, and the mind's innate drive toward maximizing complexity is released.

Our minds are created by the functioning of our brains and the ways in which information and energy flow within us and with others. The brain is genetically programmed to be social. How we have come to define the "solitary self" may often be limited to the boundaries of the skin if we have been imprisoned by rigid adaptations to prior suboptimal attachments or unresolved loss or trauma. Such a view is also reflected in a "single skull" perspective on how a lone brain's activity gives rise to the mind in isolation. In fact, the brain is hardwired to take in signals from the social environment to alter its own internal states. Our minds emerge from this interdependence of the brain and interpersonal relationships. For those with suboptimal attachment experiences, restrictive adaptations may have been required for survival and leaving them behind may feel overwhelming and dangerous. With the courage to connect and create a new pathway, patients often become conscious of their sense of belonging to a "self" that is defined as connected to *community*. Finding meaning in belonging emerges as we join with a process much larger than our individual skin-defined lives.

Therapy begins with connection. Filled with the heroism of a journey into the unknown, patients join with therapists in exploring the past, living fully in the present, and becoming the creative authors of the future chapters of their lives. Connections then emerge beyond the therapeutic dyad, freeing the patient to explore new avenues of authentic living within the mind and with others. By making sense of our lives, we become free to join with others in creating emerging layers of meaning and connection.

The Mind

Psychotherapy focuses on healing the mind. But what is the mind? One way to address this important question is by looking at the definition of the psyche. *Webster's Dictionary* defines *psyche* as follows: "1. the soul; 2. the intellect; and 3. in psychiatry—the mind considered as a subjectively perceived, functional entity, based ultimately upon physical processes but with complex processes of its own: it governs the total organism and its interaction with the environment." Within this definition one can see some profound and basic ideas. As psychotherapists, we are helping the psyche grow and develop toward psychological health. We are focusing on the soul, the intellect, the spirit and the mind. The idea of mind embraces the central importance of subjectivity (not merely objectivity), of a process (not a static entity) that has intimate origins in neurophysiological processes (the "physical") and yet with characteristics distinct from its physical origins. The profound importance of the psyche (and the mind) is underscored by its role in governing the total organism—and its interaction with the external world.

A variety of disciplines explore the nature of the mind in its ability to process information and to regulate the function of the individual in adapting to the environment. These various conceptualizations of mind often share the notion that the mind is more than a physical entity—such as brain activity alone—and yet emerges from and also regulates the "self" and the physiological processes from which it emerges.

The mind develops throughout life as we interact with others in our environment. The genetically influenced timing of the emergence of specific brain circuits during the early years of life makes this a time of exquisite importance for the influence of interpersonal relationships—with parents and other caregivers—on how the structure and function of the brain will develop and give rise to the organization of the mind. Overwhelmingly stressful experiences may have their greatest impact on the growth of the mind at the times when specific areas of the brain are in rapid periods of development and reorganization. For this reason, the early years of life may be a time of enhanced opportunity as well as of vulnerability. Trauma during the early years may have lasting effects on deep brain structures responsible for such processes as the response to stress, the integration of information, and the encoding of memory (De Bellis, 1999b; Teicher, 2002). As we will see, specific "states of mind" can also be deeply engrained as a form of memory of trauma, a lasting effect of early traumatic experience. States of fear, anger, or shame can then reemerge as a characteristic trait of the individual's responses.

The mind has an organization to its processes that can be described and studied. Mental processes such as memory, emotion, attention, behavioral regulation, and social cognition can be understood by examining the nature of brain activity. Recent technological advances have permitted truly new insights into the nature of the mind. For example, our modern view of the brain and its response to experience has shed some new light on how experience directly affects gene function, neuronal connections, and the organization of the mind (Kandel, 1998).

Three principles serve as the backbone of an interpersonal neurobiology of the mind that help us find a definition of the mind that is derived from a wide array of scientific disciplines. The first principle is that the human mind is a process that regulates patterns in the flow of two elements: energy and information. The second principle is that such a flow can occur within one brain or among two or more brains. In this way, the mind is created in the interaction between neurophysiological processes and interpersonal relationships. This is one reason why the mind is not the same as the brain: Energy and information flow may originate in neuronal processes, but can extend beyond a single brain, which is why interpersonal relationships, such as psychotherapy, can be fundamental to altering the mind. In addition, energy and information flow—the mind—can itself alter neuronal firing patterns. In this way, alterations in mind, coming in part from interpersonal communication, can create lasting changes in neuronal structure and function that can in turn powerfully transform the mind. In other words, the mind can alter the brain and the brain can alter the mind.

The idea of flow is that something changes across time. It's a dynamic process, like a river. Energy is not some magical, mystical thing; rather, it is literally the physical property of energy. It's the flow of ions, for example, down the axonal length. Energy flow is about the consumption of energy in the brain as neural circuits are becoming activated in the brain. The other entity that flows within the mind is the processing of information. This information can flow within one brain, or between brains. Deepening our understanding of these fundamental components of the mind can help us to understand others, and ourselves, and perhaps offer new ways of helping others heal.

These issues raise an important point about how experiences shape the mind, bringing us to a third basic principle: The mind emerges as the genetically programmed maturation of the brain responds to ongoing experience. This third principle enables us to examine directly the notion that both genetic information and experience directly shape the connections within the brain that shape the mind. It is not a matter of nature versus nurture, but rather it is that nature needs nurture. Experiences shape the brain connections that create the mind and enable an emerging sense of a "self" in the world.

Mind, Brain, and the Processing of Information

How do the processes of the mind emerge from the neuronal activity of the brain? Recent advances in brain imaging have been profoundly important in expanding our understanding of how the brain gives rise to the mind—but they are not the same as visualizing the mind itself or reducing the mind to only brain activity. Recent writings often focus on the mind as being essentially equivalent to the brain. That is, if you put a person in a brain scanner and the brain reveals certain activity, then somehow we are visualizing the mind. That view reveals what can be called a "single skull psychology" which does not provide a complete picture that helps us to fully understand mental health or the power of relationships to hurt or to heal.

The brain is composed of billions of cells called neurons, which are long entities with a central nucleus (containing genes) and long extensions called axons. At the axonal end, one neuron connects to others at a small space called a synapse that enables packets of neurotransmitters to be released. These chemicals can activate, or inhibit, the "downstream" post-synaptic neuronal firing. Neuromodulators, another form of chemical that can be released, can have more long-term influences on the probabilities of neuronal firing and on the creation of new synaptic connections (Le Doux, 2002). Neural firing is the equivalent of an electric current, known as an action potential, flowing to the dendritic receiving end and on to the axonal end where it will in turn lead to the release of neurotransmitters for the activation, or inhibition, of the subsequent neuron. The key to the complexity of all of this is that an average neuron connects directly to about ten thousand other neurons. Given that the adult brain has over ten billion neurons, with over two million miles of length of axonal fibers, the spiderweb-like connections create a virtually infinite variety of on-off firing patterns. It is these firing patterns, or "neural net profiles," that are believed to create mental processes.

The brain itself is composed of a massively complex network of interconnected neurons. The activity of neurons occurs in a network of activation—a certain portion of a spiderweb-like neural network active across time. It is the specific pattern of this brain activity across time that determines the nature of the mental processes created at a given moment: the timing and location of neural activation within the brain determine the "information" contained within the neural net patterns or neural "maps." Activity in sensory regions may mediate perception and the specific nature of this firing may signify the different aspects of perceptual information: a visual stimulus, auditory input, or tactile sensation, for example. Information carried within perceptual regions often becomes integrated into a larger "cross-modal" perceptual system. Such an integrating process is an example of how the brain functions as a hierarchical set of layers of relatively distinct component elements or processing modalities whose neuronal activity may become clustered together into a functional whole. This is one example of neural integration.

The brain as a system is composed of hierarchical layers of component parts that can be analyzed at a number of levels: single neurons, neuronal groups, circuits, systems, regions, and hemispheres. At birth the brain is the most undifferentiated of any "organ" in the body. As development unfolds, neural pathways are created as synapses are formed which allow for the creation of these component parts to become differentiated and to carry out such features as attention, perception, memory, and emotional regulation. A huge number of genes encode for the timing and general details of how circuits are to develop early in life. However, the creation, maintenance, and elaboration of neural connections may often also require that they be activated in a process sometimes called experience- or activity-dependent development. Experience activates specific neuronal connections and allows for the creation of new synapses and the strengthening of existing ones. In some cases, lack of use leads to impaired synaptic growth and to a dying away process—called pruning—in which connections are lost and neurons themselves may die. Such a pruning process appears to be a major event during the adolescent years, in which the huge increase in synaptic density created during the early years is then pruned to the lower densities of the adult years (Spear, 2000). How genetically encoded information interacts with environmental and interactive elements to determine the nature of this important adolescent pruning period is open to future investigation.

The differentiation of the brain during the early years of life is dependent upon both genetic information and proper experiential stimulation. It is for this reason that the early years—when the basic circuits of the brain are becoming established that mediate such processes as emotional and behavioral regulation, interpersonal relatedness, language and memory—are the most crucial for the individual to receive the experience that enables proper development to occur. Attachment studies suggest that these experiences are about the interactions between the child and the environment, especially within the child's social world, rather than merely the sensory bombardment that some parents feel pressured to offer their children in the form of visual or auditory stimulation in hopes of "building better brains." As we'll see, the experiential food for the mind is in the form of collaborative communication rather than sensory overload.

The activity of the brain processes information via patterns of neural activity, which serve to "represent" aspects of the internal or external world. This mental symbol, code, or image is conceptualized as being created within patterns of neural net firing, sometimes called a "neural net profile" or neural map. For example, when we recall a visual image, such as the house we grew up in, the firing of a pattern of neural circuits within our visual system is similar but not identical to the pattern or map that fired when we were actually there years ago. Memory, as with other mental processes including ongoing perception, is an actively constructive process that draws on a range of neural systems and is shaped by a wide variety of external and internal factors. Within the brain, the pattern of activation (energy) of distributed neurons acts as a symbol (information) of some experienced event that is constructed by the mind itself.

Let's examine one way of thinking about energy and information flow as fundamental to the neurobiological, subjective, and interpersonal nature of the mind. For example, when we speak to each other with language, we transfer information through patterns of energy flow. For spoken language, such energy flow is in the form of vibrations in air; for the written word, the energy flow is in the form of photons passing from a page or screen to the retina of the eye. In either form of communication, energy is transferred from one place to the brain, with activation of perceptual circuits that lead to more complex language processing. Watch what happens with information flow in this example. Read the following words: *Eiffel Tower*. Now close your eyes briefly and notice what happens. After you open your eyes, think about what you noticed. Did you see an image in your mind? For many people, an image of the Eiffel Tower appears in their "mind's eye." Let's look at how that might have happened.

In my brain, there is a pattern of neural activation which we will be focusing on, the idea of this architectural structure that we label with the linguistic symbol, *Eiffel Tower*. My nerves then connect to my fingers and I type the words, *Eiffel Tower*. You read these words and the visual input on your retina then activates your optic nerve and the input activates neural firing in various parts of your brain and in particular goes to the left side of your brain where there are linguistic processing centers. If you've heard the term *Eiffel Tower* before then, that energy flow has symbolic value. It contains information and then you have a whole association of mental processes that are believed to come from the activation of specific circuits in your brain. Some people may experience emotional sensations as well. Some even get hungry for a baguette. You can have all sorts of sensations and the brain is all about making associations and integrating different activation profiles. This is an example of the flow of energy and information and it comes from my mind to yours. In this way, we can see that the mind, in fact, is not just what happens in a single brain but that it can be created between brains as well.

When we focus on the brain we must remember that we never mean to separate the brain from the body. The brain is an integral part of the body that contributes to the creation of "self." Sometimes that integration of brain and body is broken, which is one aspect of the consequence of trauma. When you see the word "brain" in this chapter, you should automatically think to yourself, brain-body. We shall explore how certain parts of the brain and other areas in the body perform specific functions as part of the integrated biological system that creates the experience of mind. At times, the integration of this system may be "dis-integrated" as in dissociative experiences, which can be understood as the disconnection of anatomically distinct regions into a functional dis-association. Understanding how the brain (read "brain as an integral part of the body") functions can enable us to have a deeper understanding of the subjective experiences of the mind.

How does experience affect the brain? How can human relationships, supportive or traumatizing, influence the activity and development of the brain? What are the mechanisms by which interpersonal experience can actually shape neuronal activity and growth? Some of the more devastating effects of trauma occur within relationship-based experiences, such as domestic violence or child abuse. Grounding ourselves in a neuroscience of relationships can allow us in the field of mental health to approach our work with a deeper understanding of the central importance of interpersonal experience in creating the subjective life of the mind.

As complex systems, the mind and the brain are regulated by a process that is influenced by both internal and external variables known as constraints. Internal constraints are the nature of the synaptic connections among neurons. External constraints include environmental experiences, such as patterns of interpersonal communication with others in emotionally significant relationships. Self-regulation is a key to mental health, as we'll explore in greater detail later in the chapter. Psychotherapeutic relationships can enable external variables to be altered in the form of two-person governed self-regulation. In turn, these experiences (external constraints) can help modify the synaptic connections (internal constraints) that enable the individual to achieve new levels of flexible and balanced forms of self-regulation (self-organization enabling complexity to be achieved).

The simple idea is this: Human connections within relationships can shape the neural connections of the brain from which the mind emerges. In this manner, relationships may not only be encoded in memory, but may also shape the very circuits that enable memory to be processed and self-regulation to be achieved. This is the source of the power of relationships to nurture and to heal the mind. As relationships serve as an external constraint to modify the trajectory of the system, the internal constraints become altered and the system then changes its ability to move toward complexity and thus to achieve states of mental health.

Brain Asymmetry, Neural Integration, and Trauma

Discoveries over the last several decades have resulted in a number of fascinating notions about the divided brain and mental processes. Trevarthen (1996) as well as Tucker, Luu, and Pribram (1995) have described the ways in which the right and left hemispheres of the brain are dominant for the mediation of distinct modes of representational processing. From before birth, the brain reveals an asymmetry in its structure and development. Comparative zoology, the study of other animals besides ourselves, reveals that the nervous system is asymmetric. In humans, studies of in utero development indicate an early difference in the subcortical structures on the left and on the right in what are called dorsal and ventral trends. When the baby is born, the connections among the neurons, especially in the cerebral cortex, are very immature. There is a motivational drive from these asymmetries in the subcortex that exists in utero to push for very different processing systems in the left hemisphere versus the right.

The right hemisphere is dominant in its growth during the first three years of life. The right side of the brain processes information as nonverbal signals in a holistic, parallel, visual spatial manner. Self-soothing is also a major function of the right hemisphere. The right hemisphere is usually dominant for nonverbal aspects of language (tone of voice, gestures), facial expression of affect, the perception of emotion, the regulation of the autonomic nervous system, the registration of the state of the body, and for social cognition including the process called *theory of mind*. Some views suggest that the right hemisphere is able to experience more intense emotionally arousing states of mind. Further-more, the retrieval of autobiographical memory appears to be mediated by the right hemisphere. Also, both the registration and regulation of the body's state appear to be predominantly mediated by the right hemisphere. Recent studies of flashback conditions suggest an intense activation of the right hemisphere visual cortex and an inhibition of left hemisphere speech areas (Rauch et al., 1996).

The left side of the brain, in contrast, develops later on and is about lin-ear processing using linguistics in a logical fashion. Three L's—linear, logical, linguistic! Left hemisphere processing uses something called syllogistic reason-ing, looking for cause-and-effect relationships that can explain the rightness and wrongness of things. Now, if you think about a coherent story, what is it? It's the logical, linear telling of a sequence of events using words. Stories can be depicted using other modalities, such as drawing, but we are focusing on the language-based narratives now. The linear telling of a story is driven by the left hemisphere. In order to be autobiographical, the left side must con-nect with the subjective emotional self-experience that is stored in the right hemisphere. The proposal is this: to have a coherent story, the drive of the left to tell a logical story must draw on the information from the right. If there is a blockage, as occurs in PTSD (posttraumatic stress disorder), then the narrative may be incoherent.

When one achieves neural integration across the hemispheres, one achieves coherent narratives. The deeper healing process is the acquisition of neural in-tegration which can be achieved through the telling of coherent narratives as well as other ways. Trauma may induce separation of the hemispheres, im-pairing the capacity to achieve these complex, adaptive, self-regulatory states and revealed in incoherent narratives. Such separation may at times be due to impaired growth of the corpus callosum that connects the two hemispheres to each other, as has been recently shown to be damaged in cases of early child abuse and neglect (Teicher, 2002; De Bellis et al., 1999a, 1999b).

As we'll discuss below, impairment in representational integration in gen-eral, including the bilateral integration of information processing between right and left hemispheres in particular, may be a core deficit in unresolved trauma. Therapeutic interventions that enhance neural integration and collaborative interhemisphere function may be especially helpful in moving unresolved trau-matic states toward resolution. The strategic activation of specific information processing modalities may be a mechanism of action in the creation of coherent narratives, as can be seen as an outcome in various approaches to the treatment of individuals with PTSD. Cognitive behavior therapy (CBT), psychodynamic psychotherapy, and eye movement desensitization and reprocessing (EMDR) are approaches that each may be successful to the extent that they selectively activate representational processes that are dominant in each hemisphere and then promote their integration via simultaneous activation. Such therapeutic experiences may move the brain to link these otherwise isolated processes into a functional whole.

One of the many exciting findings of attachment research is that there is a group in adult attachment studies called "earned secure." (see Roisman et al., 2002, Phelps, Belskg, & Cmic, 1998). These are adults who appear to have had difficult childhoods, but have come to create a coherent narrative: They have made sense of their lives. The children attached to these adults have secure attachments and do well! History is not destiny—if you've come to make sense of your life. It isn't just what happened to you that determines your future—it's how you've come to make sense of your life that matters most. Moreover, the experience in later relationships can actually change the future development of the mind. It seems likely, based on indirect evidence in humans, direct evidence in animal studies, and convergent findings from a number of independent disciplines, that this effect is mediated through the impact of experience on the unfolding of brain structure. What we do in psychotherapy is to constantly work at deep levels with the body, with emotions, and with many different elements of memory, to help people make sense of their inner worlds and their interpersonal lives. Such a making-sense process may depend upon various layers of neural integration.

Brain, Genetics, and Experience

As we explore the nature of trauma, we need to focus on how traumatic experience may alter synaptic connections in a manner that impairs subsequent functioning in unresolved states. One proposal is that trauma directly impairs the capacity to integrate a range of cognitive processes into a coherent whole. When attachment experiences are not optimal, mental processes may be shaped to adapt in ways that do not promote optimal well-being. These are often organized adaptations that may restrict the flexibility of the individual to respond to new environments in the future.

In the extreme situation when an organized adaptation is not possible, such as in severe, early, and chronic abusive childhood experiences, recent research has demonstrated that several areas of brain development are significantly damaged. Recent studies of brain anatomy in abused children have demonstrated an associated reduction in overall brain size as well as the specific finding of impairments in the development of the corpus callosum, the bands of neural tissue allowing for the transfer of information between the two halves of the brain (De Bellis et al., 1999a and 1999b). In addition, the cerebellar vermis may be damaged and unable to support the inhibitory gamma amino butyric acid input to the hypothalamic nucleii in the brain stem nor to perform its soothing function on the limbic structures (Teicher, 2002). In addition, the hippocampus may be shrunken, impairing the ability to process elements into explicit memory and impair the acquisition of a sense of self in the world. These direct brain insults, likely due to excessive stress hormone secretion that is neurotoxic, produce an unfortunate cascade of recursive properties in which the child may be limited in the capacity to integrate mental processes and soothe emotional lability.

Experience can be defined as the activation of neural firing patterns in response to an internal or external stimulus. We now know that neural activation, under certain conditions, can actually lead to the turning on of genes leading to a cascade of biochemical changes in the neural cell that eventually enables proteins to be produced. In this manner, genes have two functions: They encode information in the sequence of their DNA nucleotides *and* they can be transcribed into RNA and then translated into protein which enables neural connections to be altered. In other words, experience (the activation of neural firing patterns) can activate genes (thus leading to protein production) and therefore change brain structure (Meaney, 2001; Suomi, in press).

When overwhelmingly stressful experiences occur, the brain may respond with excessive cortisol secretion which, if sustained, can lead to neuronal cell death. As neural circuitry continues to develop, it may be those areas that are growing at a particular time and those with increased cortisol receptors, such as in the hippocampus, that are especially vulnerable to the neurotoxic effects of excessive and prolonged cortisol secretion.

There is no question that genes program the maturation of the brain. But experience also shapes the structure of the brain. Kandel (1998) has demonstrated that the activation of neurons (experience) can lead to the activation of genes. The ensuing production of protein then enables new synapses to form. Recent studies in neurobiology suggest that new neurons may also be able to grow from uncommitted stem cells after birth, and perhaps throughout life (Benes, 1998). We do not yet know how experience may stimulate stem cell growth and differentiation. Experience in general alters the mind by changes in the synaptic connections among neurons. As clinicians, our goal is thus to explore the ways in which the therapeutic relationship may be able to create lasting changes in our patients by way of changes in neural connections. Experiences, such as those in psychotherapy, theoretically (this has not yet been proven) should be able to change brain structure, not merely brain function. In this chapter we are exploring some possible mechanisms by which relationship experiences may promote mental health by altering the connections among neurons.

The exciting challenge we now have as modern psychotherapists is to learn about these basic biological processes and begin the important work of determining what types of experiences for which people can produce desired changes in brain structure and therefore function. Such functional changes, if they are lasting, are likely due to changes in neuronal connectivity. Of course some conditions may require a multimodal approach, involving various dimensions of psychotherapy, family involvement, medications, and other forms of treatment such as biofeedback or occupational therapy. In the second half of this chapter, we will be focusing on the former dimension in exploring how the therapeutic relationship can be harnessed to promote healing in an individual who has experienced trauma.

As psychotherapists, understanding how anatomically separate processes can be disintegrated is useful in deepening our understanding of trauma and its treatment. That is, instead of being integrated as a whole, anatomically distinct areas responsible for the creation of particular forms of memory, for example, may be disassociated. This is one of the profound effects of trauma. But here is the great thing: Our brains are extremely social. How one brain interacts with another has important effects on how the brain functions. Social interactions are one of the most powerful forms of experience that help shape how the brain gives rise to the mind. We can come to believe this view not because we are therapists and we believe in this idea; this scientifically validated perspective is true because of evolution. The human brain reveals the fact that the processes involved in self-regulation, the creation of meaning, and interpersonal communication involve overlapping neural circuits. These are the same circuits that mediate emotion and seem to be part of the process that creates autobiographical memory. So we have this exciting finding that emotion, self-regulation, and interpersonal communication are mediated by similar regions, which tells us that we have to get out of a single skull view of mind and brain.

As described earlier, the mind can be defined as a process that regulates the flow of energy and information—not just within one person, but across individuals as well. The brain becomes literally constructed by interactions with others. As we participate in the "co-construction" of each other's minds, intimately sculpting the unfolding of our mutually created life stories, we find that our most intimate personal processes such as self are actually created by our neural machinery that is, by evolution, designed to be altered by relationship experiences. Thinking of minds in this interpersonal and neurobiological way gives us the conceptual foundation in which we can smoothly shift our focus between neurons and narratives.

The Brain in the Palm of Your Hand

In *The Developing Mind*, I offered a three-dimensional, readily accessible model of the brain. It is actually right in the folded fingers that make up your fist. Here is a brief overview of that model.

If you take your thumb and bend it into your palm and bend your fingers over the top, you will have in front of you a surprisingly accurate model of the brain! This model helps to illustrate the important relationships between structure and function in the brain. The brain has billions of interconnected neurons and trillions of synaptic connections. When you read a simple phrase, such as that "the hippocampus carries out explicit memory," it is important to be careful about oversimplifying what that actually means. Let's look at the idea of "carries out" or "is involved in" or "mediates" or "subsumes." If I write that the hippocampus mediates explicit memory, that's true, but what does that mean? It doesn't mean we take this part of the brain called the hippocampus, put it in a test tube and say "remember"; it doesn't work that way. So we have to be careful not to be reductionistic about saying this part of the brain does this and, therefore, it is the only thing that does this. A more accurate way of describing it is that the hippocampus is essential for integrating a number of crucial processes that then create the mental experience of this certain form of memory. Now that's a lot of words to use so authors use terms like *it does, it mediates, it subsumes, it's responsible* for, or *it's needed for.* For example, the hippocampus isn't fully developed until about 16–18 months of age, so you don't see explicit memory before then because this area of the brain isn't ready to handle those processes. This is an example of the utility of understanding brain structure, function, and development.

There are 10 to 20 billion neurons in the adult brain, but of course we cannot review them individually, so instead, we'll divide the brain into three major areas and talk about what role they play in the larger system. These areas are clustered together into anatomical groups with functional similarities and linkages.

To return to our "folded fist" model, if you face your fingernails toward you, this "person's" eyes would be at the two center fingernails; the ears would be coming out the side, the top of the head at the top of your bent fingers, the back of the head at the back of your fist, and the neck represented in the wrist. Here are the parts: Your wrist represents your spinal cord coming up from your back. Then coming into the center of your palm symbolizes the area of the brain stem. This first area, the lowest area of the brain, takes in information from perceptions and from the body, and it regulates states of wakefulness and sleep. This is the basic part of the brain that is going to interface with the body and the outside world. It is the first area of the brain, the lowest area, the brain stem. Some call this the "primitive" or reptilian brain. It is the place where body first meets brain.

If you raise your fingers up and look at the thumb curled into your palm, this area symbolizes the limbic structures that generally mediate emotion and generate motivational states. Evolved first in mammals, these circuits are sometimes called the old mammalian brain or limbic "system." The limbic regions serve important emotional, motivational, self-regulatory, and social functions. Mammals are social creatures, and our limbic circuits appear to make the ability to perceive and respond to the internal states of others possible. These crucial limbic functions influence processes throughout the brain; so don't just think "emotion" is only based in these limbic circuits. Emotion appears to influence virtually all neural circuits and the mental processes that emerge from them. For clinicians, there are several regions that are especially important to know. First, as we mentioned, is the hippocampus, which is important in explicit memory processing, part of the medial temporal lobe memory system. Recall that the brain is divided into a left side and a right side which we will discuss later, so there are really two hippocampi. But rather than continuing to write that there is a left and a right hippocampus, I will just write *the hippocampus* knowing that there is one on each side of the brain.

The amygdala, represented also on the second to last segment of your thumb, is more toward the center of the temporal lobe. The amygdala is important for processing a number of emotions, especially perhaps fear, sadness, and anger. *Processing* means generating the internal emotional state and the external expression as well as the perception of such states in the expressions of others. For example, the amygdala contains face recognition cells that become active in response to emotionally expressive faces. The amygdala is one of the many important appraisal centers that evaluate the meaning of incoming stimuli.

Then, toward your thumbnail, we can symbolize the anterior cingulate. Some people think of this region as the chief operating officer of the brain. It helps coordinate what we do with our thoughts and our bodies. Some authors would include the hypothalamus here too. The hypothalamus is a crucial neuroendocrine center of the brain and enables neural processes to coordinate with widely distributed areas of the body, including other areas of the brain itself, through hormonal secretion.

Putting your fingers back over your thumb will reveal what symbolizes the third major area of the brain—the cerebral cortex. Also known as the neocortex or cortex, this region sits at the top of the brain; it's the most evolved in human beings and has a number of lobes that mediate distinct functions. When you saw the Eiffel Tower in the mind's eye, for example, the occipital lobe in the back of your brain was likely activating various layers of visual processing. In mental health we are extremely interested in the frontal part of this part of the brain, called the frontal lobe. Symbolized by the front of your fingers from the second to last knuckles down to your fingernails, the frontal lobe mediates reasoning and associational processes. The front part of the frontal lobe is called the prefrontal cortex, symbolized by the part of your fingers from your last knuckles down to your fingernails.

The prefrontal cortex, like any part of the brain, can be divided in a number of ways. The two major areas we will discuss are the side parts called the dorsolateral or just lateral prefrontal cortex, where your two outside fingernails are. This subsumes working memory—the chalkboard of the mind. The middle part, sometimes called the ventromedial prefrontal cortex because it's on the belly side in the middle, is also called the orbitofrontal because it's behind the orbit of the eyes. In the hand model, the orbitofrontal region is symbolized by the middle two fingers, from the last knuckle down to the fingernails. What do you notice that is unique about this region in your hand model of the brain? This part of the brain is unique because it's the only area of the brain that is one synapse away from all three major regions of the brain. In other words, its central location anatomically enables it to integrate the cortex, limbic structures, and brain stem into a functional whole. In this manner, the orbitofrontal region is crucial in the process of neural integration. With sending and receiving neurons to and from the cortex, limbic structures, and the brain stem, the orbitofrontal cortex is the ultimate neural integrative region. This unique convergent structural position gives it a special functional role in the complex system of the brain. The orbitofrontal region is extremely important for a number of processes that we will review below.

Schore (1994) has contributed greatly to our understanding of the role of the orbitofrontal cortex in affect regulation. One of the many important functions that the orbitofrontal cortex is believed to be involved in is the regulation of the autonomic nervous system. The autonomic nervous system is basically the branch of the nervous system that goes from the brain into the rest of the body, especially controlling heart rate, respiration, and the intestines. It has two branches: one is like an accelerator, the sympathetic branch. The other is like the brakes, which is the parasympathetic branch. They come up through the brain stem and are regulated by the orbitofrontal region, especially in the right hemisphere.

Linking the cortex, the limbic system components, and the brain stem together is a powerful structural and functional role of the orbitofrontal cortex. Because of this unique position, it is a key neural integrating region. Integration may be the central process that enables self-regulation to occur. As we'll discuss further, neural integration may be a key process that is impaired in trauma; hence, such integration may be fundamental to mental health and the healing of trauma.

Here are some of the functional features of the orbitofrontal region that suggest its importance in creating complex mental processes that appear to depend upon neural integration. In addition to (a) regulating the body through the autonomic nervous system, this region is also involved in the (b) regulation of emotion; (c) emotionally attuned interpersonal communication, often involving eye contact; (d) the creation of a sense of other people's subjective experience, called social cognition and based on the processes of theory of mind or *mindsight*; (e) response flexibility, a term signifying the ability to take in data, think about it, consider various options for responding, and then producing an adaptive, flexible response as a part of executive functions; (f) the creation of self-awareness and autobiographical memory; and (g) morality.

If the orbitofrontal region is impaired in some way or temporarily shut down for some reason, the individual may experience a sense of disconnection from others and an impairment in a reflective sense of self while exhibiting the emergence of knee-jerk responses rather than flexibility of response. One can hypothesize, for example, that flashback states involve the entry into such a lower mode of responding where the mind has inhibited the involvement of the orbitofrontal region and impairs a wide range of the processes that it mediates. Another process that the orbitofrontal region is important in mediating is social cognition, the ability to look at another person and sense his/her subjective experience of mind. Sometimes for kids who are being traumatized it's important not to have mindsight and they may be motivated to not think about what is going on in the mind of the abuser. For this reason, it may be important clinically to explore how mindsight may have been affected by traumatic experiences with caregivers.

Tulving and his colleagues (1994; Wheeler, Stuss, & Tulving, 1997) have demonstrated that the orbitofrontal region is involved in autobiographical narrative and the creation of mental time travel: the integration of past, present, and anticipated future. This raises the important notion of neural integration and its role in storytelling (Siegel, 1999). It isn't that the orbitofrontal region is doing this by itself, it's that the region is in a unique anatomical and functional position to coordinate separate elements into a whole functioning process. One way of understanding unresolved trauma and unresolved grief is from the view of impairments to the process of neural integration. Looking toward the function, and dysfunction, of this important neural integrative region may help us gain insights into the mechanisms of trauma's disorganizing effects on the developing mind.

Trauma and Impairments to Neural Integration

Focusing on neural integration requires that we ask why integration would be so important. As discussed earlier, the application of complexity theory suggests that a complex system has innate tendencies toward complexity called self-organization. If the system is allowed to move in its natural direction, it will move to achieve adaptive and flexible states of self-organization that move it toward emerging states of maximizing complexity. Such a flow toward complexity is achieved by balancing the fundamental processes of differentiation and integration. A complex system view of self-organization may be the same process as a psychologist's and neuroscientist's views of self-regulation. In other words, the brain has an innate tendency of self-regulation or self-organization that moves its states of activation toward what we can functionally define as "mental health." It achieves this through neural differentiation (circuits being specialized in their functions) and neural integration (circuits being functionally clustered into a working whole). Looking toward brain regions that subsume integrative functions may thus be a useful focus as we deepen our view into the neural mechanisms of healing and mental well-being.

Similarly, as the brain gives rise to the mind, the mind itself can be seen as having an innate tendency to heal itself. Trauma from this vantage point has blocked such inherent movement toward complexity and well-being. The therapist's role can thus be seen as the process of joining with the patient's mind in releasing the trauma-induced blockages to an inborn drive toward mental health. Michelangelo once stated that his job as a sculptor was not to create a statue but rather to liberate the figure from the marble by removing the excess stone. So too is it our job as therapists to help liberate the individual from the rigid adaptations that are blocking the emergence of a differentiated and integrated individual's innate movement toward well-being.

Trauma can impair this natural self-organizational process toward complexity. Achieving such complex states requires an emerging blending of the process of integration on the one hand, with the process of differentiation on the other. The brain is genetically programmed to differentiate its circuits, which are reinforced in various unique experiences that we encounter throughout life. Integration is achieved by the brain during normal development and can be impaired by trauma. Under nontraumatic conditions, the unique combination of integration and differentiation allows for a system to move toward complexity. We'll consider these concepts in detail shortly. I believe that the natural movement of development across the life-span is to constantly be moving toward maximal complexity, but if we have experiences that are suboptimal or traumatizing, then the brain may become impaired in its ability to balance this integration–differentiation process. Its self-organizational properties are impaired; it cannot move toward maximal complexity, and that's what mental disorder can be conceptualized as involving. This is the overarching paradigm of an interpersonal neurobiology approach toward psychotherapy.

Once we embrace this general idea, then the concept of self-regulation falls into place. What we're going to look at is the way the brain—including the orbitofrontal region as part of it, and the body—in which the brain is a fundamental part, and relationships in which all of this is taking place, enable self-regulation. Self-regulation can be understood as a function of the self-organization of a complex system. The natural healing tendency of the brain is to move toward this balance of integration and differentiation within itself and with other brains.

Main and her colleagues (Main, 1999; Hesse, 1999) were able to show that the most robust predictor of a child's attachment to a parent is the coherence of that adult's autobiographical narrative. This finding has important clinical applications, public policy implications, and helps us in our quest to understand the mind, the brain, and development. We have seen that one of the hallmarks of trauma is that it leads to incoherent narratives. An interpersonal neurobiology approach to narratives enables us to look at the much deeper process of the mind that I believe creates incoherent narratives, and that is the process of impairments to neural integration.

In order to pursue the relationships among coherence and complexity, we need to explore more about how the brain becomes differentiated in its functions. Such differentiated information processing can then become a part of an integrative process that enables maximal complexity to be achieved. Such neural integration of differentiated elements is at the heart of well-being and the resolution of trauma.

Memory

Memory processes are divided into two kinds. The first is implicit memory, a form of memory that is devoid of the subjective internal experience of recalling. It doesn't have a sense of self, it doesn't have a sense of time. So, for example, when you've learned to ride a bicycle, every time you ride a bike you don't say, "Oh, I remember being seven and riding a bike and my dad did this or that," you just ride the bike. That's a behavioral aspect of implicit memory. In fact, implicit memory has a number of components. It has a behavioral component, like riding the bike, which is sometimes called procedural memory. It also has an emotional component. For example, if you were bitten by a cat when you were six months of age before you had the other kind of memory, when you see a cat you may feel fear; you just feel the fear, you don't say, "Oh, I was bitten by a cat, I remember that terrible experience." In addition, implicit memory has perceptual components such as seeing something early on in life and then having a sense of familiarity, but not the internal sensation of remembering. Bodily memory should be included in this list, but in scientific research it's not yet studied, though it meets all the criteria for implicit memory.

Implicit memory is mediated via brain circuits that do not involve the hippocampus and are present at birth, and probably before. Implicit memory also includes the finding that you do not need focal attention for encoding. Focal attention is the use of consciousness in the involvement of the dorsolateral prefrontal cortex in working memory. It also involves something called mental models or schema and the process of priming or readying the brain for acting in a certain fashion. Recent discoveries in the development and neurobiology of memory have yielded some exciting and relevant insights into the nature of how our minds respond to experience and influence later functioning (Milner, Squire, & Kandel, 1998).

Implicit memory is NOT the same as nonconscious memory in that the effects of the recall are indeed within conscious awareness but are only experienced in the "here and now" and not with the subjective sense that something is being recalled. These implicit forms of memory are thought to be carried out in areas of the brain that subsume their functions such as the amygdala and other areas of the limbic system (emotional memory), basal ganglia and motor cortex (behavioral memory), and the sensory cortex (perceptual memory). These regions are relatively well developed at birth and capable of responding to experience by alterations of the synaptic connections within their circuitry, the essence of "memory encoding."

Another important aspect of implicit memory is the ability of the mind to form schema or mental models of experience. These generalizations can be across experiences and across sensory modalities and reflect the brain's inherent capacity to function as an "anticipation machine"—deriving from ongoing experience an anticipatory model of what may occur in the future. Making mental models conscious may be a part of a "self-concept." Mental models can also be seen within the "in-between-the-lines" themes of the narratives that structure both our life stories and the manner in which we live our daily lives.

A second form of memory is called explicit memory. Explicit memory requires focal attention for its encoding and appears to activate a region of the brain called the medial temporal lobe, including the hippocampus. The post-natal maturation of parts of the hippocampus may explain the delayed onset of explicit memory until after the first year of life. When explicit memory is retrieved, it has the subjective sense of "something being recalled." When you remembered the Eiffel Tower, you might have thought "I'm remembering being there," which would reflect the tagging of explicit memory through the hippocampus with a feeling of recollection.

Explicit memory includes two major forms: semantic (factual) and episodic (autobiographical). This latter form of memory has the unique features of a sense of self and time. Recent brain imaging studies suggest that episodic memory is mediated by a number of regions including the orbitofrontal cortex. The maturation (synapse formation and myelination) of this and related parts of the prefrontal cortex during the preschool years may be the neurobiological basis for the emergence and continued development of autobiographical memory and self-awareness during this period of childhood and beyond.

Tulving and colleagues (Wheeler, Stuss, & Tulving, 1997) used the phrase "autonoetic consciousness" to refer to the ability of the mind to know the self and to carry out "mental time travel"—seeing the self in the past, present, and possible future. The development of the orbitofrontal regions during the first years of life may help us to understand the onset of this autonoetic capacity during the toddler and preschool periods. The possible ongoing development of this region may also explain the ways in which experience may continue to shape the way we come to understand ourselves and the world in which we live throughout the lifespan.

There is a tremendously exciting convergence of findings regarding the orbitofrontal region which suggest a number of highly relevant processes subsumed by this coordinating area of the brain that are relevant to autobiographical memory. As discussed earlier, the orbitofrontal cortex is located in the prefrontal cortex just behind the eyes and sits at the junction of the other limbic structures (including the anterior cingulate cortex, hippocampus, and amygdala), the associational regions of the neocortex, and the brain stem.

This convergence area receives input from and sends neural pathways to a wide array of perceptual, regulatory, and abstract representational regions of the brain. In this manner, the orbitofrontal cortex integrates information from widely distributed systems and also regulates the activity of processes ranging from memory representations to the physiological status of the body, such as heart-rate and respiration. Self-awareness and autobiographical narratives may thus be interwoven, in normal development and in trauma and its resolution, with the important mental processes of the orbitofrontal cortex. Some essential points regarding the orbitofrontal cortex include the following:

1. It has been suggested to be dependent upon attachment experience for its growth and its mediation of emotionally "attuned communication" (Schore 1994, 1996);
2. It plays a primary role in mediating autonoetic consciousness (Wheeler, Stuss, & Tulving, 1997);
3. It monitors the state of the body and regulates the autonomic nervous system as well as being a primary circuit of stimulus appraisal which evaluates "meaning" of events (Damasio, 1994);
4. It appears to be an important region subsuming social cognition and "theory of mind" processing (Baron-Cohen, 1995).

Interestingly, the orbitofrontal cortex on the right side of the brain appears to be dominant for most of these processes. Each of these basic aspects of the developing mind are mediated by the same self-regulating, experience-dependent circuits that have their initial differentiation during the early years of life but may continue to develop across the life-span.

The following proposal regarding bilateral neural integration, memory consolidation, and the resolution of trauma is based on a number of independent, empirically derived views regarding memory, brain function, and the clinical findings of posttraumatic stress disorder. This hypothesis has been offered as a possible integration of a range of convergent findings and awaits future empirical studies to support its suggestions. The background findings relevant to this hypothesis are as follows:

1. Tulving and colleagues (1994) have suggested a "hemisphere encoding and retrieval asymmetry" hypothesis which postulates that for autobiographical memory there is an encoding role for the left orbitofrontal region and a retrieval role for the right.
2. Explicit memory is thought to proceed through a series of stages of encoding that include: (a) initial registration in sensory memory (lasting

less than half a second); (b) encoding into working memory (lasting half a minute); (c) encoding into long-term memory (lasting days to months to years); and (d) the consolidation of elements of long-term memory into permanent memory (a process that may take days to months to occur and then makes these representations part of an integrated network within the associational cortex and independent of the hippocampus for later retrieval) (McClelland, 1998).

3. REM sleep is essential for the consolidation of memory in which emotional elements of past events become woven together with thematic components of memory to achieve a reintegration or "consolidation" of memory representations.

I have proposed that the autobiographical narrative process may be a fundamental part of cortical consolidation. In this manner, dreams may be seen as an emotionally driven narrative process that incorporates elements of distant and more recent past events as well as ongoing perceptions and random activations in the re-organization (not new encoding) of existing memory traces. This reveals how memory retrieval can be a form of memory modification (Bjork, 1989). Unresolved trauma can be seen as an impairment in this consolidation process of memory. Such an impairment may be revealed within the REM (rapid eye movement) sleep disturbances and nightmares so prevalent in PTSD, as well as in the incoherent narratives and intrusive implicit elements of memory that torment the individual's internal subjective world and interpersonal relationships.

Here is the proposal: Unresolved trauma involves the impairment of integration of representational processes within the brain. This impairment can lead to an array of findings within PTSD and also may make the individual vulnerable to entering inflexible, reactive "lower mode" states of heightened emotion that lack self-reflection. At the core of "unresolved trauma" is an impairment in a core process of neural integration. One expression of this impairment can be seen in the blockage of the consolidation of memory (and the resolution of the trauma) that occurs normally via a proposed bilaterally activating process in which the right hemisphere becomes activated and creates an autonoetic retrieval state. The transfer of information from the right to the left enables the left hemisphere to utilize these representations as part of its autonoetic encoding state. In essence, the reactivated autobiographical representations (right) become the basis for newly reorganized autobiographical encoding (left). Dreams function within REM to enable this consolidation process to occur. Narratives reflect an internal, nonverbal process of neural integration which may become ultimately expressed in words. Coherent narratives—nonverbal or language-based—emerge from such a bilaterally integrating process. The process of bilateral integration can thus be proposed to be one of the core elements in resolution.

The narrative process, so fundamental to many forms of psychotherapy, may also facilitate (as well as reveal) this integration across the hemispheres. It is important to note, however, that the core issue is one of representational integration. These representations or mental images may be manifested in an array of modalities, from various forms of perception (sight, hearing) to words. It is thus quite likely that therapeutic progress (increased integration) may give rise to increased coherence of autobiographical narratives. This suggests that the interpersonal sharing of the internal experience in words alone may not be the core curative feature within therapy. Such sharing may require a range of representational modalities, divided at the most basic level between the nonverbal and the verbal. The sense of safety and the emotional "holding environment" of a secure attachment within a therapeutic relationship, discussed later in the chapter, may be essential for these integrative processes to (finally) occur within the traumatized person's mind. Future research will be needed to examine whether this proposed neural integration and resolution process is associated with alterations in neural function and possibly changes in specific integrative neural circuits, such as those of the corpus callosum, cerebellum, prefrontal, hippocampal, and anterior cingulate regions.

Emotion

Researchers have addressed the topic of emotion by looking at the level of psychological function, attachment theory, and more recently at neurobiological substrates of emotional development. An interpersonal neurobiological approach examines the fundamental role of emotion by drawing on various levels of analysis—from neuronal processes to interpersonal relationships—in viewing the individual mind as a system and the relationship between individuals as a way in which two minds come to function as a dyadic system. This perspective allows us to move back and forth between neuronal activity and mental function and between individual and dyadic processes. From this vantage point, emotion is seen as a way of describing an integrative process of the mind.

Scientific views of emotion are described in many different ways. Emotion includes the categorical "feelings" like sadness, anger, shame that Darwin described 100 years ago. But emotion is much more than that. Stern (1985) wrote about "vitality affects," which are external expressions of the ebb and flow of energy levels in the mind that are shared within attuned communication. Stern was describing the expression of a central process called primary emotion, which is the way that the mind orients itself and appraises things as good or bad, and then leads to different states of arousal within the brain. These primary emotions are really what emotional communication is about during reciprocal, attuned communication fundamental to contingency. In this way, emotional communication is fundamentally integrative as it links two minds together.

Though there are a wide range of details about how researchers attempt to define emotion, many authors point to a number of common features (Sroufe, 1996; Garber & Dodge, 1991). Emotion is often considered as a way in which the mind appraises the meaning of a stimulus, is a response to engagement with the world, and prepares the self for action. Emotion is also seen as having a number of levels of manifestation, including subjective, cognitive, physiological, and behavioral components.

A fascinating recursive finding about the regulation of emotion has been noted by a number of authors: Emotion is both regulated and is regulatory. In other words, the process of emotion serves to regulate other mental processes and is itself regulated by mental processes. This view supports the more recently held perspective that there are no discernible boundaries between our "thoughts" and "feelings." Emotion influences and is influenced by a wide range of mental processes, in other words, emotion, thought, perception, memory, and action are inextricably interwoven. This linkage is exemplified by the idea that perception is the brain's preparation for action: There is no perception without the potential for action upon incoming stimuli. Thus, regions mediating "perception" are directly influenced by those which respond, internally and behaviorally, to perceptual representations. Likewise, modern views of the brain circuitry subsuming emotional processes support the view that all layers of the brain are influenced by the emotion-generating regions. In fact, recent views of the neurobiology of emotion suggest that the limbic regions—which include the orbitofrontal cortex, anterior cingulate, hippocampus, and amygdala—have no clearly definable boundaries. This suggests that the integration of a wide array of functionally segregated processes, such as perception, abstract thought, and motor action, may be a fundamental role of the brain. Such an integrative process may be at the core of what emotion does and indeed what emotion is. In other words, we can broadly define emotion as a process that emerges from neural integration.

As we've proposed, trauma may exert its effects by directly impairing the core integrative capacity of the mind. In its essence, this means that trauma may cause neuronal patterns to become engrained which restrict the ability of the brain to functionally cluster independent modes of information processing. As we'll see, such a restriction may occur within a single brain (such as functional isolation of one hemisphere from the other) or between brains (such as in rigidly constrained interpersonal communication typical of intrafamilial child abuse). Resolution of trauma, from this perspective, requires movement toward freeing the innate tendency of the mind to integrate its functions.

The brain as a system functions as a set of differentiated neuronal groups and circuits that can be clustered into a functionally integrated set of activations. Edelman (1992) has described the importance to such a cluster of interacting parts of having a "value" system that can reinforce or "select" certain stimuli and neuronal responses over others. A range of neuromodulatory systems, including the limbic regions, can be proposed to meet the criteria for a value system of the brain. Such a value system must have extensive innervation to far-reaching areas of the brain, have the effect of enhancing the excitability and activation of neurons, and influence their plasticity (the capacity to strengthen and form new neuronal connections). In this manner, the limbic regions may be conceptualized as a primary source of "value" for the brain. The central location of limbic structures, especially the orbitofrontal cortex and anterior cingulate, may allow for these areas to play a crucial role in the neural integration of neocortical, limbic, and deeper structures (responsible for states of alertness and bodily function).

What we can now say about the neuronal functions directly related to emotion is that there is believed to be an interdependence of several important domains of mental processes: stimulus appraisal (the evaluation of meaning), neural circuit activation, social communication, bodily state, and autonomic regulation each appear to be mediated by a closely linked system of neural circuits. Interestingly, these elements of the "self" appear to be fundamentally linked to the neural substrates of various forms of consciousness (Damasio, 1999). Emotion, bodily state, and a "core consciousness" of the self emerge from within the same circuitry within the brain. The significance of this finding is that it explains how communication within attachment relationships is the primary experience that regulates and organizes the development of those circuits in the brain that mediate self-regulation and social relatedness. A sense of self emerges directly from self-other interactions (Stern, 1985). Early in life, when the infant's brain is developing the circuitry responsible for these domains, attachment relationships help the experience-dependent growth of crucial neuromodulatory regions responsible for emotional regulation (Schore, 1994). Trauma during this early period, especially in those that may be genetically vulnerable to the effects of stress on the unfolding of brain structures, may have devastating effects on the development of these basic mental processes that create the self. As discussed earlier, the overwhelming stress of early abuse appears to be associated with significant alterations in brain development and function (De Bellis et al., 1999a, 1999b; Teicher, 2002).

Emotion is fundamentally an integrative process. Sharing emotional states is a direct route by which one mind becomes connected to another. The brain's evaluation of the meaning of events—the information—is linked to the activation of neural circuits—the energy. Our internal experience of emotion becomes in essence the "music of the mind"—the rhythmic flow of energy and information through our neural circuitry. Our interpersonal sharing of emotion, seen within attuned communications of secure attachments, is the way in which the flow of energy and information occurs—often nonverbally—between two individuals' minds. Such a sharing of nonverbal signals may be one way in which the right hemisphere of one person "joins" with the right hemisphere of the other. The right hemisphere may have a far greater role than the left in the regulation of bodily and emotional states as well as in mediating social and emotional communication. This attunement of right-to-right hemisphere may be crucial in establishing the secure attachment environment which may be essential for effective therapy to occur. This therapeutic process thus enables the therapist to serve in a similar role as an attachment figure: as a part of an interactive relationship that enables the *co-regulation* of internal states to eventually lead to more autonomous *self-regulation* of emotional states within the individual's own mental processes.

Within neural circuits, the systems that mediate the perception of social communication—especially the nonverbal messages within facial expressions, gestures, and tone of voice—are closely linked to those that appraise the meaning of stimuli and regulate the activation of the autonomic nervous system. These circuits appear to be predominantly in the right hemisphere. Thus, information and energy flow are directly regulated by the regions that carry out and perceive interpersonal communication! It is with this new awareness that we can see the mechanisms underlying the long-held belief in how powerful human relationships are in organizing our continually emerging minds. The nonverbal behavior of the therapist is crucial for establishing a sense of safety and security within the fragile and vulnerable conditions of psychotherapy. The distinct but equally important logical and linguistic output of the left hemispheres of patient and therapist find a different manner in which the two come to "join" in the therapeutic process, as discussed later in the chapter.

States of Mind and Self-Regulation

As discussed earlier in this chapter, the capacity of the mind to self-organize can be explored by examining the nonlinear dynamics of complex systems, or complexity theory. Modern applications of this systems view to the human mind have yielded some powerful ideas for understanding development. In essence, these applications suggest a number of relevant concepts: self-organization, the movement toward increasingly complex states of activation, and the regulation of the state of activation of a system by both internal and external factors called constraints. In early development, the parent's mind acts to alter the present state of the child's mind and to help form the neural circuits which will enable the child's brain to regulate itself in increasingly sophisticated ways as the child matures. Interaction between parent and child thus serves to help self-organization both in the interactive moment and in creating self-organizational neural capacities for the future. Parental behavior that produces disorganization within the child's mind thus may create not only an impairment in functioning in the moment, but, if repeated, a tendency to dis-integrate in the future. Such a form of self-dysregulation may be at the heart of dissociation (Siegel, 1996).

The organization of attachment relationships may reveal characteristic ways in which the state of mind of the parent becomes linked to that of the child. For example, a securely attached child-parent relationship may easily form what can be called "dyadic states" in which the minds of two individuals become "joined" and function as a single adaptive and flexible system. Such a system can be seen as both highly integrated and highly differentiated in a manner that creates maximal complexity of the system's flow of states across time. This feature of complexity theory has profound implications at a number of levels. One implication is that integration occurs when there is a functional coupling of differentiated components. In the case of secure attachments, this coupling can be seen to allow for a balance in the patterns of regularity and novelty within the flow of states of the pair that enables the achievement of maximal complexity. Such a balance is observed as "attuned" or contingent communication and from this complexity view can be said to allow the system to achieve the most flexibility and stability.

For the disorganized attachments, a child may have experienced abrupt shifts in state on the part of the parent that can result in fear and disorientation in the child's mind. The hypervigilant stance seen clinically in these children may also reveal highly coupled communication with poor differentiation that may minimize the level of complexity achievable by the dyad. The parent seems unable to perceive distress in the child and is thus unable to provide interactive regulatory experiences that would enable the child to use the parent to enter more tolerable levels of arousal. Repeated experiences within disorganized attachments have been shown to be associated with the process of dissociation in which mental processes fail to become integrated into a coherent whole (Main & Morgan, 1996; Ogawa et al., 1997; Carlson, 1998).

These findings raise the important question of the relationship between internal coherence and interpersonal communication. One finding is that interpersonal communication that is dominated by a reliable set of contingent communications is that which promotes security of attachment. In the next section, we will explore an idea of how interpersonal contingency promotes internal coherence by examining how interactions become neurally embedded in the creation of the self (Siegel, 2001a).

The Development of "Self" and Consciousness

A number of authors have offered various views of how the sense of self can be understood. Stern, a child psychiatrist, for example, has examined the ways in which the self develops from within interpersonal relationships during the first few years of life (Stern, 1985). Damasio (1999), a neurologist, has examined the neurological structures that subsume the manifestations of various aspects of consciousness at the root of three very different forms of self. In my own writing, I have examined an interpersonal neurobiology of the sense of self as it emerges from the various layers of neural integration and forms of memory. Because the conceptualization of self is so fundamental to the notion of development and psychotherapy, I will explore these and other perspectives in-depth and offer a new view of the connection of the sense of self to the mental/neural representation of self and a sense of internal coherence.

Stern has suggested that the self develops within stages during the first years of life. Each domain of self experience begins at a certain age but then continues to play an important role throughout the lifespan. From birth to two months, the infant's *emerging self* begins in which the body takes in sensory data and the infant has the sense of emerging organization of the world as directly experienced. From two to three months to seven to nine months, the infant has the onset of a sense of a *core self*, one in which the infant's sense of agency (the center of will), coherence (sensations of the body), affectivity (emotionality), and continuity (the sense of self across time in the form of memory) are all central features. From nine months to around eighteen months, the *subjective self* emerges in which there is a sense of self and self-with-other that involves the shared attention, intention, and emotion between caregiver and child. By the second birthday, the *verbal self* has begun in which words begin to be shared between self and other. Beyond this period, a "narrative self" emerges in which autobiographical narratives play a major role in defining the self.

Damasio has suggested that various neurological studies (of normal and diseased brains) can be examined to reveal three forms of *self* and two forms of consciousness. Within deep structures in the brain that represent sensory information from the outside world (perceptions) and from the body (via the "somatosensory system") a *proto-self* is created. This can be seen as a direct experience of the brain as it responds to its interaction with the outer and bodily worlds. These can be called *first-order* neural maps. Within higher circuits in the brain are the neural processes that create a *second-order* map of the proto-self as it is changed by its interaction with the world/body. In other words, these higher brain regions are able to have a neural map of the proto-self before interaction and then a proto-self just following interaction with the world/body. This second-order map is in essence a neural symbol of change: It compares the proto-self before and after the interaction. This process of change defines the *core self*. The ability of the brain to focus attention on the "object" that created the change in the proto-self—whether it is something in the world (a physical object), something in the body proper, or an image in the mind itself—creates the heightened sense of awareness Damasio calls *core consciousness*. Core consciousness is a "here-and-now" experience of focused attention that is fundamentally a measure of how the proto-self is changed by interaction with an "object" in the internal or external world.

Within this neural understanding, Damasio goes on to point out that a third grouping of neural structures is essential for what he has called "extended consciousness." Extended consciousness involves *third-order* neural maps—neural representations of the changes in the core self over time. (These are maps of the changes in the changes of the self in interaction with objects.) Such a process allows the brain to create an "autobiographical self" that records the history of the individual, compares it to present experience, and prepares for the future.

Other scientists have provided still other terms for various forms of consciousness and the neural structures that subsume their function. For example, Edelman (1992) has described a primary form of consciousness that is in the "prison of the present" and a "higher form" of consciousness that depends upon language for its functioning in liberating the self from that "prison" in creating a sense of past and future. Tulving and colleagues (Tulving et al., 1994; Wheeler et al., 1997) have described a form of "autonoetic consciousness" that permits the self to create the experience of "mental time travel" that links past, present, and future. Within this framework there is also a sense of a "noetic consciousness," a knowing of facts without the sense of self.

In my own writings, I have drawn on a number of these perspectives in examining how interpersonal experiences may shape these higher, extended, autonoetic forms of consciousness. The neural substrate that allows for the sense of self that "emerges" early in life, the foundations for the proto-self, is likely in large part to be determined by genetic and constitutional features. Thus, in neurologically normal individuals, there is likely a similar mechanism involved in the creation of an emerging proto-self experience. This sense of self is rooted in the interaction of the brain with its environment: the external world, the body proper, and the mind itself (the neural flow of energy and information within the brain). Neurologically impaired individuals may thus differ significantly in the manner in which this emerging proto-self is orga-nized and thus how the subsequent and more elaborated senses of self (core, subjective, verbal, narrative) come to be formed.

Many of these authors' views converge upon the notion, paralleled by studies of implicit memory, that the brain can create a "here-and-now" experience of self. This core ability of "living in the moment" may also have a large degree of genetically determined neural structure to it. However, as Damasio has pointed out, one view of this core self is that it is the neural mapping of the individual's changing in response to interaction with an "object" in the external or internal world. In this manner, the core self may indeed be subject to huge degrees of impact by the environment. For example, if the environment is one of trauma and stress, the core self will be impacted to a great degree. The sense of agency, coherence, affectivity, and even continuity (memory) of the self in interaction with others will be severely impaired in cases, for example, of familial child abuse (Siegel, 1995, 1996). For these reasons, the deepest sense of self-awareness, of core consciousness, may be profoundly influenced by early experiences in infancy even before explicit, autobiographical memory is available.

One aspect of the self is that of autonoesis as revealed in autobiographi-cal narratives. Attachment research shows, for example, that one of the most important predictors of an infant's attachment to the parent is the parent's au-tobiographical narrative coherence. Narrative coherence can be examined by determining the free and flexible flow of information as individuals tell the story of their lives, beginning with memories of their earliest experiences. The research instrument utilized to assess this coherence is the Adult Attachment Interview (Main, 1995; Hesse, 1999), which is a narrative review by the par-ent of her recollections of her earliest relationship experiences with her own parents. The relevant point here is that one can view such autobiographical accounts as revealing the capacity of the mind to achieve a certain amount of integration of functioning. I have called such a process one of *coherent autonoesis* that reveals how an individual has "made sense" of his or her life experiences. This integration appears to allow for the individual to have an internal sense of connection to the past, to live fully and be mindful in the present, and to prepare for the future as informed by the past and the present. In this manner, coherent autonoesis allows for the fluid flow of past, present, and future. Such fluid and flexible reflections on the past, present, and future are the hallmark of coherent autobiographical narratives.

But why should such a self-reflective process of the parent be associated with the child's security of attachment? In the next section, I will offer some possible links between the internal processes of autonoesis and the interpersonal connections of parent-child relationships within attachment experiences that can serve as a guideline for the possible processes of healing in psychotherapy.

Attachment and the Developing Mind

The process of attachment may be fundamental to the psychotherapeutic relationship. Exploring these elements of parent-child attachment may serve as a useful foundation for deepening our understanding of the therapeutic process.

Children are born with an innate need to be attached to their caregivers. This need creates a triad of developmental processes, including:

1. *proximity seeking*—children need to be physically close to their attachment figures;
2. *safe haven*—when upset, children turn to their caregivers for soothing; and
3. *secure base*—after repeated experiences with their attachment figures, children internalize these relationships for a sense of security that can be utilized when physically distant from their parents.

These basic elements of what we can provide our children to develop secure attachments are derived from research which also suggests that secure attachment is generally associated with a child's development of emotional competence, a sense of well-being, and interpersonal skills. Security of attachment enables children to feel secure and be able to explore the world around them. Studies reveal that security of attachment can change as relationships change, and so it may never be "too late" to begin to offer children these basic elements of secure attachment. Another point of optimism is that adults who have made sense of their early family experiences, even those that have been particularly difficult such as trauma or loss, can do extremely well at providing a secure attachment for their own children.

Longitudinal attachment studies in children have found that securely attached children appear to have a number of positive outcomes in their development. These include enhanced emotional flexibility, social functioning, and cognitive abilities. Some studies suggest that security of attachment conveys a form of resilience in the face of future adversity. In contrast, a number of studies suggest that the various forms of insecurity of attachment can be associated with emotional rigidity, difficulty in social relationships, impairments in reasoning, difficulty in understanding the minds of others, and risk in the face of stressful situations. Insecure attachment may predispose a child to psychological vulnerability.

What are the essential ingredients of the kinds of experiences that children need with their caregivers to develop a secure attachment? We can outline five elements:

1. *Contingent Communication:* Secure relationships are based on the ability of the parent to offer a collaborative form of transaction that involves: (a) perception of the child's signals; (b) making sense of the signals in terms of what they mean for the child; and (c) a timely and effective response. When the parent's signal is sent as a response, the child can in turn respond with these three elements, and a circle of communication is established. The child may then experience the sensation of "feeling felt" by the parent, with the child feeling that his or her mind is inside that of the parent. Contingency is thus a form of joining, of communion, connecting child and parent. Throughout life, but especially crucial during the early years, the signals being sent and received are often of the nonverbal sort and include: eye contact, facial expression, tone of voice, bodily gestures, posture, and timing and intensity of response. When communication is often (but naturally inevitably not always) contingent in some reliable manner, the core self of an individual has a sense of clarity and coherence. This may be an essential aspect of how patterns of communication with relationships promote emotional well-being and a positive sense of self.

2. *Reflective Dialogue:* Parents can also engage in focusing verbally based discussions on the contents of the mind itself. Going beyond just the discussion of outwardly visible "objective" events, parents can elaborate on the deeper layer of "subjective" human experience by focusing on the mental processes such as: thoughts, feeling, sensations, perceptions, memories, attitudes, beliefs, and intentions. By so doing, a caregiver offers the child the opportunity to develop the capacity for "mindsight"—the ability to perceive the subjective experience of others, and of themselves. Such an ability may be a cornerstone

of compassion. Reflective dialogues build on contingent forms of nonverbal communication in helping one person feel connected to another.

3. *Repair:* Each form of emotionally involving social relationship involves the inevitable rupture in the attuned, contingent communication that is the "ideal" form of transaction. Contingency is not able to occur in all interactions. We all go through phases of needing connection and then solitude. When we need connection to others and it does not occur, this is called "rupture." Sometimes ruptures occur when we are distracted, tired, or in other ways preoccupied and have missed the opportunity for connecting with others in a contingent manner. At other times, a caregiver may be setting limits on a child's behavior and not be able to "go along" with the desires of a child. In this situation, a caregiver can still acknowledge the child's inner world, though not agreeing with the desire or expressed behavior. Still other times are more difficult, even "toxic," when we may become overwhelmed with anger that directly interferes with our ability to be in tune with our children. At these times, children may become filled with a sense of shame and humiliation, being left with an urge to turn away and with a sense that the self is defective. Repair is essential when there is a rupture, especially of this latter toxic sort. Repair is an interactive process that involves an acknowledgment of the disconnection and an attempt to move forward and reconnect.

4. *Emotional Communication:* Securely attached children often have a form of emotional communication with their parents that involves: (a) the sharing and amplification of positive emotions, such as joy and excitement; and (b) the sharing and soothing of negative emotions, such as fear, sadness, and anger. This sharing of emotion allows a child to learn that emotions are tolerable internally, and can lead to a rewarding sense of closeness interpersonally. Parents may often feel the urge to quickly "solve" a problem that has produced a negative emotional state—but it is important to reflect with a child on this state before rushing to eliminate it. Negative emotions can be seen as an opportunity to deepen a child's capacity for self-regulation and self-understanding. The development of such internal processes may give rise to the interpersonal experiences of empathy and compassion.

5. *Coherent Narratives:* As children grow past their second birthdays, storytelling becomes a vital form of interpersonal communication and internal understanding. Narratives help us to "make sense" of our lives and of other people. Stories enable us to understand the complex social worlds in which we all live. Interestingly, studies have demonstrated that parents who have come to make sense of their own early life relationships have the highest likelihood of having children who are securely attached to them. It is not that the parents tell these coherent stories to their children—but rather that there is some way in which

a parent who has achieved this form of coherent self-knowledge seems to offer children the contingent communication that is at the root of the interactions that enable secure attachments to develop. Helping parents make sense of their own lives may provide a direct route to helping their children develop secure attachments (Siegel & Hartzell, 2003).

Attachment and Neural Integration

Attachment and effective psychotherapy can be proposed to promote neural integration. In insecure attachments, optimal integration is not achieved and the capacity for achieving states of complexity, within the self or with others, is compromised. One form of insecurity of attachment, called "disorganized/disoriented," has been associated with marked impairments in the emotional, social, and cognitive domains, and a predisposition toward a clinical condition known as dissociation in which the capacity to function in an organized, coherent manner is at times impaired.

Studies also have found that youths with a history of disorganized attachments are at great risk of expressing hostility with their peers and have the potential for interpersonal violence as they mature (Lyons-Ruth & Jacobwitz, 1999; Carlson, 1998). This disorganized form of attachment has been proposed to be associated with the caregiver's frightened, frightening, or disoriented behavior with the child. Such experiences create a state of alarm in the child. The parents of these children often have an autobiographical narrative finding, as revealed in the Adult Attachment Interview, of unresolved trauma or grief that appears as a disorientation in their narrative account of their own childhoods. Such linguistic disorientation occurs during the discussion of loss or threat from childhood experiences. Lack of resolution appears to be associated with parental behaviors that are incompatible with an organized adaptation on the part of the child. Lack of resolution of trauma or grief in a parent can lead to parental behaviors that create "paradoxical," unsolvable, and problematic situations for the child. The attachment figure is intended to be the source of protection, soothing, connections, and joy. Instead, the experience of the child who develops a disorganized attachment is such that the caregiver is actually the source of terror and fear, of "fright without solution," and so the child cannot turn to the attachment figure to be soothed (Main & Hesse, 1990). There is not organized adaptation and the child's response to this unsolvable problem is disorganization (see Hesse et al., this volume).

This finding provides important insights into the nature of the transmission of trauma across the generations. Helping such individuals resolve their traumatic experiences and losses may be an important therapeutic intervention in attempting to alter the course of devastation that such transgenerational trauma can create (Siegel & Hartzell, 2003).

The interweaving of findings from attachment research, complexity theory, and neurobiology yield some important ideas about integration, development, and the impact of relationships on the capacity for self-regulation. One idea is that the psychotherapy helps the system to develop the ability to self-organize utilizing the modulation of both internal and external constraints. External constraints involve the flow of energy and information between minds within interpersonal communication. Patterns of communication are the external constraint that can alter the trajectory of the system over time. Internal constraints include the synaptic connections and the neuromodulatory processes that enable the brain to regulate its states of activation, representational processes, and behavioral responses. Such a well-developed capacity for neuromodulation would be mediated by circuits capable of integrating a range of neural processes, from abstract representations to bodily states. As we've discussed, these circuits may confer "value" to stimuli and are functionally connected to the systems that mediate interpersonal communication.

Integration is a central self-organizing mechanism that links these many disparate aspects of internal and interpersonal processes. Integration is defined as the functional coupling of distinct and differentiated elements into a coherent process or functional whole. This concept has been used by a wide range of researchers including those studying group behavior ("inter-individual integration"), development across the lifespan ("individual integration"), and brain functioning ("neural integration"). Within a coherently integrated process, adaptive and flexible states are achieved as individual components remain highly differentiated *and* become functionally united. Such states may also be seen as moving toward conditions that maximize complexity.

Coherent narratives and flexible self-regulation may reflect such an integrative process within the individual mind. Interpersonal integration can be seen when the mind of one person has the free and collaborative exchange of energy and information with another mind. Such adaptive and flexible states flow between regularity and predictability on the one hand, and novelty and spontaneity on the other, to yield a maximal degree of complexity in their functional coupling. Such dyadic states may be seen within the interactions of securely attached children and their parents. The mind—defined as the flow of energy and information—can thus be conceptualized as an inherently integrating system. This system may be viewed from a wide range of levels of analysis, from groups of neurons to dyads, families, and even communities. Such a view may allow us to synthesize our understanding of the neurobiology of the individual brain with insights into the interpersonal functioning of people within dyads and larger social groups.

Another application of the concept of integration can be seen in unresolved trauma or grief. Unresolved states may be conceptualized as an ongoing impediment of the mind to achieve coherent integration. Lack of resolution thus implies a blockage in the flow of information and energy within the mind and may also manifest itself as an impairment in the capacity to achieve a coherent transfer of energy and information between minds. This may help us to understand the finding that the most robust predictor of disorganized attachment is a parent's unresolved state of mind as revealed in the adult attachment narrative.

Impairments to mental health can thus be seen to oscillate to either side of complexity and involve states of excessive rigidity (numbing, avoidance, withdrawal) and those of chaos (flashbacks, intrusive memories and emotions). One example of this failure to achieve integration is in the various forms of dissociation that may accompany lack of resolution. For example, unresolved states may involve the intrusion of elements of implicit memory, such as emotions, behaviors, and perceptions, in the absence of an explicit memory counterpart for aspects of past traumatic experiences (Siegel, 1995). Such "dis-associations" of mental processes may be at the core of clinical "dissociation" and an outcome of both trauma and earlier histories of disorganized attachments.

As discussed previously, a further application of the concept of integration can be seen in an analysis of the nature of our life-stories. The structure of the narrative process itself may reveal the central role of integration in states of mental health and emotional resilience. Within the brain, the neural integration of the processes dominant in the left hemisphere with those dominant in the right can be proposed to produce a "bihemispheric" integration which enables many functions to occur, ranging from perceptual processes to motor coordination. Another process that can be proposed to depend upon bilateral integration is that of coherent narrativization. The left hemisphere functions as what has been called an "interpreter," searching for cause-effect relationships in a linear, logical mode of cognition. The right hemisphere is thought to mediate autonoetic consciousness and the retrieval of autobiographical memory. Also dominant on the right side of the brain is the social cognition or theory of mind module of information processing. Coherent narratives can thus be proposed to be a product of the integration of left and right hemisphere processes: the drive to explain cause-effect relationships (left) and the capacity to understand the minds of others and of the self within autonoetic consciousness (right). In this manner coherent narratives reflect the mind's ability to integrate its processes across time and across the representational processes of both hemispheres.

Perhaps impediments to this central process of the mind's capacity for integration, both internal and interpersonal, are at the core of the deficit in unresolved traumatic experience. Perhaps such an integrative capacity is at the heart of mental health. Finding ways to facilitate an integrative process within and between individuals may enable us to help others grow and develop.

Information Processing and the Resolution of Trauma

Lack of resolution of trauma can be seen as impairment in the innate capacity of the mind to balance the differentiation and integration of energy and information flow. Integration can be defined as the functional clustering of independent subcomponents into a cohesive whole at a given moment in time. Integration also exists across time, and can be described as enabling the mind to achieve coherence across its many states of mind. Within the brain, neural integration can involve a wide range of layers of differentiated components, including clusters of neurons, neural circuits, systems, and hemispheres. With names such as vertical, lateral, dorsal-ventral, and spatiotemporal integration, the nature of this neural process can be described in quite specific detail. At the core of neural integration is the process called emotion. Balanced emotion is inherently integrative: It links subcomponents together in a functional whole. Unbalanced emotion may be revealed in inflexible or chaotic states, as seen in various forms in posttraumatic stress disorder and reflecting an inability to achieve complexity. Emotion is also a fundamental part of self-regulation. In this manner, we can see that the proposal that unresolved trauma exerts its effects by an impairment of integration implies that lack of resolution is a form of self-dysregulation and emotional disequilibrium. Integration, self-regulation, and emotion are thus inextricably intertwined neural processes that are impaired in unresolved traumatic conditions.

Patterns in the flow of energy and information that become ingrained as restrictive or chaotic states reveal a lack of resolution of trauma. As we've discussed, such an impairment in the system's movement toward complexity directly interferes with its ability to adapt to changes in the internal or external environment. Such impaired flexibility leads to dysfunction in both the internal and interpersonal worlds of the individual.

A general approach to psychotherapy for individuals with unresolved trauma would be to attempt to enhance the mind's innate tendency to move toward complexity, both within the brain and within interpersonal relationships. The measure of efficacy for such an approach would be an enhancement in self-regulation and emotional processing. In addition to the dissolution of the many and varied symptoms of posttraumatic stress disorder, we could also predict a number of other fundamental changes in the individual's functioning. From a systems perspective, therapeutic improvement would be revealed as a more adaptive flexibility of the mind to respond to changes in the internal and external environments. Stability of mood would replace emotional lability. Increased capacity to experience a wider range and intensity of emotion would emerge with an enhanced tolerance for change. Resolution would also be revealed as a movement of the individual toward more differentiated abilities while at the same time participating in more "joining" experiences. This increased individual differentiation and interpersonal integration would reflect the mind's movement toward increasingly complex states. Overall, these changes would reflect not only the freedom from posttraumatic symptomatology, but the enhanced capacity of the individual to achieve integration (internal and interpersonal) and thus more adaptive and flexible self-regulation.

One outcome of this enhanced integration would be revealed within more coherent autobiographical narratives for specific traumatic events as well as for the life of the individual as a whole. Such a narrative process can be seen in both the personal stories that are told, as well as the ways in which the individual's life is lived. This latter aspect, called *narrative enactment*, would be seen as the manner in which life decisions are made and the quality in which daily life is experienced.

Contingency, Coherence, and Psychotherapy

In general, psychotherapy is a form of attachment relationship in which the patient seeks proximity to the therapist, has a safe haven (is soothed when upset), and achieves an internal working model of security based on the patterns of communication between therapist and patient. Healing within psychotherapy can thus be seen as the ways in which the innate, hard-wired attachment system of the brain is utilized to enable the patient's mind to achieve more functional self-regulation. As with attachment in general, interactive regulation is first required to enable the mind to achieve more autonomous (and adaptive) self-regulation. The five elements of secure attachments described earlier can be directly applied to the psychotherapy process. These include contingency, reflective dialogue, repair, emotional communication, and coherent narratives. The patterns of communication that have been found to be the most effective in secure attachments are those that involve reciprocal, contingent, collaborative communication. When such processes are disrupted, as they inevitably will be, interactive repair is essential. Contingency and repair involve a give-and-take of signals between the two members of the interacting pair. Right-to-right and left-to-left hemisphere patterns of communication can be described, involving nonverbal and verbal components, respectively.

As discussed above, interpersonal contingency can promote internal coherence. Both processes reflect movement of the system toward complexity. As the sense of a core self emerges out of contingent communication with a therapist, the pathway is established for the development of a coherent autobiographical self. From a consciousness point of view, as we offer our clients a here-and-now form of contingency, they are then able to develop a sense of here-and-now consciousness that is cohesive. As these relationship experiences evolve over time and are coupled with reflective dialogues that examine the past and potential future in light of present experiences, these cohesive and connecting core self-transactions enable the creation of a past-present-future conscious experience and the creation of a coherent autobiographical self. In other words, as here-and-now consciousness builds a cohesive self in the moment, a past-present-future consciousness enables a coherent autobiographical self to emerge.

At the core of effective therapy of many forms may be the manner in which patient and therapist are able to engage in contingent communication. For individuals with unresolved trauma, this therapeutic attachment relationship enables the patient's mind to enter terrifying states that can then process information which before may have led to excessively restrictive or chaotic patterns in the flow of energy and information. These rigidly constrained or disorganized states, at the core of unresolved trauma, can then have the opportunity within this interpersonal communicative experience to be dramatically—and permanently—altered. Note that the essential feature is not that all of the details of trauma be related with words, but rather that the patient be given the sense of safety that such traumatic states can be re-experienced, communicated if possible, and altered into more adaptive patterns in the future. What emerges from such a process are new levels of integration of information and energy flow. If such a process involves the bilateral integration of information across the hemispheres combined with the integration of here-and-now with past-present-future consciousness, an increased coherence of autobiographical narratives may result. Note that the creation or communication of such a narrative may not be essential for resolution, but rather may reveal resolution.

In unresolved traumatic states various representational processes may have remained quite functionally independent, an isolation that may have preserved the ability of the individual to function in the face of traumatic experiences. Now, perhaps for the first time, these representational processes are being activated within the brain simultaneously in the therapeutic experience. This simultaneous activation will be occurring at the same time as the initiation of focal attention within these orienting processes. Such a "synchronic" activation may be necessary, but not sufficient, to begin the process of neural integration. In therapy, this may take the form of the patient focusing on the here-and-now experience with the therapist while simultaneously focusing on the past-present-future elements of memory. Furthermore, focusing in therapy on elements of both the right (imagery, bodily state, emotion, autobiographical memory) and left hemispheres (words, self-concepts, logical understanding of the cause-effect relationships among events in a linear analysis such as a narrative) enables a multidimensional representational activation that may be essential for promoting integration beyond earlier restrictive processes. The nature of the processing that occurs during the simultaneous activation of these previously functionally isolated representational processes can make a significant difference in the direction of information processing and therapeutic outcome.

The process from initial orientation (of attention) to subsequent arousal and appraisal of the mental representations is termed "primary emotion." These primary emotions are expressed as vitality affects (Stern, 1985) and are the "background" emotional processes (Damasio, 1999) that serve as the initial patterns of activations that then may become elaborated into more complex ("specific" or categorical) emotions. Primary emotions, reflected in the profiles of energy activation within the brain, are at the core of how the mind evaluates the significance and meaning of a stimulus. These are the initial aspects of emotional processing. The neural mechanisms underlying this process are proposed to involve neuromodulatory circuits discussed earlier that have a number of properties: (a) they increase the excitability and activation of neurons, (b) they enhance neural plasticity via the growth of synaptic connections, (c) they are widely distributed throughout the brain and enhance integration through their extensive enervation of distinct brain regions, and (d) they are thus fundamental to self-regulation.

Focusing attention in therapy may thus initiate primary emotional processes that enable both internal alteration of representational isolation as well as promote a form of interpersonal emotional connection through the attunement of primary emotion.

The fundamental role of emotion in all aspects of mental life can be seen within the processes by which therapy focuses the patient's orientation toward a particular set of representations. This focus of attention then influences the direction of the "emotional" processing of the varied layers of subjective mental life, from ongoing perceptions to autobiographical representations. As initial orientation is followed by the arousal/appraisal process, a sense of hedonic tone may unfold in which there is an internal sense of good/approach or bad/withdrawal. As the process emerges, these primary emotional states may become elaborated into the categorical or universal emotions of fear, sadness, anger, joy, surprise, disgust, and shame. Such internal states may be apparent as externally expressed affect. Whatever the level of external communication, the patient's internal experience of these emotional states reflects the subjective core of the flow of information processing and the achievement of new levels of integration as therapy proceeds.

In this manner, effective psychotherapy can be seen fundamentally as an emotionally engaging and transformative experience that enables new levels of representational integration to occur. Emotion is inherently integrative. In this manner, one can see how impaired integration, as reflected within emotional dysregulation present in unresolved states, may move toward balanced self-regulation as the emotionally involving therapy progresses.

States of Mind

The simultaneous clustering of functionally distributed representational processes enables the brain to achieve a particular state of mind. In unresolved trauma, a particular activation of elements within focal attention may create a semi-stable state—usually nonconsciously avoided or intrusively flooding and disabling outside of therapy—that can now be a primary focus of treatment. The brain is now being "primed," that is, being made more likely, to activate new associations of representational processes. In fact, the therapist's strategic clustering of these multilayered elements of cognition creates a unique state of mind that may enable new directions of information processing to occur. The impediments to the acquisition of these new forms of processing, as we've discussed above, can be proposed to be embedded in either an excessively restricted, rigid pattern in the flow of states, or a chaotic, flooding, and disorganizing flow of states. Either condition has led to an impairment in the adaptive, flexible response to internal or external factors. Such inflexibility is the greatest challenge at this moment in therapy. This inflexibility may be at the foundation of the "getting stuck" or "going blank" that may have occurred in the patient's life, as well as in moments within the therapy process itself. Such "stuck" points can be seen as the emergence of the rigid patterns of the flow of information processing and energy in the brain. They are ingrained patterns in dire need of change.

One way in which these past stuck points can be altered is that these new multilayered simultaneous activations within focal attention/working memory contain within them intense emotional elements that are potentially open to change. The setting of a secure patient-therapist relationship may create a sense of safety that allows the discomfort, anxiety, fear, or outright terror to become more tolerable. Offering relaxation techniques can enable a patient to focus attention on these traumatic elements while simultaneously having the intensely negative affective component be soothed to some degree. The overall effect would be to enable multiple layers of focal processing, alter the subjective experience of the state of mind, and enable such states to be better tolerated. The re-encoding of these representational elements in this setting of less distressful affect would then allow for a less distressing emotional charge to become associated with the "reconstructed" memory representation. Future retrieval would then reveal such a newly reorganized memory configuration which, in turn, would be more easily tolerated. The repeated process of such activation, multilayered focal attention, encoding, reactivation, and encoding, would modify the memory into a more tolerated, integrated, and perhaps "resolved" configuration that no longer had such devastating effects on the flexibility of the system's flow of states.

The Central Role of Integration

As described in the first half of this chapter, we can propose that the traumatic impairments to neural integration have many layers of effects. One layer is on the isolation of the representational processes of the right and left hemispheres. These two regions have asymmetries in the developing embryo that give rise to quite distinct modes of constructing reality (Tucker, Luu, & Pribram, 1995; Trevarthen, 1996). In reviewing a range of research findings from laterality studies, emotion, and memory, the proposal can be made (as summarized earlier in this chapter) that the process of integrating the modalities from the left and right hemispheres enables traumatic memories to be processed in a new manner that allows resolution to occur. This process may be a component of the emotionally attuned communication and coconstruction of narratives that are a foundation of numerous forms of therapy. In this manner, both nonverbal and verbal communication enable patient and therapist to "resonate" with each other in a fashion that begins to promote internal "resonance" or integration within each person's mind. The patient and the therapist are both impacted by the experience of psychotherapy. Coherent narratives emerge from such an integrative process and can be proposed to reveal, as well as promote, the resolution of trauma.

One view of development is that it involves the organization, disorganization, and re-organization of patterns in the flow of states of mind.

In this manner, development requires periods of disequilibrium in order to move forward in its ever-changing trajectory. In unresolved trauma, such forward movement has stopped. Restrictive or chaotic states preclude adaptive development from occurring. Such states inhibit the movement toward complexity and reveal a "stressed" system. Therapeutic interventions that create new associations of representations related to traumatic experiences are a start. Enabling more global changes in the flow of states across time based on these representational activations is one aspect of change that neural integration may be catalyzing. Such integration may indeed occur within emotionally attuned, coconstructing therapeutic relationships that encourage the processing of information in both the verbal and nonverbal domains.

We have the ability to have "observer" or "participant" recollections, possibly reflecting our noetic and autonoetic reflections on personally experienced events, respectively. Some suggest that the noetic, semantic, or factual elements of memory are stored predominantly in the left hemisphere, whereas autobiographical (the sense of the self in the past, not merely the knowledge of such an experience) representations are stored in the right hemisphere. As discussed earlier, flashbacks appear to involve the intense activation of the right hemisphere (visual cortex) in the setting of left hemisphere (speech area) deactivation. In this manner, focusing attention on verbal and nonverbal dimensions of memory may "force" the activation of both hemispheres in the therapeutic process of integrating autobiographical and semantic representations of traumatic events. For some patients, the therapeutic technique of facilitating the synchronous process of representational activation involving the circuits of each hemisphere (as discussed above) may be sufficient to produce excellent results. Others may require additional therapeutic approaches to promote healing. Neural integration may be at the heart of resolution, but the therapeutic strategies necessary to achieve it may vary depending on the particular needs of a given individual.

One example of a strategic focus on neural integration involves the psychotherapeutic processing of representations from both sides of the brain. Such a process, as described above, seems to evoke a noetic/autonoetic encoding and retrieval state that enables memory to be processed in an accelerated fashion. As the structure of memory may be layered by a wide range of explicit components, such as periods of life, thematic elements, specific experiences, and evaluative components, as well as the implicit elements of emotion, behavioral impulse, perception, and bodily sensation, the therapeutic processing of traumatic memory may involve the integration of a wide array of mental processes. These activated representations can then be functionally linked to each other in truly new combinations that are likely mediated by the creation of new synaptic linkages. Effective therapy does not only involve an intensely emotional experience in the moment, but probably involves lasting changes in brain structure and function.

Central in the encoding and retrieval of autobiographical memory appears to be the region of the prefrontal cortex we've discussed at length earlier in the chapter, the orbitofrontal cortex. As a region of the brain in the unique position of receiving and sending input from and to a wide range of important regions, the orbitofrontal cortex plays a crucial role in neural integration. Researchers have recently proposed that post traumatic stress disorder may involve disruptions in the functioning of medial aspects of the prefrontal cortex, including the orbitofrontal region (Bremner, 2002). The findings that this region is essential in attachment, autobiographical memory, representation and regulation of bodily state, social cognition, and the expression and regulation of emotion, further highlight the probable importance of this area in the resolution of trauma. The ways in which the brain comes to modulate states of mind in a more flexible manner, to tolerate a wider range of emotional states, to gain access to and consolidate autobiographical memory, and to enable more complex levels of interpersonal relatedness may each be mediated in large part by this region of the brain. When we look to the mechanisms of resolution of trauma as being rooted in neural integration, we may be well advised to look toward the integrative orbitofrontal region in mediating the acquisition of mental coherence.

Resolution: Response Flexibility, Autonoetic Consciousness, and Integration

Response flexibility is an important integrative process also mediated by the orbitofrontal region. Response flexibility refers to the capacity of the brain to respond to changes in the internal or external environment with a flexibly adaptive range of behavioral or cognitive responses. A number of studies point to the central role of the orbitofrontal region in carrying out such a capacity (Nobre et al., 1999; Mesulam, 1998). One can propose that this ability requires the integrative capacities of the orbitofrontal region in order to functionally link elements from widely distributed input and output circuits. As discussed earlier, this region is uniquely positioned to link the major regions of the brain, including the associational cortex, limbic circuits, and brain-stem areas. In this manner, the orbitofrontal region enables the more complex "higher order" processing of the neocortex to be integrated with the "lower order" functions of the deeper structures. Autonoetic consciousness may reveal one example of this "higher mode" of integrative processing, one that permits mental time travel and a deep sense of self-awareness.

One extension of this view is that the mind is capable of a mode of information processing that does not involve the higher mode of processing. In such a "lower mode" (or, as some of my students have preferred to call it, a "low road") of processing, response flexibility is suspended along with other integrative functions such as autonoetic consciousness and impulse control (Siegel, 2001a). In this lower mode, behaviors become reflexive and the mind becomes filled with deeply engrained, inflexible patterns of response. In such a condition, emotions may flood the mind and make rational thought and mindful behavior quite impaired. We can propose that one effect of trauma is to make such a lower mode of processing more likely to occur. While each of us may be vulnerable to entering such states given the "proper" stressful situations, unresolved trauma may make entry into such states more frequent, more intense, and more likely to occur with minimal provocation. Recovery from such states that have moved beyond a "window of tolerance" may also be especially difficult in unresolved traumatic conditions. In this situation, the individual may remain "on the low road" for more extended durations as well as with increased frequency.

The neurobiology of such a lower mode of processing can be proposed to involve the state-dependent inhibition of the prefrontally-mediated neural integration of neocortical input from that of the limbic and brain-stem regions of the brain. In such a condition, the individual may be driven by the lower regions of the brain and dominated by intense emotions as well as elements of implicit memory. Implicit processes, such as behaviors, emotions, perceptual biases, and mental models, may become activated without the sense of something being recalled. Such a state may be present, we can propose, in flashback conditions as well as in intense emotional responses to trauma-related stimuli from the external or internal environment. Entry into such states can produce excessive emotional reactions, inner turmoil, dread, or terror as well as an ensuing sense of shame and humiliation. In such conditions, the individual may be prone to "infantile rage" and aggressive, intrusive, or outright violent behavior. Interpersonally, the entrance into such states directly impairs the capacity of the individual to maintain collaborative communication. In this way, the tendency to have an impairment in response flexibility and autonoetic consciousness may be at the core of how parents with unresolved trauma engage in the frightened and/or frightening behaviors that lead to disorganized attachment in their offspring. Lower mode states do not allow for the sensitive, contingent communication that secure attachments require. Herein may lie the core elements in the intergenerational transfer of trauma as its devastating effects leave a wake of pain across the boundaries of space and time that separate one mind from another.

As psychotherapeutic interventions promote neural integration, we can imagine that the integrative orbitofrontal region may become more actively involved in the global functioning of the individual. We can also propose that this outcome would be especially evident during the activation of representations related to traumatic memories. In unresolved states, trauma-related stimuli may activate a cascade of mental representations that produce an inhibition of response flexibility and autonoetic consciousness. As discussed earlier, this impairment may take the form of either excessively rigid or of disorganized patterns in the flow of states of mind across time. In this way, the blockage of orbitofrontally mediated integration during trauma-related conditions may be the mechanism of impaired flexibility of response. Resolution would thus involve the repair of such impediments to flexible self-regulation.

Psychotherapeutic processes may facilitate the resolution of trauma by altering the constraints on the flow of states of mind within the individual. At the most basic level of analysis, this alteration in the pattern of neural firing is likely to be mediated by changes in synaptic strengths among widely distributed neurons in the brain. These changes may be especially evident in the function of the neuromodulatory circuits. The growth of new synaptic connections as well as of neurons themselves may be revealed with the integrative fibers of regions such as the hippocampus that have been recently shown to develop throughout the lifespan (Benes, 1998). We might also want to look toward the corpus callosum, cerebellum, and the anterior cingulate as other integrative regions that may respond positively with new development as a result of effective treatment and the resolution of trauma. Future research can help to illuminate exactly how psychotherapeutic interventions create lasting changes in an individual's brain, and thus the mind, in enabling the process of mental well-being to develop. The more global effects of resolution would be seen in how the mind functions as a complex system, now allowing for the more complex flow of energy and information within itself and in connection to other minds. Such a healing process is thus far more than the modification of the degree of distress associated with traumatic memories. Instead, the resolution of trauma can be viewed as enabling the mind to regain the natural process of the integration of differentiated processes across time and across states of mind. Successful resolution creates a deep sense of coherence within the individual. Enhanced autonoetic consciousness would be the outcome of such a resolution process and revealed as a more flexible capacity of the individual to reflect on the past, live fully in the present, and have an active sense of the self in the future.

This new level of mental coherence can be revealed within autobiographical narratives that "make sense" of past experiences and their impact on present functioning as well as allowing the mind to create a sense of hope for the future.

An individual moves from being the passive victim of trauma to the active author of the ongoing story of his or her life. Integrating coherence, though, is not a final achievement. Rather, it is a process that enables the person to engage in the spontaneous and flexible flow of energy and information within the mind, as well as within meaningful and invigorating connections with others.

This perspective allows us to be in a position to base our clinical efforts in a scientific foundation that supports the important work we do as therapists with the subjective lives of people in trying to help them heal. We need to understand how the mind and brain function, such as in knowing the difference between implicit and explicit memory, in order to help people make sense of their internal worlds and their interpersonal actions. As we help to focus attention on both the here-and-now and on the integration of the past, the present, and the future, we can promote a deep sense of coherent self-knowledge. This focus on connecting layers of subjective internal experiences across time is not just some idle preoccupation we have as therapists, but a neurologically based process of integration that allows the potentially activated representations of the brain to be able to have an adaptive and fluid flow as the mind is created. In trauma, rigidities to this flow of energy and information have developed as adaptations that can lead to various difficulties as the mind flows to the extremes of either order and sameness, or rigidity and chaos. An oscillation between these two poles prevents the individual from achieving the highly complex internal or interpersonal states that can be seen as the essence of mental health. Our role in treating individuals with unresolved trauma clearly has important implications for the next generation. Attachment research has pointed the way to the idea that if an individual has unresolved trauma or grief, conditions we know are treatable, then we need to lend ourselves to facilitating the individual's innate healing process so that we can try to help not only this generation but also the well-being of future generations.

References and Suggested Reading

Aitken, K. J., & Trevarthen, C. (1997). Self-other organization in human psychological development. *Development and Psychopathology, 9,* 653–678.

Baron-Cohen S. (1995). *Mindblindness: An essay on autism and theory of mind.* Cambridge, MA: MIT Press.

Bauer, P. J. (1996). What do infants recall of their lives? Memory for specific events by one- to two-year-olds. *American Psychologist, 51,* 29–41.

Beebe B., & Lachman F. (1994). Representation and internalization in infancy: Three principles of salience. *Psychoanalytic Psychology, 11,* 127–166.

Benes, F. M. (1998). Human brain growth spans decades. *American Journal of Psychiatry, 155,* 1489.

Bjork, R. (1989). Retrieval inhibition as an adaptive mechanism in human memory. In H. L. Roediger & F. I. M. Craik (Eds.), *Varieties of memory and consciousness: Essays in honor of Endel Tulving* (pp. 283–288). London: Wiley.

Boldrini, M., Placidi, G. P. A., & Marazziti, D. (1998). Applications of chaos theories to psychiatry: A review and future perspectives. *International Journal of Neuropsychiatric Medicine, 3*, 22–29.

Bowlby, J. (1969). *Attachment and loss. Volume 1: Attachment.* New York: Basic Books.

Bremner, J. D. (2002). *Does stress damage the brain?* New York: Norton.

Bremner, J. D., & Narayan, M. (1998). The effects of stress on memory and the hippocampus throughout the life cycle: Implications for childhood development and aging. *Development and Psychopathology, 10*, 871–888.

Carlson, E. A. (1998). A prospective longitudinal study of disorganized/disoriented attachment. *Child Development, 69*, 1107–1128.

Cicchetti, D., & Rogosch, F. A., (editors) (1997). *Self-Organization: Special Issue, Development and Psychopathology, 9*, 595–929.

Corbetta, M., Akbudak, E., Conturo, T. E., Snyder, A. Z., Ollinger, J. M., Drury, H. A., Lineweber, M. R., Petersen, S. E., & Van Essen, D. C. (1998). A common network of functional areas for attention and eye movements. *Neuron, 21*, 761–773.

Cozolino, L. (2002). *The neuroscience of psychotherapy: Building and rebuilding the brain.* New York: Norton.

Damasio, A. (1994). *Descartes' error: Emotion, reason, and the human brain.* New York: Grosset/Putnam.

Damasio, A. (1999). *The Feeling of what happens: Emotion and the body in the making of consciousness.* New York: Harcourt Brace.

De Bellis, M. (1999). *The neurobiology of trauma.* Presentation at the Annual Meeting of the American Academy of Child and Adolescent Psychiatry, Chicago.

De Bellis, M. D., Baum, A. S., Birmaher, B., Keshavan, M. S., Eccard, C. H., Boring, A. M., Jenkins, F. J., & Ryan, N. D. (1999a). A. E. Bennett Research Award. Developmental traumatology. Part I: Biological stress systems. *Biological Psychiatry, 45*(10), 1259–1270.

De Bellis, M. D., Keshavan, M. S., Clark, D. B., Casey, B. J., Giedd, J. N., Boring, A. M., Frustaci, K., & Ryan, N. D. (1999b). A. E. Bennett Research Award. Developmental traumatology. Part II: Brain development. *Biological Psychiatry, 45*(10),1271–1284.

Dolan, R. J. (1999). On the neurology of morals. *Nature Neuroscience 2*, 927–929.

Edelman G. (1992). *Bright air, brilliant fire.* New York: Basic Books.

Fogel, A., Lyra, M. C. D. P., & Valsiner, J. (editors) (1998). *Dynamics and indeterminism in developmental and social processes.* Mahwah, NJ: Erlbaum.

Fonagy, P., & Target, M. (1997). Attachment and reflective function: Their role in self-organization. *Development and Psychopathology, 9*, 679–700.

Garber, J., & Dodge, K. A. (Eds.) (1991). *The Development of emotion regulation and dysregulation.* Cambridge, U.K.: Cambridge University Press.

Hesse, E. (1999). The adult attachment interview: Historical and current perspectives. In J. Cassidy & P. Shaver (Eds.), *Handbook of attachment* (pp. 395–433). New York: Guilford Press.

Hofer, M. A. (1994). Hidden regulators in attachment, separation, and loss. In N. A. Fox (Ed.), *The development of emotion regulation: biological and behavioral considerations. Monographs of the Society for Research in Child Development, 240*(59), 192–207.

Kandel, E. R. (1998). A new intellectual framework for psychiatry. *American Journal of Psychiatry, 155*, 457–469.

Kinsbourne, M. (1972). Eye and head turning indicates cerebral lateralization. *Science, 176*, 539–541.

Kinsbourne, M. (1974). Direction of gaze and distribution of cerebral thought processes. *Neuropsychologia, 12* (2), 279–281.

Le Doux, J. (2002). *The synaptic self.* New York: Viking Press.

Llinas, R. R. (1990). Intrinsic electrical properties of mammalian neurons and CNS function. *Fidia Research Foundation Neuroscience Award Lectures, 4,* 175–194.

Lyons-Ruth, K., & Jacobwitz, D. (1999). Attachment disorganization: Unresolved loss, relational violence, and lapses in behavioral and attentional strategies. In J. Cassidy and P. R. Shaver (Eds.), *Handbook of attachment: Theory, research, and clinical applications* (pp. 520–554). New York: Guilford Press.

Main M. (1991). Metacognitive knowledge, metacognitive monitoring, and singular (coherent) versus multiple (incoherent) models of attachment: Findings and directions for future research. In C. M. Parkes, J. Stevenson-Hinde, & P. Marris (Eds.), *Attachment across the life cycle* (pp. 127–159). London: Routledge.

Main, M. (1995). Attachment: Overview, with implications for clinical work. In S. Goldberg, R. Muir, & J. Kerr (Eds.), *Attachment theory: Social, developmental and clinical perspectives* (pp. 407–474). Hillsdale, NJ: Analytic Press.

Main, M., & Hesse, E. (1990). Parents' unresolved traumatic experiences are related to infant disorganized status: Is frightened and/or frightening parental behavior the linking mechanism? In M. Greenberg, D. Cicchetti, & M. Cummings (Eds.), *Attachment in the preschool years* (pp. 161–182). Chicago: University of Chicago Press.

Main, M., & Morgan, H. (1996). Disorganization and disorientation in infant strange situation behavior: Phenotypic resemblance to dissociative states. In L. K. Michelson & W. J. Ray (Eds.), *Handbook of dissociation: Theoretical, empirical, and clinical perspectives.* New York: Plenum Press.

McClelland, J. L. (1998). Complementary learning systems in the brain: A connectionist approach to explicit and implicit cognition and memory. *Annals of the New York Academy of Sciences, 843,* 153–178.

Meaney, M. J. (2001). Maternal care, gene expression, and the transmission of individual differences in stress reactivity across generations. *Annual Review of Neuroscience 24,* 1161–1192.

Mesulam, M. M. (1998). Review article: From sensation to cognition. *Brain, 121,* 1013–1052.

Milner, B., Squire, L. R., & Kandel, E. R. (1998). Cognitive neuroscience and the study of memory. *Neuron, 20,* 445–468.

Nobre, A. C., Coull, J. T., Frith, C. D., & Mesulam, M. M. (1999). Orbitofrontal cortex is activated during breaches of expectation in tasks of visual attention. *Nature Neuroscience, 2,* 11–12.

Ogawa, J. R., Sroufe, L. A., Weinfeld, N. S., Carlson, E. A., & Egeland, B. (1997). Development and the fragmented self: Longitudinal study of dissociative symptomatology in a nonclinical sample. *Development and Psychopathology, 9,* 855–880.

Phelps, J. L., Belskg, J., & Cmic, K. (1998). Earned security, daily stress, and parenting: A comparison of five alternative models. *Development and Psychopathology, 10,* 21–38.

Rauch, S. L., van der Kolk, B. A., Fisler, R. E., Alpert, N. M., Orr, S. P., Savage, C. R., Fischman, A. J., Jenike, M. A., & Pitman, R. K. (1996). A symptom provocation study of posttraumatic stress disorder using positron emission tomography and script-driven imagery. *Archives of General Psychiatry, 53,* 380–387.

Roisman, G. I., Padron, E., Sroufe, L. A., Egeland, B. (2002). Earned-secure attachment status in retrospect and prospect. *Child Development, 73*(4), 1204–1219.

Schore, A. N. (1994). *Affect regulation and the origin of the self: The neurobiology of emotional development*. Hillsdale, NJ: Erlbaum.

Schore, A. N. (1996). The experience-dependent maturation of a regulatory system in the orbital prefrontal cortex and the origin of developmental psychopathology. *Development and Psychopathology, 8*, 59–87.

Siegel, D. J. (1995). Memory, trauma, and psychotherapy: A cognitive science view. *Journal of Psychotherapy Practice and Research, 4*, 93–122.

Siegel, D. J. (1996). Cognition, memory, and dissociation. *Child and Adolescent Clinics of North America, 5*, 509–536.

Siegel, D. J. (1999). *The developing mind: Toward a neurobiology of interpersonal experience*. New York: Guilford Press.

Siegel, D. J. (2001a). Toward an interpersonal neurobiology of the developing mind: Attachment relationships, "mindsight," and neural integration. *Infant Mental Health Journal, Special Edition on Contributions of the Decade of the Brain to Infant Psychiatry, 22*, 67–94.

Siegel, D. J. (2001b). Memory, An overview, with emphasis on developmental, interpersonal, and neurobiological aspects. *Journal of the American Academy of Child and Adolescent Psychiatry, 40*(9), 997–1011.

Siegel, D. J. (2002). *Mindsight: Making sense of life from the inside out*. Unpublished manuscript.

Siegel, D. J., & Hartzell, M. (2003). *Parenting from the inside-out*. New York: Penguin/Putnam.

Siegel, D. J., & Hartzell, M. (2003). Parenting from the Inside Out: How a deeper self-understanding can help you raise children who thrive, New York: Penguin/Putnam.

Spear, L. P. (2000). The adolescent brain and age-related behavioral manifestations. *Neuroscience and Biobehavioral Reviews, 24*, 417–463.

Sroufe, L. A. (1996). *Emotional development: The organization of emotional life in the early years*. New York: Cambridge University Press.

Stern, D. N. (1985). *The interpersonal world of the infant*. New York: Basic Books.

Suomi, S. J. (in press). How gene-environment interactions can shape the development of socioemotional regulation in rhesus monkeys. In Socioemotional regulation: Dimensions, developmental trends, and influences. Ed. B. S. Zuckerman and A. F. Lieberman, Skillman, NJ: Johnson and Johnson.

Teicher, M. (2002). Scars that will not heal: The neurobiology of child abuse. *Scientific American, 286*(3), 68–75.

Tononi, G., & Edelman, G. M. (1998). Consciousness and complexity. *Science, 282*, 1846–1851.

Trevarthen, C. (1996). Lateral asymmetries in infancy: Implications for the development of the hemispheres. *Neuroscience and Biobehavioral Reviews, 20*, 571–586.

Tucker, D. M., Luu, P., & Pribram, K. H. (1995). Social and emotional self-regulation. *Annals of the New York Academy of Sciences, 769*, 213–239.

Tulving, E., Kapur, S., Craik, F. I. M., Moscovitich, M., & Houle, S. (1994). Hemispheric encoding/retrieval asymmetry in episodic memory: Positron emission tomography findings. *Proceedings of the National Academy of Sciences USA, 91*, 2016–2020.

Whalens, T. (1999). *Institute chair, Institute on Advanced Psychopharmacology: Contemporary Issues in Clinical Care*. 1999 Annual Meeting of the American Academy of Child and Adolescent Psychiatry, Chicago.

Wheeler, M. A., Stuss, D. T., and Tulving, E. (1997). Toward a theory of episodic memory: The frontal lobes and autonoetic consciousness. *Psychological Bulletin, 121*(3), 331–354.

Wilson, E. O. (1998). *Consilience: The unity of knowledge*. New York: Vintage.

2

Unresolved States Regarding Loss or Abuse Can Have "Second-Generation" Effects: Disorganization, Role Inversion, and Frightening Ideation in the Offspring of Traumatized, Non-Maltreating Parents*

Erik Hesse, Mary Main, Kelley Yost Abrams, and Anne Rifkin

THE INFLUENCE OF early development on later psychological functioning is a central focus of attachment theory and of much clinical theory as well. Attachment theory and its accompanying research paradigms differ from most traditional clinical perspectives, however, in focusing on (a) the evolutionary origins and adaptive, or biological, function of the infant's endeavors to maintain proximity to its caregiver, and relatedly (b) both observational and experimental

*We are grateful to the American Psychoanalytic Foundation, the Harris Foundation of Chicago, and the Kohler-Stiftung Foundation of Munich for their financial assistance in support of this project.

approaches to research. Early empirical work in attachment centered on direct observation of behavior with infants, young children, and their parents (e.g., Ainsworth, 1967; Robertson & Bowlby 1952; Heinicke & Westheimer, 1966). Beginning in the 1980s, however, new methods for systematically approaching aspects of representational processes in both adults and children were developed (Main, Kaplan, & Cassidy, 1985).

Partially as a result of this shift to the investigation of the "internal" processes responsible for variations in attachment relationships, the study of attachment is gaining the attention of clinicians. This is due in good part to the creation of language-based methodologies such as the Adult Attachment Interview, which emphasizes individual differences in narrative and specific aspects of conversational (discourse) usages during discussion of past experiences. This methodology has advanced the potential for designing and testing clinical hypotheses in adults and latency-aged children[1] (AAI protocol, George, Kaplan, & Main, 1984, 1985, 1996; AAI system of analysis, Main & Goldwyn, 1984–1998; Main, Goldwyn, & Hesse, 2002; see Hesse, 1999a, for overview). Concurrently, fine-grained research regarding attachment-related behavior in parents and infants has continued against the backdrop of the Ainsworth strange situation procedure (Ainsworth, Blehar, Waters, & Wall, 1978) and its middle-childhood equivalents (e.g., Main & Cassidy, 1988). By combining these methodologies, researchers are investigating relations between representational and behavioral/emotional processes in caregivers, and behavioral/emotional and (later) representational processes in their offspring. It is therefore becoming possible to systematize attachment-related precursors to a variety of clinical outcomes.

Using traditional attachment theory and some of its recent extensions, this presentation focuses on the confusing, disorganizing, and disorienting effects which repeated experiences involving *fear of the parent* should at times engender among attached infants. In some cases, of course, an infant will be fearful as a result of physical abuse. Here, however, we address the implications of

---

[1] As Hesse's (1999a) overview indicated, three studies employing the AAI with children have been carried out. Maureen Gaffney at Trinity College has recently reported that interviews conducted with a small sample of 11-year-old children in Dublin have a match above 70% to those of their mothers, coming close to the average match previously reported in a meta-analysis of mother-infant samples (Gaffney, personal communication; van IJzendoorn, 1995; Hesse, 1999). Massimo Ammaniti and his colleagues at the University of Rome have found secure vs. insecure attachment status stable from 10 to 14 years of age (Ammaniti, van IJzendoorn, Speranza, & Tambelli, 2000), while in a blinded study Judith Trowell and her colleagues at the Tavistock Clinic in London have found the AAI categories sharply discriminated 42 sexually abused children (6–14 years) from their matches (20 community and 20 community mental health controls). All three research groups have used the Main and Goldwyn (1984–1998) system of interview analysis. Trowell (personal communication, 1997) found that the interview works well with children 10 years of age and older, but may be difficult for those younger children independently found to experience difficulties with language comprehension.

interacting with a *traumatized but nonabusive* parent who may in many cases be normally sensitive and responsive. We will also suggest that, presumably resulting from their own traumatic experiences or frightening ideation, some such parents might sporadically but repeatedly alarm the infant via (often involuntary or unconscious) exhibition of frightened or dissociative behavior. We report that sporadic but ongoing interactions of this kind are associated with the infant becoming "disorganized/disoriented" (D) under the stress of Ainsworth's separation-and-reunion procedure (Main & Solomon, 1990; Ainsworth et al., 1978), and that D attachment status with the mother during infancy has been associated with increased vulnerability to psychopathology in adolescence (see Carlson, 1998).

This given, clinicians might want to consider whether overwhelming events experienced by some patient's *parents* have indirectly become associated with the patient's symptomatology, especially where it is difficult to identify more direct experiential origins of the patient's mental state. Support for the existence of this kind of "second-generation effect" with respect to a parent's traumatic experiences has of course depended upon empirically linking the parent's traumatized state to difficulties exhibited by the offspring. This link was first uncovered in a sample studied by Main and Hesse (1990, 1992), and has been replicated by many succeeding investigators. In these studies, the parent's unresolved/ traumatized state is identified via marked *lapses in the monitoring of reasoning or discourse* during the discussion of potentially traumatic experiences within the Adult Attachment Interview (AAI). Parents exhibiting these lapses are found more likely than others to have infants judged disorganized/disoriented with them in Ainsworth's strange situation procedure. Discourse or reasoning lapses during the AAI are presently being found associated with *frightened, dissociative, or threatening (FR) parental behavior* observed in the home or in laboratory play sessions, and FR parental behavior has now in fact repeatedly been found predictive of disorganized/disoriented (D) infant strange situation behavior. Thus, the central argument of this chapter is that lapses in the monitoring of reasoning or discourse during discussions of loss or trauma may (a) be subtle indicators of sporadic representational/ mental disturbances, which (b) mediate proportionally subtle anomalous parental behaviors, that (c) can in turn have adverse effects upon the offspring, even in the presence of otherwise sensitive parenting.

Disorganized Attachment Status in Infancy: Unfavorable Sequelae

The Ainsworth strange situation is a structured laboratory procedure in which one-year-old infants are observed responding to two brief separations from, and reunions with, the parent (Ainsworth et al., 1978; see also Main, 2000). While behavioral responses to this procedure lead a majority of infants in low-risk samples to be classified according to Ainsworth's original three "organized" attachment patterns (secure, avoidant, or ambivalent), a substantial minority are now placed in a fourth, disorganized/disoriented attachment category. The D classification is assigned to infants exhibiting any of a wide variety of odd, inexplicable, conflicted, or apprehensive behaviors in the parent's presence, such as leaning sobbing with head on wall and gaze averted, rocking on hands and knees specifically in response to the return of the parent, interrupting an approach to the parent by falling huddled to the floor, or freezing all movement with a trancelike expression (Main & Solomon, 1990). In short, D is assigned when an infant with no known neurological impairment[2] exhibits an observable "collapse of attentional and behavioral strategies" (Main & Hesse, 1992; see Hesse, 1999b). Infants are generally found to exhibit disorganized behavior in the presence of *only one* of the two parents, and by 1999, multiple studies had failed to find indices of distinct temperamental or constitutional components in D strange situation responses (van IJzendoorn, Schuengel, & Bakermans-Kranenburg, 1999; but see Lakatos et al., 2000).

In neurologically normal high-risk and low-risk samples, D attachment status with mother during infancy has been associated with aspects of psychopathology from middle childhood to late adolescence. Early disorganization has been shown to be associated with unusual levels of aggression (i.e., disruptive/aggressive or "externalizing" disorders) in both high- and low-risk samples (see Lyons-Ruth, 1996, and Lyons-Ruth & Jacobvitz, 1999, for a narrative overview; see van IJzendoorn, et al., 1999, for a meta-analysis of these studies).

In a finding the author termed "unprecedented," Carlson (1998) reported that overall psychopathology at age 17 was predictable from D strange situation behavior with the mother during infancy (the K-SADS-E interview was used to assess psychopathology in this large, high-risk Minnesota poverty sample). In keeping with a proposal advanced by Liotti (1992), Carlson found infant D attachment also specifically associated with dissociative-like *behavior* observed in both elementary school and high school, and dissociative *experiences* as described to the K-SADS interviewer. Within the same sample, Ogawa and colleagues (1997) additionally found early disorganization predictive of self-reports of dissociative experiences using a brief "pencil and paper" inventory

---

[2] Some such behaviors are of course common in atypical samples, e.g., infants or young children diagnosed with Downs syndrome or autism (Main & Solomon, 1990; see also Pipp-Siegel, Siegel, & Dean, 1999).

at age 19, but only if the young adult had also experienced intervening trauma (Ogawa and his colleagues used Carlson & Putnam's DES self-report inventory, 1993).

Infant disorganization has, then, been linked with specific child and adolescent diagnostic categories. Additionally, in a low-risk middle-class sample, disorganized (as opposed to secure, avoidant, or ambivalent) infant attachment status was already known to predict role inversion with the parent in many children by age six, and also response inhibition, dysfluent discourse, and narratives involving "catastrophic" fantasies (Main et al., 1985). With respect to role-inversion, Main and Cassidy (1988) reported that, seen on reunion following a one-hour separation, children (age 6) previously disorganized with a particular parent tended to be controlling of that same parent. Some of these children harshly ordered the parent about ("Sit down! I said, sit down!", "I told you what to do—now do it!") or humiliated the parent by remaining silent in the face of the parent's repeated overtures—responses termed Controlling-punitive. Others inverted roles with the parent by becoming excessively solicitous ("Did you have a nice time while you were gone? Would you like to sit down and have me bring you something?"), responses which were termed Controlling-caregiving (Main & Cassidy, 1988). The development of D-Controlling behavior during middle childhood in children judged D with the same parent during infancy has been replicated in three further studies (Wartner et al., 1994; Jacobsen et al., 1997, Jacobsen et al., 1992; and Steele, Steele, & Fonagy, 1996b.), and D-Controlling behavior is now used to identify disorganization in later childhood (van IJzendoorn et al., 1999; a system developed by Cassidy & Marvin, 1992, also utilizes this category).

Viewed at the behavioral level, then, early disorganization following brief separations from an unresolved caregiver appears to have vanished by middle childhood, having been replaced by organized (albeit controlling) behavior. When these same children are asked to respond to imagined child-parent separations, however, states of fear and disorientation reappear (Kaplan, 1987; see also Main et al., 1985). Using interview transcripts taken from an adaptation of Hansburg's Separation Anxiety Test (SAT; 1972; see also Klagsbrun & Bowlby, 1976), Kaplan presented six-year-olds with pictures involving separations ranging from a goodnight kiss to a two-week parental leave-taking. The child was asked what he or she thought the pictured child would do, and how the child might feel in response to these pictured separations. Responses were transcribed verbatim. In "blind" analyses (i.e., working without knowledge of early strange situation classifications), Kaplan identified the majority of the six-year-olds who had been judged D with the mother during infancy Fearful-Disorganized/disoriented (D-fearful). Indeed, many D children now demonstrated signs of being *"inexplicably afraid and unable to do anything about it"* (Kaplan, 1987, p. 109).

The central responses leading to D-Fearful placement in Kaplan's study were:

(a) *Direct descriptions of fearful events.* These included markedly catastrophic fantasies. For example, asked what the pictured child would *feel*, one previously disorganized child (who had herself had no loss experiences to date) said:

> She's afraid.
> (*Why is she afraid?*).
> Her dad might die and then she'll be by herself.
> (*Why is she afraid of that?*).
> Because her mom died and if her mom died, she thinks that her dad might die.

Asked what the pictured child would *do*, another previously disorganized child—also with no personal loss experiences—responded:

> Probably gonna lock himself up.
> (*Lock himself up?*).
> Yeah, probably in his closet.
> (*Then what will he do?*)
> Probably kill himself.
> (Kaplan, 1987, pp. 109–110)

Other investigators have also noted the chaotic, flooded, catastrophic quality of response to (doll-play) separations in D children (e.g., Solomon, George, & DeJong, 1995). Here, for example, is one D-controlling six-year-old responding to a query regarding what might happen during an overnight parent-child separation:

> And see, and then, you know what happens? Their whole house blows up. See . . . they get destroyed and not even their bones are left. Nobody can even get their bones. Look. I'm jumping on a rock. This rock feels rocky. Aahh! Guess what? The hills are alive, the hills are shakin' and shakin'. Because the hills are alive. Uh huh. The hills are alive. Ohh! I fall smack off a hill. And got blowed up in an explosion. And then the rocks tumbled down and smashed everyone. And they all died. (Solomon & George, 1999, p. 17)

(b) *Voicelessness and resistance.* Indices of a continuing state of fear and disorientation were observed in children who, responding to queries regarding parent-child separations, suddenly fell silent, began whispering, refused the task, or appeared too distressed to complete it.

(c) *Disorganization in language or behavior.* Some former D infants responded to the presentation of pictured parent-child separations by suddenly using nonsense language ("yes-no-yes-no-yes-no-yes-no"), making contradictory statements without acknowledging the contradiction, or becoming behaviorally disorganized. For example:

> Happy.
> (*What's he happy about?*)
> 'Cause he likes his grandfather coming. (Child jumps on back of stuffed animal in the playroom and hits it.) Bad lion! (Hits it more). Bad lion!
> (Kaplan, 1987, pp. 110–111)

The association between the D-Fearful responses and infant D attachment with the mother was marked, suggesting to Kaplan that, because many of the D children in this sample had parents (termed *unresolved/disorganized* on the AAI) who were still experiencing frightening ideation involving their own loss experiences, questions about separation might have had a disorganizing effect on their offspring. In essence, Kaplan proposed that the children's fearful fantasies, silences, and disorganized language or behavior regarding parent-child separations could well have been the product of repeated interactions with parents who were themselves still fearful and confused regarding an important loss.

Jacobsen and her colleagues have replicated the relation between infant D attachment status and Kaplan's D-Fearful responses to separation pictures at ages 6 or 7 (Jacobsen et al., 1997; Jacobsen & Hofmann, 1997; see also Jacobsen, Edelstein, & Hofmann, 1994). Jacobsen and colleagues (1994) reported that D-Fearful 7-year-olds in a large Icelandic sample had negative feelings about themselves, and (perhaps due to anxiety) had notable problems in drawing the correct deductions to verbally administered reasoning tasks in adolescence. Employing doll play with 6-year-olds, Steele and colleagues (1995) also found themes of violence, hurt, and illness significantly associated with infant disorganized attachment with the mother (Steele et al., 1995). In a concurrent sixth-year assessment which utilized Main and Cassidy's (1988) *D-Controlling* category, Solomon's group (1995) replicated Kaplan's early findings with respect to the appearance of both catastrophic, chaotic fantasies in some children, and silence or response inhibition in others (the children were termed *D-Fearful*).

Additional indices of continuing fear specific to children classified D with mother appeared in a substantial portion of their family drawings (Kaplan &

Main, 1986,[3] replicated in the Minnesota poverty sample by Carlson & Levy, 1999). Drawings by former D children included, for example, floating, dismembered body parts, directly frightening elements (in one case, skeletons), and scratched-out figures. Some D children were so dissatisfied with their original drawing that they scratched it out, or else demanded another sheet of paper (see Main, 1995, for overview).

Another characteristic of child-mother and child-father dyads with whom the child had been disorganized in the strange situation procedure was "dysfluent" conversation. Here, based on transcripts taken from Main and Cassidy's sixth-year reunion procedure (1988), the child/parent conversation typically involved one or both partners stumbling in their sentences, while the child rather than the parent (as is usual) provided conversational guidance or "scaffolding." An example (drawn from Hesse & Main, 2000, p. 1107) is as follows:

Child: Gosh, you were, uh, gone a long time, you look . . . Come sit down, Mom. Where—where were you?

Mother: I was with . . . with . . . I've forgotten her name . . .

Child: Rachel, you were with Rachel . . .

Mother: . . . right, Rachel, and she was asking me a lot of questions. And you're with . . .

Child: . . . Emma. You remember, this is Emma, and she showed me this sandbox.

Mother: . . . oh, is that it in the corner? Oh, it's really cute, hon, you must have had fun.

Child: No, the sandbox is *here*. That's the toy-box. Want to see it?

Mother: No, uh, no. We're going to—I think they want us to leave now.

Child: Well, we—we can't leave yet, Mom. You have to sign the forms.

In identifying and distinguishing former D from the remaining strange situation dyads on the basis of conversational dysfluency, Strage (then a graduate student in psycholinguistics) worked exclusively and deliberately from

---

[3] Researchers with access to standard behavior-based (for example, Ainsworth strange situation procedures, or Main and Cassidy's sixth-year reunion procedure) assessments of attachment in their sample can write to Dr. Nancy Kaplan, c/o the Social Development Project, the Department of Psychology, The University of California at Berkeley, Berkeley, CA, 94720 to obtain training in the Kaplan and Main (1986) drawing system for 6-year-olds. We do not recommend use of this system in the absence of better validated and established assessments, and it should be noted that many secure young children seen outside of our standardized laboratory assessment deliberately draw frightening pictures (for example, at Halloween), or scratch out aspects of their pictures (in a search for improvement).

transcripts devoid of any accompanying cues to nonverbal behavior, to "prosody," or to emotional tone (Strage & Main, 1985).[4] Strage and Main found that children who had been disorganized with one parent (mother or father) but not with the second parent were dysfluent in their conversation only with the first parent (see Main, 1995). In sum, while previously disorganized children in the Bay Area sample had developed an "organized" behavioral strategy for dealing with the stress of separation from the parent via role-inverted or controlling behavior, marked indices of disorganization, fear, and chaos remained evident at the level of representation.

Although to this point we have been concerned exclusively with predictions from infancy to middle childhood, we should note that we have now been able to follow 15 former D infants to age 19, when we have administered the AAI (Main, 2001: Main & Hesse, in preparation). Although a majority of these young adults had been give an alternative "secure" classification during infancy (i.e., D/secure—as infants, then, they would therefore have been classified as "secure" prior to the recognition of D attachment), 14 out of the 15[5] were found insecure on the AAI by a "blind" coder who had had no part in our earlier projects, and several were judged Cannot Classify (see Hesse, 1996, and p. 87). Another interesting finding emerging from our study at age 19 was the reappearance in some former D infants of disorganized behavior (e.g., facial grimace, upward eye roll) when videotaped responding to an unexpected request to visualize themselves (Main, 2001).

The import of these findings to child clinicians is clear. However, this report may additionally be of interest to those working with older individuals, since during therapy the offspring of a traumatized caregiver might be expected to exhibit difficulties consonant with the sequelae to early disorganization described above. As adult patients, then, some such individuals may exhibit:

1. Recurring catastrophic fantasies (e.g, fear of death of important persons or the self, or other catastrophies [including fear of nervous breakdown, see Hesse & Main, 1999] based on no earlier or current experience discernible to self or clinician);

---

[4] The reader may note that Strage and Main (1985) has yet to be submitted for publication. This is because in the strange situations to which conversational styles were being linked, one of the four major categories (Group C, "insecure-ambivalent," see below) was virtually absent, and we have yet to replicate our original results with a sample having sufficient members of this category to identify a pattern.

[5] Twelve of these young adults had been assigned directly to the D classification in infancy: All 12 were judged insecure on the AAI. Three had been assigned an alternative D classification (of these, one was secure on the AAI), but because our original (1986) strange situation coding had been conservative with respect to D, we presently include alternative D as "D" in our studies of this sample (Abrams et al., submitted; Main, 2001). The coder for these interviews was Dr. Isabel Bradburn.

2. Attempts to control the clinician at times by becoming punitive or excessively solicitous, especially when feeling frightened of, or perhaps even frightened for, the clinician or other important persons; and,

3. In more extreme cases, cognitive confusion and blank spells (see Liotti, 1993).

The discovery of disorganized attachment is embedded in a complex theoretical and empirical background. To understand the category, its correlates, and its implications for psychopathology, therefore, an introduction to the field is necessary. This includes, first, the evolutionary links between attachment behavior, fear, and survival. We then turn to studies of the association between parental state of mind and parent-infant interaction, describing the frightening, if often involuntary, behaviors appearing in the parents of D infants, which are also associated with that same parent's language and reasoning slippages during the discussion of loss (or, especially in high-risk samples, abuse) experiences in the AAI.

Our central position is that, as long as the infant is not directly frightened by the parent, "insensitive" parenting in itself will not lead to disorganization, but rather to the formation of "organized" (avoidant or resistant/ambivalent) insecure attachments (see Main, 1990, 2000). *Fear of the parent*, in contrast, is anticipated to lead to disorganized attachment.

The Evolutionary Background to Attachment Theory

Elsewhere (e.g., Main, 1995; Hesse, 1999b) we have described the field of attachment as developing in three principle phases. In the first, drawing on evolutionary theory and observations of nonhuman primates, Bowlby (1969) called attention to the functioning of an "attachment behavioral system" which, having primary and immediate responsibility for regulating infant safety in the environments of evolutionary adaptedness (i.e., those in which we originally evolved), unavoidably still leads the infant to continually monitor the physical and psychological accessibility of attachment figure(s). The attachment system is now understood to be present in adults as well, as illustrated in the "secure base" behavior which leads each member of a well-functioning couple to turn to the other in times of stress (see especially Bowlby, 1988). Responses to death of a spouse or partner also highlight the continuing functioning of the attachment system during adulthood (Bowlby, 1980).

In the first volume of his trilogy, Bowlby (1969) presented and described the role which he believed evolution must play in human motivation, and specifically with regard to the functioning of the attachment behavioral system, which he viewed as central to understanding mental health. However, Bowlby had other aims as well. Until then, the clinician's primary source of data had been the speech, dreams, and retrospective accounts of adults. Bowlby urged that a more prospective—and simultaneously, observational—approach to the development of repression, defense, splitting, and other processes should be undertaken, permitting theoreticians and researchers alike to work forward from a particular experience to its sequelae. He took as his own point of entrée protracted parent-child separations, in which a toddler was placed for periods ranging from weeks to several months in an unfamiliar (usually, hospital or "residential nursery") setting. The sequelae to repeated or protracted experiences of this kind were found to include not only anxiety and ambivalence with respect to previously loved figures, but eventually a state of "detachment" in which ties to attachment figures were no longer acknowledged, and previously affectionate (and hostile) feelings were thought to have become repressed (Robertson & Bowlby 1952; Heinicke & Westheimer, 1966). During these traumatic separations, some young children also become disorganized (Main & Solomon, 1990; see also Solomon & George, 1999).

The behavioral manifestations of human attachment are familiar to all of us, and while most adults as well as (virtually all) infants are presumed to have attachment figures (persons to whom they are likely to turn in situations of stress), attachment behavior is perhaps most readily observed in the intense concern with the whereabouts of parental figures exhibited in young children. As Ainsworth (1967) demonstrated, during infancy attachment is identified with:

1. an insistent interest in *maintaining proximity* to one or a very few selected persons, usually but by no means necessarily biological relatives;
2. the tendency to use these individuals as a *secure base* for exploration of unfamiliar environments; and
3. *flight to the attachment figure as a haven of safety in times of alarm.*

These behaviors also appear in modified form in adults.

First attachments are ordinarily formed by seven months, develop with respect to only a few persons, and are generally believed to be based upon contingent social interactions (see Main, 1999b). The capacity for forming attachments is regarded as a matter of population genetics and, like language, emerges in the face of varied, or even sparse, environmental input. Attachment will then occur as readily as a product of interactions with maltreating as with sensitively responsive persons, and the biologically based proclivity to form attachments even on the basis of very restricted interactions ensures that it is only in truly extremely anomalous circumstances that a child will be found unattached.

Bowlby articulated the biological background to the human infant's attachment in part by drawing attention to highly similar behavior patterns observed in young, ground-living monkeys and apes, and in human hunters and gatherers studied by anthropologists. Guided to then-current evolutionary thinking by the Cambridge biologist Robert Hinde (Bretherton, 1992), Bowlby eventually ascribed the development of these central behavioral patterns to the functioning of an attachment behavioral system acting to heighten the probability of *"immediate" individual survival*—and hence, ultimately, the likelihood of reproductive success. He postulated that this system—as deeply genetically ingrained within our inherited emotional and behavioral response programming as feeding and reproduction—would have had *primary responsibility for regulating infant safety and survival* in the environments in which our species evolved (Main, 1995; Hesse & Man, 1999).

Initially, Bowlby considered the function of attachment behavior (proximity-seeking and proximity-maintaining behavior focused on specific figure[s]) as a source of protection from predation. Maintenance of proximity to caregivers is now believed to further act as an immediate aid to survival by increasing the likelihood that the infant will be sheltered from exposure to the elements, defended against the attacks of conspecifics, and able to keep up with the movements of the troop as well (as, e.g., Main, 1979b).

Maintaining proximity to a selected, older conspecific is, then, the infant's primary mechanism for heightening its chances of survival, and separation from attachment figures will presumably ensure a far more rapid death than will, for example, lack of access to food. Human as well as other ground-living primate infants therefore characteristically monitor the accessibility of their attachment figures, attempt to maintain a reasonable degree of proximity even in relatively nonthreatening situations, and seek the attachment figure as a haven of safety in times of perceived alarm.

Bowlby also pointed out that we differ from other animals (and even most mammals) in that gaining proximity to a *person*, as opposed to a *place*, provides our primary solution to situations of fear (Bowlby, 1958, 1969). For many mammalian young, frightening situations often lead to rapid flight to a *place* associated with safety, such as a den or burrow. In contrast, for human and other ground-living nomadic primates, it is not a place but a *selected individual* who provides the primary "solution" to conditions that elicit fright. Because it appears that the human infant has no haven of safety beyond its attachment figure(s), we have taken this proposition one step further and addressed the question of what will occur when the attachment figure itself—the person we "run to"—becomes a direct source of alarm (Hesse & Main, 1999; Hesse, 1999b; Hesse & Main, 2000).

While at first glance an inherent propensity to approach the location of alarm appears irrational, it is helpful to recall Darwin's observations regarding the Galapagos sea lizard, an animal able to move about with ease on both land and sea, who exhibited the peculiar behavioral feature that, when frightened, it would not enter the water. To further his understanding of this phenomenon, Darwin repeatedly threw one lizard into the water. Oddly enough, although possessed "of perfect powers of diving and swimming," the sea lizard invariably returned in a direct line to the promontory of land on which its attacker stood. Darwin speculatively solved this conundrum by consideration of the animal's evolutionary history or *phylogeny*:

> Perhaps this singular piece of apparent stupidity may be accounted for by the circumstance, that this reptile has no [natural] enemy whatever on shore, whereas at sea it must often fall a prey to the numerous sharks. Hence, probably, urged by a fixed and hereditary instinct that the shore is its place of safety, whatever the emergency may be, it there takes refuge. (1839/1962 p. 335)

Turning now to human evolution, note that (in parallel to Darwin's sea lizard), the human infant alarmed by its attachment figure *also has no inherent (i.e., instinctively organized) means for separating the location of its "attacker" from the location of its haven of safety.* Confronted with circumstances unanticipated within its evolutionary history, then, it should experience strong propensities to approach (as well as flee from) the place of threat. Thus, obtaining proximity to or contact with the attachment figure is the young infant's normal solution to all experiences of fright.

Here, we describe the "fright without solution" (Kaplan, 1987; Main & Hesse, 1992) which, then, might well occur when the parent—normally the infant's biologically channeled "haven of safety"—simultaneously becomes the source of its alarm (Hesse & Main, 1999, 2000). Such experiences should be inherently disorganizing, effecting emotion, behavior, and attention; it would not be surprising if vulnerability to psychopathology is significantly increased in the face of repeated early experiences of unsolvable fear.

The "Organized" Categories of Strange Situation Behavior: Patterns of Relationship with Parents who are not Directly Frightening

In attempting to describe how the infant comes to organize its attachment to selected persons under normal conditions, Mary Ainsworth embarked upon systematic observations of infant-mother interaction in the home across the first year of life. These studies were undertaken initially in Uganda (Ainsworth, 1967) and later in Baltimore (26 dyads, Ainsworth, Bell, & Stayton, 1971; Ainsworth et al., 1978). In conjunction with these investigations, Ainsworth (and other researchers; see especially Schaffer & Emerson, 1964) observed that specific or "focused" attachments usually develop by the third quarter of the first year of life, and appear to be the outcome of contingent social interactions. It was noted that—precisely because attachments are based on contingent social interactions—infants can develop attachments to nonrelated individuals, including of course those who do not participate in their primary care. For many infants, two or more attachment figures are eventually selected.

Ainsworth, like Bowlby (1969), believed that all infants but those raised in extremely anomalous circumstances would form an attachment by the end of the first year of life. This given, the central question regarding a normally raised toddler's parenting experience was not *whether* she or he had become attached, but *how the attachment to the primary caregiver(s) had become organized.* Considering the relation between attachment and survival, the infants of insensitive and even maltreating parents were expected to be as fully (or "strongly") attached as the infants of sensitive and responsive parents (see, e.g., Crittenden & Ainsworth, 1989). In contrast, the *organization* of the infant's attachment to a particular parent, determined in part by examining the circumstances in which attachment behavior was displayed, terminated, or else inhibited, was expected to differ across dyads.

Via exactingly recorded home observations across the first year of life (approximately 66 waking hours per dyad), ending with the brief, structured, strange situation procedure (Ainsworth et al., 1978). Ainsworth and her colleagues described three organized patterns of infant attachment behavior that were predictable from specific interaction patterns between the mother and child ($N = 26$ Baltimore dyads seen in the home, 23 seen in the strange situation as well). The strange situation is a 15–20 minute procedure where a parent and infant (12–18 months old) are brought into an unfamiliar playroom; a stranger is introduced to the dyad; and the parent twice leaves, and twice returns (the infant is first left with the stranger and then left alone during the second separation). The procedure was designed to combine several "natural clues to danger," as previously identified by Bowlby (1969, 1973), including unfamiliar persons and settings, separation from the attachment figure, and being left entirely alone.

In keeping with Bowlby's theorizing, Ainsworth had anticipated that by the time of the second separation, all home-reared 12-month-old infants would exhibit some form of attachment behavior, such as calling and crying (Ainsworth, personal communication, 1988). Once the dyad was reunited, however, the mother's presence was expected to provide sufficient security to permit the infant to return to exploration and play. While the majority of Ainsworth's Baltimore infants displayed this pattern of behavior (now termed secure, "B"), two "insecure" patterns of attachment behavior were also noted (termed A and C). Approximately 26% of infants showed few or no signs of missing the mother on separation, often even when left entirely alone. When reunited, they actively ignored and avoided the mother, moving away, turning away, and, if picked up (often, subtly), leaning out of the mother's arms, indicating a wish to be put down. This attachment pattern was termed insecure-avoidant ("A"). The remaining 17% of infants were distressed and preoccupied with the mother throughout the procedure. In keeping with their persistent focus upon the mother, many showed little or no interest in the toys or other aspects of the environment. Sometimes exhibiting anger toward the mother, these infants were unable to settle upon reunion, and were termed insecure-resistant/ambivalent ("C").

In later years, the worldwide proportions of infants judged secure, avoidant, or resistant in strange situation studies have been found to be highly similar to those seen in Ainsworth's original sample (van IJzendoorn & Kroonenberg, 1988), and strange situation response patterning appears to be independent of sex and birth order. Most important, strange situation response is found predictable from maternal caregiving behavior in the home over the first year of life, with sensitive and responsive caregiving predicting secure attachment, rejecting caregiving predicting insecure-avoidant attachment, and inconsistent caregiving predicting insecure-resistant/ambivalent attachment (Ainsworth et al., 1978; see De Wolff & van IJzendoorn, 1997 for a meta-analysis of existing studies; see also Pederson, Gleason, Moran, & Bento, 1998). Several subsequent investigations have found attachment to the mother stable to at least 6 years of age (Main & Cassidy, 1988; Jacobsen et al., 1992, 1997; Wartner, Grossmann, Fremmer-Bombik, & Suess, 1994; Ammaniti, Speranza, & Candelori, 1996).

Stability of response to the same person, however—even if indicative of continuing emotional security with respect to that person—does not inform us as to whether security of attachment influences emotional well-being in settings in which the attachment figure is absent. This critical question was addressed in a series of studies of a large, high-risk poverty sample pioneered by Sroufe, Egeland, and their colleagues, that included extensive longitudinal observations of children in school and camp settings. Here, children judged secure with mother during infancy were found to be more ego-resilient, more popular with peers, more competent, and happier than formerly insecure children (Weinfield, Sroufe, Egeland, & Carlson, 1999; see also Main, 1973, and

Troy & Sroufe, 1987). In most samples,[6] the infant's attachment to its mother and father were found independent (i.e., the same infant was often secure with one parent, but insecure with the other). Finally, a series of critical investigations provided little support for the otherwise reasonable supposition that genetic factors might contribute substantially to the "organized" categories of infant attachment (Sroufe, 1985; van IJzendoorn, et al., 1992; Vaughn & Bost, 1999; van IJzendoorn, 2000).

In addition, Main and colleagues (1985) had shown that each of the organized categories of infant strange situation behavior is predictable from parental discourse within the Adult Attachment Interview (AAI), a structured, hourlong procedure in which individuals are asked to describe and evaluate early attachment-related experiences and their effects upon personality and current functioning (see Hesse, 1999a, for overview). The interview (George, Kaplan, & Main, 1984, 1985, 1996) is transcribed verbatim and, utilizing a system developed by Main and Goldwyn (e.g., Main & Goldwyn, 1984, 1998; Main et al., 2002), most transcripts in low-risk samples can be assigned to one of three "organized" categories or "states of mind with respect to attachment"—secure-autonomous, insecure-dismissing, and insecure-preoccupied.[7] Using the three-way analysis of the "organized" categories, these adult attachment categories appear to provide discourse parallels to the three "organized" infant categories[8] of strange situation behavior, and an overview is provided in Table 2.1. Secure-autonomous parents repeatedly have been found most likely to have secure infants, and dismissing parents to have avoidant infants. Additionally, preoccupied parents have ambivalent/resistant infants markedly more frequently than expected by chance (see Hesse, 1999a; see also van IJzendoorn, 1995). As noted earlier, however, some speakers—while acceptably organized elsewhere within the interview—show indications of disorganization and/or disorientation in reasoning or discourse specifically in response to queries regarding potentially traumatic events. These linguistic "slippages" predict

---

[6] Van IJzendoorn and his colleagues reported that, across samples, only a very small association can be uncovered (van IJzendoorn & De Wolff 1997).

[7] Transcripts are assigned to the secure-autonomous category when the speaker remains coherent, consistent, and collaborative throughout the interview, whether early life experiences were favorable or unfavorable. Dismissive and preoccupied speakers lack the attentional flexibility and coherence evidenced in secure speakers, with dismissing speakers being especially striking for their failure to provide adequate support for positive descriptions of early experience, and preoccupied speakers seeming so excessively involved in early experiences with parents as to fail to simultaneously monitor the discourse context (Hesse, 1996).

[8] In direct parallel to "unclassifiable" infant attachment status as noted by Main and Weston (1981), a few transcripts have insufficient overall organization to permit assignment to the dismissing, secure, or preoccupied categories. These are currently termed "cannot classify" (see Hesse, 1996).

TABLE 2.1
AAI Classifications and Corresponding Patterns of Infant
Strange Situation Behavior

ADULT STATE OF MIND WITH RESPECT TO ATTACHMENT	INFANT STRANGE SITUATION BEHAVIOR
SECURE/AUTONOMOUS (F)	SECURE (B)
Coherent, internally consistent, and clear discourse. The speaker is seen as "valuing" of attachment, while seeming objective regarding any particular event/relationship. Description and evaluation of attachment-related experiences is consistent, whether experiences are favorable or unfavorable. Discourse does not notably violate any of Grice's maxims.	While the parent is present in the early episodes of the strange situation, the infant explores the room and toys with interest. Signs of missing the parent on separation, often cries by the time of the second separation. Obvious preference for parent over stranger. Greets parent actively, usually initiating physical contact. May maintain physical contact briefly by second reunion, then settles and returns to play.
DISMISSING (Ds)	AVOIDANT (A)
Not coherent. Dismissing of attachment-related experiences and relationships. Normalizing ("excellent, very normal mother"), with generalized representations of history unsupported or actively contradicted by episodes recounted. Thus, violating of Grice's maxim of quality. Transcripts also tend to be excessively brief (occasionally an attachment figure is contemptuously dismissed from discussion), violating the maxim of quantity.	Like secure infants, explores in the early episodes of the procedure. However, fails to cry on separation from parent, then actively avoids and ignores parent on reunion, i.e., by moving away, turning away, or leaning out of arms when picked up. Little or no proximity or contact seeking, no distress and no anger. Response to parent appears unemotional. Focuses on toys or environment throughout procedure.
PREOCCUPIED (E)	RESISTANT (C)
Not coherent. Preoccupied with or by past attachment relationships/experiences, speaker appears angry, passive, or fearful. Sentences often long, grammatically entangled, or filled with vague usages ("dadadada," "and that"). Thus, violating of Grice's maxims of manner and relevance. Transcripts often excessively long, violating quantity.	May be wary or distressed even prior to separation, with little exploration. Preoccupied with parent throughout procedure, may seem angry or passive. Fails to settle and take comfort in parent on reunion, and usually continues to focus on parent and cry. May alternately seek and then resist contact. Fails to return to exploration after reunion.

(continued)

TABLE 2.1
Continued

ADULT STATE OF MIND WITH RESPECT TO ATTACHMENT	INFANT STRANGE SITUATION BEHAVIOR
UNRESOLVED/DISORGANIZED (U/d)	DISORGANIZED/DISORIENTED (D)
During discussions of loss or abuse, individual shows striking lapse in the monitoring of reasoning or discourse. For example, individual may briefly indicate a dead person is believed still alive in the physical sense, or was killed by a childhood thought. Individual may lapse into prolonged silence, or eulogistic speech. The speaker will ordinarily otherwise fit to Ds, E, or F categories.	The infant displays disorganized and/or disoriented behaviors in the parent's presence, suggesting a temporary collapse of behavioral strategy. For example, the infant may freeze with a trancelike expression, hands in air; may rise at parent's entry then fall prone and huddled on the floor; or may cling while crying hard and leaning away with gaze aversion. Infant will ordinarily otherwise fit to A, B, or C categories.

Note: Two-week training institutes in the analysis of both the organized and disorganized categories of infant strange situation behavior are taught yearly by Alan Sroufe and Elizabeth Carlson of the Institute of Child Development, University of Minnesota, Minneapolis, MN, 55455. Two-week training institutes in the analysis of the Adult Attachment Interview are held regularly by several certified trainers. A list of available AAI institutes can be obtained from the first author.

Source: Permission to reprint an earlier version of this table, taken from Hesse (1999a), had been obtained from Guilford Press. Descriptions of the Adult Attachment Classification System are taken from Main, Kaplan, Cassidy (1985) and from Main and Goldwyn (1984–1998). Descriptions of infant ABC categories are taken from Ainsworth and colleagues (1978), and description of the infant D category is taken from Main and Solomon (1990). Information regarding a fifth, "cannot classify" category not described here (but prominent in clinically distressed and violent samples) can be found in Hesse (1996). This table is updated from that printed in Hesse and Main (1999).

disorganized/disoriented infant attachment status with 57%, of such speakers having disorganized infants across samples and markedly higher associations being reported when the researchers had had more training in identifying infant D attachment status.

Disorganized Infant Strange Situation Behavior

An early description of the disorganized/disoriented attachment category (now the fourth category of strange situation behavior, and utilized in virtually all laboratories studying strange situation behavior) first appeared in 1986, and was well elaborated by 1990 (Main & Solomon, 1986, 1990). This new category emerged through the meeting of two branches of inquiry which involved (a) the direct observation of conflict behaviors in infants and toddlers (Main, 1973, 1979a; Main & Stadtman, 1981) and (b) the recognition that some infants seen in the strange situation were difficult or impossible to classify (e.g., Main & Weston, 1981; see Main & Solomon, 1998, for review).

Drawing on descriptions of what ethologists term *conflict behaviors*—that is, those behaviors which appear to result from the simultaneous activation of incompatible systems (see, e.g., Hinde, 1966; Tinbergen, 1951)—the second author had begun to code conflict behaviors in the toddlers observed in her doctoral thesis by 1972, and by 1974 undertook a second investigation of conflict behaviors, focusing on the narrative records from Ainsworth's Baltimore sample (see Main, 1973; Main & Stadtman, 1981). Finally, utilizing a third (Bay Area) sample, a scale assessing "disordered/disoriented" behaviors was developed (Main, 1979a, utilized in Grossmann, 1997; see Main & Solomon, 1990, pp. 154–155).

As early as 1981, Main and Weston reported that approximately 13% of infants in their low-risk Bay Area sample were *unclassifiable* within Ainsworth's original, tripartite system. This finding was in keeping with that of many investigators working with maltreatment and high-risk samples who were not only finding that many maltreated infants were unclassifiable, but additionally that when these infants were 'forced' into one of the three available categories, many were best-fitting to 'secure' (see Main & Solomon, 1990, for review).

With the aim of better understanding unclassifiable attachment status, Main and Solomon reviewed 200 anomalous ("unclassifiable") strange situation videotapes (Main & Solomon, 1990). Rather than revealing any new patternings across the course of the procedure, unclassifiable infants were found to display a diverse array of inexplicable, odd, or overtly conflicted behaviors. One unclassifiable infant, for example, cried loudly while attempting to gain her mother's lap, then suddenly fell silent and stopped moving for several seconds. Others were observed approaching the parent with head averted; moving away from the parent to the wall when apparently frightened by the stranger; raising hand to mouth in an apprehensive gesture immediately upon seeing the parent at the door when reunited; and while in an apparently good mood slowly swiping at the parent's face with a trancelike expression.

The most striking theme running through the behaviors observed was that of *disorganization*, a contradiction in movement patterns indicative of contradictions of observed/inferred intention or plan (Main & Solomon, 1990). As an extreme example, here is the immediate response to reunion of one infant whose strange situation behavior was otherwise very secure. The case suggests, as do only a few, the possibility of an alteration in executive control (see Hilgard, 1977):

> Creeping rapidly forward to father as though to greet him at the doorway, the infant suddenly stops and turns her head 90 degrees to the side. Gazing blankly at the wall with face expressionless and eyes half closed, she slaps her hand on the floor three times. These gestures appear aggressive, yet they have a ritualized quality. The baby then looks forward again, smiles, and resumes her approach to her father, seeking to be picked up. (Main & Morgan, 1996, pp. 108–109)

The term *disorientation* was added to describe behavior which, while not overtly disorganized, nonetheless indicated a lack of orientation to the present environment (such as immobilized behavior accompanied by a dazed expression).[9] The following is an example:

> Upon reunion, a mother picks up her very active son, and sits down with him on her lap. He sits still and closes his eyes. His mother calls his name, but he does not stir. Still calling his name, she bounces him on her knee, and gently shakes him, but he remains limp and still. After several seconds, he opens his eyes, slides off her lap and darts across the room to retrieve a toy. (Main & Morgan, 1996, p. 124)

In total, Main and Solomon delineated seven "thematic headings" for the identification of disorganized/disoriented behavior. These are presented in Table 2.2.

Bouts of disorganized/disoriented behavior sufficient for assignment to the D category are often quite brief (not infrequently consisting of one episode lasting 10 to 30 seconds). For example, if an infant froze inexplicably in a posture which required physical effort to maintain (e.g., with one hand partially extended) for 20 seconds or more, it would be classified as D. As has already been noted, the D category is always assigned together with a best-fitting, alternate avoidant, secure, or resistant category (e.g., disorganized/avoidant or disorganized/secure).[10, 11] Lyons-Ruth and her colleagues have found that the second best-fitting category may ultimately be related to differing precursors,

---

[9] Directions for judging infants as disorganized were developed and refined through repeated study of 200 infant strange situation videotapes designated "unclassifiable" within the original three-part system—half drawn from low-risk and half from high-risk and/or maltreatment samples.

[10] Also, some infants are alternately unclassifiable or cannot classify.

[11] Acceptable levels of reliability and stability were established for the disorganized strange situation category in this and succeeding independent investigations, and, additionally, across studies, no significant sex differences have been found (van IJzendoorn, Schuengel, & Bakermans-Kranenburg, 1999).

TABLE 2.2
Disorganized/Disoriented Behavior Observed During the Strange Situation

STRANGE SITUATION BEHAVIOR IS JUDGED DISORGANIZED WHEN IT FITS TO ONE OF THE FOLLOWING THEMATIC HEADINGS:

1. *Sequential display of contradictory behavior patterns.* For example, the infant may dash crying to parent, then inexplicably fall silent and turn away to the wall.

2. *Simultaneous display of contradictory behavior patterns.* For example, the infant may approach the parent with head averted, or lean sharply away while clinging. Also, while smiling and in an apparent good mood the infant suddenly strikes or claws at the parent's face.

3. *Undirected, misdirected, incomplete, and interrupted movements and expressions.* For example, the infant may turn and brightly greet the stranger at parent entrance, or move sobbing to the wall rather than toward the parent when distressed.

4. *Stereotypies, asymmetrical movements, mistimed movements, and anomalous postures.* For example, the infant may rock hard on hands and knees immediately on reunion, greet the parent with a one-sided smile, or repeatedly raise arms straight forward at shoulder height, eyes closed.

5. *Freezing, stilling, and slowed movements and expressions.* For example, the infant may move very slowly toward the parent, as though moving under water or against physical resistance. Or, the infant may freeze all movements for 20 seconds, hands in air.

6. *Direct indices of apprehension regarding the parent.* For example, the infant may place hands to mouth at parent entrance with a frightened expression, or may back against the wall with a fearful smile.

7. *Direct indices of disorganization and disorientation.* For example, the infant may wander about the room in a disorganized fashion, turning in circles. Or, immediately upon parent entrance the infant may turn and brightly greet the stranger, raising arms.

Note: Disorganized/disoriented behavior is scored by instance on a 9-point scale, and infants scoring above a 5 are placed in the disorganized category. Training in the identification of disorganized/disoriented behavior is provided yearly by Elizabeth Carlson at the Institute of Child Development, University of Minnesota.

Source: The above descriptions of disorganized/disoriented infant strange situation behavior are adapted from Main and Solomon (1990), and from Hesse and Main (1999).

that is, the behavior of the mothers of disorganized/secure infants may differ markedly from those who are disorganized/insecure (see Lyons-Ruth, Alpern, & Repacholi, 1993; Lyons-Ruth, 1996; see Lyons-Ruth & Jacobvitz, 1999 for overview).

Despite the overtly unusual nature of many of these behaviors, a meta-analytic overview of studies of neurologically normal samples found no indication of a temperamental or constitutional component in disorganized strange situation responses while, as with the "organized" patterns of attachment, infants generally exhibit disorganized behavior in the presence of *only one* of two parents (van IJzendoorn et al., 1999). (Recently, however—as predicted by Main, 1995, 1999—an association between a particular genetic allele and infant disorganization has been described, though the data suggest the importance of environmental factors as well, since many of the infants carrying the allele were not disorganized [Lakatos et al., 2000].) Disorganized behavior has also been observed in infants and older individuals who are neurologically atypical (Main & Solomon, 1990; see also Pipp-Siegel, Siegel, & Dean, 1999), isolated, or simply overwhelmed or overstimulated by repeated or extended separations (Heinecke & Westheimer, 1966; Robertson & Robertson, 1971; Main & Solomon, 1990; Solomon & George, 1999; see Hesse, 1999b for overview). In addition, D behavior (e.g., stereotypies and "freezing") can result from pharmacological interventions (see Hesse, 1999b).

However, since disorganization and disorientation also result from conflicting behavioral tendencies (Hinde, 1966), it is not surprising that disorganized behavior has been observed in experimental settings in which toddlers are deliberately given conflicting signals (Volkmar & Siegel, 1979; Volkmar, Hoder, & Siegel, 1980), subjected to abrupt and confusing changes in interactional behavior, or else exposed to "inescapable" situations involving, for example, shame or embarrassment (see Main & Solomon, 1990, and Hesse, 1999b). Disorganized behavior in the presence of a particular parent may also result from transient circumstances in the parent's life, which lead to frightened behavior only temporarily (a case of this kind in which an otherwise secure parent had just had a life-threatening experience is discussed extensively by Ainsworth & Eichberg, 1991). Because conflict arising in these latter situations is, however, either the product of experimental procedures or presumed temporary, a focus upon ongoing and potentially disorganizing aspects of parental behavior was initiated.

In 1990, Main and Hesse hypothesized that behavioral, emotional, and attentional organization can ordinarily be maintained under the stress of the strange situation procedure only so long as the attachment figure—whether sensitive or insensitive to infant signals and communications in the home—has not been a direct source of alarm or fright (Main & Hesse, 1990, 1992). It was proposed, however, that organization might well break down in the face of repeated exposure to the inherently highly conflictual situation in which the attachment figure becomes alarming.

In keeping with this proposal, disorganized behavior has been observed in the great majority (77%) of maltreated infants studied in the strange situation in two large independent samples (Carlson, Cicchetti, Barnett, & Braunwald, 1989; Lyons-Ruth, Repacholi, McLeod, & Silva, 1991; see van IJzendoorn, Schuengel, & Bakermans-Kranenburg, 1999, Table 5). Further, a post-strange situation rise in salivary adrenocortisal (a physiological index of stress for which the individual has no immediate behavioral strategy) has been found in disorganized infants in two independent studies (Spangler & Grossmann, 1993; Hertsgaard, Gunnar, Erickson, & Nachmias, 1995).

It is nevertheless necessary to account for the fact that 15% of infants observed in low-risk samples ($N = 2,104$; van IJzendoorn et al., 1999) are disorganized, and that in several studies the proportion of middle-class infants judged disorganized has ranged above 30% (e.g., Ainsworth & Eichberg, 1991). Further, direct maltreatment is unlikely to provide explanation for the fact that in a study of children of mothers suffering from anxiety disorders, 65% of offspring were found disorganized (Manassis, Bradley, Goldberg, Hood, & Swinson, 1994). While of course it would be naïve to argue that maltreatment is absent in low-risk samples, or that it might not occur in some parents with anxiety disorders, it is highly unlikely that, for example, 65% of mothers suffering from anxiety disorders would also be maltreating.

These findings, then, leave open the question of (a) what the parental correlates of disorganized attachment might ordinarily be in nonmaltreating populations, and (b) how disorganization arises under circumstances that do not involve directly maltreating behavior. Ultimately, Main and Hesse concluded that *frightened, dissociative,* and *anomalous forms of (merely) "threatening"* parental behavior could place the infant in a conflict situation similar to one involving physically agonistic parental behavior (Main & Hesse, 1990; Hesse & Main, 1999; Hesse, 1999b), and that behavior of this kind could be anticipated in parents in low-risk samples who are still frightened, unresolved, and/or disoriented with respect to their own experiences of loss or abuse.

Unresolved (Ud) Adult Attachment Status: Discourse/Reasoning Lapses During the Discussion of Traumatic Events

Initial indirect support for the above was provided by an early investigation of the upper-middle-class Bay Area sample (Main & Hesse, 1990). Here we found a substantial association between the infant's disorganized/disoriented behavior during the strange situation as conducted with a given parent and *linguistic slippages* observed in that same parent's discussion of potentially traumatic events sufficient to warrant placement in the *unresolved/disorganized* AAI category (Main & Goldwyn, 1984, 1998; see Hesse, 1999a, Hesse & Main, 1999, and Hesse & Main, 2000, for an overview). In this study, it was reported that 91% of mothers classified as substantially unresolved on the basis of discourse/reasoning lapses had had disorganized infants five years earlier. In contrast, only 16% of mothers who had *experienced* a loss, but showed little or no indication of disorganized mental processes in discussing the loss, had had disorganized infants.

Ainsworth and Eichberg (1991) provided the first replication of the Bay Area findings. Using a sample of 50 mother-infant dyads where coders of both the AAI and the strange situation were blind to the alternative procedure, these authors found that *mothers who had simply experienced a loss—even a major loss of a family member—were no more likely than other mothers to have disorganized infants*. However, *all eight* mothers whose lapses in reasoning or discourse during the AAI identified them as unresolved/disorganized had infants who were judged D with them in the strange situation.

This study provided a particularly illustrative example of a lapse in the monitoring of reasoning in a high-functioning mother. Immediately upon being queried regarding loss experiences, she responded "Yes, there was a little man..." and then began to cry. The person lost was an elderly man who had worked briefly for her parents when she was eight years old. Jokingly, he had asked her to marry him when she grew up, and she had replied, "No, you'd be dead." Not long after this exchange, he died unexpectedly of a brain hemorrhage. Crying, this mother told the interviewer that it was she who had killed him—"with one sentence" (Ainsworth & Eichberg, 1991, p. 175). This lapse in reasoning was left unmonitored, leading to placement in the unresolved/disorganized adult attachment category and, as expected, the infant's strange situation behavior was independently classified as disorganized. The reader should note: (a) the existence of frightening ideation (having killed someone with a thought) in this otherwise high-functioning mother, (b) whose loss experience would not normally have been considered traumatic.

By 1994, unresolved/disorganized parental attachment status had predicted infant D attachment in five further samples (summarized in van IJzendoorn, 1995). In four, the AAI had been administered *prior to the birth of the first child* and the parent's attachment status was compared to infant strange situation response to the same parent at 12 months (Benoit & Parker, 1994; Fonagy, Steele & Steele, 1991; Radojevic, 1992; Ward & Carlson, 1995; the latter is a high-risk sample.[12] Six additional investigations of the relation between un-resolved parental attachment status and infant D attachment have been conducted since this original meta-analysis, with highly significant linkages reported for the majority (Hesse, 1999b).

To summarize, many independent investigators have found that (1) isolated, brief *linguistic* indices of disorganization and disorientation in the parent's AAI occurring specifically in response to queries regarding loss or abuse experiences (the majority of *unresolved* AAI's are otherwise acceptably organized, whether secure or insecure), predict (2) usually brief bouts of *behavioral* disorganization and disorientation in the infant. An overview of this system of linguistic analysis is provided in Table 2.3.

Frightened/Frightening (FR) Behavior in Non-Maltreating Parents

The initial step leading toward the proposal that disorganized behavior might result not only from direct physical abuse and other maltreatment (i.e., as a *direct* effect of trauma) but also as a *second-generation effect* of a frightened men-tal state mediated by more subtle forms of parental behavior (Main & Hesse, 1990, 1992) came about via a closer examination of AAI passages where "un-resolved/disorganized" slippages had been identified. Here it was found that in most cases questions regarding a potentially traumatic event appeared to have sparked or induced a momentary but dramatic alteration in the speaker's mental state. Many of the more marked slippages suggested that the speaker was experiencing either (a) high levels of absorption involving events which had not undergone normal processing (Hesse & van IJzendoorn, 1999) or (b) intrusions from a secondary (normally dissociated) ideational system re-garding those experiences, which was incompatible with an ordinarily more prominent view regarding these same events (Main & Hesse, 1990, 1992).[13] As Table 2.3 indicates, examples of absorption include unusual attention to detail during the discussion of a loss, or a sudden shift to eulogistic (funereal) speech. Lapses in reasoning indicating intrusions from a secondary, incompatible belief system also appeared—for example, in statements indicating that a deceased

---

[12] Interestingly, the strength of the association is highly related to the amount of training researchers have had in assessing disorganized strange situation behavior (van IJzendoorn, 1995).

[13] States of absorption and intrusions from secondary systems are compatible with Hilgard's analysis of hypnotic phenomena and trancelike states (Hilgard, 1977) and with Bowlby's analysis of a case of unresolved mourning in an adolescent girl ("Geraldine," see Bowlby, 1980).

TABLE 2.3
Identifying Unresolved/Disorganized Attachment Status Within the Adult Attachment Interview: Lapses in the Monitoring of Discourse and Reasoning

LAPSES IN THE MONITORING OF *DISCOURSE* MAY TAKE THE FOLLOWING FORMS, AMONG OTHERS:

1. Sudden changes in speech register (e.g., shifting from normal speaking patterns into eulogistic/funereal speech, as, "She was young, she was lovely, and she was torn from us by that most dreaded of diseases, tuberculosis");

2. Falling silent for 2 minutes in mid-sentence, then continuing on unrelated topic;

3. Giving extreme attention to details surrounding a loss or other potentially traumatic experience inappropriate to the interview context (e.g., a 10-minute discussion involving minute details of a loss including time of day, furnishings of the room, car taken to the funeral, and clothing worn by each family member).

LAPSES IN THE MONITORING OF *REASONING* MAY TAKE THE FOLLOWING FORMS, AMONG OTHERS:

1. Subtle or direct indications that a deceased individual is believed simultaneously dead and alive in the physical (not religious or metaphysical) sense (e.g., "It was almost better when she died, because then *she could get on with being dead,* and I could get on with raising my family," or, "My (deceased) mother definitely wants me to study law");

2. Placement of the timing of a death at several widely separated periods (e.g., ages 9, 11, and 15 given for same loss experience at differing places in the interview);

3. Indications that self was responsible for the death where no material cause was present (e.g., death caused by having thought something negative near the time of the death);

4. Claims to have been absent at the time of the death, juxtaposed with claims to having been present (e.g., stating regret at having been at home when other family members were present at a drowning, then later speaking as though the self had been present: "and we tried, but none of us could swim to her").

Note: Transcripts can also be assigned to unresolved/disorganized attachment status on the basis of reports of extreme (disorganized/disoriented) behavioral reactions to loss or abuse: however, these are very rare in samples of the kind discussed here. Training in identifying these lapses is provided in conjunction with training in the Adult Attachment Interview (See Table 2.1).

Source: The above examples of lapses in the monitoring of reasoning and discourse are taken from Main and Goldwyn (1998), and further adapted from Hesse and Main (1999).

person was believed still alive in the physical (as opposed to metaphorical, metaphysical, or religious) sense. It appeared reasonable to speculate, then, that *similar state-shifts could occur in such individuals in other settings*, being activated by (a) involuntary intrusions from alarming memories or ideation and/or (b) aspects of the environment idiosyncratically associated with those ideas or memories.

Thus, a theory was developing which might provide an explanation for how a parent's unintegrated or quasidissociated state could become associated with disorganized behavior in the infant (Main & Hesse, 1990, 1992; Hesse & Main, 1999). Entering such a state, the parent might exhibit

(1) anomalous forms of frightening or threatening (but nonphysically abusive) behavior;
(2) frightened behavior; or
(3) overtly dissociative behavior.

Each of the above subtypes of behavior was expected to be frightening to the infant (Hesse & Main, 1999). Depending on the nature and intensity of their own traumatic experiences, it was reasoned that some unresolved parents might also

(4) exhibit sexualized behavior,
(5) treat the infant deferentially, timidly, or as a protector, or
(6) become unpredictably behaviorally disorganized and/or disoriented for brief periods of time, as had been previously observed only in infants (Main, 1979a; Main & Stadtman, 1981; Main & Solomon, 1986, 1990).

Although it was supposed that these latter three subtypes of anomalous behavior (4, 5, and 6) might not be frightening in themselves, they would nonetheless be unlikely to occur if the parent had not entered some kind of an "altered" or dissociated state. Thus, the same parent could potentially become directly frightening, frightened, or overtly dissociative at other times as well.

These ideas necessitated empirical testing, which led to the development of a coding system for identifying such parental behaviors (hereafter termed FR behavior; Main & Hesse, 1992–1998). An overview of this system is presented in Table 2.4.

Unresolved/Disorganized Adult Attachment Status as Predictive of "FR" Parental Behavior

Presently, at least three laboratories have investigated the relation between unresolved/disorganized (parental) attachment status on the AAI and FR behavior as observed in home or play settings. In the first study of this kind,

TABLE 2.4
Precis of the Six Central Categories of the System for Coding
FR Behaviors[a,b]

I. Direct indices of entrance into a dissociative state. For example, parent suddenly completely "freezes" with eyes unmoving, half-lidded,
despite nearby movement; parent addresses infant in an "altered"
tone with simultaneous voicing and devoicing ("haunted" sound, as
is produced by elongating the sounds of "Hi," "huh," or "ah" while
pulling in on diaphragm).

II. Threatening behavior inexplicable in origin and/or anomalous in form.
For example, in nonplay contexts and in the absence of "meta"-
signals of play, stiff-legged "stalking" of infant on all fours; exposure
of canine teeth; hissing or deep growls directed at infant.

III. Frightened behavior patterns inexplicable in origin and/or anomalous in form. Sudden frightened look (fear mouth, exposure of whites
of eyes) in absence of environmental change. Also, a quick, stammering, alarmed retreat accompanied by indications that the infant
must not follow, or approaching infant apprehensively as though a
potentially dangerous object.

IV. Timid/deferential (role-inverting) behavior. For example, parent is
submissive to infant aggression, hands folded, head bowed, while
infant engages in obviously painful slapping, hitting, or hair-pulling.
Also, turning to the offspring as a haven of safety when alarmed.

V. Sexualized behavior toward infant. For example, deep kissing of infant, exhibition or encouragement of sexualized caressing.

VI. Disorganized/disoriented behaviors compatible with Main and
Soloman's (1990) infant system. For example, mis-timed movements,
anomalous postures, approaching infant with head averted, or any
observable "collapse of behavioral (caregiving) strategy," such as
becoming motionless while infant is crying.

[a] Exclude from consideration simple disciplinary actions, even if somewhat harsh, insensitive,
or momentarily frightening (e.g., shouting, or slapping of hand), or accidents involving the
parent that momentarily frighten the infant (e.g., stumbling and bumping infant's head on wall),
as long as parent's state does not appear anomalous (see text pp. 88–89).

[b] Readers interested in a more complete description of this system should write to the first
author at Berkeley. Training institutes in the identification and scoring of FR behavior are being
planned.

Source: This table is adapted from an earlier table published in Psychoanalytic Inquiry (Hesse
& Main, 1999).

Schuengel and his colleagues in Leiden videotaped 85 mothers and infants for approximately four hours across the course of two home visits (Schuengel, van IJzendoorn, & Bakermans-Kranenburg, 1997). Observations were made at 10.5 months, with no instructions being given to mothers to engage in any particular type of interaction. An association between unresolved/disorganized attachment status and maternal FR behavior was found, but only when the mother's alternative or "best-fitting" AAI classification was insecure (Schuengel et al., 1997; Schuengel, van IJzendoorn, & Bakermans-Kranenburg, 1999). This suggested the possibility of a protective factor operating to inhibit the expression of FR behavior in unresolved mothers whose underlying adult attachment classification was secure.

At the University of Texas, Jacobvitz, Hazen, and Riggs (1997; Jacobvitz, 1998) administered the AAI to 113 mothers prenatally. In contrast to the Leiden study mothers were required to feed their babies, play with them, and change their clothing on camera. In this more stressful procedure, unresolved/secure and unresolved/insecure mothers were both found far more likely to exhibit FR behaviors, as compared to either secure or insecure mothers who were not unresolved.

Similar results have been obtained in a study of middle-class Bay Area families where frightened/frightening behavior was observed in mothers and (separately) fathers during a brief (30-minute) laboratory parent-infant play session (Abrams, Rifkin, & Hesse, submitted). The parents of a substantial number of infants in this study had been seen in the AAI five years following the play sessions and strange situations.[14] In the Abrams and colleagues study, assignment to unresolved/disorganized attachment status was based entirely on discourse surrounding the discussion of *loss* experiences (abuse experiences were not included as there were too few cases), and was also confined to individuals who experienced losses prior to the play session.

As in previous investigations, FR behavior was found significantly related to unresolved/disorganized status on the AAI. Moreover, there was a tendency for unresolved/disorganized parents to display more *dissociative* (or dissociative-like) behavior in particular than parents not judged unresolved/disorganized. This finding appears consistent with the supposition that language and reasoning "slippages" in the AAI, which identify unresolved attachment status, are most likely subtle indications of absorption and other "altered states of consciousness" as described above. Relatedly, Hesse and van IJzendoorn (1999)

---

[14] This indeliberate sequencing of events is based on the fact that the AAI was not devised until the children in this study were 6 years of age.

had discovered a significant relation between unresolved/disorganized attachment status on the AAI and elevated scores on Tellegens' Absorption Scale (Tellegan, 1982; Tellegan & Atkinson, 1974).

Frightened/Frightening Parental Behavior and Infant Disorganized Attachment

Using a system for coding frightening and disruptive, confusing maternal behavior termed AMBIENCE (the method includes several categories from an early version of Main and Hesse's FR system), Lyons-Ruth and her colleagues examined maternal behavior *within* the Ainsworth strange situation, utilizing a high-risk sample. The aim of the study was to look for behaviors specific to the mothers of infants found disorganized within the same procedure. Here, FR behavior (as well as disrupted maternal communication and withdrawal) was found associated with infant disorganization, and the parents of disorganized infants whose alternative best-fitting classification was secure differed from those whose alternative best-fitting classification was insecure in that the former were more likely to exhibit frightened/withdrawn behavior (Lyons-Ruth, Bronfman, & Parsons, 1999).

In addition, several investigators have now examined the relation between FR behavior in the home, field, or laboratory, and infant disorganized attachment status assessed in independent strange situations. In the Leiden study mentioned above, FR behavior observed in the home at 10.5 months predicted disorganized attachment in strange situations conducted 2 to 3 months later (Schuengel et al., 1999). Using a simplified assessment of FR behavior, researchers have also investigated the attachment and caregiving behaviors of members of the Dogan ethnic group in Mali, West Africa (True, Pisani, & Oumar, 2001). True and her colleagues found maternal FR behavior observed in the home and clinic settings substantially correlated with infant D attachment status in the strange situation.

The Bay Area study of 50 infant-mother and 25 infant-father dyads was the first to use the most recent (1998) version of the FR coding system (Abrams et al., (submitted); the full coding system is available as an appendix to Hesse, 1999b). Here, parents and infants were videotaped in the laboratory in 18 minutes of free play, but—to create an opportunity for observing infant obedience—parents were instructed to keep the infant away from certain locations and objects. Free play was followed by Main and Weston's (1981) 12-minute Clown Session, and coders, scoring across the full 30 minutes of these two procedures, were blind to infant strange situation behavior. The match between parental FR free play/Clown Session classifications and infant D strange situation classifications was substantial for both mother-infant dyads and (independently) father-infant dyads (each dyad, then, was observed both in the play session, and again in the strange situation). In analyses of the six subcategories of frightened/frightening parental behavior, *dissociative* or dissociative-like behavior emerged as the primary predictor of infant disorganization. This result was anticipated, since dissociation has been conceptualized as an alteration in consciousness in response to overwhelming psychological trauma and fear (e.g., Breuer & Freud, 1895/1960; Liotti, 1992; Putnam, 1985; Spiegel, 1990).

Frightened/Frightening Parental Behavior and "Cannot Classify" Infant Attachment Status

Earlier, it was mentioned that the D strange situation category evolved via the discovery that a substantial proportion of infants could not be classified in Ainsworth's original tripartite system. Although almost all previously "unclassifiable" infants are now found to display disorganized or disoriented behavior sufficient for placement in the D category, a (very) few remain who do not meet these criteria. Thus, while showing few or no indices of disorganization or disorientation, some infants still do not fit into Ainsworth's three-part classification system, and in our laboratory are termed "cannot classify" (CC).

The AAI classification system developed by Main and Goldwyn, and extended by Hesse (Main et al., 2002), includes a fifth (rare) "cannot classify" category (CC). The category is utilized when speakers exhibit a mix of discourse strategies and thus qualify for placement in two different attachment categories (e.g., dismissing and preoccupied; see Table 2.1). Individuals are also judged CC within the AAI when they fail to display *any* specific discourse strategy. The apparent inability of adults placed in this AAI category to mobilize a consistent discourse strategy is conceptually similar—at a global level—to the local breakdowns in strategy characteristic of disorganized infants and unresolved adults (see Hesse, 1996). Yet, CC appears to be a separate category in its own right, being relatively rare in middle-class low risk samples and having been found associated with severe pathological outcomes (see Hesse, 1996, 1999a, 1999b).

As attachment is conceived of as a relational process between caregiver and infant, it would seem likely that in parent-child interactions leading to *infant* CC status experiences similar to (albeit perhaps more extreme or anomalous than) precursors to the D category might be found. Relatedly, Abrams and colleagues (2002) found that both of the parents of the CC infants in their sample were judged FR within the play session.

Taken as a whole, these studies provide correlational[15] support for the hypothesis that FR behavior might be one important mediator in the relation between unresolved (adult) and disorganized (infant) attachment status. It should be noted that (a) FR behavior may be most likely to appear in stressful settings; and consequently (b) these conditions will produce stronger relations between unresolved maternal and disorganized infant attachment status. In other words, parents who are vulnerable to lapses in organization/emotion regulation might, when stressed, display breakdowns or a collapse in caregiving strategy which is manifest as frightened/frightening behavior. Stress might also elicit breakdowns in care-seeking strategies on the part of disorganized infants.

The following is a general description of frightening and frightened parental behaviors which are *not* expected to produce disorganization. (A more extensive description is found in Hesse & Main, 1999.) Discussion includes the behaviors delineated in the six categories of the FR system presented in Table 2.4, and illustrative case examples. We also consider the ways in which each type of FR behavior may be directly (categories 1 to 3) or indirectly (categories 4 to 6) frightening and/or disorganizing to the offspring. The reader should recall that in all studies (other than the original 1990 report by Main & Hesse, which focused on nonblind anecdotal observations), observers of parental behavior were blind to both the AAI and infant strange situation behavior.

Frightened and Threatening Parental Behaviors Not Expected to Produce Disorganization

Maltreating parental behavior normally arises from pathological conditions. There are, however, several forms of frightened and threatening parental behavior that occur frequently but would not be anticipated to produce disorganization (Hesse & Main, 1999). For example, Campos and his colleagues have demonstrated that infants as young as 11 months are highly alert to frightened expressions on the part of the parent which indicate danger. In Campos's studies infants have, for example, been observed to monitor and respond to parental expressions of apprehension or alarm as the infant approaches what appears to be a dangerous "visual" cliff by inhibiting further movement (see Klinnert, Campos, Sorce, Emde, & Svedja, 1983; Kermoian & Campos, 1988).

Fearful parental expressions in the "real" world can also, of course, indicate approaching danger (e.g., the appearance of a potentially aggressive animal), or the possibility that the infant's actions may have immediately dangerous

---

[15] Ultimately, experimental evidence will be needed. One form of evidence which could readily be collected would involve observing physiological (and perhaps also facial) responses to varying FR behaviors (e.g., haunted voice, "predatory" movements) in adults.

consequences (e.g., the toddler's movement toward oncoming traffic). In circumstances such as these, however, what is alarming—that is, the source of the alarm—is *external* to the parent. The alarming stimulus will therefore ordinarily be both discernible and comprehensible, as will be made obvious in the parent's orientation, and the infant will be free to approach the parent. Moreover, when most parents themselves accidentally do something to frighten the infant, they are ordinarily likely to immediately provide comfort, contact, or (in clinical terms) "repair" (see especially Lyons-Ruth & Jacobvitz, 1999, and Lyons-Ruth et al., 1999).

Consider in addition the "normal" contexts in which threatening parental behavior arises. It is not unusual for a parent to become angry and/or threatening in disciplinary interactions—for example, when the child runs out into the street. At such times, the parent may not only sharply raise his or her voice, but even spank the child, or slap the child's hand. Here again, however, the motivation or stimulus for the parent's behavior is both external to the parent and readily comprehensible. In addition, via compliance the infant or child can in principle terminate the "frightening" parental behavior. Finally, the child is often subsequently able to (or even encouraged to) approach the parent, since the ultimate aim of such interactions is usually protective. This too provides an opportunity for "repair." Thus, parental expressions of fright or threat as just described, are discernible and comprehensible, while the expressions themselves are not anomalous (Hesse & Main, 1999).

Parental Behavior Likely to Be Directly Frightening and Disorganizing: Dissociative Behavior, Anomalous Threat, and Anomalous Expressions of Fright

If our line of reasoning is correct, in direct contrast to the above, parental behaviors which are mediated primarily by internal factors related to unresolved experiences of trauma and fear should in general interfere with the regulated functioning of the offspring's attachment behavioral system. This is because the parent's psychological state will most likely be "altered" when these behaviors occur. The behaviors themselves can be delineated as follows.

DISSOCIATIVE PARENTAL BEHAVIOR

The phenomena of dissociation have intrigued psychologists since the turn of the last century (e.g., Breuer & Freud, 1895/1960; James, 1890/1983; Janet, 1907/1965; and Prince, 1905/1978). Careful consideration of the phenomena has been made available through the work of Hilgard (1977), Kihlstrom (1997), Liotti (1992, 1993, 1999), Putnam (1985), and Spiegel (1990), among others.

Some aspects of dissociative experiences are subjective, and are there-fore difficult to identify. These include depersonalization, amnesia, and the subjective sense of the existence of alternative identity states. Other aspects of dissociation are, in contrast, overtly observable, for example, trance states, and certain kinds of altered, anomalous facial and vocal expressions. The ex-tremes of dissociative phenomena, such as dissociative identity disorder and fugue states, have frequently been associated with a history of trauma, and by implication with fear (Putnam, 1985).

Dissociative parental behaviors were first found informally related to dis-organized infant attachment status by Main and Hesse (1990) who, for ex-ample, described the simultaneous voicing and devoicing intonation some parents use in greeting their (disorganized) infants. This intonation most of-ten has a haunted quality as when "Hi . . . iiiii" is spoken while pulling in on the diaphragm. In a more recent study, one mother of a disorganized infant used a devoiced "haunted" whisper ("*aaaaaa . . .   . ahhh,* get the blocks") in addressing her infant. This mother was also sometimes observed whispering instructions to herself just prior to speaking the *same* words in a normal con-versational tone (Abrams et al., submitted), and these instances of apparent "self-coaching" prior to normal speech also had a devoiced or "haunted" qual-ity. Another mother of a disorganized infant grunted and growled in a deep, aggressive, male voice while smiling and apparently pleasantly attempting to engage her infant in play. These sounds were sufficiently anomalous that ear-lier observers of the same videotape had assumed they were mechanical, and originated from outside of the room.

Another type of behavior which most observers would consider indicative of entrance into a dissociative state consists in lengthy "freezing" of all move-ment, including half-closed, unblinking eyes. Here the parent is completely unresponsive to, or appears to be unaware of, the external environment, includ-ing the movements and vocalizations of his or her infant. We have observed several unresolved/disorganized parents freeze all movement as just described, and recently Jacobvitz (see Lyons-Ruth & Jacobvitz, 1999) has reported ob-serving an unresolved/disorganized mother enter a trance while being filmed in a feeding interaction in the home. This mother sat immobilized in an uncom-fortable position with hand in air, blankly staring into space for 50 consecutive seconds. In total, she entered apparently altered states for 5 out of the 20 min-utes of feeding. Dissociative or trancelike behavior this pronounced is assumed to be rare in low-risk samples, and would receive the highest score (9) on the 1 to 9 point FR scale.

In a recent Bay Area study of 75 middle-class parent-infant dyads, a marked relation between FR scores assigned specifically for dissociative-like behavior in the free play/Clown Session and the degree to which the infant had shown

disorganization with the same parent in the Ainsworth strange situation procedure was found for both mother-infant and father-infant dyads (Abrams et al.,
2002; see also the significant relation between maternal dissociative behavior
and infant disorganization found in the Leiden sample by Schuengel et al.,
1997a, 1997b).

Clearly it seems plausible that at high levels of intensity and/or in stressful
situations, dissociative parental behavior could in itself be sufficiently alarming
to leave the infant without a strategy for maintaining behavioral, emotional,
and attentional organization. For example, in three separate instances in which
a parent used devoicing ("haunted") tones in addressing the infant, the infant's
behavior immediately became disorganized. Similarly, two infants seen in the
strange situation immediately "froze" (Main & Solomon's [1990] guidelines
identify freezing and stilling as forms of disorganized/disoriented behavior) as
soon as the parent entered a trancelike state. When marked, then, many types
of dissociative behavior might be alarming, while at the same time leaving the
infant with "nowhere to go" (since the parent appears to be "absent"). Thus, a
state of "fright without solution" could well be created.

Anomalous Forms of Threatening Parental Behavior

Main and Hesse (1990) called attention to unusual movement patterns observed during the strange situation in some parents of disorganized infants
(see also Hesse & Main, 1999). These included startling, unpredictable inva-
sions of "personal space"—for example, while seated behind the infant, some
parents silently and abruptly slid their hands across the infant's face or throat.
In addition, Main and Hesse informally noted non-gamelike movements or
postures that resembled a hunt or chase-pursuit sequence in the parents of
some disorganized infants.

In more recent, formal investigations utilizing home or laboratory free-play
observations, other researchers have similarly described the sudden appearance
of animal-like forms of threatening behavior in the parents of disorganized
infants. Some parents have abruptly begun "stalking" movements toward the
infant on all fours, silent and stiff-legged, in the absence of all "meta-signals"
of play. In the Leiden study, one unresolved mother of a disorganized infant
crawled toward her infant and then, simulating "mauling" behavior, turned
her over with fingers extended like claws (see Schuengel, van IJzendoorn,
Bakermans-Kranenburg, & Blom, 1997a). Another mother clawed repeatedly
toward her infant's face, while the mother of an unclassifiable infant[16] tossed
her toddler in the air while making growl-like sounds and baring her teeth.

---

[16] As noted earlier, the identification of disorganized infant strange situation behavior evolved out
of an examination of infants whose strange situation behavior was unclassifiable. Schuengel and his

Recent observations in the free-play laboratory context by Abrams and colleagues (submitted) and in the home by Jacobvitz at Texas (Jacobvitz, Hazen, & Riggs, 1997; Jacobvitz, 1998; see also Lyons-Ruth & Jacobvitz, 1999) have continued to confirm the existence of anomalous forms of threat behavior in parents independently identified as having disorganized infants. These behaviors have included not only teeth-baring but additionally hissing, deep growls, and even one-sided lip-raising (in essence, vestigial canine exposure, a threat gesture noted by Darwin in 1872). None of these behaviors and expressions appeared to be playful, and most seemed to arise "out of nowhere," and then disappear.

The approach-flight conflict leading to disorganization within the context of (anomalous) threatening parental behavior should, of course, be similar to that described earlier in cases of battering. Because most of the anomalous forms of parental threat just described appear suddenly, briefly, and without apparent context, we infer that fleeting affects—frightening, partially dissociated memories or thoughts associated with the parent's own trauma or fearful ideation—may drive the abrupt appearance and disappearance of these behaviors. It should be noted that in the Bay Area study of 75 infant-parent dyads described earlier (Abrams et al., submitted), scores for these anomalous forms of parental behavior were in themselves found moderately associated with infant disorganization.

ANOMALOUS FRIGHTENED PARENTAL BEHAVIOR

We now discuss the more subtle and initially confusing problem of why particular anomalous manifestations of *fright* are also likely to lead to disorganization in the offspring (see also Hesse & Main, 1999). Ultimately, we suspect that the operative mechanism also involves alterations in normal consciousness originating from the parent's traumatized state of mind. However, as noted earlier, and as Lyons-Ruth's findings have implied (Lyons-Ruth and Jacobvitz, 1999; Lyons-Ruth et al., 1999), these behaviors are not intrinsically incompatible with parenting, which is otherwise relatively sensitive and responsive.

Anomalous forms of frightened behavior presumed to result from events associated with the parent's unresolved state of mind. The stimuli resulting in expressions of fright stemming from a parent's traumatic experiences should most often be internal or idiosyncratically associated with the environment and therefore unlocatable

---

colleagues described this infant's strange situation behavior as not only failing to fully fit to the traditional A, B, and C attachment categories, but to the D category as well (Schuengel et al., 1997). Our own (still informal) ongoing analyses of strange situation behavior are continuing to suggest that unclassifiable infant strange situation attachment status has correlates similar to that of disorganized attachment status.

and incomprehensible to the infant. Under these conditions the infant might "sense" impending danger which is indiscernible or incomprehensible as to source. Providing one example of behavior of this type, Main and Hesse (1990) described the parent of a disorganized toddler who responded with an immediate, frightened intake of breath as he began moving a toy car across the room, and then exclaimed "Uh-oh! Gonna have an *accident!* Everybody's gonna get *killed!!*" Although no access to this parent's history was available, the anxiety implied by the intake of breath combined with the particular statement made could well suggest some connection to earlier personal or familial experiences of loss through automobile or other accidents. This is, of course, only one example. A parent who suddenly looks about or reacts to an unchanged benign environment with fear provides a more general illustration.

Although a parent engaged in an anomalous display of fright may or may not also be in a dissociative state, it is reasonable to speculate that this kind of unintegrated fear could be the product of a somewhat altered and anomalous state of consciousness. The fearful parent might therefore be *simultaneously alarming and unavailable*, placing the infant in a disorganizing situation involving "fright without solution" (Kaplan, 1987; Main & Hesse, 1992).

Frightened Behavior where the Infant Becomes the Source of the Parent's Alarm

In some cases a parent who remains frightened by partially dissociated experiences may come to confuse or identify the infant with the original traumatic experience. One (unresolved/disorganized) parent was observed backing away from their infant during the separation episode of the strange situation, while stammering in an unusual voice: "D-don't follow me, d-don't" (Main & Hesse, 1990). During the succeeding reunion, the infant stilled against the parent with eyes dazed for over one full minute, and was judged disorganized. Parents have also been seen stepping cautiously from place to place as though attempting to keep the offspring at the greatest possible distance, or even trying to "escape" by moving out of reach as if the infant was, for example, a potentially dangerous animal.

How can such anomalous responses to an infant be accounted for? Consider the unresolved mother of a disorganized infant discussed by Ainsworth and Eichberg (1991). This mother appeared to retain the childhood belief that, at age eight, she had killed her caretaker "with one sentence!" Thus, if at times this speaker believes that children have the power to kill through thoughts or words, the idea *that it is possible to be killed by one's own offspring* could also be present. "Anniversary" reactions occurring when an offspring reaches the age at which the parent lost an important person may therefore not only be mediated by, for example, the renewed onset of depression, but also in some situations by the re-arousal of anxiety and fright. Fear *of the offspring* in traumatized parents is therefore perhaps not as unlikely an outcome as might be imagined (see Hesse & Main, 1999).

In a case where the source of danger is thought by the parent to emanate from the infant, the infant's position would become especially perplexing and disorganizing, and could lead to the following experiences, observations, or suppositions, however inaccessible to consciousness and/or infantile in form:

1. *Attempts to increase proximity to the parent, may result in increasing parent-offspring distance.* Efforts to approach a parent where fears are centered on the infant might trigger parental inclinations (however subtle) to increase parent-offspring distance. Moreover, rather than appearing simply indifferent (neglecting), the retreating parent might appear alarmed.

2. *Danger which emanates from within the self is paradoxically inescapable.* Thus, the disorganizing need to take flight from the self could arise.[17] Main and Hesse (1992; see Hesse, 1999b) have suggested that in extreme cases one "solution" to the approach/flight paradox caused by an alarming parent could be the "creation" of two selves or executors—one to approach, and one to take flight. Similarly, the ultimate "solution" to the more perplexing situation currently under discussion could also at times necessitate the creation of segregated systems or multiple executors (see Bowlby, 1980, Hilgard, 1977; Main, 1999). Here, however, rather than simply requiring two "selves" to perform contradictory actions (as in the case of extreme abuse), two selves are required in order for one to retreat from the second. While undoubtedly a rare outcome, these circumstances provide a particularly compelling backdrop for less extreme "splitting" or dissociative sequelae in the event of future trauma.

3. Finally, as is inferred from observations of animals, *flight behavior on the part of one individual can be a stimulus provoking attack or hunt-chase behavior on the part of a second* (T. Johnson, personal communication, 1994). A parent who exhibits fear or inclinations to take flight in response to infant approach could therefore also provoke aggressive or "chase/pursuit" tendencies. This could gradually stimulate inclinations to "attack" the parent, and contribute to the intensification of frightening and aggressive ideation. As infant disorganization has been found predictive of

---

[17] This condition may await the development of a sense of self and cognitive abilities which appear shortly after infancy.

aggressive, "externalizing" behaviors (e.g. see van IJzendoorn et al., 1999, for meta-analysis), this suggestion is intriguing. However, without an understanding of disorganized attachment the origin of an adult's intrusive, aggressive ideation, insofar as it has resulted from early interactions with a subtly frightened parent, might be difficult to identify.

Other Parental Behaviors Likely to Be Associated with Unresolved Mental States: Timid/Deferential, Sexualized, and Disorganized/Disoriented Behavior

The final three subcategories delineated in the FR coding system may not in themselves lead directly to an approach-flight paradox for the infant. Nonetheless, they each suggest alterations in normal consciousness which should increase the likelihood that the anomalous behaviors capable of directly producing disorganization will appear at other times. This was the case in the 30-minute laboratory observations of parental FR behavior discussed above, where the majority of parents who displayed timid, sexualized, or disorganized behaviors also displayed more directly frightening (threatening, frightened, or dissociative) behaviors (Abrams, 2000; Abrams et al., submitted).

TIMID/DEFERENTIAL BEHAVIOR, AND (ROLE-INVERTING) TENDENCIES TO UTILIZE THE OFFSPRING AS AN ATTACHMENT FIGURE

In our original observations (Main & Hesse, 1990) of the strange situation behavior of the parents of disorganized infants, we noted "extreme timidity" in one mother's handling of her infant. During a reunion episode, another unresolved/disorganized mother had welcomed her daughter with extended hands; however, when the infant made an impatient gesture, the mother responded by slumping her shoulders, folding her hands, and assuming a "humbled" posture, accompanied by a pleading expression. Similar timid/deferential behavior was observed in the Leiden study (Schuengel et al., 1997) in a mother classified unresolved regarding a parental suicide. We have also noted more extreme examples, such as deferential submission to obviously painful slapping, hitting, or hair-pulling on the part of the infant. In these latter more extreme cases, the infant was definitively disorganized, or else unclassifiable.

The above behaviors may suggest that some parents at times feel the infant to be "superior" and/or to have relatively greater power. This accords with George and Solomon's (1996) interview-based finding, that the parents of disorganized children sometimes report that the child has supernatural capabilities, and that (as identified from a caregiving interview) these parents feel helpless with respect to their offspring who are, correspondingly, perceived as powerful.

Because an infant in fact has no capacity to control, harm, or protect the parent, we may ask why, from an evolutionary vantage point, behavior of this type would arise. Recall, then, that in ground-living nomadic primates at least two relatively universal tendencies are assumed to be aroused in conjunction with heightened states of alarm.[18] The first is to take flight from the perceived source of danger, and the second is to gain proximity to an attachment figure who provides protection. Thus, *the parent* as well as the infant should experience a volition to seek a haven of safety if sufficiently alarmed. In most parents it seems likely that any propensities to seek the offspring as a haven of safety are either absent or are over-ridden, so that alarm stemming from an environmental source most often elicits a protective, as opposed to a protection-seeking, response (Cassidy, 1999).

Some parents in unresolved mental states may at times nevertheless experience a disoriented volition to seek the offspring when alarmed (Hesse & Main, 1999). This anomalous inclination would no doubt be involuntary, and intended to reduce parental fear. If acted upon, however—even as a momentary inclination—the infant's immediate confusion and fear could easily be heightened. If, then, the frightened (hence, frightening) parent approaches the infant for protection, an approach-flight paradox could well be created, since the source of the infant's alarm (the frightened, proximity-seeking parent) will stimulate strong simultaneous inclinations to increase proximity as well as distance.

SEXUALIZED BEHAVIOR

We have rarely observed overtly sexualized parental behavior in parent/child dyads in low-risk Western strange situation samples. Nevertheless, mild forms of these behaviors do occur. For example, Abrams (2000) noted one parent of a D infant who suddenly and briefly, grunted and twisted her body suggestively towards her infant with a "come-hither" expression. In a few samples, intimate kissing of the infant has been observed.

It is difficult to imagine that individuals in the particular Westernized nations where these studies were conducted could (a) enter a state where they appear to lack the ability to monitor their actions sufficiently to "suppress" sexualized behavior toward their infants without (b) having had experiences rendering them vulnerable to exhibiting overtly dissociated and/or frightened or frightening behavior in other contexts.

---

[18] In older individuals, both the protective and agonistic systems may also become activated.

DISORGANIZED PARENTAL BEHAVIORS COMPATIBLE WITH THE INFANT D CODING SYSTEM

From the outset, the FR system has included parental behaviors which had been identified as disorganized/disoriented in the infants originally studied by Main and Solomon (1986, 1990), and some such behaviors, even during infancy, have been regarded as (at least phenotypically) dissociated (Liotti, 1992; Main & Morgan, 1996). Abrams and colleagues (submitted) found that two mothers of disorganized infants momentarily appeared "blind" (both facially and by changes in movement pattern) during the play session, whereas to that point the functioning of their eyes had appeared normal. A "sudden blind look to eyes" had previously been identified only in infants. Another parent of a D infant abruptly began to move in a stiff, asymmetrical, robotlike manner indicative of neurological impairment. Assuming no momentary neurological interference (the mother moved normally at other times) this behavior was inexplicable, suggesting a momentary "collapse of attentional and behavioral strategy" (Main & Hesse, 1992; see Hesse, 1999b). Abrams and her colleagues speculated that this "dissociation of movement" could have been caused by a lapse in procedural memory (e.g., memory for muscle movement), perhaps comparable to the concept of a lapse in explicit (verbal) memory.

These findings regarding the varying subtypes of frightened/frightening parental behavior, as well as the broader findings and results discussed earlier (e.g., Jacobvitz, 1998; Schuengel et al., 1997, 1999; Abrams et al., submitted; Lyons-Ruth & Jacobvitz, 1999; Lyons-Ruth et al., 1999) suggest that observational research using the FR system will continue to yield new and intriguing information regarding sporadic and anomalous "lapses" in parental action.

Many theories focusing on early development would of course concur that parental behaviors which frighten the offspring will increase the likelihood of untoward effects. It is specifically attachment theory, however, which posits that the biological function of the child's tie to its primary caregiver(s) is protection, and that among ground-living primates, the attachment figure is the infant's primary solution to situations of fear (Bowlby, 1969; Hesse & Main, 1999). Attachment theory has, then, created a compelling theoretical framework for the proposal that parental behavior which frightens the infant will not only drive the infant *away from* but also *toward* the parent. It is suggested that this "unsolvable" experience will often lead to disorganization and disorientation for the infant.

In addition, we have suggested that fear of the parent may cause a disruption or "dysregulation" of attention and emotion and, relatedly, temporarily restrict or alter the child's capacity for normal conscious processing. Alterations in consciousness in the face of an approach-flight paradox may, in other words, be associated with difficulties in maintaining normal information-processing (as suggested by Liotti, 1992). This proposition needs further exploration, but it may provide a means of enhancing our understanding of the psychological vulnerabilities[19] being found associated with disorganized attachment (see Main and Hesse [1992] in Hesse [1999b] for a discussion of serial vs. parallel informational processing in this context).

Conclusion

Although D attachment in infancy is clearly a risk factor, we by no means believe that all, or even most individuals who have been disorganized will not fare well in later development. Nonetheless, within this presentation (see also Hesse & Main, 1999), outlined a pathway from certain anomalous forms of parental behavior to a variety of unfavorable outcomes for the offspring, which may otherwise have appeared untraceable with respect to a direct experimental source. First, by studying the lapses in the monitoring of discourse or reasoning which occurred as parents of disorganized infants discussed loss or abuse experiences within the AAI, we discovered "parapraxes"[20] or slips in the parents' *language* which were predictive of parapraxes in the *infant's actions* (Main & Hesse, 1990). It was presumed that these slips in language or reasoning stemmed from sources internal to the parent; that they resulted from states of mental disorganization and conflict surrounding frightening experiences; and that they would be found associated with the sporadic appearance of corresponding (frightened/frightening) *parental actions*. Above, we have reviewed a number of recent studies providing corroboration for each of these hypotheses.

In essence, we have advanced an extension of attachment theory (Hesse & Main, 1999, 2000; Main & Hesse, 1990) which focuses upon a previously underemphasized aspect of the role of fear within the attachment relationship. Correspondingly, we have suggested a new mechanism by which the traumatic experiences of one individual can indirectly affect the development of a second. Specifically, it has been proposed that the infant repeatedly frightened by its

---

[19] Intellectual, introspective, artistic, and other advantages may at times be primed by early disorganized attachment. A disscussion of these "positive" outcomes (potentially driven, for example, by increased capacties for absorption) is, however, beyond the scope of this paper.

[20] Readers outside of the analytic community may be less familiar with the term "parapraxis," indicating a "... faulty action due to the interference of some conflict, or train of thought." Freud (1901/1960) used parapraxes (often but not always slips of the tongue or slips of the pen) to demonstrate the existence of unconscious mental processes in healthy individuals.

parent does not just experience negative and disturbing emotion(s) or ordinary conflict, but additionally is subjected to a biologically channeled paradox in which simultaneous propensities to approach and to take flight from the parent which cannot be over-ridden ("regulated") are activated. Finally, we have extended Bowlby's emphasis upon the role which direct experience plays in the development of psychopathology in the individual (Bowlby, 1969, 1980) by pointing to the powerful indirect influence of events which occurred in the previous generation and have become associated with (sometimes anomalous) fears and fantasies.

Thus, as first suggested by van IJzendoorn (personal communication, 1997), we have broadened our understanding of what "real" events are to include a parent's (often indeliberately) fear-evoking responses to aspects of their own histories; these parental behaviors responses that are predictive of specifiable "second-generation" effects for the child. From this point of view, the parents' frightening experience itself is of course not "real" for the second generation. What is real, however, is the developing child's interaction with a parent whose behavior at times reflects their own original traumatic experiences and/or ideation.

References

Abrams, K. Y. (2000). *Pathways to disorganization: A study concerning varying types of parental frightened and frightening behaviors as related to infant disorganization.* Unpublished doctoral dissertation, University of California at Berkeley.

Abrams, K. Y., Rifkin, A., & Hesse, E. (submitted). *Dissociative parental behavior observed in a laboratory play session predicts disorganized infant attachment.*

Ainsworth, M. D. S. (1967). *Infancy in Uganda: Infant care and the growth of love.* Baltimore, MD: The Johns Hopkins Press.

Ainsworth, M. D. S., Bell, S. M., & Stayton, D. J. (1971). Individual differences in Strange Situation behavior of one-year-olds. In H. R. Schaffer (Ed.), *The origins of human social relations* (pp. 17–57). London: Academic Press.

Ainsworth, M. D. S., Blehar, M. C., Waters, E., & Wall, S. (1978). *Patterns of attachment: A psychological study of the Strange Situation.* Hillsdale, NJ: Erlbaum.

Ainsworth, M. D. S., & Eichberg, C. G. (1991). Effects on infant-mother attachment of mother's unresolved loss of an attachment figure or other traumatic experience. In P. Marris, J. Stevenson-Hinde, & C. Parkes (Eds.), *Attachment across the life cycle* (pp. 160–183). New York: Routledge.

Ammaniti, M., Speranza, A. M., & Candelori, C. (1996). Stability of attachment in children and intergenerational transmission of attachment (Stabilita dell'attaccamento infantile e trasmissione intergenerazionale dell'attaccamento). *Psichiatria dell'Infanzia e dell'Adolescenza, 63,* 313–332.

Ammaniti, M., van IJzendoorn, M. H., Speranza, A. M., & Tambelli, R. (2000). Internal working models of attachment during late childhood and early adolescence: An exploration of stability and change. *Attachment and Human Development, 2*(3), 328–346.

Benoit, D., & Parker, K. (1994). Stability and transmission of attachment across three generations. *Child Development 65*, 1444–1456.

Bowlby, J. (1958). The nature of the child's tie to his mother. *International Journal of Psychoanalysis, 39*, 350–373.

Bowlby, J. (1969). *Attachment and loss: Vol. 1. Attachment*. New York: Basic Books.

Bowlby, J. (1973). *Attachment and loss: Vol. 2. Separation*. New York: Basic Books.

Bowlby, J. (1980). *Attachment and loss: Vol. 3. Loss*. New York: Basic Books.

Bowlby, J. (1982). *Attachment and loss: Vol. 1. Attachment* (2d ed.). New York: Basic Books.

Bowlby, J. (1988). *A secure base: Parent-child attachment and healthy human development*. New York: Basic Books.

Bretherton, I. (1992). The origins of attachment theory: John Bowlby and Mary Ainsworth. *Developmental Psychology 28*, 759–775.

Breuer, J., & Freud, S. (1960). *Studies in hysteria*. Boston: Beacon. (Original work published 1895)

Carlson, E. A. (1998). A prospective longitudinal study of disorganized/disoriented attachment. *Child Development, 69*, 1970–1979.

Carlson, E. B., & Putnam, F. W. (1993). An update on the Dissociative Experiences Scale. *Dissociation, 7*, 16–27.

Carlson, V., Cicchetti, D., Barnett, D., & Braunwald, K. (1989). Disorganized/disoriented attachment relationships in maltreated infants. *Developmental Psychology 25*, 525–531.

Cassidy, J. (1999). The nature of the child's ties. In J. Cassidy & P. R. Shaver (Eds.), *Handbook of attachment: Theory, research and clinical applications* (pp. 3–20). New York: Guilford Press.

Cassidy, J., & Marvin, R. S., with the MacArthur Working Group on Attachment (1992). *Attachment organization in three and four year olds: Procedures and coding manual*. Unpublished manuscript, University of Virginia.

Crittenden, P. M., & Ainsworth, M. D. S. (1989). Child maltreatment and attachment theory. In D. Cicchetti & V. Carlson (Eds.), *Child maltreatment: Theory and research on the causes and consequences of child abuse and neglect* (pp. 432–463). New York: Cambridge University Press.

Darwin, C. (1962). *The voyage of the Beagle*. Garden City NY: Doubleday. (Original work published in 1839)

Darwin, C. (1979). *The expression of emotions in man and animals*. New York: St. Martin's Press. (Original work published in 1872)

De Wolff, M. S., & van IJzendoorn, M. H. (1997). Sensitivity and attachment: A meta-analysis on parental antecedents of infant attachment. *Child Development 68*, 571–591.

Fonagy, P., Steele, H., & Steele, M. (1991). Maternal representations of attachment during pregnancy predict the organization of infant-mother attachment at one year of age. *Child Development, 62*, 891–905.

Freud, S. (1960). The psychopathology of everyday life. In J. Strachey (Ed. & Trans.), *The standard edition of the complete psychological works of Sigmund Freud* (Vol. 6, pp. 1–279) London: Hogarth Press. (Original work published 1901)

George, C., Kaplan, N., & Main, M. (1984, 1985, 1996). *Adult Attachment Interview*. Unpublished protocol, Department of Psychology, University of California, Berkeley.

George, C., & Solomon, J. (1996). Representational models of relationships: Links between caregiving and attachment. *Infant Mental Health, 17*, 198–216.

Grossmann, K. E. (1997, September). *The development of attachment and psychological adaptation from the cradle to the grave*. Invited lecture, VIII European Conference on Developmental Psychology, Rennes, France.

Hansburg, H. G. (1972). *Adolescent separation anxiety: A method for the study of adolescent separation problems.* Springfield, IL: Thomas.

Heinicke, C., & Westheimer, I. (1966). *Brief separations.* New York: International Universities Press.

Hertsgaard, L., Gunnar, M., Erickson, M. F., & Nachmias, M. (1995). Adrenocortical responses to the Strange Situation in infants with disorganized/disoriented attachment relationships. *Child Development, 66,* 1100–1106.

Hesse, E. (1996). Discourse, memory and the Adult Attachment Interview: A note with emphasis on the emerging Cannot Classify category. *Infant Mental Health Journal, 17,* 4–11.

Hesse, E. (1999a). The Adult Attachment Interview: Historical and current perspectives. In J. Cassidy and P. R. Shaver (Eds.), *Handbook of attachment: Theory, research, and clinical applications* (pp. 395–433). New York: Guilford Press.

Hesse, E. (1999b). *Unclassifiable and Disorganized Responses in the Adult Attachment Interview and in the Infant Strange Situation Procedure: Theoretical proposals and empirical findings.* Ph. D. diss., Leiden University.

Hesse, E., & Main, M. (1999). Second-generation effects of unresolved trauma as observed in non-maltreating parents: Dissociated, frightened and threatening parental behavior. *Psychoanalytic Inquiry, 19,* 481–540.

Hesse, E., & Main, M. (2000). Disorganization in infant and adult attachment: Descriptions, correlates and implications for developmental psychopathology. *Journal of the American Psychoanalytic Association, 48* (4), 1097–1127.

Hesse, E., & van IJzendoorn, M. H. (1998). Parental loss of close family members and propensities towards absorption in offspring. *Developmental Science, 1,* 299–305.

Hesse, E., & van IJzendoorn, M. H. (1999). Propensities towards absorption are related to lapses in the monitoring of reasoning or discourse during the Adult Attachment Interview: A preliminary investigation. *Attachment and Human Development, 1,* 67–91.

Hilgard, E. R. (1977/1986). *Divided consciousness: Multiple controls in human thought and action.* New York: Wiley.

Hinde, R. A. (1996). *Animal behaviour: A synthesis of ethology and comparative psychology.* New York: McGraw-Hill.

Hinde, R. A. (1974). *Biological bases of human social behavior.* New York: McGraw-Hill.

Hrdy, S. (1999). *Mother nature: A history of mothers, infants, and natural selection.* New York: Pantheon.

Jacobsen, T., Edelstein, W., & Hofmann, V. (1994). A longitudinal study of the relation between representations of attachment in childhood and cognitive functioning in childhood and adolescence. *Developmental Psychology, 30,* 112–124.

Jacobsen, T., & Hofmann, V. (1997). Children's attachment representations: Longitudinal relations to school behavior and academic competency in middle childhood and adolescence. *Developmental Psychology, 33,* 703–710.

Jacobsen, T., Huss, M., Fendrich, M., Kruesi, M. P., & Ziegenhain, U. (1997). Children's ability to delay gratification: Longitudinal relations to mother-child attachment. *Journal of Genetic Psychology 158,* 411–426.

Jacobsen, T., Ziegenhain, U., Muller, B., Rottmann, U., Hofmann, V., & Edelstein, W. (1992, September). *Predicting stability of mother-child attachment patterns in day-care children from infancy to age 6.* Poster presented at the Fifth World Congress of Infant Psychiatry and Allied Disciplines, Chicago.

Jacobvitz, D. (1998, March). *Frightening caregiving: Links with mother's loss and trauma.* Paper presented at the biennial meeting of the Southwestern Society for Research in Human Development, Galveston, TX.

Jacobvitz, D., Hazen, N. L., & Riggs, S. (1997). *Disorganized mental processes in mothers, frightened/frightening behavior in caregivers, and disoriented, disorganized behavior in infancy.* Paper presented at the biennial meeting of the Society for Research in Child Development, Washington, D. C.

James, W. (1983). *The principles of psychology.* Cambridge, MA: Harvard University Press. (Original work published 1890)

Janet, P. (1965). *The major symptoms of hysteria.* New York: Hafner. (Original work published 1907)

Kaplan, N. (1987). *Individual differences in six-year-old's thoughts about separation: Predicted from attachment to mother at age one.* Ph. D. diss., University of California at Berkeley.

Kaplan, N., & Main, M. (1984, 1986). *Assessment of attachment organization through children's family drawings.* Unpublished manuscript, Department of Psychology, University of California at Berkeley.

Kermoian, R., & Campos, J. J. (1988). Locomotor experience: A facilitator of spatial cognitive development. *Child Development, 59,* 595–624.

Kihlstrom, J. F. (1997). Consciousness and me-ness. In J. D. Cohen & J. W. Schooler (Eds.), *Scientific approaches to consciousness* (pp. 451–468). Hillsdale, NJ: Erlbaum.

Klagsbrun, M., & Bowlby, J. (1976). Responses to separation from parents: A clinical test for children. *British Journal of Projective Psychology, 21,* 7–21.

Klinnert, M. D., Campos, J. J., Sorce, J. F., Emde, R., & Svedja, M. (1983). Emotions as behavior regulators: Social referencing in infancy. In R. Plutchik & H. Kellerman (Eds.), *The emotions, Vol 2.* San Diego: Academic Press.

Lakatos, K., Toth, I., Nemoda, Z., Ney, K., Sasvari-Szekely, M., & Gervai, J. (2000). Dopamine D4 receptor (DRD4) gene polymorphism is associated with attachment disorganization in infants. *Molecular Psychiatry. 5,* 633–637.

Liotti, G. (1992). Disorganized/disoriented attachment in the etiology of the dissociative disorders. *Dissociation, 5,* 196–204.

Liotti, G. (1993). Disorganized attachment and dissociative experiences: An illustration of the developmental-ethological approach to cognitive therapy. In H. Rosen & K. T. Kuehlwein (Eds.), *Cognitive therapy in action* (pp. 213–239). San Francisco: Jossey-Bass.

Liotti, G. (1999). Disorganization of attachment as a model for understanding dissociative psychopathology. In J. Solomon & C. George (Eds.), *Attachment disorganization* (pp. 291–317). New York: Guilford Press.

Lyons-Ruth, K. (1996). Attachment relationships among children with aggressive behavior problems: The role of disorganized early attachment patterns. *Journal of Consulting and Clinical Psychology, 64,* 64–73.

Lyons-Ruth, K., Alpean, L., & Repacholi, B. (1993). Disorganized infant attachment classification and maternal psychosocial problems as predictors of hostile-aggressive behavior in the preschool classroom. *Child Development, 64,* 572–585.

Lyons-Ruth, K., Bronfman, E., & Parsons, E. (1999). Maternal disrupted affective communication, maternal frightened or frightening behavior, and disorganized infant attachment strategies. In J. Vondra & D. Barnett (Eds.), *Atypical patterns of infant attachment: Theory, research, and current directions* (pp. 67–96). *Monographs of the Society for Research in Child Development, 64*(3).

Lyons-Ruth, K., & Jacobvitz, D. (1999). Attachment disorganization: Unresolved loss, relationship violence, and lapses in behavioral and attentional strategies. In J. Cassidy & P. R. Shaver (Eds.), *Handbook of attachment: Theory, research and clinical applications* (pp. 520–554). New York: Guilford Press.

Lyons-Ruth, K., Repacholi, B., McLeod, S., & Silva, E. (1991). Disorganized attachment behavior in infancy: Short-term stability, maternal and infant correlates, and risk-related sub-types. *Development and Psychopathology, 3*, 377–396.

Main, M. (1973). *Exploration, play, and cognitive functioning as related to child-mother attachment.* Ph. D. diss., Johns Hopkins University.

Main, M. (1979a). *Scale for disordered/disoriented infant behavior in response to the Main and Weston Clown Session.* Unpublished manuscript, University of California at Berkeley.

Main, M. (1979b). The ultimate causation of some infant attachment phenomena: Further answers, further phenomena and further questions. *The Behavioral and Brain Sciences, 2*, 640–643.

Main, M. (1981). Avoidance in the service of attachment: A working paper. In K. Immelmann, G. Barlow, L. Petrinovitch, & M. Main (Eds.), *Behavioral development: The Bielefeld interdisciplinary project* (pp. 651–693). New York: Cambridge University Press.

Main, M. (1990). Cross-cultural studies of attachment organization: Recent studies, changing methodologies and the concept of conditional strategies. *Human Development, 33*, 48–61.

Main, M. (1995). Recent studies in attachment: Overview, with implications for clinical work. In S. Goldberg, R. Muir, & J. Kerr (Eds.), *Attachment theory: Social, developmental and clinical perspectives* (pp. 407–474). Hillsdale, NJ: Analytic Press.

Main, M. (1999). Epilogue. Attachment theory: Eighteen points with suggestions for future studies. In J. Cassidy & P. R. Shaver (Eds.), *Handbook of attachment: Theory, research, and clinical applications* (pp. 845–888). New York: Guilford Press.

Main, M. (2000). The Adult Attachment Interview: Fear, attention, safety and discourse processes. *Journal of the American Psychoanalytic Association, 48* (4), 1055–1096.

Main, M. (2001, April). *Attachment to mother and father in infancy, as related to the Adult Attachment Interview and a self-visualization task at age 19.* Poster presented at the biennial meeting of the Society for Research in Child Development, Minneapolis, MN.

Main, M., & Cassidy, J. (1988). Categories of response to reunion with the parent at age six: Predicted from infant attachment classifications and stable over a one-month period. *Developmental Psychology, 24*, 415–426.

Main, M., & Goldwyn, R. (1984–1998). *Adult attachment scoring and classification system.* Unpublished manuscript, Department of Psychology, University of California at Berkeley.

Main, M., Goldwyn, R., & Hesse, E. (2002). *Adult attachment scoring and classification system.* Unpublished manuscript, Department of Psychology, University of California, Berkeley.

Main, M., & Hesse, E. (1990). Parents' unresolved traumatic experiences are related to infant disorganized attachment status: Is frightened and/or frightening parental behavior the linking mechanism? In M. T. Greenberg, D. Cicchetti, & E. M. Cummings (Eds.), *Attachment in the preschool years: Theory, research, and intervention* (pp. 161–182). Chicago: University of Chicago Press.

Main, M., & Hesse, E. (1992–1998). *Frightening, frightened, dissociated, deferential, sexualized and disorganized parental behavior: A coding system for frightening parent-infant interactions.* Unpublished manuscript, University of California at Berkeley.

Main, M., & Hesse, E. (1992). Disorganized/disoriented infant behavior in the strange situation, lapses in the monitoring of reasoning and discourse during the parent's Adult Attachment Interview, and dissociative states. In M. Ammaniti & D. Stern (Eds.), *Attachment and psychoanalysis* (pp. 86–140). Rome: Guis, Lateza, & Figli.

Main, M., Kaplan, N., & Cassidy, J. (1985). Security in infancy, childhood, and adulthood: A move to the level of representation. In I. Bretherton & E. Waters (Eds.), *Growing points of attachment theory and research* (pp. 66–104). *Monographs of the Society for Research in Child Development,* 50 (Serial No. 209).

Main, M., & Morgan, H. (1996). Disorganization and disorientation in infant Strange Situation behavior: Phenotypic resemblance to dissociative states? In L. Michelson & W. Ray (Eds.), *Handbook of dissociation: theoretical, empirical and clinical perspectives* (pp. 107–138). New York: Plenum Press.

Main, M., & Solomon, J. (1986). Discovery of a new, insecure-disorganized/ disoriented attachment pattern. In T. B. Brazelton & M. W. Yogman (Eds.), *Affective development in infancy* (pp. 95–124). Norwood, NJ: Ablex.

Main, M., & Solomon, J. (1990). Procedures for identifying infants as disorganized/disoriented during the Ainsworth strange situation. In M. T. Greenberg, D. Cicchetti, & E. M. Cummings (Eds.), *Attachment in the preschool years: Theory, research, and intervention* (pp. 121–160). Chicago: University of Chicago Press.

Main, M., & Stadtman, J. (1981). Infant response to rejection of physical contact by the mother: Aggression, avoidance and conflict. *Journal of the American Academy of Child Psychiatry,* 20, 2992–3007.

Main, M., & Weston, D. R. (1981). The quality of the toddler's relationship to mother and to father: Related to conflict behavior and the readiness to establish new relationships. *Child Development,* 52, 932–940.

Manassis, K., Bradley, S., Goldberg, S., Hood, J., & Swinson, R. P. (1994). Attachment in mothers with anxiety disorders and their children. *Journal American Academy of Child and Adolescent Psychiatry,* 33, 1106–1113.

Ogawa, J. R., Sroufe, L. A., Weinfield, N. S., Carlson, E. A., & Egeland, B. (1997). Development and the fragmented self: Longitudinal study of dissociative symptomatology in a nonclinical sample. *Development and Psychopathology,* 9, 855–879.

Pederson, D. R., Gleason, K. E., Moran, G., & Bento, S. (1998). Maternal attachment representations, maternal sensitivity and the infant-mother attachment relationship. *Developmental Psychology,* 34, 925–933.

Pipp-Siegel, S., Siegel, C. H., & Dean, J. (1999). Neurological aspects of the disorganized/disoriented attachment classification system: Differentiating quality of the attachment relationship from neurological impairment. In J. I. Vondra & D. Barnett (Eds.), *Atypical attachment in infancy and early childhood among children at developmental risk* (pp. 25–44). *Monographs of the Society for Research in Child Development* 64 (3).

Prince, M. (1978). *The dissociation of a personality.* New York: Oxford University Press. (Original work published 1905)

Putnam, F. W. (1985). Dissociation as a response to extreme trauma. In R. P. Kluft (Ed.), *The child antecedents of multiple personality* (pp. 65–97). Washington, DC: American Psychiatric Press.

Rudke-Yarrow, M., Cummings, E. M., Kuczynski, L., & Chapman, M. (1985). Patterns of attachment in two- and three-year olds in normal families and families with parental depression: *Child Development,* 56, 884–893.

Radojevic, M. (1992, July). *Predicting quality of infant attachment to father at 15 months from pre-natal paternal representations of attachment: An Australian contribution.* Paper presented at the XXV International Congress of Psychology, Brussels, Belgium.

Robertson, J., & Bowlby, J. (1952). Responses of young children to separation from their mothers. *Courrier Centre Internationale Enfance,* 2, 131–142.

Robertson, J., & Robertson, J. (1971). Young children in brief separation: A fresh look. *Psychoanalytic Study of the Child,* 26, 264–315.

Schaffer, H. R., & Emerson, P. E. (1964). *The development of social attachments in infancy. Monographs of the Society for Research in Child Development,* 29 (94).

Schuengel, C., van IJzendoorn, M. H., & Bakermans-Kranenburg, M. J. (1997). Attachment and loss: Frightening maternal behavior linking unresolved loss and disorganized infant attachment. In C. Schuengel, *Attachment, loss, and maternal behavior: A study on intergenerational transmission* (pp. 40–58). Ph.D. diss., Leiden University.

Schuengel, C., van IJzendoorn, M. H., & Bakermans-Kranenburg, M. J. (1999). Frightening maternal behavior linking unresolved loss and disorganized infant attachment. *Journal of Consulting and Clinical Psychology* 67, 54–63.

Schuengel, C., van IJzendoorn, M. H., Bakermans-Kranenburg, M. J., & Blom, M. (1997, March). *Frightening, frightened and/or dissociated behavior, unresolved loss and infant disorganization.* Paper presented at the biennial meeting of the Society for Research in Child Development, Washington, DC.

Siegel, D. (1999). *The developing mind: Towards a neurobiology of interpersonal experience.* New York: Guilford Press.

Solomon, J., & George, C. (1999). The place of disorganization in attachment theory: Linking classic observations with contemporary findings. In J. Solomon & C. George (Eds.), *Attachment disorganization* (pp. 3–32). New York: Guilford Press.

Solomon, J., George, C., & DeJong, A. (1995). Children classified as controlling at age six: Evidence for disorganized representational strategies and aggression at home and at school. *Development and Psychopathology, 7*, 447–463.

Spangler, G., & Grossmann, K. E. (1993). Biobehavioral organization in securely and insecurely attached infant. *Child Development, 64*, 1439–1450.

Spiegel, D. (1990). Hypnosis, dissociation and trauma: Hidden and overt observers. In J. Singer (Ed.), *Repression and dissociation: Implications for personality theory, psychopathology, and health* (pp. 121–142). Chicago: University of Chicago Press.

Sroufe, L. A. (1985). Attachment classification from the perspective of infant-caregiver relationships and infant temperament. *Child Development, 56*, 1–14.

Sroufe, L. A., Carlson, E. A., Levy, A. K., & Egeland, B. Implication of attachment theory in developmental psychopathology. *Development and Psychopathology, 11*(1), 1–13.

Steele, M., Fonagy, P., Yabsley, S., Woolgar, M., & Croft, C. (1995, March). *Maternal representations of attachment during pregnancy predict the quality of children's doll play at five years of age.* Presented at the biennial meeting of the Society for Research in Child Development, Indianapolis, IN.

Steele, H., Steele, M., & Fonagy, P. (1996a). Associations among attachment classifications of mothers, fathers and infants: Evidence for a relationship-specific perspective. *Child Development, 2*, 541–555.

Steele, H., Steele, M., & Fonagy, P. (1996b, August). *Attachment in the sixth year of life.* Paper presented at the meetings of the International Congress of Psychology, Montreal.

Strage, A., & Main, M. (1985, March). *Attachment and parent-child discourse patterns.* In M. Main (Chair), *Attachment: A move to the level of representation.* Paper presented at the biennial meeting of the Society for Research in Child Development, Toronto.

Tellegen, A. (1982). *Brief manual for the Differential Personality Questionaire.* Unpublished manuscript, University of Minnesota, Minneapolis.

Tellegen and Atkinson, G. (1974). Openness to absorbing and self-altering experiences ("absorption"), a trait related to hypnotic susceptibility. *Journal of abnormal psychology, 83*, 268–277.

Tinbergen, N. (1951). *The study of instinct.* Oxford, U.K.: Clarendon Press.

Troy, M., & Sroufe, L. A. (1987). Victimization among pre-schoolers: The role of attachment-relationship theory. *Journal of the American Academy of Child and Adolescent Psychiatry 26*, 166–172.

True, M., Pisani, L., & Oumar, F. (2001). Infant-mother attachment among the Dogon in Mali. *Child Development, 75*(5), 1451–1466.

Trowell, J. (1997). Attachment in Children: Development from study of sexually abused girls (Association for Child Psychology & Psychiatry Occurred Paper, No. 14). London: Association for Child & Psychiatry.

van IJzendoorn, M. H. (1995). Adult attachment representations, parental responsiveness and infant attachment: A meta-analysis on the predictive validity of the Adult Attachment Interview. *Psychological Bulletin, 117*, 387–403.

van IJzendoorn, M. H., & Bakermans-Kranenburg, M. (1996). Attachment representations in mothers, fathers, adolescents and clinical groups: A meta-analytic search for normative data. *Journal of Clinical and Consulting Psychology, 64*, 8–21.

van IJzendoorn, M. H., & De Wolff, Marianne S. (1997). In search of the absent father—meta-analysis of infant-father attachment: A rejoinder to our discussants. *Child Development, 68*, 604–609.

van IJzendoorn, M. H., & Kroonenberg, P. M. (1988). Cross-cultural patterns of attachment: A meta-analysis of the Strange Situation. *Child Development, 63*, 840–858.

van IJzendoorn, M. H., Moran, G., Belsky, J., Pederson, D., Bakermans-Kranenburg, M., & Fisher, K. (2000). The similarity of siblings' attachments to their mother. *Child Development, 71*(4): 1086–1098.

van IJzendoorn, M. H., Schuengel, C., & Bakermans-Kranenburg, M. J. (1999). Disorganized attachment in early childhood: Meta-analysis of precursors, concomitants and sequelae. *Development and Psychopathology, 11*, 225–249.

Vaughn, B. E., & Bost, K. K. (1999). Attachment and temperament: Redundant, independent, or interacting influences on interpersonal adaptation and personality development? In J. Cassidy & P. R. Shaver (Eds.), *Handbook of attachment: Theory, research, and clinical applications* (pp. 198–225). New York: Guilford Press.

Volkmar, F. R., Hoder, E. L., & Siegel, A. E. (1980). Discrepant social communications. *Developmental Psychology, 16*, 495–505.

Volkmar, F. R., & Siegel, A. E. (1979). Young children's responses to discrepant social communications. *Journal of Child Psychology and Psychiatry, 20*, 139–149.

Ward, M. J., and Carlson, E. A. (1995). The predictive validity of the adult attachment interview for adolescent mothers. *Child Development, 66*, 69–79.

Wartner, U. G., Grossmann, K., Fremmer-Bombik, E., & Suess, G. (1994). Attachment patterns at age six in South Germany: Predictability from infancy and implications for preschool behavior. *Child Development, 65*, 1014–1027.

Weinfield, S., Sroufe, L. A., Egeland, B., & Carlson, E. A. (1999). The nature of individual differences in infant-caregiver attachment. In J. Cassidy & P. R. Shaver (Eds.), *Handbook of attachment: theory, research and clinical applications* (pp. 68–88). New York: Guilford Press.

3

Early Relational Trauma, Disorganized Attachment, and the Development of a Predisposition to Violence

Allan N. Schore

IN THE INTRODUCTION to Karr-Morse and Wiley's landmark book on the early roots of violence, *Ghosts From the Nursery* (1997), the pediatrician Berry Brazelton stated, "experiences in infancy which result in the child's *inability to regulate strong emotions* [italics added] are too often the overlooked source of violence in children and adults" (p. xiii). When a child commits a violent act, it means that his or her developmental trajectory has gone seriously askew so very early in the lifespan. The fact that he can't even make it through the next developmental stage (much less the later challenges of adulthood) is a direct outcome of a severe growth-inhibiting environment in his very beginnings, in his first relationship, the one in the nursery. In their book, Karr-Morse and Wiley turned to new findings in what was then "the decade of the brain" that directly related to the problem of why interpersonal deprivations and failures in the earliest stages of human development serve as a primordial matrix for a personality that is at high risk for violence.

Despite overall decreases in violent crime in this country, statistics document that increases in the juvenile homicide rate have surpassed those of adults (Helmuth, 2000). A large proportion of referrals to child and adolescent clinical services have involved serious antisocial behaviors (Kazdin, Siegel, & Bass, 1990). This alarming trend compels us to look for the underlying causal mechanisms of violence, mechanisms that are already fully operational in childhood. A growing body of studies indicates that traumatic childhood experiences provide the contexts for the roots of adult violence. But now we are confronted with an increasing number of violent offenders who are still in their first decade of life, "early onset antisocial youth" (Loeber & Farrington, 2000), and this is telling us that we must look even earlier, indeed, to the literal beginnings for the essential causal factors.

In this Chapter I focus on the events in the nursery, not metaphorically, but through the lenses of developmental neuroscience, attachment theory, and infant psychiatry. In recent contributions I have modeled how severe traumatic attachments result in structural limitations of the early developing right brain, expressed in a number of enduring functional deficits, including a fundamental inability to regulate emotional states under stress (Schore, 1998c, 1998f, 1999b, 1999c, 2000c, 2001b, 2001f, 2002b, 2003a, 2003b). It is well established that the loss of the ability to regulate the intensity of affects is the most far-reaching effect of early traumatic abuse and neglect. Theoretical and clinical studies are now focusing on the direct connections between early traumatic attachment experiences and the inability of certain personalities to regulate fear-terror states, leading to developing a high risk for posttraumatic stress disorders (PTSD) (Schore, 1997a, 2001b, 2002b).

Here I want to suggest that another affect that can become dysregulated by early relational trauma is aggression. If PTSD represents a dysregulation of the brain "flight" systems, aggression disorders represents a dysregulation of the brain's "fight" centers. Each represents a dysregulation of a pattern of autonomic nervous system (ANS) sympathetic hyperarousal, one associated with intense terror, the other with intense rage. These impairments are manifest at early ages in personalities who are at high risk for psychiatric disorders. Research has indicated that "exposure to early life stress is associated with neurobiological changes in children and adults, which may underlie the increased risk of psychopathology" (Heim & Nemeroff, 2001, p. 1023).

This general principle also applies to early trauma-associated psychopathologies of aggression dysregulation, including borderline and antisocial personality disorders. The American Psychiatric Association (1994) described antisocial (psychopathic) personality disorder as showing "irritability and aggressiveness, as indicated by frequent physical fights and assaults," while borderline personality disorder manifests "inappropriate, intense anger or dif-ficulty controlling anger (e.g., frequent displays of temper, constant anger, recurrent physical fights)." Both are therefore capable of violence, episodes of intense aggressive emotional states, psychobiologically driven by a subcortical psychobiological core, that are dysregulated in both intensity and duration and cut off from feedback systems in the internal and external environment.

The interpersonal aspect of violence is highlighted in its definition as "aggression that has extreme harm as its goal (e.g., death)" and the intra-personal aspect in its association with aggressive personalities (Anderson & Bushman, 2002). I shall later argue that the psychopathic personality is sus-ceptible to "cold blooded" predatory rage, while the borderline personality to "hot blooded" impulsive rage. The excessively impulsive, undermodulated state of blind rage is described by Horowitz:

> Not thinking, all feeling. He wants to demolish and destroy persons who frustrate him. He is not aware of ever loving or even faintly liking the object. He has no awareness that his rage is a passion that will decline. He believes he will hate the object forever. (1992, p. 80)

I further propose that it is impossible to make definitive statements about the early roots of violence without knowledge of what we now know about the early roots of human life, the process of development itself. Why are the experiences that take place in the nursery, the very earliest events of human life, so critical to everything that follows? But in addition, I argue that we know enough about the structural biological development of the brain that we must go beyond purely functional psychological theories of the development of a predisposition to violence. A consensus statement on an understanding of violence concluded, "As is the case of all human behaviors, it is crucial to remember that an understanding of the organ producing the behavior cannot be overlooked" (Filley et al., 2001, p. 12).

This leads to the questions, how do early attachment experiences positively impact maturing brain structures and thereby the developmental process, and by what mechanisms do early relational traumatic attachment experiences neg-atively impact brain development and deflect the developmental trajectory? Childhood traumatic maltreatment not only results in enduring brain deficits, but also acts as a risk factor for the development of personality disorders in early adulthood (Johnson, Cohen, Brown, Smailes, & Bernstein, 1999). In other words, a deeper understanding of the genesis of a high risk for personality dis-orders of aggression dysregulation must integrate both the psychological and biological realms. The concept of trauma, which is by definition psychobio-logical, is a bridge between the domains of both mind and body.

Introduction

The idea that early trauma has an indelible negative impact upon the developing personality has a long history in psychology. In his last writings Freud (1940/1964) asserted that trauma in early life affects all vulnerable humans because "the ego . . . is feeble, immature and incapable of resistance." It should be emphasized that in current literature trauma in human infancy includes both abuse and neglect (Schore, 2001b, 2002b). Physically abused infants show high levels of negative affect, while neglected infants demonstrate flattened affect (Gaensbauer & Hiatt, 1984). There is evidence indicating that neglect may be even more damaging than abuse, and that there is a link between neglect in childhood and antisocial personality disorders in later life (Hildyard & Wolfe, 2002). But the "worst case scenario" is, not infrequently, found in a child who experiences both abuse and neglect (Post & Weiss, 1997). There is agreement that severe trauma of interpersonal origin may override any genetic, constitutional, social, or psychological resilience factor (De Bellis, 2001).

Furthermore, the perpetrator of abuse or neglect is most often one of the primary caregivers (Graham, Heim, Goodman, Miller, & Nemeroff, 1999). Such developmental trauma is relational, usually not a singular event but "cumulative," a characteristic feature of an impaired attachment relationship (Schore, 2001b). Ongoing repetitive relational stressors embedded in a severely misattuned attachment relationship indicate that the infant is experiencing not acute but chronic stress in the first two years of life. In an editorial on child abuse in the *Journal of Trauma and Dissociation*, Chu asserted:

> The child protective service statistics do not differentiate cases of single episodes of abuse from repetitive abuse, and it is particularly important to identify children who are chronically abused and victims of multiple types of abuse. These traumatized children are the most likely to go on to develop impairments in psychological functioning, specific psychiatric symptomatology, and changes in brain function. (2001, p. 3)

Similarly, the consensus statement of the panel on an understanding of violence at the Aspen Neurobehavioral Conference concludes that violence in children may be a product of "negative experiences such as early maternal rejection and unstable family environment" and that "child abuse, particularly that involving physical injury, may be especially damaging." Furthermore, "exposure to emotionally traumatic or violent experiences may exert a profound effect on behavior, presumably through their actions on the developing brain" (Filley et al., 2001, p. 7). These authors then go on to specify the brain systems involved in violence, specifically the temporolimbic areas of the subcortical amygdala that are involved in the expression of aggressive states, and the corticolimbic areas in the orbitofrontal (ventromedial) cortex that control aggression.

A large body of studies in neurobiology indicates that an impairment of the orbitofrontal cortex is a central mechanism in the behavioral expression of violence (e.g., Best, Williams, & Coccaro, 2002; Brower & Price, 2000; Fornazzari, Farenik, Smith, Heasman, & Ischise, 1992; Grafman, Schwala, Warden, Pridgen, Brown, & Salazar, 1996; Miller, Darby, Benson, Cummings, & Miller, 1997; Mitchell, Colledge, Leonard, & Blair, 2002; Raine et al., 1998; Raine, Stoddard, Bihrle, & Buchsbaum, 1998; Schore, 1994, 1999a, 2001b, 2001c; Starkstein & Robinson, 1997; Volavka, 1999). It is well established that neurological damage of this system is associated with "neurologically acquired sociopathy" (Tranel, 1994; Blair & Cipolotti, 2000), that focal damage to the orbitofrontal cortex represents a neural basis of sociopathy (Damasio, 2000), and that neurological impairment of this prefrontal system in the first 18 months of life is associated with abnormal development of social and moral behavior and a syndrome, later in life, resembling psychopathy (Anderson, Bechara, Damasio, Tranel, & Damasio, 1999).

I have suggested that the neurological trauma embedded in early relational abuse and neglect can also produce an impaired orbitofrontal system, and therefore a "developmentally acquired sociopathy" (Schore, 1999a, 2001e). An entire issue of the journal *Biological Psychiatry* was devoted to development and vulnerability, and in it De Bellis, Keshavan, and colleagues concluded, "the overwhelming stress of maltreatment in childhood is associated with adverse influences on brain development" (1999, p. 1281). We know that early psychosocial stressors, specifically from a severely missattuned maternal environment, can negatively impact brain development, including brain systems involved in aggression regulation (Glaser, 2000; Schore, 1994, 1996, 1997a, 1997b, 1998c, 2000d, 2001b, 2002b).

In current writings on the origins of violence, Cairns and Stoff state,

> It is highly unlikely that the problem of aggression and violence can be reduced to a single gene or dysfunction . . . of a nerve cell. More than likely, multiple biological systems are involved and these systems act in concert with . . . the social realm. (1996, p. 349)

The most in-depth investigations of the "social realm" occur within the province of attachment theory, "the dominant approach to understanding early socioemotional and personality development during the past quarter-century of research" (Thompson, 2000, p. 145). Recall that the first work published by Bowlby, the creator of attachment theory, was a study of the early histories of "Forty four juvenile thieves" (1944).

The current explosion of developmental studies is relevant to why certain personalities are at high risk for violence. Prolonged and frequent episodes of intense and unregulated stress in infants and toddlers have devastating effects on "the establishment of psychophysiological regulation and the development of stable and trusting attachment relationships in the first year of life" (Gaensbauer & Siegel, 1995, p. 294). These effects endure: a "type D" disorganized/disoriented insecure attachment pattern seen in abused and neglected infants predicts later chronic disturbances of affect regulation, stress management, and hostile-aggressive behavior (Lyons-Ruth & Jacobovitz, 1999). Although other organized insecure attachment patterns are associated with limitations in coping with aggressive states, this attachment pattern is involved in the etiologies of a high risk for both posttraumatic stress disorder and a predisposition to relational violence (Schore, 1997a, 1998f, 1999a, 1999b, 1999c, 2000d, 2001b, 2001e, 2001f, 2002b, 2003a). Main (1996) argued that "disorganized" forms of insecure attachment are primary risk factors for the development of psychiatric disorders. This includes disorders of aggression dysregulation (Schore, 1994).

Relational Trauma and Right Brain Development

My own work in developmental affective neuroscience and developmental neuropsychiatry integrates recent psychological data of attachment theory and the current data of developmental neurobiology. This psychoneurobiological perspective focuses on the first two years of life, when the human brain grows faster than any other stage of the life cycle. This period exactly overlaps the period of attachment so intensely studied by contemporary developmental psychology. A fundamental tenet of Bowlby's (1969) model is that, for better or worse, the infant's "capacity to cope with stress" is correlated with certain maternal behaviors.

The central thesis of my work is that the early social environment, mediated by the primary caregiver, directly influences the final wiring of the circuits in the infant brain that are responsible for the future social and emotional coping capacities of the individual. The attachment relationship thus directly shapes the maturation of the infant's right brain, which comes to perform adaptive functions in both the assessment of visual and auditory socio-emotional communicative signals and the human stress response (Adolphs, 2002; Dimberg & Petterson, 2000; Gur et al., 2002; Keil et al., 2002; Nakamura et al., 1999; Pizzagalli et al., 2002; Stoll, Hamann, Margold, Huf, & Winterhoff-Spurk, 1999; Wittling, 1997; Zald & Pardo, 2002). The ultimate product of this social-emotional development is a particular system in the prefrontal areas of the right brain that is capable of regulating emotions (Schore, 1994, 1996, 1998a, 1998d, 1999d, 2000a, 2000c, 2000e, 2001a, 2001c, 2001d; Hariri, Bookheimer, & Mazziotta, 2000), including positive emotions such as joy and interest as well as negative emotions such as fear and aggression.

This work bears directly upon the problem of the etiology of violent personalities. The early traumatic dysregulating transactions with the social environment lead to more than an insecure attachment; they negatively impact the maturation of the brain during its growth spurt from the last trimester of pregnancy through the middle of the second year (Dobbing & Sands, 1973). This exact interval represents a period of accelerated growth of the right hemisphere: "The right hemisphere is more advanced than the left in surface features from about the 25th (gestational) week and this advance persists until the left hemisphere shows a post-natal growth spurt starting in the second year" (Trevarthen, 1996, p. 582). Thus, traumatic attachments act as a growth-inhibiting environment for the experience-dependent maturation of the right hemisphere, which is in a critical period of growth in the first year of life and dominant for the first three (Chiron et al., 1997). An MRI study of infants reported that the volume of the brain increases rapidly during the first two years, that normal adult appearance is seen at 2 years and all major fiber tracts can be identified by age 3, and that infants under 2 years show higher right than left hemispheric volumes (Matsuzawa et al., 2001).

There is agreement that the enduring effects of early abuse are specifically reflected in the impaired processing of both social and bodily information. In a number of works I offered data which indicate that early trauma alters the development of the right brain, the hemisphere that is dominant for the unconscious processing of socioemotional information, the regulation of bodily states, the capacity to cope with emotional stress, and the corporeal and emotional self (Schore 1994, 1996, 2000b, 2000c, 2001a). The right brain is specialized to process socioemotional information at levels beneath awareness, and so it is dominant for unconscious processes and fast-acting regulatory operations.

It is clear that threat-related cues associated with danger are nonconsciously processed (LeDoux, 1996) and that the autoregulation of aggression involves the operation of a self-regulatory mechanism operating at a preconscious level (Berkowitz, 1990). Consequently, an enduring developmental impairment of the right brain would be expressed as a severe limitation in the ability, at levels beneath conscious awareness, to self-regulate negative states, such as fear and aggression. Hostile destructiveness (as opposed to nondestructive aggression) is associated with the dysregulated experience of excessive bodily pain and distress, is self-protective, and is present in its most primitive form in infancy (Parens, 1987).

In over two dozen contributions I offered experimental and clinical data characterizing the central role of the highest limbic level of the right brain, the right hemispheric orbitofrontal system, in the regulation of adaptive affective, motivational, and cognitive functions. Referring back to Brazelton's suggestion that the child's inability to regulate strong emotions is associated with violence, a growing body of evidence implicates the central role of the prefrontal areas of the right brain in affect regulation. A developmentally mature hierarchical orbitofrontal system regulates lower areas in the right brain that generate positive and negative affective states, including aggressive states, but a developmentally impaired right prefrontal cortex is vulnerable, especially under interpersonal stress, to disorders of aggression regulation. Thus,

> [D]epending on the presence of other social triggers and *early stressful environmental circumstances* [italics added], increased right hemisphere subcortical activity could predispose the individual to experience negative affect which fosters aggressive feelings and which in turn act as a general predisposition to violent behavior. (Raine, Melroy, et al., 1998, p. 329)

The maturation of the orbitofrontal areas, the brain's central emotion regulating system, occurs completely postnatally, and their development is positively or negatively shaped by attachment experiences. The enduring functional coping deficits of the disorganized/disoriented insecure attachment pattern that are associated with infant abuse and neglect thus reflect a severe structural defect of the orbitofrontal cortex (Schore, 2001b, 2002b), the brain system involved in "critical human functions, such as social adjustment and the control of mood, drive and responsibility, traits that are crucial in defining the 'personality' of an individual" (Cavada & Schultz, 2000, p. 205). But it is also thought that "The orbitofrontal cortex represents a brain region of particular interest with respect to violence because dysfunction in this brain area results in personality and emotional deficits that parallel criminal psychopathic behavior" (Raine, Stoddard, et al., 1998, p. 5). This frontolimbic cortex is expanded in the right hemisphere (Falk et al., 1990), and is known as the "senior executive" of the social emotional right brain. A structural limitation of the right brain is responsible for the individual's inability to regulate emotion, which is a central deficit in aggressive personalities.

Indeed, the self-regulation of negative emotions is low in aggressive personalities. Furthermore, neurological studies with adult patients reveal that lesions in the right, but not left, orbitofrontal areas produce increased unregulated aggression (Grafman et al., 1996), and that "acquired sociopathy" results from neurological trauma to the right orbitofrontal region (Blair & Cipolotti, 2000). In neuropsychological research, Raine and his colleagues found that "reductions in right orbitofrontal functioning may be a particularly important predisposition to violence" (Raine, Stoddard, et al., 1998, p. 6), and observe reduced right hemisphere activation during a working memory task in severely abused violent offenders (Raine et al., 2001).

In the following I elaborate upon this psychoneurobiological model of the early etiology of a predisposition to violence. A fundamental principle of the discipline of developmental psychopathology is that we need to understand normal development in order to understand abnormal development. Abuse and neglect not only expose the immature infant to threatening experiences, they also deprive the developing brain/mind/body of vital growth-facilitating interpersonal experiences that are requisite for the continuing experience-dependent maturation of the right brain.

So, in this chapter I briefly outline the brain events of a secure attachment and the resultant organization of an adaptive regulatory system in the prefrontal areas of the right hemisphere. I then describe the neuropsychology of a disorganized/disoriented insecure attachment pattern found in traumatized infants and children with aggressive behavior problems, the inhibitory effects of early trauma on the development of prefrontal systems involved in aggression regulation, the continuity of aggression dysregulation over the course of the lifespan, and a model of the etiology of the patterns of violence potential in borderline and antisocial personality disorders. I conclude with a few words on the implications of this model for early intervention programs. These psychoneurobiological models are offered as heuristic proposals that can be evaluated by experimental and clinical research.

Overview of the Affective Psychology of a Secure Attachment

The essential task of the first year of human life is the creation of a secure attachment bond of emotional communication between the infant and the primary caregiver. Within episodes of affect synchrony (Feldman, Greenbaum, & Yirmiya, 1999), parents engage in intuitive, nonconscious, facial, vocal, and gestural preverbal communications. These experiences, which the parent carries out "unknowingly and can hardly control consciously," " . . . provide young infants with a large amount of episodes—often around 20 per minute during parent-infant interactions—in which parents make themselves contingent, easily predictable, and manipulatable by the infant" (Papousek, Papousek, Suomi, & Rahn, 1991, p. 110).

In order to do this, the mother must be psychobiologically attuned to the dynamic crescendos and decrescendos of the infant's bodily-based internal states of arousal. Within a context of visual-facial, auditory-prosodic, and gestural preverbal communication, each partner learns the rhythmic structure of the other and modifies his or her behavior to fit that structure, thereby cocreating a specifically fitted interaction. The synchronizing caregiver facilitates the infant's unique information-processing capacities by adjusting the mode, amount, variability, and timing of the onset and offset of stimulation to the infant's actual integrative capacities, his "windows of tolerance" (Siegel, 1999).

In this interactively regulated context, the more the mother tunes her activity level to the infant during periods of social engagement, the more she allows him to recover quietly in periods of disengagement, and the more she attends to the child's reinitiating cues for reengagement, the more synchronized their interaction. In play episodes, the pair are in affective resonance, and in such, an amplification of vitality affects and a positive state occur, especially when the mother's psychobiologically attuned external sensory stimulation frequency coincides with the infant's genetically encoded endogenous rhythms.

When an attuned dyad cocreates a resonant context within an attachment transaction, the behavioral manifestation of each partner's internal state is monitored by the other, and this results in the coupling between the output of one partner's loop and the input of the other's to form a larger feedback configuration and an amplification of the positive state in both. In order to enter into this communication, the primary caregiver must also monitor her own internal signals and differentiate her own affective state, as well as modulate nonoptimal high or low levels of stimulation which would induce supra-heightened or extremely low levels of arousal in the infant.

In these exchanges of affect synchrony, as the mother and infant match each other's temporal and affective patterns, each recreates an inner psychophysiological state similar to the partner's. Stern (1983) described moment-to-moment state sharing, feeling the same as the other (interactive regulation), and state complementing, responding in one's unique way to stimuli coming from the other (autoregulation). In contexts of "mutually attuned selective cueing," the infant learns to preferentially send social cues to which the mother has responded, thereby reflecting "an anticipatory sense of response of the other to the self, concomitant with an accommodation of the self to the other" (Bergman, 1999, p. 96).

And in moments of interactive repair, the "good-enough" primary caregiver who induces a stress response in her infant through a misattunement reinvokes in a timely fashion a reattunement, a regulation of the infant's negative state. Active parental participation in state regulation is critical to enabling the child to shift from the negative affective states of hyperaroused protest or hypoaroused despair to a reestablished state of positive affect. Again, the key to this is the caregiver's capacity to monitor and regulate her own affect, especially negative affect. Maternal sensitivity thus acts as an external organizer of the infant's biobehavioral regulation (Spangler, Schieche, Ilg, & Ackerman, 1994).

If attachment is the regulation of interactive synchrony, stress is defined as an asynchrony in an interactional sequence, and, following this, a period of reestablished synchrony allows for stress recovery and coping. The regulatory processes of affect synchrony that create states of positive arousal and interactive repair that modulates states of negative arousal are the fundamental building blocks of attachment and its associated emotions, and resilience in the face of stress is an ultimate indicator of attachment security. Attachment, the outcome of the child's genetically encoded biological predisposition and the particular caregiver environment, thus represents the regulation of biological synchronicity between organisms, and imprinting, the learning process that mediates attachment, is defined as synchrony between sequential infant-maternal stimuli and behavior (Schore, 2000a, 2000b, 2001b). The attachment mechanism, the dyadic regulation of emotion, thus psychobiologically modulates positive states, such as excitement and joy, but also negative states, such as fear and aggression.

In regard to the developmental regulation of aggression, it is especially important to emphasize that subsequent to the child's formation of attachment to the mother in the first year, the child forms another—in the second year to the father (Schore, 1994). According to Herzog, "the biorhythmicity of man with infant and woman with infant" affords the infant "interactive, state-sharing, and state-attuning experiences with two different kinds of caregivers" (2001, p. 55). He further asserted that this paternal function is "entirely contingent on the presence of homeostatic-attuned caregiving by the mother." Indeed, developmental researchers observe the formation of a second attachment system to the father that emerges in the second year (Schaffer & Emerson, 1964), as the child now expresses a separation response to the absence of either parent. Research demonstrated that the quality of the toddler's attachment to the father is independent of that to the mother (Main & Weston, 1981), and that at 18 months both a "mother attachment system" and a "father attachment system" are operational (Abelin, 1971).

In parallel work, classical developmental psychoanalytic observational research indicated that in the second year the child shows more intense interest in the father's emotional availability (Mahler, Pine, & Bergmann, 1975), and that an "early experience of being protected by the father and caringly loved by him becomes internalized as a lifelong sense of safety" (Blos, 1984, p. 3). At this point he takes over from the early mother some significant portions of infantile attachment emotions, but in particular, he is critically involved in the development of the toddler's regulation of aggression. This is true of both sexes, but particularly of boys, who are born with a greater aggressive endowment (Maccoby, 1966). Herzog pointed out that through the father's careful use of his own aggression he helps the boy to modulate and integrate his own burgeoning aggression, and states that his "stimulating, gear-shifting, disruptive, limit-setting play" mobilizes intense affect, and facilitates "radical reorganization and further developmental progression" (2001, p. 261).

Overview of the Neurobiology of a Secure Attachment

The "developmental progressions" of emerging functions observed in the first two years of human life occur during stages of the brain growth spurt. It is thought that "the intrinsic regulators of human brain growth in a child are specifically adapted to be coupled, by emotional communication, to the regulators of adult brains" (Trevarthen, 1990, p. 357). And so these face-to-face emotional communications impact the developing brain, especially rapidly developing limbic areas (Kinney, Brody, Kloman, & Gilles, 1988) and cortical association areas of the right brain that myelinate in the first two years. These right lateralized structures are specialized for assessing familiar faces and processing visual and auditory mother-infant emotional communicative signals and mutual gaze (Acerra, Burnod, & de Schonen, 2002; Deruelle & de Schonen, 1998; Lorberbaum et al., 2002; Nakamura et al., 1999, 2000; Ricciardelli, Ro, & Driver, 2002; Tzourio-Mazoyer et al., 2002; Watanabe, Miki, & Kakigi, 2002; Wicker, Michel, Henaff, & Decety, 1998).

According to Buck,

> This spontaneous emotional communication constitutes a conversation between limbic systems . . . It is a biologically based communication system that involves individual organisms directly with one another: the individuals in spontaneous communication constitute literally a biological unit. The direct involvement with the other intrinsic to spontaneous communication represents an attachment that may satisfy deeply emotional social motives. (1994, p. 266)

These moments of imprinting, the very rapid form of learning that irreversibly stamps early experience upon the developing nervous system and mediates attachment bond formation, are described in the neuroscience literature:

> When the child is held and hugged, brain networks are activated and strengthened and firing spreads to associated networks; when the child is sung to, still other networks are strengthened to receive sounds and interpret them as song. The repeated appearance of the mother provides a fixation object . . . as in imprinting. (Epstein, 2001, p. 45)

More specifically, during the imprinting of play episodes mother and infant show sympathetic cardiac acceleration and then parasympathetic deceleration in response to the smile of the other, and thus the language of mother and infant consists of signals produced by the autonomic, involuntary nervous system in both parties (Schore, 2002a). The attachment relationship mediates the dyadic regulation of emotion (Sroufe, 1996), wherein the mother coregulates the infant's postnatally developing autonomic nervous system. Also known as the vegetative nervous system, from the Latin, *vegetare*, to animate or bring to life, its variations of form, intensity, and timing are responsible for the generation of what Stern (1985) called vitality affects.

In this manner, the optimally regulated communications embedded in secure attachment experiences directly imprint the postnatally maturing central nervous system (CNS) limbic system that processes and regulates social-emotional stimuli and the autonomic nervous system (ANS) that generates the somatic aspects of emotion. The limbic system derives subjective information in terms of emotional feelings that guide behavior (MacLean, 1985), and functions to allow the brain to adapt to a rapidly changing environment and organize new learning (Mesulam, 1998). The higher regulatory systems of the right hemisphere form extensive reciprocal connections with the limbic and autonomic nervous systems (Erciyas, Topalkara, Topaktas, Akyuz, & Dener, 1999; Spence, Shapiro, & Zaidel, 1996; Tucker, 1992; Wittling, Block, Schweiger, & Genzel, 1998; Yoon, Morillo, Cechetto, & Hachinsti, 1997). Both the ANS and the CNS continue to develop postnatally, and the assembly of these limbic-autonomic circuits (Rinaman, Levitt, & Card, 2000) in the right hemisphere, which is dominant for the human stress response (Wittling, 1997), is directly influenced by the attachment relationship (Schore, 1994; 2000a, 2000b, 2001a, 2001c, 2001d, 2003a, 2003b). In this manner, maternal care regulates the development of the infant's stress response:

> [T]he transmission of individual differences in stress reactivity from mother to offspring can provide an adaptive level of "preparedness" for the offspring . . . These responses promote detection of potential threats, avoidance

learning, and the mobilization of energy reserves that are essential under the increased demands of the stressor. (Caldji, Diorio, & Meaney, 2000, p. 1170)

As Bowlby suggested, the mother shapes the infant's stress coping systems.

Developmental researchers have observed that a consequence of the attachment is the infant's development of a finely articulated schema, a mental image of the mother, especially her face (Mussen, Conger, & Kagan, 1969). Furthermore, studies of the psychobiology of attachment indicated:

> The mother initially provides an external regulating mechanism for many of the physiological mechanisms that the infant possesses but does not regulate itself. These effects are mediated by effects of the mother on the infant's neurobiological processes. At some point in development the infant becomes self-regulating through the development of internal regulatory mechanisms entrained to the stimuli that the mother provides. (Kraemer, Ebert, Schmidt, & Mckinney, 1991, p. 561)

The Development of an Aggression Regulation System in the Orbitofrontal Cortex

Bowlby asserted that attachment behavior is organized and regulated by means of a "control system" in the brain, and that the maturation of this control system is influenced by the particular environment in which development occurs (Schore, 2000a, 2000b). In a number of works I offered evidence to show that the right hemisphere is dominant for inhibitory control (Garavan, Ross, & Stein, 1999), and that the orbitofrontal cortex, which acts in "the highest level of control of behavior, especially in relation to emotion" (Price, Carmichael, & Drevets, 1996) is the attachment control system.

The observations that the right orbitofrontal region is centrally involved in self-regulation (Schore, 1994; Stuss & Levine, 2002) in the recognition of a pleasant facial expression associated with social reward (Gorno-Tempini et al., 2001), and in the short-term storage of icon-like representations of visual objects (Szatkowska, Grabowska, & Szymanska (2001), and that the human orbitofrontal cortex encodes "a primary reinforcer that can produce affectively positive emotional responses" (Rolls, 2000), support the idea that the visual image of the loving mother's positive emotional face as well as the imprint of the mother's regulatory capacities are inscribed into the circuits of this lateralized prefrontal system.

The orbitofrontal regions are not functional at birth, but as a result of attachment experiences this system begins to mature in the last quarter of the first year, the same time that internal working models of attachment are first measured. Socialization experiences in the second year also influence its maturation, a period when the toddler develops a second attachment, to the father, and these lead to further orbitofrontal development.

This ventromedial prefrontal cortex is a convergence zone, where the lower subcortical areas of the brain that generate emotional states interface with the higher cortical areas that regulate these states. The fact that it receives multimodal visual, auditory, and tactile input from all sensory areas of the posterior cortex enables this prefrontal cortex to be responsive to events in the external environment, especially the social environment. But in addition, due to its direct connections into dopaminergic, noradrenergic, and serotonergic nuclei in the subcortical reticular formation, it processes information from the internal environment, by acting as a senior executive of arousal, an essential component of all emotional states.

This regulation of internal states is also due to orbitofrontal connections into the subcortical hypothalamus, the head ganglion of the ANS, thereby allowing for cortical control of the autonomic sympathetic and parasympathetic somatic responses associated with emotional experiences (Schore, 1994; Craig, 2002). An efficient mature orbitofrontal system can adaptively regulate both sympathoadrenomedullary catecholamine (Euler & Folkow, 1958) and corticosteroid levels (Hall & Marr, 1975), and therefore autonomic hyper- and hypoarousal. In this manner, this prefrontal system is centrally involved in the regulation of autonomic responses to social stimuli (Zald & Kim, 1996), and in the control of autonomic responses associated with emotional events (Cavada et al., 2000).

More specifically, the orbital prefrontal cortex is situated at the hierarchical apex of the emotion processing limbic system, above lower limbic centers in the anterior cingulate and insula, and the amygdala (see Schore, 2001a, Figure 3). All these limbic structures interconnect into the hypothalamus and the reticular formation, centers that generate arousal and psychobiological state. Although the early maturing amygdala acts as a sensory gateway to the limbic system, amygdala processing, although very rapid, is crude compared to the more complex processing of affective stimuli by later maturing corticolimbic areas (Adolphs, 2002). Even without conscious awareness, both are activated by emotional stimuli (Vuilleumier et al., 2002). In optimal developmental environments the orbitofrontal cortex takes over amygdala functions and "provides a higher level coding that more flexibly coordinates exteroceptive and interoceptive domains and functions to correct responses as conditions change" (Derryberry & Tucker, 1992, p. 335). The interactions between the cortical orbital prefrontal cortex and the subcortical amygdala enable individuals "to avoid making choices associated with adverse outcomes, without their first having to experience adverse outcomes" and therefore this circuit is of "immense biological significance" (Baxter, Parker, Lindner, Izquierdo, & Murray, 2000, p. 4317).

Right limbic-autonomic circuits allow for cortically processed information concerning the external environment (such as visual, auditory, tactile stimuli emanating from an attachment object) to be integrated with subcortically processed information regarding the internal visceral environment (such as concurrent changes in the bodily self-state). The operations of the right orbitofrontal control system involve a rapid subcortical evaluation of the regulatory significance of an external environmental stimulus, a processing of feedback information about the current internal state in order to make assessments of coping resources, and a moment-to-moment updating of context-appropriate response outputs in order to make adaptive adjustments to particular environmental perturbations (Schore, 1998a).

This cortical-subcortical system also specializes in coping with threatening environmental stressors that trigger aggressive states, products of the fight-flight centers in the hypothalamus. Studies have shown that orbitofrontal areas specifically respond to angry faces (Elliott, Dolan, & Frith, 2000), yet are also involved in the regulation of "motivational control of goal-directed behavior" (Tremblay & Schultz, 1999). Indeed, the orbitofrontal region is centrally involved in the regulation of motivational states, including aggressive states. More specifically, basic neurobiological studies indicate that the orbitofrontal cortex exerts an inhibitory control over hypothalamic sites from which aggression can be elicited by electrical stimulation (Kruk, Van der Poel, & De Vos-Frerichs, 1979), and that it is implicated in the suppression of aggression in dyadic encounters (De Bruin, 1990). Notice that the same system that is shaped by the attachment relationship regulates aggression.

The orbital prefrontal region is expanded in the right cortex, and it comes to act in the capacity of a "Senior Executive" of the social-emotional right brain. Studies have demonstrated that "self-related" material and "self-recognition" are processed in the right hemisphere (Keenan, Nelson, O'Connor, & Pascual-Leone, 2001; Kircher et al., 2001; Miller et al., 2001; Ruby & Decety, 2001) and that the right brain plays a fundamental role in the maintenance of "a coherent, continuous, and unified sense of self" (Devinsky, 2000). The right brain, the locus of the corporeal and emotional self, is also dominant for the ability to understand the emotional states of other human beings, that is, empathy (Schore, 1994; Perry et al., 2001). Empathy is, of course, a moral emotion, and so attachment experiences thus directly impact the neurobiological substrate of moral development. The prefrontal areas are now referred to as a "frontal moral guidance system" (Bigler, 2001).

The right hemisphere stores, in implicit-procedural memory (Hugdahl, 1995), an internal working model of the attachment relationship that determines the individual's characteristic strategies of affect regulation (Schore, 1994). Unconscious internal working models of the maternal (and paternal) attachment relationship thus function as right hemispheric coping strategies for dealing with stressors in the social environment (Schore, 1994, 2000a, 2000b). In light of the principle that coping strategies have the greatest potential when they are initiated before the actual stimulus (Tulving, 1985), these models, acting at nonconscious levels, act to guide appraisals of experience (Main, Kaplan, & Cassidy, 1985) before conscious knowledge does (Bechara, Damasio, Tranel, & Damasio, 1997).

The right hemisphere contains "a unique response system preparing the organism to deal efficiently with external challenges," and so its adaptive functions mediate the human stress response (Wittling, 1997, p. 55). It, and not the "speaking" left hemisphere, is centrally involved in the vital functions that support survival and enable the organism to cope actively and passively with stress. The right brain contains a circuit of emotion regulation that is involved in "intense emotional-homeostatic processes" (Porges, Doussard-Roosevelt, & Maiti, 1994), and in the regulation of not only the biologically primitive positive emotions such as excitement and joy, but also negative emotions of terror, disgust, shame, hopeless despair, and rage. The dysregulation of rage states is, of course, central to the expression of violence.

The orbitofrontal system that is fundamentally involved in "the emotional modulation of experience" (Mesulam, 1998) plays a unique role in the adjustment or correction of emotional responses, that is, affect regulation. Orbitofrontal coping functions are most observable in contexts of uncertainty, in moments of emotional stress (Elliott et al., 2000), when they support "the early mobilization of effective behavioral strategies in novel or ambiguous situations" (Savage et al., 2001). It acts as a recovery mechanism that efficiently monitors and regulates the duration, frequency, and intensity of not only negative but also positive states. The functioning of the "self-correcting" right hemispheric system is central to self-regulation, the ability to flexibly regulate emotional states through interactions with other humans in interconnected contexts via a two-person psychology, or autoregulation in independent, autonomous contexts via a one-person psychology.

It is thought that the "nonconscious mental systems perform the lion's share of the self-regulatory burden" (Bargh & Chartrand, 1999), that the autoregulation of aggression involves the operation of a self-regulatory mechanism operating at a preconscious level (Berkowitz, 1990), and that aggression dysregulation is associated with specifically altered orbitofrontal function

(Fornazzari et al., 1992; Grafman et al., 1996; Miller et al., 1997; Raine, Meloy, et al., 1998; Raine, Stoddard, et al., 1998; Schore, 1994; Starkstein & Robinson, 1997). These data lead to the questions, how does attachment trauma impair the development of this regulatory system, and how does an early relational environment of abuse and/or neglect engender personality organizations that are unable to adaptively regulate aggressive states?

The Neurobiology of
The Disorganized/Disoriented Attachment

It is important to stress the fact that the developmental attainment of a secure attachment bond of emotional communication and an efficient internal system that can adaptively regulate various emotional states only evolve in a growth-facilitating emotional environment. The good-enough mother of the securely attached infant permits access after a separation and shows a tendency to respond appropriately and promptly to his or her emotional expressions. She also allows for the interactive generation of high levels of positive affect in coshared play states. These regulated events allow for an expansion of the child's coping capacities, and thus security of the attachment bond is the primary defense against trauma-induced psychopathology (Glaser, 2000; Schore, 2001b).

In contrast to this scenario of a contingent, easily predictable, and manipulatable primary caregiver, the abusive and/or neglecting caregiver not only shows less play with her infant, she also induces traumatic states of enduring negative affect in the child. Affective communications, so central to the attachment dynamic, are distorted in the abused/neglected infant-caregiver relationship (Gaensbauer & Sands, 1979). Because her attachment is disorganized, she provides little protection against other potential abusers of the infant, such as the father. This caregiver is inaccessible and reacts to her infant's stressful emotions inappropriately and/or rejectingly, and shows minimal or unpredictable participation in the various types of affect regulating processes. Instead of modulating, she induces extreme levels of stimulation and arousal, and because she provides no interactive repair the infant's intense negative states last for long periods of time. Prolonged negative states are toxic for infants, and although they possess some capacity to modulate low-intensity negative affect states, these states continue to escalate in intensity, frequency, and duration.

It is established that the infant's psychobiological response to trauma is composed of two sequential response patterns—hyperarousal and dissociation

(Schore, 2001b). Infant researchers observed instances of "mutually escalating overarousal" between mother and infant, an experimental analog of abuse:

> Each one escalates the ante, as the infant builds to a frantic distress, may scream, and, in this example, finally throws up. In an escalating overarousal pattern, even after extreme distress signals from the infant, such as ninety-degree head aversion, arching away...or screaming, the mother keeps going. (Beebe, 2000, p. 436)

In this initial stage of threat, the intensity, amount, and timing of the mother's stimulation shatter the upper boundary of the infant's "window of tolerance." Extremely high visual, auditory, and tactile (pain) levels breach the infant's still fragile stimulus barrier, thereby suddenly inducing a startle reaction. This intensely stressful dysregulation triggers an alarm response, in which the sympathetic component of the ANS is suddenly and significantly activated, resulting in increased heart rate, blood pressure, and respiration. This same psychobiological pattern is expressed in states of pain (Liebeskind, 1991). Distress is vocally expressed in crying and then screaming.

This state of fear-terror, dysregulated sympathetic hyperarousal, reflects increased levels of the major stress hormone, corticotropin releasing factor, which in turn up-regulates central monoaminergic activity (Graham et al., 1999) as well as sympathetic catecholamine activity (Brown et al., 1982), and so brain adrenaline, noradrenaline, and dopamine levels are significantly elevated. The resultant rapid and intensely elevated catecholamine levels trigger a hypermetabolic state within the developing brain. Catecholamines are among the first neurochemicals to respond to stressors in response to perceived threat, and repeated stress triggers their persistent activation (Sabban & Kvetnansky, 2001). In such "kindling" states high levels of the excitatory neurotransmitter, glutamate, are also released in the limbic system.

In addition, increased amounts of vasopressin, a hypothalamic neuropeptide associated with sympathetic activation, are expressed (Kvetnansky et al., 1989, 1990). This condition is specifically triggered when an environment is perceived to be unsafe and challenging, and resultant elevated levels of vasopressin potentiate immobilization responses via sympathetic activation, behaviorally expressed as fear (Porges, 2001). Interestingly, heightened levels of this neuropeptide are associated with nausea (Koch, Summy-Long, Bingaman, Sperry, & Stern, 1990), a finding that may explain the hyperarousal behaviors observed by Beebe.

But a second, later forming reaction to infant trauma is seen in dissociation, in which the child disengages from stimuli in the external world and attends to an "internal" world. Tronick and Weinberg (1997) characterized contexts of hypoarousal and dissociation in the still-face procedure, an experimental analog of neglect:

> [W]hen infants' attempts fail to repair the interaction infants often lose postural control, withdraw, and self-comfort. The disengagement is profound even with this short disruption of the mutual regulatory process and break in intersubjectivity. The infant's reaction is reminiscent of the withdrawal of Harlow's isolated monkey or of the infants in institutions observed by Bowlby and Spitz. (p. 56)

Guedeney and Fermanian (2001) reported an infant assessment scale of sustained withdrawal, associated with disorganized attachment, manifest in a fixed, frozen, absent facial expression, total avoidance of eye contact, immobile level of activity, absence of vocalization, absence of relationship to others, and the impression that the child is beyond reach.

This massive disengagement is mediated by the parasympathetic dominant state of conservation-withdrawal (Kaufman & Rosenblum, 1967; Schore, 1994), one that occurs in helpless and hopeless stressful situations in which the individual becomes inhibited and strives to avoid attention in order to become "unseen." This primitive defensive state is a primary hypometabolic regulatory process, used throughout the lifespan, in which the stressed individual passively disengages in order "to conserve energies . . . to foster survival by the risky posture of feigning death, to allow healing of wounds and restitution of depleted resources by immobility" (Powles, 1992, p. 213). It is this parasympathetic mechanism that mediates the "profound detachment" (Barach, 1991) of dissociation. If early trauma is experienced as "psychic catastrophe" (Bion, 1962), dissociation represents "a last resort defensive strategy" (Dixon, 1998), "detachment from an unbearable situation" (Mollon, 1996), "the escape when there is no escape" (Putnam, 1997).

The neurobiology of the later forming dissociative reaction is different than the initial hyperarousal response. In this passive state, pain numbing and blunting endogenous opiates (Fanselow, 1986) and behavior-inhibiting stress hormones, such as cortisol, are elevated. Furthermore, activity of the dorsal vagal complex in the brainstem medulla increases dramatically, decreasing blood pressure, metabolic activity, and heart rate, despite increases in circulating adrenaline (Schore, 2001b, 2002b). This elevated parasympathetic arousal, a basic survival strategy (Porges, 1997), allows the infant to maintain homeostasis in the face of the internal state of sympathetic hyperarousal.

The traumatized infant's sudden state switch from sympathetic hyperarousal into parasympathetic dissociation is reflected in Porges's characterization of "the sudden and rapid transition from an unsuccessful strategy of struggling requiring massive sympathetic activation to the metabolically conservative immobilized state mimicking death associated with the dorsal vagal complex" (1997, p. 75). The child's dissociation in the midst of terror involves numbing, avoidance, compliance, and restricted affect, the same symptom cluster found in adult PTSD.

The massive autonomic dysregulation of both hyperarousal and dissociation induce severe disturbances in the infant's nascent psychophysiological systems, especially the cardiovascular system. Sympathetic hyperarousal is accompanied by significant increases in heart rate, while dissociation involves severe alterations of parasympathetic dorsal vagal tone that dramatically decrease heart rate and blood pressure. Basic research showed that simultaneous stimulation of both autonomic components produces an even greater cardiac output and aortic blood flow (Koizumi, Terui, Kollai, & Brooks, 1982). Behaviorally this is like "riding the gas and the brake at the same time," and the simultaneous activation of hyperexcitation and hyperinhibition results in the "freeze response" (Schore, 2001b, 2001g, 2002b).

But cumulative, ambient relational trauma also negatively impacts brain development: "dissociation at the time of exposure to extreme stress appears to signal the invocation of neural mechanisms that result in long-term alterations in brain functioning" (Chambers et al., 1999, p. 274). Because trauma in infancy occurs in a critical period of growth of the emotion-regulating limbic system, it negatively affects the maturation of the brain systems that modulate stress and regulate affect, including aggressive affective states. In other words, infants who experience abuse and/or neglect and little interactive repair are at high risk for developing aggression dysregulation in later stages of life. An early relational environment of maternal neglect and paternal abuse (insecure maternal *and* paternal attachments) would be a particularly potent matrix for generating inefficient control systems that would be high-risk for developing later disorders of aggression dysregulation.

The Neuropsychology of Maternal and Paternal Abuse and Neglect

As mentioned earlier, a type D disorganized/disoriented insecure attachment pattern occurs in abused and neglected infants, and it predicts later hostile-aggressive behavior (Lyons-Ruth & Jacobovitz, 1999). This pattern is found in 80% of maltreated infants (Carlson, Cicchetti, Barnett, & Braunwald, 1989). The infant, instead of finding a haven of safety in the relationship, is alarmed by the parent, and thereby in an irresolvable paradox in which it can neither approach, shift its attention, or flee (Main & Solomon, 1986). At 12 months in the Strange Situation attachment measure, type D infants show contradictory behavior patterns, such as backing toward the parent rather than approaching face-to-face, apprehension and confusion, and behavioral stilling and freezing.

This disorganization and disorientation is a "collapse" of behavioral and attentional strategies, and phenotypically resembles dissociative states (Hesse & Main, 2000; Main & Morgan, 1996). These infants experience low stress tolerance, and at the most basic level, they are unable to generate a coherent behavioral coping strategy to deal with this interactive stress (Main & Solomon, 1986). Indeed, in the Strange Situation this group of toddlers exhibits higher heart rates and stress hormones than all other attachment classifications (Spangler & Grossman, 1999), and are at greatest risk for impaired hypothalamo-pituitary-adrenocortical axis stress responding (Hertsgaard, Gunnar, Erickson, & Nachimias, 1995).

More specifically, as episodes of relational trauma commence, the infant is processing information from the external and internal environments. The mother's face is the most potent visual stimulus in the child's world, and it is well known that direct gaze can mediate not only loving but powerful aggressive messages. In coding the mother's frightening behavior, Hesse and Main (1999, p. 511) described "in non-play contexts, stiff-legged 'stalking' of infant on all fours in a hunting posture; exposure of canine tooth accompanied by hissing; deep growls directed at infant."

The image of the mother's aggressive face, as well as the chaotic alterations in the infant's autonomic (bodily) state and the disengagement-dissociative defenses that are associated with it, are indelibly imprinted into the infant's developing limbic circuits as a "flashbulb memory." These episodes are processed and stored in imagistic implicit-procedural memory in the visuospatial right hemisphere, which is dominant for the autonomic conditioning of aggressive facial emotional expressions (Johnsen & Hugdahl, 1993), and the sympathetic and parasympathetic components of the physiological and cognitive components of emotional processing (Spence et al., 1996). Recall, dysregulated aggression reflects intense activation of subcortical "fight" centers, and sympathetic hyperarousal.

But within the traumatic interaction the infant is presented with another affectively overwhelming facial expression, a maternal expression of fear-terror that represents a different pattern of sympathetic hyperarousal associated with hyperactivation of subcortical "flight" centers in the mother's brain. Main and Solomon (1986) noted that this occurs when the mother withdraws from the infant as though the infant were the source of the alarm, and they report that dissociated, trancelike, and fearful behavior is observed in parents of type D infants. Studies have shown a specific link between frightening, intrusive maternal behavior and "unsolvable fear" and disorganized infant attachment (Schuengel, Bakersmans-Kranenburg, & van IJzendoorn, 1999). Again, dissociation, the escape when there is no escape, is inscribed into the right hemisphere, which is specialized for withdrawal and avoidance (Davidson & Hugdahl, 1995).

In both cases, dysregulated maternal aggressive and fearful states, the infant is propelled into massive sympathetic hyperarousal, the immediate precipitant of dissociation. It is now thought that "dissociation, at its first occurrence, is a consequence of a 'psychological shock' or high arousal" (Meares, 1999). From the moment of the switch into the dissociative state, the infant loses the capacity to efficiently process information from the external environment (the abusive caregiver's face and voice) and the internal environment (his chaotic bodily state). It is important to note that these dysfunctional coping patterns persist—the type D attachment classification has been observed to utilize dissociative behaviors in later stages of life (van IJzendoorn, Schuengel, & Bakermans-Kranenburg, 1999), and are found in over 70% of hostile-aggressive preschoolers (Lyons-Ruth, Alpern, & Repacholi, 1993).

These instances of maternal relational trauma in the first year may be continue, in different form, in the second. In discussing maladaptive manifestations of aggression in relation to attachment, Lieberman (1996) described "aggressive" attributions of sons of single mothers with a history of abusive relationships:

> These mothers tend to attribute to their sons the same violent impulses acted out by the adult males in their lives . . . [T]hey distort the meaning of (age-appropriate) discrete angry behaviors on the son's part as evidence that the boy has an aggressive core to his personality and will grow up to be violent. These mothers exert very direct pressure on their sons to comply with their attributions. They tease the boy until he loses control and strikes out . . . they ignore or ridicule his signals of anxiety and vulnerability . . . and they are consistently rough and bossy with him. Paradoxically, when the boy does strike out . . . the mother is at a loss to put an effective stop to his behavior. (p. 287)

Lieberman pointed out that these mothers are giving their toddlers the early training to become violent when they grow up.

Where the mother continues in an abusive marital relationship, the child's maternal abuse may be compounded by later paternal trauma. Aggression dysregulation disorders are, of course, more common in males than females, and so it is necessary to further elaborate the role of the father's abuse and/or neglect in the etiology of aggression dysregulation in males. For the toddler, paternal abuse again involves terror, but perhaps even more physical pain than in maternal abuse. Herzog (2001) reported a study of infants seen in the emergency room for croup, or vaginal or anal infection in cases of suspected abuse. In the context of a play group, abused children who did not suffer physical pain during abuse, termed "therapists," assisted other children in distress in a precocious fashion. In contrast, those who had been physically hurt the most and dissociated during the abuse, labeled " 'abusers', seem to fall on an injured or otherwise compromised child and thus inflict even greater burden...In such a situation, identification with the aggressor seemed to be the resultant patterning" (Herzog, 2001, p. 90).

In a secure paternal-infant attachment system the father serves as an interactive regulator of fear and aggression, thereby providing a growth-facilitating environment for the maturation of the boy's regulatory system that is responsible for "a lifelong sense of safety" (Blos, 1984). Thus, paternal neglect and an insecure attachment with the father would preclude the boy's access to this regulation, and therefore be manifest as "father thirst" (Abelin, 1971) or "father hunger" (Herzog, 1980). Increased paternal attachment activation has been observed in toddlers who are deprived of contact with father.

Recall Herzog's (2001) description of "the biorhythmicity of man with infant and woman with infant." During episodes of maternal and paternal relational trauma, both abuse and neglect, the infant is matching the rhythmic structures of these states, and this synchronization is registered in the firing patterns of the right corticolimbic brain regions that are in a critical period of growth. Importantly, it is not just the trauma but the infant's defensive response to the trauma, the regulatory strategy of dissociation that is inscribed into the infant's right brain implicit-procedural memory system. According to Mollon, "If childhood trauma or abuse is repeated, and if the abuser is a caregiver, so that the child has nowhere to run and no one to turn to, then internal escape is resorted to—the child learns to dissociate more easily and in a more organized way (2001, p. 218). In light of the fact that many of these parents have suffered from unresolved trauma themselves (Famularo, Kinscherff, & Fenton, 1992; McCauley et al., 1997), this spatiotemporal imprinting of terror, rage, and dissociation is a primary mechanism for the intergenerational transmission of violence (see Schore, 2001b, 2003a for a detailed discussion).

This imprinting, the learning mechanism of attachment, is "burnt into" developing right prefrontal circuits (Stuss & Alexander, 1999), and thereby inscribed into long-term implicit memory. Clinical data and research findings now indicate that" preverbal children, even in the first year of life, can establish and retain some form of internal representation of a traumatic event over significant periods of time" (Gaeusbauer, 2002, p. 259).

In an earlier work I sketched out the long-term effects of a severely compromised attachment relationship on the future developmental trajectory of the self system:

> If . . . an infant, especially one born with a genetically-encoded altered neurophysiologic reactivity, does not have adequate experiences of being part of an open dynamic system with an emotionally responsive adult human, its corticolimbic organization will be poorly capable of coping with the stressful chaotic dynamics that are inherent in all human relationships. Such a system tends to become static and closed, and invested in defensive structures to guard against anticipated interactive assaults that potentially trigger disorganizing and emotionally painful psychobiological states. Due to its avoidance of novel situations and diminished capacity to cope with challenging situations, it does not expose itself to new socioemotional learning experiences that are required for the continuing experience-dependent growth of the right brain. This structural limitation, in turn, negatively impacts the future trajectory of self-organization. (Schore, 1997a, p. 624)

Corticolimbic Psychopathogenesis and Aggression Dysregulation

The disorganized/disoriented attachment represents a pathological attachment pattern, and this pathology is expressed in both function and structure. Type D behaviors often take the form of stereotypies that are found in neurologically impaired infants. Indeed, relational trauma interferes with the maturation of, particularly, the right brain. A fundamental precept of developmental neurology is that the developing infant is maximally vulnerable to nonoptimal and growth-inhibiting environmental events during the period of most rapid brain growth. During a critical period of regional brain growth, genetic factors are expressed in an initial overproduction of synapses. This is followed by an environmentally driven process, the pruning and maintenance of synaptic connections, and the organization of circuits. The principle is, "cells that fire together, survive together, and wire together," but in the case of inadequate environmental input, increased programmed cell death occurs (Voigt, Baier, & de Lima, 1997). Post and his colleagues reported a study of infant mammals demonstrating maternal deprivation induces cell death in the developing brain (Zhang et al., 2002). Maternal neglect is the behavioral manifestation of maternal deprivation and this alone or in combination with paternal physical abuse is devastating to developing limbic subsystems. (see Schore in press a, for a detailed discussion).

The brain of an infant who experiences frequent intense attachment disruptions and little interactive repair is chronically exposed to states of impaired homeostasis which he or she shifts into in order to maintain basic metabolic processes for survival. If the caregiver does not participate in reparative functions that reduce stress and reestablish psychobiological equilibrium, the limbic connections that are in the process of developing are exposed to a toxic chemistry that negatively impacts a developing brain. Developmental psychobiological studies indicate that hyperaroused attachment stressors are correlated with elevated levels of the arousal-regulating catecholamines and hyperactivation of the excitotoxic N-methyl-D-aspartate (NMDA)-sensitive glutamate receptor, a critical site of neurotoxicity and synapse elimination in early development (Guilarte, 1998; McDonald, Silverstein, & Johnston, 1988; Noh et al., 1999; Portera-Cailliau, Price, & Martin, 1997). High levels of glutamate and cortisol are known to specifically alter the growth of the developing limbic system. During critical periods, dendritic spines, potential points of connection with other neurons, are particularly vulnerable to long pulses of glutamate (Segal, Korkotian, & Murphy, 2000) that trigger severely altered calcium metabolism and therefore "oxidative stress" and synaptic apoptosis (Mattson, Keller, & Begley, 1998; Park, Bateman, & Goldberg, 1996; Schore, 1994, 1997a, 2001b).

Furthermore, basic research has shown that adverse social experiences during early critical periods result in permanent alterations in opiate, corticosteroid, corticotropin releasing factor, dopamine, noradrenaline, and serotonin receptors (Coplan et al., 1996; Ladd, Owens, & Nemeroff, 1996; Lewis, Gluck, Beauchamp, Keresctury, & Mailman, 1990; Martin, Spicer, Lewis, Gluck, & Cork, 1991; Meerlo et al., 2001; Rosenblum et al., 1994; van der Kolk, 1987). Such receptor alterations are a central mechanism by which "early adverse developmental experiences may leave behind a permanent physiological reactivity in limbic areas of the brain" (Post, Weiss, & Leverich, 1994, p. 800). Impairments in the limbic system, and in dopamine, noradrenaline, and serotonin receptors have all been implicated in aggression dysregulation (Dolan, Deakin, Roberts, & Anderson, 2002; Oquendo & Mann, 2000; Siever & Trestman, 1993).

Because the early maturing (Geschwind & Galaburda, 1987; Schore, 1994) right hemisphere is more deeply connected into the limbic system than the left (Tucker, 1992; Borod, 2000; Gainotti, 2000), this enduring reactivity is inscribed into corticolimbic circuits of the right brain, the hemisphere dominant for the regulation of the stress hormones cortisol and corticotropin releasing factor (Wittling & Pfluger, 1990; Kalogeras et al., 1996). Elevated corticotropin releasing factor is known to initiate seizure activity in the developing brain (Wang, Dow, & Fraser, 2001), and so this circuit hyperreactivity may be expressed at later periods as "psychogenic nonepileptic seizures," a syndrome etiologically associated with "physical assault or other extreme trauma" and "traumatic loss in childhood" (Sirven & Glosser, 1998).

The right frontal cortex is at the top of a cortical hierarchy for the processing of prolonged emotionally stressful inputs, where it adaptively modulates the activity of subcortical dopamine neurons (Sullivan & Szechtman, 1995; Sullivan & Gratton, 2002). But dopamine rapidly increases under stress (Bertolucci-D'Angio, Serrano, Driscoll, & Scatton, 1990), and can induce DNA mutations in brain tissue (Spencer et al., 1994) and cell death (Hoyt, Reynolds, & Hastings, 1997). Perinatal distress leads to dopamine hypofunction and a blunting of the stress regulating response of the right (and not left) prefrontal cortex that is manifest in adulthood (Brake, Sullivan, & Gratton, 2000). A study in *Molecular Psychiatry* reported that 12-month-old type D infants, categorized in the Strange Situation, show a less sensitive D4 dopamine receptor, and the authors conclude that this leads to a blunted dopamine response that reduces the value of the mother and prevents the infant from organizing an appropriate coping response (Lakatos et al., 2000).

Orbitofrontal–Amygdala Dysfunction and Rage States

The dysregulating events of both abuse and neglect create chaotic biochemical alterations in the infant brain that intensify the normal process of apoptotic programmed cell death (Schore, 1994, 1997a, 1997b, 2001b, 2002b). A trauma-induced developmental overpruning of a corticolimbic system, especially one that contains a genetically encoded underproduction of synapses, represents a scenario for high-risk conditions. It is now established that "psychological" factors "prune" or "sculpt" neural networks in the postnatal brain (Schore, 1994). Trauma-induced excessive pruning of hierarchical right cortical-subcortical circuits operates in the etiology of a vulnerability to later extreme disorders of affect regulation, including disorders of aggression dysregulation.

Earlier in this chapter, I described a hierarchical sequence of interconnected limbic areas in the orbitofrontal cortex, anterior cingulate-insula, and amygdala (Devinsky, Morrell, & Vogt, 1995) that acts as a complex circuit of emotion regulation (Davidson, Putnam, & Larson, 2000; Schore, 1997a, 2000c, 2001b). The three components of this "rostral limbic system" all interconnect with each other and with brainstem bioaminergic neuromodulatory and hypothalamic neuroendocrine nuclei. These corticolimbic circuitries ontogenetically progress from the simplest system in the amygdala, which is on-line at birth, through the cingulate (areas 24, 25, and 32), which begins a maturation period at the end of the second month, to the orbitofrontal cortex, which begins its critical period at the end of the first year (Schore, 1994, 2001b). This means that excessive prenatal stressors would most negatively impact the amygdala (Cratty, Ward, Johnson, Azzaro, & Birkle, 1995) via elevated levels of corticotropin releasing factor, a neuropeptide that contributes to shorter gestational lengths and altered fetal development (Glynn, Wadhwa, & Sandman, 2000). Relational trauma in the second and third quarters of the first year would impair the development of the insula, an area involved in representations of the physiological state at the body, and the anterior cingulate, an area involved in social behavior and gating of amygdala activity.

The orbitofrontal areas of the right hemisphere undergo an experience-dependent maturation from the last quarter of the first through the last of the second year (Schore, 1994). Research has documented that disorganized infant attachment strategies increase in frequency from 12 to 18 months (Lyons-Ruth et al., 1993). Relational trauma at this time interferes with the organization of the orbitofrontal regions and compromises such functions as attachment, empathy, the capacity to play, and affect regulation. In other words, due to a poor orbitofrontal organization, the achievement of emotional control, including aggression control, is precluded in these infants. As previously mentioned, an impressive body of neurological evidence now indicates that at all points in the lifespan, aggression dysregulation is associated with specifically altered orbitofrontal function (Anderson et al., 1999; Best, Williams, & Coccaro, 2002; Brower & Price, 2001; Fornazzari et al., 1992; Grafman et al., 1996; Miller et al., 1997; Mitchell, Colledge, Leonard, & Blair, 2002; Starkstein & Robinson, 1997; van Honk, Hermans, Putman, Montagne, & Schutter, 2002).

A number of converging studies from psychiatry and neuroscience underscore the centrality of the orbitofrontal cortex in the regulation and dysregulation of aggression. In an entire edition of the journal *Science* devoted to "Violence: A new frontier for scientific research," Davidson and his colleagues offered an article on "Dysfunction in the neural circuitry of emotion regulation—A possible prelude to violence," in which they conclude that dysregulation of an orbitofrontal-anterior cingulate-amygdala circuit of emotion regulation is associated with a risk for violence and aggression (Davidson et al., 2000). An article in the *American Journal of Psychiatry* reported that a functional alteration of the orbitofrontal cortex is present in individuals with pathological aggressive behavior (Pietrini, Guazzelli, Basso, Jaffe, & Grafman, 2000). And in the neuroscience journal *Brain* a study described how right orbitofrontal impairment is associated with difficulties in emotional recognition of angry facial expressions, as well as with high levels of aggression (Blair & Cipolotti, 2000).

More specifically, an inefficient right orbitofrontal system would be unable to regulate subcortical limbic structures through an early excessive parcellation of right cortical-subcortical connections (Schore, 1994, 1997a, 2001b, 2003a). Of special importance are the connections between the orbitofrontal areas and the hypothalamus, the head ganglion of the ANS and control system for fight-flight responses, and the amygdala, a major fear (La Bar, Gatenby, Gore, LeDoux, & Phelps, 1998) and aggression (Bear, 1989) center in the brain. Studies have shown two types of aggression: "affective," "impulsive," "reactive," "defensive," or "hot-blooded" aggression (an uncontrolled and emotionally charged response to physical or verbal aggression initiated by another), in contrast to "predatory," "proactive," "stalking," "attack," or "cold-blooded" aggression (controlled, purposeful aggression lacking in emotion), and each is mediated by a distinct neuroanatomical pathway (see Schore, 2001b, 2002b, 2003a). Affective rage involves the hypothalamic sympathetic ventromedial nucleus, and predatory attack the parasympathetic lateral hypothalamus, an area also involved in "tonic immobility" or dissociation (Adamec, 1990; Panksepp, 1998; Siegel, Roeling, Gregg, & Kruk, 1999). An excessive developmental parcellation of either of these orbitofrontal-hypothalamic circuitries would thus lead to a limited capacity of higher corticolimbic system to modulate these hypothalamically driven aggressive states (Egger & Flynn, 1967).

The reciprocal connections between the orbitofrontal areas in the prefrontal lobe, the amygdala in the temporal lobe, and the diencephalic hypothalamus develop postnatally (Bouwmeester, Smits, & Van Ree, 2002; Bouwmeester, Wolterink, & Van Ree, 2002; Fisher & Almli, 1984; Nair, Berndt, Barrett, & Gonzalez-Lima, 2001). These interconnections are directly influenced by the attachment relationship (Braun, & Poeggel, 2001; Helmeke, Ovtscharoff, Poeggel, & Braun, 2001; Helmeke, Poeggel, & Braun. 2001; Schore, 1999).

An excessive traumatic attachment-induced developmental parcellation of the orbitofrontal and cingulate inhibitory pathways that gate the amygdala would seriously interfere with the ability of higher limbic inputs to regulate amygdala-driven affective rage. In this manner, "Temporolimbic dysfunction could conduce to hyperarousal in response to environmental stimuli, while prefrontal deficits might lead to inhibitory failures, with either or both contributing to aggressive dyscontrol" (Brower & Price, 2000, p. 147).

An efficient mature orbitofrontal system can facilitate or inhibit the defense reactions of the amygdala (Timms, 1977), and thereby adaptively regulate amygdala-driven autonomic hyperarousal or hypoarousal. But stress may also take the prefrontal areas "off-line," allowing the "more habitual" responses mediated by the subcortical structures to regulate behavior (Arnsten & Goldman-Rakic, 1998). This occurs all too frequently in a severely developmentally compromised immature frontolimbic system, one that can not shift back to orbitofrontal dominance in a timely fashion:

> In the absence of the contribution from orbitofrontal cortex, the original encoding is more difficult to alter and exerts a stronger control over behavior. In other words, behavior becomes more rigid and less amenable to control by changing contingencies and more subtle contextual features of the enviroment. (Schoenbaum, Chiba, & Gallagher, 2000, p. 5189)

In light of the fact that social stressors are more detrimental than nonsocial aversive stimuli, relational trauma, perceived in facially expressed aggressive signals at even nonconscious levels, may expose this impaired cortical-subcortical regulatory system. According to Adolphs, Tranel, and Damasio, "The amygdala's role appears to be of special importance for social judgement of faces that are normally classified as unapproachable and untrustworthy, consistent with the amygdala's demonstrated role in processing threatening and aversive stimuli" (1998, p. 472).

Previously I wrote of the infant's right brain temporolimbic imprinting of the abusive, untrustworthy caregiver's threatening face into implicit-procedural memory in the right hemisphere, the hemisphere dominant for the nonconscious processing of untrustworthy, fearful, aggressive facial emotional expressions (Dimberg & Petterson, 2000; Johnsen & Hugdahl, 1993; Peper & Karcher, 2001; Winston, Strange, O'Doherty, & Dolan, 2002). But the abused infant also imprints the defenses against arousal dysregulating abuse or neglect, and this operation also involves the amygdala. The amygdala's connections with the dorsolateral periaqueductal gray mediates the freeze response (Vianna, Graeff, Brandao, & Landeira-Fernandez, 2001) and its connections with the vagal complexes mediate the dissociative response (Schore, 2001b).

The amygdala interacts with and modulates the fusiform gyri, the visual area that decodes facial patterns (George et al., 1999). It is established that the right amygdala, a dynamic emotional stimulus detection system (Wright et al., 2001) that is specialized to respond to high arousal negative stimuli (Garavan, Pendergrass, Ross, Stein, & Risinger, 2001), is activated by the nonverbal facial and vocal expressions of fear (Phillips et al., 1998) and involved in the representations of fearful faces and the expression of emotionally influenced memory of aversive experiences (Coleman-Mesches & McGaugh, 1995; Morris, Ohman, & Dolan, 1999). Partial kindling of the right and not left amygdala induces long-lasting increases in anxiety-like behavior (Adamec, 1999). Research now demonstrates that the right prefrontal cortex processes fear (Kalin, Larson, Shetton, & Davidson, 1998), that single neurons in the human right ventromedial cortex respond to facial expressions of fear in 120–160 ms (Kawasaki et al., 2001), and that the right orbitofrontal cortex shows an enhanced re-sponse to anger expressions which correlate with expression intensity (Blair, Morris, Frith, Perrett, & Dolan, 1999). The automatic emotional associative learning of threat-related facial stimuli is now understood to be the combined effect of opponent mechanisms that include both a right amygdalocortical ex-citatory process and prefrontal inhibitory influences (Peper & Karcher, 2001).

Thus, an inefficient right orbitofrontal system would be unable to modulate the response of the right amygdala to emotionally significant and stressful stimuli, such as an aggressive face. These findings suggest that, under stress, the limbic system of these individuals is regulated not by the right cortical areas, but by the subcortical right amygdala, a structure that also connects into the reticular formation and hypothalamus and is specialized to process "unseen fear" (Morris et al., 1999). This enduring pattern, associated with destructive, defensive rage, was imprinted into an immature, inefficient orbitofrontal system in contexts of early relational trauma: "If, during early childhood, the lower brain has been overstimulated through exposure to continual traumatic stress, while the upper brain has received scant amounts of nurturing, the scales will be tipped strongly in favor of violence" (Verny, 2002, p. 199).

Continuity Between Infant, Childhood, Adolescent, and Adult Aggression Dysregulation

Earlier in this chapter, I contended that severe disorders of aggression regula-tion may have their roots in not only neurological damage in infancy (neurolog-ically acquired sociopathy) but in relational trauma of abuse and neglect (de-velopmentally acquired sociopathy). Barnett and his colleagues (1999) found that infants with congenital conditions involving nervous system damage are also classified as disorganized/disoriented attachments. They concluded:

> [C]hildren with neurological disorders demonstrate indices of disorganiza-tion under lower levels of stress that are typically required to evoke such behaviors in children with normal nervous systems. It also may be the case that living under chronically stressful conditions in which comfort is rarely present contributes to congenitally healthy children developing neurological damage. (pp. 205–206)

The origin of an environmentally impaired right brain system for regulating aggressive affective states thus all too frequently lies in early relational trauma and the intergenerational transmission of an insecure disorganized/disoriented attachment pattern.

Furthermore, attachment outcome is the result of the genetically encoded psychobiological predisposition of the infant and the nature of the caregiver environment (Schore, 1994, 2000b, 2003a). Basic research has shown that the degree of genetic predisposition interacts with the extent of early induced environmental defect, and that environmental stress exaggerates a "developmental lesion" to produce an enduring vulnerability to stress (Lipska & Weinberger, 1995). A particularly potent negative caregiver environment for generating high risk for aggression dysregulation would be pre- and/or postnatal maternal alcohol or cocaine use, a documented generator of disorganized/disoriented attachments (Espinosa, Beckwith, Howard, Tyler, & Swanson, 2001; O'Connor, Sigman, & Brill, 1987). Another would be maternal neglect followed by paternal abuse and humiliation.

This means that a type D attachment results from a combination of genetic-constitutional vulnerability *and* psychosocial environmental stressors, and that this interaction is involved in the genesis of a high-risk scenario for future aggression dysregulation. Indeed, birth complications combined with maternal rejection at age 1 predispose to violent crime at 18 years, and both early neuromotor deficits and unstable family environments are associated with high rates of violence, crime, and behavioral and academic problems in adolescent and adult males (Raine, Brennan, & Mednick, 1994).

The aggression dysregulation of such personalities may be detected early in life. Infants who experience intense amounts of negative emotion (Dawson, Panagiotides, Grofer Klinger, & Hill, 1992) and crying (Fox & Davidson, 1988) present a pattern of right frontal electroencephalogram (EEG) activation under resting conditions at 10 months. A pattern of hitting, biting, kicking, and temper tantrums common to all toddlers, peaks at 18 to 24 months and then declines. This maturational decline would not be seen in personalities, especially males, with severe attachment pathologies. Thus, early warning signs are specifically disruptive behaviors, such as temper tantrums and aggression that persist beyond the first 2 to 3 years of life, and that are more frequent and severe than other children of the same age (Loeber & Farrington, 2000).

Indeed, toddlers who exhibit severe disturbances are observed to physically assault others, and to engage in self-destructive behaviors (Causey, Robertson, & Elam, 1998). Children maltreated as toddlers are more angry, hyperactive, distractible, inattentive, noncompliant, and aggressive in preschool and kindergarten (Erikson, Egeland, & Pianta, 1989). Continuity between disorganized/disoriented attachment in infancy and hostile-aggressive behavior in the preschool classroom has been well documented (Lyons-Ruth et al., 1993). Furthermore, greater right than left resting frontal activation at 3 years is associated with a lack of empathy (Jones, Field, & Davalos, 2000), and at $4\frac{1}{2}$ years with oppositional defiant disorder (Baving, Laucht, & Schmidt, 2000).

In an important body of research on early markers of risk Raine and his colleagues (Raine, Reynolds, et al., 1998) found that fearlessness, stimulation seeking, and large body size predispose to childhood aggression at age 11. This group also reported that, at 3 years, low arousal, reflected in low resting heart rate, is a diagnostically specific early biological marker for later aggressive behavior (Raine, Venables, Mednick, 1997). (Recall that dissociation, the infant's response to relational trauma, is reflected in decreased heart rate.) Raine and colleagues (1997) pointed out that low heart rate, which is found in no other psychiatric disorder, is also a marker of fearless behavior. According to these researchers:

[L]ow arousal represents an aversive physiological state . . . antisocial, aggressive individuals seek out stimulation to increase their arousal levels back to optimal or normal levels. Aggressive behavior may be viewed as a form of stimulation seeking in that behaviors such as outbursts of anger, fighting, swearing, and cruelty could be stimulating to some children. (p. 1463)

These outbursts, dysfunctions of affect regulation, are most obvious under stressful and challenging conditions that call for behavioral flexibility. In such unstable systems, small disruptions associated with interpersonal stresses could too easily become rapidly amplified into intense negative states. This would be subjectively experienced as a sudden transition into rapidly shifting and intensely affective states. A good example of this occurs in the rapid escalation of rage seen in response to humiliation and in aggressive eye gaze, a very common trigger of interpersonal rage. Exposure to shame-humiliation is a very frequent accompaniment of early child abuse, and it may serve as an interpersonal matrix for interpersonal rage (shame-rage; Schore, 1994, 1998b).

Blair and his colleagues demonstrated that boys with psychopathic tendencies, as young as 9 years, show impairments in processing fearful and sad (but not aggressive) faces (Blair, Colledge, Murray, & Mitchell, 2001) and orbitofrontal dysfunction (Blair, Colledge, & Mitchell, 2001). As mentioned, this prefrontal cortex is centrally involved in the individual's appraisal of the safety or danger of interactive contexts. Early traumatic experiences bias this system toward insecurity and aggression, and this negatively tinged perceptual bias powerfully influences the way in which a male, abused early in childhood, would see the world during moments of stress. A growing literature demonstrates that neglected children have difficulty recognizing emotion in faces, and that physically abused children display a response bias for angry facial expressions (Pollak, Cicchetti, Hornung, & Reed, 2000).

Developmental research also has revealed that "hostile attributional biases" among aggressive boys are specifically exacerbated under conditions of threat to the self. Dodge and Somberg (1987) suggested that early experiences of physical abuse, exposure to aggressive models, and insecure attachments lead a child to develop memory structures that contain a hostile world schema and an aggressive response repertoire. Later, when the child is presented with provocative stimuli, such as peer teasing and humiliation, these structures lead him to attend to hostile cues and to engage in aggressive behavior. These dynamics characterize "early onset antisocial youth," which spans 7 through 11 years (Loeber & Farrington, 2000).

Multiple psychological changes are seen in adolescence, a time in the life-span when the commission of violence is highest (Reiss & Roth, 1993). The brain undergoes a significant reorganization during this period. Adolescence is second only to the neonatal period in terms of both rapid biopsychosocial growth and changing environmental characteristics and demands. After a relatively long period of slowed growth during early childhood, the adolescent brain undergoes extensive repruning and a prominent developmental transformation. It has been suggested that the reorganization of amygdala and prefrontal limbic areas that innervate the hypothalamus and modulate emotional reactivity drive the reorganization of the adolescent brain (Spear, 2000). Notice that these systems are the same ones involved in aggression and its regulation.

Although adolescence can be potentially growth enhancing for certain personalities, for others with developmentally overly pruned cortical-subcortical circuits, this stage of the lifespan can be emotionally overwhelming and disorganizing. A brain that in infancy had to chronically shift into hypometabolic survival modes had little energy available for growth, and a repruning of already developmentally thinned-down cortical-subcortical connections exposes earlier forming regulatory deficits. This would be particularly so for type D personalities (identified on the Adult Attachment Interview as "unresolved/disorganized") who show inefficient capacities for regulating rage states. Excessive pruning is thought to be a primary mechanism in other "neurodevelopmental" disorders, where large reductions in frontal connectivity are associated with the emergence of circuit pathology that mediates dysfunctional symptoms (Hoffman & Dobscha, 1989).

In other words, early structural defects of aggression regulation circuits would become even more apparent during this stressful transitional period. In support of this principle, neurological damage of the orbitofrontal cortex in the first year-and-a-half can result, in adolescence, in a syndrome that resembles psychopathy (Anderson et al., 1999), and infants who experience perinatal complications show orbitofrontal dysfunction in adolescence (Kinney et al., 2000). Psychiatric diagnoses of sociopathy are also first made at this time. The "frontal lobe maturational lag" of juvenile delinquents (Pontius & Ruttiger, 1976) thus reflects what Anderson and colleagues (2000) described as a "long-term sequelae of prefrontal cortex damage acquired in early childhood" that results in "a failure to ever develop specific cognitive and behavioral competencies," and what Bechara's group (2001) termed "a developmentally hypo-functioning ventromedial cortex." A "developmentally hypo-functioning ventromedial cortex" thus underlies a "developmentally acquired sociopathy."

Borderline Personality Disorder and Affective-Impulsive Versus Antisocial Personality Disorder and Predatory-Stalking Aggression

Teicher and colleagues (1996) reported that children who have suffered early physical abuse show EEG abnormalities in frontal brain regions, and conclude that stress alters the development of the prefrontal cortex, arrests its development, and prevents it from reaching a full adult capacity. I suggest that the ambient relational trauma embedded in type D disorganized/disoriented attachments induces an apoptotic excitotoxic alteration of neural circuitry (Mattson & Duan, 1999; Schore, 2003a), a severe overpruning of reciprocal orbitofrontal (and anterior cingulate) connections with the amygdala. In earlier works I have outlined the role of this mechanism in the etiology of PTSD and borderline personality disorders (BPD) (Schore, 2001b). Both of these groups show neuropsychological deficits and abnormal amygdala and orbitofrontal function (Corrigan, Davidson, & Heard, 2000; Goxer, Konicki, & Schulz, 1994; Herpetz, et al., 2001; Schore, 2001b, 2002b; Zelkowitz, Paris, Guzder, & Feldman, 2001). This conception further suggests that like PTSD, borderline, and antisocial personality organizations that manifest dysregulated aggression each represent an "environmentally induced complex developmental disorder" (DeBellis, 2001).

A large body of studies demonstrates disrupted early attachments and early trauma and abuse in the histories of children and adults diagnosed as borderline personality disorder (Lyons-Ruth & Jacobvitz, 1999). Zanarini and colleagues (1997) reported that 91% of borderline patients report childhood abuse. In an overview of the literature, Paris summarized the developmental data and asserts "the weight of the research evidence supports the hypothesis that abuse during childhood is an important risk factor for borderline personality disorder" (1995, p. 15). The maladaptive deficits of affect regulation that accompany pathological dissociation, a primitive defense against overwhelming affects, are well documented in borderline personality disorder (Golynkina & Ryle, 1999).

In the trauma literature, Herman and van der Kolk (1987) asserted that this personality organization manifests a bias to use dissociation when under stress, and experiences massive disturbances in affect regulation, interpersonal difficulties, self-integration, and impulse control. The impulse control and aggression dysregulation deficits of borderline personality disorders have been well documented in the psychoanalytic literature by Kernberg (1975), who stated that the excess (unregulated) endogenous aggression of this group of patients is due to "severe chronic traumatic experiences" (1988).

I suggest that such early traumatic attachments induce apoptosis and circuit overpruning in the developing limbic system and represent the origins of the enduring structural impairments of both borderline and antisocial (sociopathic) personality disorders. This would lead to a deficit of the higher right brain regulation of lower right subcortically driven aggressive states. Indeed, neuroimaging studies now confirm that both predatory and affective murderers show excessively high right subcortical activity (Raine, Meloy, et al., 1998). Furthermore, the severe disturbances in affect regulation and impulse control of borderline personality disorders are manifestations of aggression dysregulation, specifically of "affective," "impulsive," "reactive" aggression. On the other hand, "predatory," "stalking," "proactive" aggression characterizes antisocial (sociopathic) personality disorders, a group known to show limbic abnormalities in affective processing (Kiehl et al., 2001).

Indeed, borderline personality disorder is linked specifically to impulsive aggression (Dougherty, Bjork, Huckabee, Moeller, & Swann, 1999; Gurvits, Koenigsberg, & Siever, 2000; Oquendo & Mann, 2000), children manifesting reactive relative to proactive aggression show higher levels of physical abuse (Dodge, Lochman, Harnish, & Bates, 1997), and psychopathic adults are known to exhibit predatory violence, while nonpsychopathic adults manifest affective-impulsive violence (Raine, Meloy, et al., 1998). These differences would be seen most clearly not in a basal resting state, but under exposure to a personally meaningful stressor.

I also hypothesize that although both experience disorganized-disoriented insecure attachments and severe alterations of arousal, a history of maternal abuse-hyperarousal is dominant in the borderline, and neglect-hypoarousal in the antisocial personality. During a critical period of corticolimbic limbic-hypothalamic connectivity, an excessive developmental parcellation and/or cell death in the hypothalamic sympathetic ventromedial nuclei would lead to a borderline organization and a predisposition to affective-reactive rage, while a severe parcellation of the parasympathetic lateral hypothalamus would lead to an antisocial personality organization and a predisposition to predatory-proactive rage.

In addition, excessive developmental cell death in specific groups of face processing neurons in the developing right fusiform gyrus, the area that decodes facial stimuli (George et al., 1999), would be associated with the borderline's inability to efficiently process aggressive faces and the psychopath's mindblindness to fearful faces. Relational trauma-induced excessive developmental cell death of neurons in the human right ventromedial cortex that respond to facial expressions of fear (Kawasaki et al., 2001) would also account for this mindblindness. Indeed, children with psychopathic tendencies can respond appropriately to angry facial expressions, but not to fearful (or sad) expressions (Blair, 1999). The etiology of a failure to mobilize an appropriate autonomic response to fearful or aggressive facial expressions traces back to the previously described traumatic episodes of sympathetic hyperarousal triggered by maternal aggressive and fearful states, and the infant's defensive switch into dissociation. Extended periods of hypometabolism during a critical period of face processing neuron connectivity could later mediate a dissociative response to fearful or aggressive faces.

Furthermore, different patterns of critical period parcellation of various orbitofrontal connections into subcortical autonomic arousal systems would account for the high resting arousal of borderline and low resting arousal of sociopathic personalities. In other words, although the borderline would oscillate between supra-low arousal (abandonment depression) and supra-high arousal (uncontrolled rage), the psychopath's ANS would fix at low resting arousal levels. Earlier I mentioned that physically abused infants show high levels of negative affect, while neglected infants demonstrate flattened affect (Gaensbauer & Hiatt, 1984) and low cortisol levels (Gunnar & Vazquez, 2001). This psychobiological alteration endures—habitually violent offenders with antisocial personality show low cortisol levels (Virkkunen, 1985).

In this conceptualization, infant neglect would be associated with severe hypoarousal, the same low arousal found in children who are high risk for later fearless aggressive behavior (Raine et al., 1997). Recall that the idea that maternal neglect is the most severe form of maternal deprivation, and the principles that "maternal deprivation induces cell death" (Zhang et al., 1997), and "cells that fire together, survive together, and wire together." I suggest that severe neglect induces an overpruning of CNS-ANS limbic-autonomic connections, producing the unique pattern of low resting heart rate, the best-replicated biological marker for antisocial personalities who are high risk for aggression (see Schore, 2002b, for a model of the de-evolution of the autonomic nervous system).

This reduced autonomic arousal has been hypothesized by Blair (1999) to be associated with the psychopath's "failure to develop" a "Violence Inhibition Mechanism." Furthering Blair's developmental speculation, in the earlier discussion of the psychobiology of relational trauma, I described the infant's intense disengagement during dissociation, psychobiologically expressed as a severe alteration of vagal tone and a dramatic decrease of heart rate and blood pressure. Vagal tone is defined as "the amount of inhibitory influence on the heart by the parasympathetic nervous system" (Field, Pickens, Fox, Nawrocki, & Gonzalez, 1995, p. 227). Vagal activity has long been known to decelerate heart rate, but it is now established that there are two parasympathetic vagal systems, a late developing "mammalian" or "smart" system in the nucleus ambiguus which allows for the ability to communicate via facial expressions, vocalizations, and gestures via contingent social interactions, and a more primitive early developing "reptilian" or "vegetative" system in the dorsal motor nucleus of the vagus that acts to shut down metabolic activity (Porges, 1997, 2001). Both the ventral and dorsal vagal systems are right lateralized (Porges, Doussard-Roosevelt, & Maiti, 1994), and so during early critical periods of regional synaptogenesis prolonged episodes of dorsal vagal dissociation have growth-inhibiting effects, especially in the right brain which specializes in withdrawal and contains a vagal circuit of emotion regulation (Davidson & Hugdahl, 1995; Porges et al., 1994).

I have suggested that in growth-facilitating socioemotional environments, the orbitofrontal system enhances its connections with the nucleus ambiguus vagal system and therefore expands its affect regulatory capacities, but in traumatic growth inhibiting environments, this "smart" system never optimally develops, and the "vegetative" system dominates (Schore, 2001b). I propose that Blair's adaptive Violence Inhibition Mechanism is driven by a ventral vagal dominant parasympathetic mechanism, while the low arousal system of the psychopath reflects elevated levels of dorsal vagal activity.

The orbitofrontal system directly connects into the body via its direct connections into the ANS (Neafsey, 1990), and its modulation of the parasympathetic branch of the ANS is achieved via descending axons that synapse on dendritic fields of the hypothalamus, the head ganglion of the ANS, and vagal areas of the medulla. An extensive parcellation or developmentally impoverished synaptic connections in adolescence would lead to reduced orbitofrontal ventral vagal connectivity, and thereby a loss of higher cortical inhibition of subcortical sympathetic hyperexcitatory states. Panic attacks in late adolecence, accompanied by a subjective fear of madness or dying, are associated with high rates of antisocial personality disorder (Goodwin & Hamilton, 2002). Parcellation could also lead to increased prefrontal neuronal death and a predominance, especially under stress, of hypometabolic dorsal vagal over ventral vagal systems. This conception fits nicely with recent observations of reduced prefrontal gray matter, severely altered autonomic activity, and significantly reduced heart rate in individuals diagnosed with antisocial personality disorder (Raine, Lencz, Bihrler, LaCasse, & Colletti, 2000).

Thus, developmentally acquired sociopathy, like neurologically acquired sociopathy, would result in an adult orbitofrontal system that is unable to express autonomic responses (somatic markers) to social stimuli, and therefore a lack of empathy (Damasio, Tranel, & Damasio, 1990; van Honk et al., 2002). This deficit is a hallmark of psychopathy, and reflects a dysfunction of the orbitofrontal system's critical role in emotional moral behavior (Moll, de Oliveira-Souza, Bramati, & Grafman, 2002). Impairments in this prefrontal system are responsible for a personality organization that is primarily guided by immediate prospects and insensitive to future consequences, a "myopia for the future," one that has "difficulties learning from previous mistakes, as reflected by repeated engagement in decisions that lead to negative consequences" (Bechara, Tranel, & Damasio, 2000, p. 2,189). They are also associated with a high risk for drug and alcohol dependence, both of which show amygdala and orbitofrontal impairment (Franklin et al., 2002; Hill et al., 2001; Rogers et al., 1999).

I have earlier presented ideas on the association between dysregulation of attachment-associated infantile rage reactions and the structural impairments of the orbitofrontal cortex seen in "primitive" personality disorders (Schore, 1994). In total, this body of work supports the hypothesis that the orbital cortex, the prefrontal system that is central to "defining the 'personality' of an individual" (Cavada & Schultz, 2000), shows a "preferential vulnerability" to psychiatric disorders (Barbas, 1995), including borderline and psychopathic personality disorders (Blair, 2001; Goyer, Konicki, & Schulz, 1994; LaPierre, Braun, & Hodgins, 1995). Interestingly, the American Psychiatric Association (1994) lists "inability of function as a responsible parent" as a characteristic of psychopathic personality. Child abuse and neglect is the most direct expression of irresponsible parenting. With regard to borderline personalities, parents who attempt suicide and kill their children manifest impulsive aggression (Lindberg, Asberg, & Sunquist-Stensman, 1984).

At the beginning of this chapter, I cited research which indicates that reductions in right orbitofrontal functioning may be a particularly important predisposition to violence (Raine, Stoddard, et al., 1998), and that reduced right hemisphere activation during a working memory task in severely abused violent offenders (Raine et al., 2001). In this latter work Raine and his colleagues concluded:

Abused individuals who go on to perpetrate serious violence have right hemisphere dysfunction that predisposes to violence via poor fear conditioning, reduced pain perception, faulty processing of emotions, and a deficit in the withdrawal system (2001, p. 126).

Epilogue and Implications for Early Intervention

Within the context of the preceding information, it is extremely important to emphasize the point now being made by Verny (2002):

> Most emotionally neglected or traumatized children do not turn into violent criminals or sociopaths. Usually, if these children have had some positive relationships—for example with a grandparent or cherished teacher—they will manage to function, even prosper. However, those not so lucky will most likely suffer a sense of emptiness and loneliness, because they are unable to connect with others. Others connect, but only through relationships that are destructive or disturbed. (p. 201)

This observation underscores the critical import of even a single timely, attuned, benign positive relationship in both altering a developmental trajectory away from violence, and diverting a child from a pathway leading to the fixed organization of a sociopathic personality that is unable to emotionally connect or a borderline personality that forms pathological connections with other humans.

Returning to Raine's proposition that an optimally functioning right hemisphere is a protective factor against a risk for violence, recall that this hemisphere is dominant for the first years of human life, the time of the human brain growth spurt. The critical period hypothesis (Schore, 1994), which applies to the experience-dependent maturation of the right brain systems that regulate aggression, strongly supports the notion that "treatment and intervention studies need to begin much earlier in life than hitherto in order for success to be maximized in preventing violence" (Raine et al., 1997, p. 1463). Neurobiological, neuropsychiatric, and attachment data clearly indicate that prevention and intervention should begin even before the nursery, during pregnancy, and extend through the perinatal and postnatal period, the interval of the brain growth spurt. Standardized, reliable diagnostic protocols for identifying maternal and infant risk factors, and dyads that experience intense and prolonged negative affective states need to be established on a broad basis. These standards should take gender differences into account (see Schore, 2000b).

Following Brazelton's suggestion that the "inability to regulate strong emotions" is the source of violence, developing right brain regulatory functions and coping capacities need to be assessed. Classification of disorganized/ disoriented insecure infants must be made well before 12 months, and these high-risk infants need to be followed throughout the stages of infancy. Because "harsh touch" in infancy is implicated in the genesis of later aggressive behavior (Weiss, Wilson, St. Jonn Seed, & Paul, 2001), early tactile experience of low birth weight children needs to be evaluated. Screenings for sustained withdrawal and dissociation (Guedeney & Fermanian, 2001) and low resting heart rate are obviously essental in high-risk children.

In light of the known function of the right frontal system in mobilizing an adaptive stress reponse, a neurobiologically oriented diagnostic program should include infant right frontal EEG risk markers (Field, Diego, Hernandaz-Reif, Schanberg, & Kuhn, 2002). Indeed, an increasing amount of evidence suggests that the biological risk factor of right hemisphere dysfunction, when combined with the psychosocial risk factor of early abuse predisposes to violence (Raine, 2002). Neuroimaging investigations of cortical and subcortical limbic structures (orbitofrontal, cingulate, insula, amygdala) under resting and attachment stress conditions at different critical periods would provide a neurobiological picture of the developmental process.

Digital videotape assessments of the infant's capacity for recognition of positive and negative visual and auditory facial expressions need to measure the high-risk infant's autonomic responses to the mother's face in the first year and to his/her own face in the second year. Ultimately, assessments that concurrently measure brain, behavioral, and bodily changes in both members of the dyad will give the most clinically relevant information about the adaptive and maladaptive nature of the right brain regulatory functions mediated by the attachment relationship (for further ideas on this theme, see Schore, 2000b, 2003a, 2003b).

Interventions directed toward ameliorating relational trauma should focus on improving the efficiency of psychobiological communications within the bodily-based attachment relationship, and on optimizing the maturation of limbic-autonomic circuits and the higher right brain prefrontal systems involved in affect regulation. Treatment programs that impact the early intergenerational transmission of traumatic abuse and neglect also transform a growth-inhibiting interpersonal context that generates dense negative affect and frequent episodes of aggression dysregulation, thereby reducing the incidence of personality disorders that are high risk for violence. These programs should also include home visitations (Eckenrode et al., 2000).

In fact, infant mental health workers are devising interventions that effectively alter the regulatory capacities of effective parenting, and thereby the attachment experiences and psychobiological functions of high-risk infants (Cohen, Lojkasek, Muir, Muir, & Parker, 2002; Lieberman & Zeanah, 1999;

Osofsky & Fenichel, 1994; van IJzendoorn, Juffer, & Duyvesteyn, 1995). These programs are creating a developmental context for the transformation of insecure into secure attachments, thereby facilitating the experience-dependent neurobiological maturation of the right brain, which is centrally involved in the adaptive regulation of motivational states, including aggressive states, and in enabling the individual to cope with stress. This effort must involve a joint cooperation of developmental researchers and the spectrum of clinicians from pediatrics, child psychiatry, child psychology, social work, as well as the other professions that constitute the interdisciplinary field of infant mental health.

The mental health field must move from late intervention to early prevention in order to address the problem of violence in children, a growing concern of a number of societies. In these tragic cases the seemingly invisible "ghosts from the nursery" reappear in horrifyingly sharp outline during the ensuing stages of childhood, where they not only haunt and destroy individual lives but negatively impact entire communities and societies. The "ghosts from the nursery" that are associated with the early roots of violence, described by Karr-Morse and Wiley, are in essence the enduring right brain imprints of the nonconscious intergenerational transmission of relational trauma. According to a very recent study, there are 3 million diagnosed antisocial personality disorders in this country (Narrow, Rae, Robins, & Reiger, 2002). The answer to the fundamental question of why certain humans can, in certain contexts, commit the most inhuman of acts, must include practical solutions to how we can provide optimal early social-emotional experiences for larger and larger numbers of our infants, the most recent embodiments of our expression of hope for the future of humanity.

References

Abelin, E. (1971). The role of the father in the separation-individuation process. In J. B. McDevitt & C. F. Settlage (Eds.), *Separation-Individuation* (pp. 229–252). New York: International Universities Press.

Acerra, F., Burnod, Y., & de Schonen, S. (2002). Modelling aspects of face processing in early infancy. *Developmental Science, 5,* 98–117.

Adamec, R. E. (1990). Role of the amygdala and medial hypothalamus in spontaneous feline aggression and defense. *Aggressive Behavior, 16,* 207–222.

Adamec, R. E. (1999). Evidence that limbic neural plasticity in the right hemisphere mediates partial kindling induced lasting increases in anxiety-like behavior: effects of low frequency stimulation (Quenching?) on long-term potentiation of amygdala efferents and behavior following kindling. *Brain Research, 839,* 133–152.

Adolphs, R. (2002). Recognizing emotion from facial expressions: Psychological and neurological mechanisms. *Behavioral and Cognitive Neuroscience Reviews, 1,* 21–62.

Adolphs, R., Tranel, D., & Damasio, A. R. (1998). The human amygdala in social judgment. *Nature, 393,* 470–474.

Amercian Psychiatric Association (1994). *Diagnostic and Statistical Manual of Mental Disorders.* Washington, DC: American Psychiatric Association.

Anderson, C. A., & Bushman, B. J. (2002). Human aggression. *Annual Review of Psychology, 53,* 27–51.

Anderson, S. W., Bechara, A., Damasio, H., Tranel, D., & Damasio, A. R. (1999). Impairment of social and moral behavior related to early damage in human prefrontal cortex. *Nature Neuroscience, 2,* 1032–1037.

Anderson, S. W., Damasio, H., Tranel, D., & Damasio, A. R. (2000). Long-term sequelae of prefrontal cortex damage acquired in early childhood. *Developmental Neuropsychology, 18,* 281–296.

Arnsten, A. F. T., & Goldman-Rakic, P. S. (1998). Noise stress impairs prefrontal cortical cognitive function in monkeys. Evidence for a hyperdopaminergic mechanism. *Archives of General Psychiatry, 55,* 362–368.

Barach, P. M. M. (1991). Multiple personality disorder as an attachment disorder. *Dissociation, IV:* 117–123.

Barbas, H. (1995). Anatomic basis of cognitive-emotional interactions in the primate prefrontal cortex. *Neuroscience and Biobehavioral Reviews, 19,* 499–510.

Bargh, J. A., & Chartrand, T. L. (1999). The unbearable automaticity of being. *American Psychologist, 54,* 462–479.

Barnett, D., Hunt, K. H., Butler, C. M., McCaskill, J. W., Kaplan-Estrin, M., & Pipp-Siegel, S. (1999). Indices of attachment disorganization among toddlers with neurological and non-neurological problems. In J. Solomon & C. George (Eds.), *Attachment disorganization* (pp. 189–212). New York: Guilford Press.

Baving, L., Laucht, M., & Schmidt, M. H. (2000). Oppositional children differ from healthy children in frontal brain activation. *Journal of Abnormal Child Psychology, 28,* 267–275.

Baxter, M. G., Parker, A., Lindner, C. C. G., Izquierdo, A. D., & Murray, E. A. (2000). Control of response selection by reinforcer value requires interaction of amygdala and orbital prefrontal cortex. *Journal of Neuroscience, 20,* 4311–4319.

Bear, D. (1989). Hierarchical neural regulation of aggression: Some predictable patterns of violence. In D. A. Britzer & M. Crowner (Eds.), *Current approaches to the prediction of violence* (pp. 85–100). Washington, DC: American Psychiatric Press.

Bechara, A., Damasio, H., Tranel, D., & Damasio, A. R. (1997). Deciding advantageously before knowing the advantageous strategy. *Science, 275,* 1293–1295.

Bechara, A., Dolan, S., Denburg, N., Hindes, A., Anderson, S. W., & Nathan, P. E. (2001). Decision-making deficits, linked to a dysfunctional ventromedial prefrontal cortex, revealed in alcohol and stimulant abusers. *Neuropsychologia, 39,* 376–389.

Bechara, A., Tranel, D., & Damasio, H. (2000). Characterization of the decision-making deficit of patients with ventromedial prefrontal cortex lesions. *Brain, 123,* 2189–2202.

Beebe, B. (2000). Coconstructing mother-infant distress: The microsychrony of maternal impingement and infant avoidance in the face-to-face encounter. *Psychoanalytic Inquiry, 20,* 412–440.

Bergman, A. (1999). *Ours, yours, mine: Mutuality and the emergence of the separate self.* Northvale, NJ: Analytic Press.

Berkowitz, L. (1990). On the formation and regulation of anger and aggression. *American Psychologist, 45,* 494–503.

Bertolucci-D'Angio, M., Serrano, A., Driscoll, P., & Scatton, B. (1990). Involvement of mesocorticolimbic dopaminergic systems in emotional states. *Progress in Brain Research, 85,* 405–417.

Best, M., Williams, J. M., & Coccaro, E. F. (2002). Evidence for a dysfunctional prefrontal circuit in patients with an impulsive aggressive disorder. *Proceedings of the National Academy of Science of the United States of America, 99,* 8448–8453.

Bigler, E. D. (2001). Frontal lobe pathology and antisocial personality disorder. *Archives of General Psychiatry, 58,* 609–611.

Bion, W. R. (1962). *Learning from experience.* London: Heinemann.

Blair, R. J. R. (1999). Responsiveness to distress cues in the child with psychopathic tendencies. *Personality and Individual Differences, 27,* 135–145.

Blair, R. J. R. (2001). Neurocognitive models of aggression, the antisocial personality disorders, and psychopathy. *Journal of Neurology, Neurosurgery, and Psychiatry, 71,* 727–731.

Blair, R. J. R., & Cipolotti, L. (2000). Impaired social response reversal. A case of "acquired sociopathy." *Brain, 123,* 1122–1141.

Blair, R. J. R., Colledge, E., & Mitchell, D. G. V. (2001). Somatic markers and response reversal: Is there orbitfrontal cortex dysfunction in boys with psychopathic tendencies? *Journal of Abnormal Child Psychology, 29,* 499–511.

Blair, R. J. R., Morris, J. S., Frith, C. D., Perrett, D. I., & Dolan, R. J. (1999). Dissociable neural responses to facial expressions of sadness and anger. *Brain, 122,* 883–893.

Blair, R. J. R., Colledge, E., Murray, L., & Mitchell, D. G. V. (2001). A selective impairment in the processing of sad and fearful expresions in children with psychopathic tendencies. *Journal of Abnormal Child Psychology, 29,* 491–498.

Blair, R. J. R., Morris, J. S., Frith, C. D., Perrett, D. I., & Dolan, R. J. (1999). Dissociable neural responses to facial expressions of sadness and anger. *Brain, 122,* 883–893.

Blos, P. (1984). Sons and fathers. *Psychoanalytic Study of the Child, 32,* 301–324.

Borod, J. (2000). *The neuropsychology of emotion.* New York: Oxford University Press.

Bouwmeester, H., Smits, K., & Van Ree, J. H. (2002). Neonatal development of projections to the basolateral amygdala from prefrontal and thalamic structures in the rat. *Journal of Comparative Neurology, 450,* 241–255.

Bouwmeester, H., Wolterink, G., & Van Ree, J. H. (2002). Neonatal development of projections from the basolateral amygdala to prefrontal, striatal, and thalamic structures in the rat. *Journal of Comparative Neurology, 442,* 239–249.

Bowlby, J. (1944). Forty-four juvenile thieves: Their character and home life. *International Journal of Psychoanalysis, 25,* 1–57, 207–228.

Bowlby, J. (1969). *Attachment and loss. Vol. 1: Attachment.* New York: Basic Books.

Brake, W. G., Sullivan, R. M., & Gratton, A. (2000). Perinatal distress leads to lateralized medial prefrontal cortical dopamine hypofunction in adult rats. *Journal of Neuroscience, 20,* 5538–5543.

Braun, K., & Poeggel, G. (2001). Recognition of mother's voice evokes metabolic activation in the medial prefrontal cortex and lateral thalamus of *Octodon degus* pups. *Neuroscicence, 103,* 861–864.

Brazelton, T. B. (1997). Introduction. In R. Karr-Morse & M. S. Wiley, *Ghosts from the nursery* (pp. xiii–xiv). New York: Atlantic Monthly Press.

Brower, M. C., & Price, B. H. (2000). Epilepsy and violence: When is the brain to blame? *Epilepsy & Behavior, 1,* 145–149.

Brower, M. C., & Price, B. H. (2001). Neuropsychiatry of frontal lobe dysfunction in violent and criminal behaviour: A critical review. *Journal of Neurology, Neurosurgery, and Psychiatry, 71,* 720–726.

Brown, M. R., Fisher, L. A., Spiess, J., Rivier, C., Rivier, J., & Vale, W. (1982). Corticotropin-releasing factor: actions on the sympathetic nervous system and metabolism. *Endocrinology, 111,* 928–931.

Buck, R. (1994). The neuropsychology of communication: Spontaneous and symbolic aspects. *Journal of Pragmatics, 22,* 265–278.

Cairns, R. B., & Stoff, D. M. (1996). Conclusion: A synthesis of studies on the biology of aggression and violence. In D. M. Stoff & R. B. Cairns (Eds.), *Aggression and violence: genetic, neurobiological, and biosocial perspectives* (pp. 337–351). Mahwah, NJ: Erlbaum.

Caldji, C., Diorio, J., & Meaney, J. (2000). Variations in maternal care in infancy regulate the development of stress reactivity. *Biological Psychiatry, 48,* 1164–1174.

Carlson, V., Cicchetti, D., Barnett, D., & Braunwald, K. (1989). Disorganized/disoriented attachment relationships in maltreated infants. *Developmental Psychology, 25,* 525–531.

Causey, D. L., Robertson, J. M., & Elam, S. M. (1998). Characteristics of toddlers and preschoolers exhibiting severe psychiatric disturbance. *Child Psychiatry and Human Development, 29,* 33–48.

Cavada, C., Company, T., Tejedor, J., Cruz-Rizzolo, & Reinoso-Suarez-Suarez, F. (2000). The anatomical connections of the macaque monkey orbitofrontal cortex. A review. *Cerebral Cortex, 10,* 220–242.

Cavada, C., & Schultz, W. (2000). The mysterious orbitofrontal cortex. Foreword. *Cerebral Cortex, 10,* 205.

Chambers, R. A., Bremner, J. D., Moghaddam, B., Southwick, S. M., Charney, D. S., & Krystal, J. H. (1999). Glutamate and post-traumatic stress disorder: Toward a psychobiology of dissociation. *Seminars in Clinical Neuropsychiatry, 4,* 274–281.

Chiron, C., Jambaque, I., Nabbout, R., Lounes, R., Syrota, A., & Dulac, O. (1997). The right brain hemisphere is dominant in human infants. *Brain, 120,* 1057–1065.

Chu, J. A. (2001). A decline in the abuse of children? *Journal of Trauma and Dissociation, 2,* 1–4.

Cohen, N. S., Lojkasek, M., Muir, E., Muir, R., & Parker, C. J. (2002). Six-month follow-up of two mother-infant psychotherapies: convergence of therapeutic outcomes. *Infant Mental Health Journal, 23,* 361–280.

Coleman-Mesches, K., & McGaugh, J. L. (1995). Differential involvement of the right and left amygdalae in expression of memory for aversively motivated training. *Brain Research, 670,* 75–81.

Coplan, J. D., Andrews, M. W., Rosenblum, L. A., Owens, M. J., Gorman, J. M., & Nemeroff, C. B. (1996). Increased cerebrospinal fluid CRF concentrations in adult non-human primates previously exposed to adverse experiences as infants. *Proceedings of the National Academy of Sciences of the United States of America, 93,* 1619–1623.

Corrigan, F. M., Davidson, A., & Heard, H. (2000). The role of dysregulated amygdalic emotion in borderline personality disorder. *Medical Hypotheses. 54,* 574–579.

Craig, A. D. (2002). How do you feel? Interoception: The sense of the physiological condition of the body. *Nature Reviews Neuroscience, 3,* 655–666.

Cratty, M. S., Ward, H. E., Johnson, E. A., Azzaro, A. J., & Birkle, D. L. (1995). Prenatal stress increases corticotropin-releasing factor (CRF) content and release in rat amygdala minces. *Brain Research, 1995,* 675–302.

Damasio, A. R. (2000). A neural basis for sociopathy. *Archives of General Psychiatry, 57,* 128–129.

Damasio, A. R., Tranel, D., & Damasio, H. (1990). Individuals with sociopathic behavior caused by frontal damage fail to respond autonomically to social stimuli. *Behavioral Brain Research, 41,* 81–94.

Davidson, R. J., & Hugdahl, K. (1995). *Brain asymmetry*. Cambridge, MA: MIT Press.

Davidson, R. J., Putnam, K. M., & Larson, C. L. (2000). Dysfunction in the neural circuitry of emotion regulation—a possible prelude to violence. *Science, 289,* 591–594.

Dawson, G., Panagiotides, H., Grofer Klinger, L., & Hill, D. (1992). The role of frontal lobe functioning in the development of infant self-regulatory behavior. *Brain & Cognition, 20,* 152–175.

De Bellis, M. D. (2001). Developmental traumatology: The psychobiological development of maltreated children and its implications for research, treatment, and policy. *Development and Psychopathology, 13,* 539–564.

De Bellis, M. D., Baum, A. S., Birmaher, B., Keshavan, M. S., Eccard, C. H., Boring, A. M., Jenkins, F. J., & Ryan, N. D. (1999). Developmental traumatology part I: Biological stress systems. *Biological Psychiatry, 45,* 1259–1270.

De Bellis, M. D., Keshavan, M. S., Clark, D. B., Casey, B. J., Giedd, J. N., Boring, A. M., Frustaci, K., & Ryan, N. D. (1999). Developmental traumatology part II: Brain development. *Biological Psychiatry, 45,* 1271–1284.

de Bruin, J. P. C. (1990). Social behaviour and the prefrontal cortex. *Progress in Brain Research, 85,* 485–500.

Derryberry, D., & Tucker, D. M. (1992). Neural mechanisms of emotion. *Journal of Clinical and Consulting Psychology, 60,* 329–338.

Deruelle, C., & de Schonen, S. (1998). Do the right and left hemispheres attend to the same visuospatial information within a face in infancy? *Developmental Neuropsychology, 14,* 535–554.

Devinsky, O. (2000). Right cerebral hemisphere dominance for a sense of corporeal and emotional self. *Epilepsy & Behavior, 1,* 60–73.

Devinsky, O., Morrell, M. J., & Vogt, B. A. (1995). Contributions of anterior cingulate cortex to behaviour. *Brain, 118,* 279–306.

Dimberg, U., & Petterson, M. (2000). Facial reactions to happy and angry facial expressions: Evidence for right hemisphere dominance. *Psychophysiology, 37,* 693–696.

Dixon, A. K. (1998). Ethological strategies for defense in animals and humans: Their role in some psychiatric disorders. *British Journal of Medical Psychology, 71,* 417–445.

Dobbing, J., & Sands, J. (1973). Quantitative growth and development of human brain. *Archives of Diseases of Childhood, 48,* 757–767.

Dodge, K. A., Lochman, J. E., Harnish, J. D., & Bates, J. E. (1997). Reactive and proactive aggression in school children and psychiatrically impaired chronically assaultive youth. *Journal of Abnormal Psychology, 106,* 37–51.

Dodge, K. A., & Somberg, D. R. (1987). Hostile attributional biases among aggressive boys are exacerbated under conditions of threat to the self. *Child Development, 58,* 213–224.

Dolan, M., Deakin, W. J. F., Roberts, N., & Anderson, I. (2002). Serotonergic and cognitive impairment in impulsive aggressive personality disordered offenders: are there implications for treatment? *Psychological Medicine, 32,* 105–117.

Dougherty, D. M., Bjork, J. M., Huckabee, H. C. G., Moeller, F. G., & Swann, A. C. (1999). Laboratory measures of aggression and impulsivity in women with borderline personality disorder. *Psychiatry Research, 85,* 315–326.

Eckenrode, J., Ganzel, B., Henderson, C. R., Jr., Smith, E., Olds, D. L., Powers, J., Cole, R., Kitzman, H., & Sidora, K. (2000). Preventing child abuse and neglect with a program of nurse home visitation. The limiting effects of domestic violence. *Journal of the American Medical Association, 284,* 1385–1391.

Egger, M. D., & Flynn, J. P. (1967). Further studies on the effects of amygdaloid stimulation and ablation on hypothalamically elicited attack behavior in cats. *Progress in Brain Research, 27,* 165–182.

Elliott, R., Dolan, R. J., & Frith, C. D. (2000). Dissociable functions in the medial and lateral orbitofrontal cortex: evidence from human neuroimaging studies. *Cerebral Cortex, 10,* 308–317.

Epstein, H. T. (2001). An outline of the role of brain in human cognitive development. *Brain and Cognition, 45,* 44–51.

Erciyas, A. H., Topalkara, K., Topaktas, S., Akyuz, A., & Dener, S. (1999). Suppression of cardiac parasympathetic functions in patients with right hemispheric stroke. *European Journal of Neurology, 6,* 685–690.

Erikson, M., Egeland, B., & Pianta, R. (1989). The effects of maltreatment on the development of young children. In D. Cichetti & V. Carlson (Eds.), *Child maltreatment: Theory and research on the causes and consequences of child abuse and neglect* (pp. 647–684). New York: Cambridge University Press.

Espinosa, M., Beckwith, L., Howard, J., Tyler, R., & Swanson, K. (2001). Maternal psychopathology and attachment in toddlers of heavy cocaine-using mothers. *Infant Mental Health Journal, 22,* 316–333.

Euler, U. S. von, & Folkow, B. (1958). The effect of stimulation of autonomic areas in the cerebral cortex upon the adrenaline and noradrenaline secretion from the adrenal gland in the cat. *Acta Physiologica Scandinavica, 42,* 313–320.

Falk, D., Hildebolt, C., Cheverud, J., Vannier, M., Helmkamp, R. C., & Konigsberg, L. (1990). Cortical asymmetries in frontal lobes of Rhesus monkeys (*Macaca mulatta*). *Brain Research, 512,* 40–45.

Famularo, R., Kinscherff, R., & Fenton, T. (1992). Psychiatric diagnoses of abusive mothers. A preliminary report. *Journal of Nervous and Mental Disease, 180,* 658–661.

Fanselow, M. S. (1986). Conditioned fear-induced opiate analgesia: A compelling motivational state theory of stress analgesia. In Kelly, D. D. (Ed.), *Stress-induced analgesia* (pp. 40–54). New York: The New York Academy of Sciences.

Feldman, R., Greenbaum, C. W., & Yirmiya, N. (1999). Mother-infant affect synchrony as an antecedent of the emergence of self-control. *Developmental Psychology, 35,* 223–231.

Field, T., Diego, M., Hernandoz-Reif, M., Sohanberg, S., & Kuhn, C. (2002). Relative right verses left frontal EEG in neonates. *Developmental Psychobiology, 41,* 147–155.

Field, T., Pickens, J., Fox, N. A., Nawrocki, T., & Gonzalez, J. (1995). Vagal tone in infants of depressed mothers. *Development and Psychopathology, 7,* 227–231.

Filley, C. M., Price, B. H., Nell, V., Antoinette, T., Morgan, A. S., Bresnahan, J. F., Pincus, J. H., Gelbort, M. M., Weisberg, M., & Kelly, J. P. (2001). Toward an understanding of violence: Neurobiobehavioral conference consensus statement. *Neuropsychiatry, Neuropsychology, and Behavioral Neurology, 14,* 1–14.

Fisher, R. S., & Almli, C. R. (1984). Postnatal development of sensory influences on labeled hypothalamic neurons of the rat. *Developmental Brain Research, 12,* 55–75.

Fornazzari, L., Farenik, K., Smith, I., Heasman, G. A., & Ischise, M. I. (1992). Violent visual hallucinations and aggression in frontal lobe dysfunction: Clinical manifestations of deep orbitofrontal foci. *Journal of Neuropsychiatry and Clinical Neuroscience, 4,* 42–44.

Fox, N. A., & Davidson, R. J. (1988). Patterns of brain electrical activity during facial signs of emotion in 10-month-old infants. *Developmental Psychology, 24,* 230–236.

Francis, D. D., & Meaney, M. J. (1999). Maternal care and the development of stress responses. *Current Opinion in Neurobiology, 9,* 128–134.

Franklin, T. R., Acton, P. D., Maldjian, J. A., Gray, J. D., Croft, J. R., Dackis, C. A., O'Brien, C. P., & Childress, A. R. (2002). Decreased gray matter concentration in insular, orbitofrontal, cingulate, and temporal cortices of cocaine patients. *Biological Psychiatry, 51,* 134–142.

Freud, S. (1964). An outline of psychoanalysis. In J. Strachey (Ed. & Trans.), *Standard edition of the complete psychological works of Sigmund Freud* (Vol. 23, pp. 141–207) London: Hogarth Press. (Original work published 1940)

Gaensbauer, T. J., & Hiatt, S. (1984). Facial communication of emotion in early infancy. In N. Fox & R. Davidson (Eds.), *The psychobiology of affective development* (pp. 207–230). Hillsdale, NJ: Erlbaum.

Gaensbauer, T. J. (2002). Representations of trauma in infancy: clinical and theoretical implications for the understanding of early memory. *Infant Mental Health Journal, 23*, 259–277.

Gaensbauer, T. J., & Sands, K. (1979). Distorted affective communications in abused/neglected infants and their potential impact on caretakers. *Journal of the American Academy of Child Psychiatry, 18*, 238–250.

Gaensbauer, T. J., & Siegel, C. H. (1995). Therapeutic approaches to posttraumatic stress disorder in infants and toddlers. *Infant Mental Health Journal, 16*, 292–305.

Gainotti, G. (2000). Neuropsychological theories of emotion. In J. Borod (Ed.), *The neuropsychology of emotion*. New York: Oxford University Press.

Garavan, H., Pendergrass, J. C., Ross, T. J., Stein, E. A., & Risinger, R. C. (2001). Amygdala response to both positively and negatively valenced stimuli. *Neuro Report, 12*, 2779–2783.

Garavan, H., Ross, T. J., & Stein, E. A. (1999). Right hemisphere dominance of inhibitory control: An event-related functional MRI study. *Proceedings of the National Academy of Sciences of the United States of America, 96*, 8301–8306.

George, N., Dolan, R. J., Fink, G., Baylis, G. C., Russell, C., & Driver, J. (1999). Human fusiform gyrus extracts shape-from-shading to recognize familiar faces. *Nature Neuroscience, 2*, 574–580.

Geschwind, N., & Galaburda, A. M. (1987). *Cerebral lateralization: Biological mechanisms, associations, and pathology*. Boston: MIT Press.

Glaser, D. (2000). Child abuse and neglect and the brain—A review. *Journal of Child Psychology and Psychiatry, 41*, 97–116.

Glynn, L. M., Wadhwa, P. D., & Sandman, C. A. (2000). The influence of corticotropin-releasing hormone on human fetal development and parturition. *Journal of Prenatal and Perinatal Psychology and Health, 14*, 243–256.

Golynkina, K., & Ryle, A. (1999). The identification and characteristics of the partially dissociated states of patients with borderline personality disorder. *British Journal of Medical Psychology, 72*, 429–435.

Goodwin, R. D., & Hamilton, S. P. (2002). The early-onset fearful panic attack as a predictor of severe psychopathology. *Psychiatry Research, 109*, 71–79.

Gorno-Tempini, M. L., Pradelli, S., Serafini, M., Pagnoni, G., Baraldi, P., Porro, C., Nicoletti, R., Umita, C., & Nichelli, P. (2001). Explicit and incidental facial expression processing an FMRI study. *NeuroImage, 14*, 465–473.

Goyer, P. F., Konicki, P. E., & Schulz, S. C. (1994). Brain imaging in personality disorders. In K. R. Silk (Ed.), *Biological and neurobehavioral studies of borderline personality disorder* (pp. 109–125). Washington, DC: American Psychiatric Press.

Grafman, J., Schwab, K., Warden, D., Pridgen, A., Brown, H. R., & Salazar, A. M. (1996). Frontal lobe injuries, violence, and aggression: a report of the Vietnam Head Injury Study. *Neurology, 46*, 1231–1238.

Graham, Y. P., Heim, C., Goodman, S. H., Miller, A. H., & Nemeroff, C. B. (1999). The effects of neonatal stress on brain development: Implications for psychopathology. *Development and Psychopathology, 11*, 545–565.

Guedeney, A., & Fermanian, J. (2001). A validity and reliability study of assessment and screening for sustained withdrawal in infancy: The alarm distress scale. *Infant Mental Health Journal, 22*, 559–575.

Guilarte, T. R. (1998). The N-methyl-D-aspartate receptor: physiology and neurotoxicology in the developing brain. In W. Slikker & L. W. Chang (Eds.), *Handbook of developmental neurotoxicology* (pp. 285–304). San Diego: Academic Press.

Gunnar, M. R., & Vazquez, D. M. (2001). Low cortisol and a flattening of expected daytime rhythm: potential indices of risk in human development. *Development and Psychopathology, 13,* 515–538.

Gur, R. C., Schroeder, L., Turner, T., McGrath, C., Chan, R. M., Turetsky, B. I., Alsop, D., Maldjian, J., & Gur, R. E. (2002). Brain activation during facial emotion processing. *Neuro Image, 16,* 651–662.

Gurvits, I. G., Koenigsberg, H. W., & Siever, L. J. (2000). Neurotransmitter dysfunction in patients with borderline personality disorder. *Psychiatric Clinics of North America, 23,* 27–40.

Hall, R. E., & Marr, H. B. (1975). Influence of electrical stimulation of posterior orbital cortex upon plasma cortisol levels in unanesthetized sub-human primate. *Brain Research, 93,* 367–371.

Hariri, A. R., Bookheimer, S. Y., & Mazziotta, J. C. (2000). Modulating emotional responses: effects of a neocortical network on the limbic system. *Neuro Report, 11,* 43–48.

Heim, C., & Nemeroff, C. B. (2001). The role of childhood trauma in the neurobiology of mood and anxiety disorders: Preclinical and clinical studies. *Biological Psychiatry, 49,* 1023–1039.

Helmeke, C., Ovtscharoff, W. Jr., Poeggel, G., & Braun, K. (2001). Juvenile emotional experience alters synaptic input on pyramidal neurons in the anterior cingulate cortex. *Cerebral Cortex, 11,* 717–727.

Helmeke, C., Poeggel, G., & Braun, K. (2001). Differential emotional experience induces elevated spine densities on basal dendrites of pyramidal neurons in the anterior cingulate cortex of *Octodon degus. Neuroscience, 104,* 927–931.

Helmuth, I. (2000). Has America's tide of violence receded for good? *Science, 289,* 582–585.

Herman, J. L., & van der Kolk, B. A. (1987). Traumatic antecedents of borderline personality disorder. In B. A. van der Kolk (Ed.), *Psychological trauma* (pp. 111–126). Washington, DC: American Psychiatric Press.

Herpetz, S., Dietrich, T. M., Wenning, B., Krings, T., Erberich, S. G., Wilmes, K., Thron, A., & Sass, H. (2001). Evidence of abnormal amygdala functioning in borderline personality disorder: A functional MRI study. *Biological Psychiatry, 50,* 292–298.

Hertsgaard, L., Gunnar, M., Erickson, M. F., & Nachimias, M. (1995). Adrenocortical responses to the strange situation in infants with disorganized/disoriented attachment relationships. *Child Development, 66,* 1100–1106.

Herzog, J. M. (1980) Sleep disturbance and father hunger in 18- to 28-month-old boys: The Erlkonig Syndrome. *Psychoanalytic Study of the child, 35,* 219–233.

Herzog, J. M. (2001). *Father hunger: Explorations with adults and children.* Hillsdale, NJ: Analytic Press.

Hesse, E., & Main, M. M. (1999). Second-generation effects of unresolved trauma in nonmaltreating parents: dissociated, frightened, and threatening parental behavior. *Psychoanalytic Inquiry, 19,* 481–540.

Hesse, E., & Main, M. (2000). Disorganized infant, child and adult attachment: Collapse in behavioral and attentional strategies. *Journal of the American Psychoanalytic Association, 48,* 1097–1028.

Hildyard, K. L., & Wolfe, D. A. (2002). Child neglect: Developmental issues and outcomes. *Child Abuse & Neglect, 26,* 679–695.

Hill, S. Y., De Bellis, M. D., Keshavan, M. S., Lowers, L., Shen, S., Hall, J., & Pitts, T.

(2001). Right amygdala volume in adolescent and young adult offspring from families at high risk for developing alcoholism. *Biological Psychiatry, 49,* 894–905.

Hoffman, R. E., & Dobscha, S. K. (1989). Cortical pruning and the development of schizophrenia: A computer model. *Schizophrenia Bulletin, 15,* 477–490.

Horowitz, M. J. (1992). Formulation of states of mind in psychotherapy. In N. G. Hamilton (Ed.), *From inner sources: New directions in object relations psychotherapy* (pp. 75–83). Northvale, NJ: Jason Aronson.

Hoyt, K. R., Reynolds, I. J., & Hastings, T. G. (1997). Mechanisms of dopamine-induced cell death in cultured rat forebrain neurons: Interactions with and differences from glutamate-induced cell death. *Experimental Neurology, 143,* 269–281.

Hugdahl, K. (1995). Classical conditioning and implicit learning: The right hemisphere hypothesis. In R. J. Davidson & K. Hugdahl (Eds.), *Brain asymmetry* (pp. 235–267). Cambridge, MA: MIT Press.

Johnsen, B. H., & Hugdahl, K. (1993). Right hemisphere representation of autonomic conditioning to facial emotional expressions. *Psychophysiology, 28,* 154–162.

Johnson, J. G., Cohen, P., Brown, J., Smailes, E. M., & Bernstein, D. P. (1999). Childhood maltreatment increases risk for personality disorders during early development. *Archives of General Psychiatry, 56,* 600–605.

Jones, A., Field, T., & Davalos, M. (2000). Right frontal EEG asymmetry and lack of empathy in preschool children of depressed mothers. *Child Psychiatry and Human Development, 30,* 189–204.

Kalin, N. H., Larson, C., Shelton, C. E., & Davidson, R. J. (1998). Asymmetric frontal brain activity, cortisol, and behavior associated with fearful temperament in rhesus monkeys. *Behavioral Neuroscience, 112,* 286–292.

Kalogeras, K. T., Nieman, L. K., Friedman, T. C., Doppman, J. L., Cutler, G. B. Jr., Chrousos, G. P., Wilder, R. L., Gold, P. W., & Yanovski, J. A. (1996). Inferior petrosal sinus sampling in healthy human subjects reveals a unilateral corticotropin-releasing hormone-induced arginine vasopressin release associated with ipsilateral adrenocorticotropin secretion. *Journal of Clinical Investigation, 97,* 2045–2050.

Karr-Morse, R., & Wiley, M. S. (1997). *Ghosts from the nursery: Tracing the roots of violence.* New York: Atlantic Monthly Press.

Kaufman, I. C., & Rosenblum, L. A. (1967). The reaction to separation in infant monkeys: Anaclitic depression and conservation-withdrawal. *Psychosomatic Medicine, 40,* 649–675.

Kawasaki, H., Adolphs, R., Kaufman, O., Damasio, H., Damasio, A. R., Granner, M., Bakken, H., Hori, T., & Howard, M. A. (2001). Single-neuron responses to emotional visual stimuli recorded in human ventral prefrontal cortex. *Nature Neuroscience, 4,* 15–16.

Kazdin, A. E., Siegel, T. C., & Bass, D. (1990). Drawing upon clinical practice to inform research on child and adolescent psychotherapy: A survey of practioners. *Professional Psychology: Research and Practice, 21,* 189–198.

Keenan, J. P., McCutcheon, B., Freund, S., Gallup, G. C., Jr., Sanders, G., & Pascual-Leone, A. (1999). Left hand advantage in a self-face recognition task. *Neuropsychologia, 37,* 1421–1425.

Keenan, J. P., Nelson, A., O'Connor, M., & Pascual-Leone, A. (2001). Self-recognition and the right hemisphere. *Nature, 409,* 305.

Keil, A., Bradley, M. M., Hauk, O., Rockstroh, B., Ellert, T., & Liang, P. N. (2002). Large-scale neural correlates of affective picture processing. *Psychophysiology, 39,* 641–649.

Kernberg, O. (1975). *Borderline conditions and pathological narcissism.* New York: Jason Aronson.

Kernberg, O., (1998). Developer of an object relations psychoanalytic therapy for borderline personality disorder (by L. K. McGinn). *American Journal of Psychotherapy, 52* (2).

Kiehl, K. A., Smith, A. M., Hare, R. D., Mendrek, A., Forster, B. B., Brink, J., & Liddle, P. F. (2001). Limbic abnormalities in affective processing by criminal psychopaths as revealed by functional magnetic resonance imaging. *Biological Psychiatry, 50,* 677–684.

Kinney, H. C., Brody, B. A., Kloman, A. S., & Gilles, F. H. (1988). Sequence of central nervous system myelination in human infancy. II. Patterns of myelination in autopsied infants. *Journal of Neuropathology and Experimental Neurology, 47,* 217–234.

Kircher, T. T. J., Senior, C., Phillips, M. L., Rabe-Hesketh, S., Benson, P. J., Bullmore, E. T., Brammer, M., Simmons, A., Bartels, M., & David, A. S. (2001) Recognizing one's own face. *Cognition, 78,* B1–B15.

Koch, K. L., Summy-Long, J., Bingaman, S., Sperry, N., & Stern, R. M. (1990). Vasopressin and oxytocin responses to illusory self-motion and nausea in man. *Journal of Clinical and Endocrinological Metabolism, 71,* 1269–1275.

Koizumi, K., Terui, N., Kollai, M., & Brooks, C. M. (1982). Functional significance of coactivation of vagal and sympathetic cardiac nerves. *Proceedings of the National Academy of Sciences of the United States of America, 79,* 2116–2120.

Kraemer, G. W., Ebert, M. H., Schmidt, D. E., & McKinney, W. T. (1991). Strangers in a strange land: A psychobiological study of infant monkeys before and after separation from real or inanimate mothers. *Child Development, 62,* 548–566.

Kruk, M. R., Van der Poel, A. M., & De Vos-Frerichs, T. P. (1979). The induction of aggressive behavior by electrical stimulation in the hypothalamus of male rats. *Behaviour, 70,* 292–321.

Kvetnansky, R., Dobrakovova, M., Jezova, D., Oprsalova, Z., Lichardus, B., & Makara, G. (1989). Hypothalamic regulation of plasma catecholamine levels during stress: Effect of vasopressin and CRF. In G. R. Van Loon, R. Kvetnansky, R. McCarty, & J. Axelrod, (Eds.), *Stress: neurochemical and humoral mechanisms* (pp. 549–570). New York: Gordon and Breach Science Publishers.

Kvetnansky, R., Jezova, D., Oprsalova, Z., Foldes, O., Michjlovskij, N., Dobrakovova, M., Lichardus, B., & Makara, G. B. (1990). Regulation of the sympathetic nervous system by circulating vasopressin. In J. C. Porter & D. Jezova, (Eds.), *Circulating regulatory factors and neuroendocrine function* (pp. 113–134). New York: Plenum Press.

La Bar, K. S., Gatenby, J. C., Gore, J. C., Le Doux, J. E., & Phelps, E. A. (1998). Human amygdala activation during conditioned fear acquisition and extinction: A mixed-trial fMRI study. *Neuron, 20,* 937–945.

Ladd, C. O., Owens, M. J., & Nemeroff, C. B. (1996). Persistent changes in corticotropin-releasing factor neuronal systems induced by maternal deprivation. *Endocrinology, 137,* 1212–1218.

Lakatos, K., Toth, I., Nemoda, Z., Ney, K., Sasvari-Szekely, M., & Gervai, J. (2000). Dopamine D4 receptor (DRD4) polymorphism is associated with attachment disorganization in infants. *Molecular Psychiatry, 5,* 633–637.

Lapierre, D., Braun, C. M. J., & Hodgins, S. (1995). Ventral frontal deficits in psychopathy: neuropsychological test findings. *Neuropsychologia, 33,* 139–151.

LeDoux, J. E. (1996). *The emotional brain.* New York: Simon and Schuster.

Lewis, M. H., Gluck, J. P., Beauchamp, A. J., Keresztury, M. F., & Mailman, R. B. (1990). Long-term effects of early social isolation in *Macaca mulatta:* Changes in dopamine receptor function following apomorphine challenge. *Brain Research, 513,* 67–73.

Lieberman, A. F. (1996). Aggression and sexuality in relation to toddler attachment: Implications for the caregiving system. *Infant Mental Health Journal, 17,* 276–292.

Lieberman, A. F., & Zeanah, C. H. (1999). Contributions of attachment theory to infant-parent psychotherapy and other interventions with infants and young children. In J. Cassidy

& P. Shaver (Eds.), *Handbook of attachment theory and research* (pp. 555–574). New York: Guilford Press.

Liebeskind, J. C. (1991). Pain can kill. *Pain, 44,* 3–4.

Lindberg, L., Asberg, M., & Sunquist-Stensman, M. (1984). 5–hydroxyindoleacetic acid levels in attempted suicides who have killed their children [letter]. *Lancet 2,* 928.

Lipska, B. K., & Weinberger, D. R. (1995). Genetic variation in vulnerability to the behavioral effects of neonatal hippocampal damage in rats. *Proceedings of the National Academy of Sciences of the United States of America, 92,* 8906–8910.

Loeber, R., & Farrington, D. P. (2000). Young children who commit crime: Epidemiology, developmental origins, risk factors, early interventions, and policy implications. *Development and Psychopathology, 12,* 737–762.

Lorberbaum, J. P., Newman, J. D., Horwitz, A. R., Dubno, J. R., Lydiard, R. B., Hamner, M. B., Bohning, D. E., & George, M. S. (2002). A potential role for thalamocingulate circuitry in human maternal behavior. *Biological Psychiatry. 51,* 431–445.

Lyons-Ruth, K., Alpern, L., & Repacholi, B. (1993). Disorganized infant attachment classification and maternal psychosocial problems as predictors of hostile-aggressive behavior in the preschool classroom. *Child Development, 64,* 572–585.

Lyons-Ruth, K., & Jacobvitz, F. (1999). Attachment disorganization: Unresolved loss, relational violence and lapses in behavioral and attentional strategies. In J. Cassidy & P. R. Shaver (Eds.), *Handbook of attachment theory and research* (pp. 520–554). New York: Guilford Press.

Maccoby, E. (1966). *The development of sex differences.* Stanford: Stanford University Press.

MacLean, P. D. (1985). Evolutionary psychiatry and the triune brain. *Psychological Medicine, 15,* 219–221.

Mahler, M., Pine, F., & Bergman, A. (1975). *The psychological birth of the human infant.* New York: Basic Books.

Main, M. (1996). Introduction to the special section on attachment and psychopathology: 2. Overview of the field of attachment. *Journal of Consulting and Clinical Psychology, 64,* 237–243.

Main, M., Kaplan, N., & Cassidy, J. (1985). Security in infancy, childhood and adulthood: A move to the level of representation. *Monographs of the Society for Research in Child Development, 50,* 66–104.

Main, M., & Morgan, H. (1996). Disorganization and disorientation in infant strange situation: Phenotypic resemblance to dissociative states. In L. K. Michelson & W. J. Ray (Eds.), *Handbook of dissociation: Theoretical, empirical, and clinical perspectives* (pp. 107–138). New York: Plenum Press.

Main, M., & Solomon, J. (1986). Discovery of an insecure-disorganized/disoriented attachment pattern: Procedures, findings and implications for the classification of behavior. In T. B. Brazelton & M. W. Yogman (Eds.), *Affective development in infancy* (pp. 95–124). Norwood, NJ: Ablex.

Main, M., & Weston, D. R. (1981). The quality of the toddler's relationship to mother and to father: Related to conflict behavior and the readiness to establish new relationships. *Child Development, 52,* 932–940.

Martin, L. J., Spicer, D. M., Lewis, M. H., Gluck, J. P., & Cork, L. C. (1991). Social deprivation of infant rhesus monkeys alters the chemoarchitecture of the brain: 1. Subcortical regions. *Journal of Neuroscience, 11,* 3344–3358.

Matsuzawa, J., Matsui, M., Konishi, T., Noguchi, K., Gur, R. C., Bilker, W., & Miyawaki, T. (2001). Age-related changes of brain gray and white matter in healthy infants and children. *Cerebral Cortex, 11,* 335–342.

Mattson, M. P., & Duan,W. (1999). "Apoptotic" biochemical cascades in synaptic compartments: roles in adaptive plasticity and neurodegenerative disorders. *Journal of Neuroscience Research, 58,* 152–166.

Mattson, M. P., Keller, J. N., & Begley, J. G. (1998). Evidence for synaptic apoptosis. *Experimental Neurology, 153,* 35–48.

McCauley, J., Kern, D., Kolodner, K., Dill, L., Schroeder, A., DeChant, H., Ryden, J., Derogatis, L., & Bass, L. (1997). Clinical characteristics of women with a history of childhood abuse. *Journal of the American Medical Association, 277,* 1362–1368.

McDonald, J. W., Silverstein, F. S., & Johnston, M. V. (1988). Neurotoxicity of *N*-methyl-D-aspartate is markedly enhanced in developing rat central nervous system. *Brain Research, 459,* 200–203.

Meares, R. (1999). The contribution of Hughlings Jackson to an understanding of dissociation. *American Journal of Psychiatry, 156,* 1850–1855.

Meerlo, P., Horvath, K. M., Luiten, P. G. M., Angelucci, L., Catalani, A., & Koolhaas, J. M. (2001). Increased maternal corticosterone levels in rats: Effects on brain 5–HT1A receptors and behavioral coping with stress in adult offspring. *Behavioral Neuroscience, 115,* 1111–1117.

Mesulam, M.-M. (1998). From sensation to cognition. *Brain, 121,* 1013–1052.

Miller, B. L., Darby, A., Benson, D. F., Cummings, J. L., & Miller, M. H. (1997). Aggressive, socially disruptive and antisocial behaviour associated with fronto-temporal dementias. *British Journal of Psychiatry, 170,* 150–155.

Miller, B. L., Seeley, W. W., Mychack, P., Rosen, H. J., Mena, I., & Boone, K. (2001). Neuroanatomy of the self. Evidence from patients with frontotemporal dementia. *Neurology, 57,* 817–821.

Mitchell, D. G. V., Colledge, E., Leonard, A., & Blair, R. J. R. (2002). Risk decisions and response reversal: Is there evidence of orbitofrontal cortex dysfunction in psychopathic individuals? *Neuropsychologia, 40,* 2013–2022.

Moll, J., deOliveira-Souza, R., Bramati, I. E., & Grafman, J. (2002). Functional networks in emotional moral and nonmoral social judgments. *Neuro Image, 16,* 696–703.

Mollon, P. (1996). *Mutliple selves, multiple voices: Working with trauma, violation and dissociation.* Chichester, U.K.: Wiley.

Mollon, P. (2001). *Releasing the self. The healing legacy of Heinz Kohut.* London and Philadelphia: Whurr Publishers.

Morris, J. S., Ohman, A., & Dolan, R. J. (1999). A subcortical pathway to the right amygdala mediating "unseen" fear. *Proceedings of the National Academy of Sciences of the United States of America, 96,* 1680–1685.

Mussen, P. H., Conger, J. J., & Kagan, J. (1969). *Child development and personality.* New York: Harper and Row.

Nair, H. P., Berndt, J. P., Barrett, D., & Gonzalez-Lima, F. (2001). Maturation of extinction behavior in infant rats: Large-scale regional interactions with medial prefrontal cortex, orbitofrontal cortex, and anterior cingulate cortex. *Journal of Neuroscience, 21,* 4400–4407.

Nakamura, K., Kawashima, R., Ito, K., Sato, N., Nakamura, A., Sugiura, M., Kato, T., Hatano, K., Ito, K., Fukuda, H., Schorman, T., & Zilles, K. (2000). Functional delineation of the human occipito-temporal areas related to face and scene processing. A PET study. *Brain, 123,* 1903–1912.

Nakamura, K., Kawashima, R., Ito, K., Sugiura, M., Kato, T., Nakamura, A., Hatano, K., Nagumo, S., Kubota, K., Fukuda, H., & Kojima, S. (1999). Activation of the right inferior frontal cortex during assessment of facial emotion. *Journal of Neurophysiology, 82,* 1610–1614.

Narrow, W. E., Rae, D. S., Robins, L. N., & Reiger, D. A. (2002). Revised prevalence estimates of mental disorders in the United States. *Archives of General Psychiatry, 59,* 115–123.

Neafsey, E. J. (1990). Prefrontal cortical control of the autonomic nervous system: Anatomical and physiological observations. *Progress in Brain Research, 85*, 147–166.

Noh, J. S., Kim, E. Y., Kang, J. S., Kim, H. R., Oh, Y. J., & Gwag, B. J. (1999). Neurotoxic and neuroprotective actions of catecholamines in cortical neurons. *Experimental Neurology, 159*, 217–224.

O'Connor, M. J., Sigman, M., & Brill, N. (1987). Disorganization of attachment in relation to maternal alcohol consumption. *Journal of Consulting and Clinical Psychology, 55*, 831–836.

Oquendo, M. A., & Mann, J. J. (2000). The biology of impulsivity and suicidality. *The Psychiatric Clinics of North America, 23*, 11–25.

Osofsky, J. D., & Fenichel, E. (Eds.), (1994). Caring for infants and toddlers in violent environments: Hurt, healing, hope. Arlington, VA: Zero to three.

Panksepp, J. (1998). *Affective neuroscience: the foundations of human and animal emotions.* New York: Oxford University Press.

Papousek, H., Papousek, M., Suomi, S. J., & Rahn, C. W. (1991). Preverbal communication and attachment: Comparative views. In J. L. Gewirtz & W. M. Kurtines (Eds.), *Intersections with attachment* (pp. 97–122). Hillsdale, NJ: Erlbaum.

Parens, H. (1987). *Aggression in our children.* Northvale, NJ: Jason Aronson.

Paris, J. (1995). Memories of abuse in borderline patients: true or false? *Harvard Review of Psychiatry, 3*, 10–17.

Park, J. S., Bateman, M. C., & Goldberg, M. P. (1996). Rapid alterations in dendrite morphology during sublethal hypoxia or glutamate receptor activation. *Neurobiology of Disease, 3*, 215–227.

Peper, M., & Karcher, S. (2001). Differential conditioning to facial emotional expressions: Effects of hemispheric asymmetries and CS identification. *Psychophysiology, 38*, 936–950.

Perry, R. J., Rosen, H. R., Kramer, J. H., Beer, J. S., Levenson, R. L., & Miller, B. L. (2001). Hemispheric dominance for emotions, empathy and social behaviour: Evidence from right and left handers with frontotemporal dementia. *Neurocase, 7*, 145–160.

Phillips, M. L., Young, A. W., Scott, S. K., Calder, A. J., Andrew, V., Giampietro, S. C. R., Williams, E. T., Bullmore, M., Brammer, M., & Gray, J. A. (1998). Neural responses to facial and vocal expressions of fear and disgust. *Proceedings of the Royal Society of London, B, 265*, 1809–1817.

Pietrini, P., Guazzelli, M., Basso, G., Jaffe, K., & Grafman, J. (2000). Neural correlates of imaginal aggresssive behavior assessed by positron emission tomography in healthy subjects. *American Journal of Psychiatry, 157*, 1772–1781.

Pincus, J. H., Gelbort, M. M., Weissberg, M., & Kelly, J. P. (2001). Toward an understanding of violence: Neurobehavioral aspects of unwarranted physical aggression: Aspen Neurobehavioral Conference Consensus statement. *Neuropsychiatry, Neuropsychology, and Behavioral Neurology, 14*, 1–14.

Pizzagalli, D. A., Lehmann, D., Hendrick, A. M., Regard, M., Pascual-Marqui, R. D., & Davidson, R. J. (2002). Affective judgments of faces modulate early activity ($\sim$160 ms) within the fusiform gyri. *Neuro Image, 16*, 663–677.

Pollak, S. D., Cicchetti, D., Hornung, K., & Reed, A. (2000). Recognizing emotion in faces: developmental effects of child abuse and neglect. *Developmental Psychology, 36*, 679–688.

Pontius, A. A., & Ruttiger, K. F. (1976). Frontal lobe system maturational lag in juvenile delinquents shown the narratives test. *Adolescence, 11*, 509–518.

Porges, S. W. (1997). Emotion: An evolutionary by-product of the neural regulation of the autonomic nervous system. *Annals of the New York Academy of Sciences, 807*, 62–77.

Porges, S. W. (2001). The polyvagal theory: Phylogenetic substrates of a social nervous system. *International Journal of Psychophysiology, 42*, 29–52.

Porges, S. W., Doussard-Roosevelt, J. A., & Maiti, A. K. (1994). Vagal tone and the physiological regulation of emotion. *Monographs of the Society for Research in Child Development, 59,* 167–186.

Portera-Cailliau, C., Price, D. L., & Martin, L. J. (1997). Excitotoxic neuronal death in the immature brain is an apoptosis-necrosis morphological continuum. *Journal of Comparative Neurology, 378,* 70–87.

Post, R., & Weiss, S. (1997). Emergent properties of neural systems: How focal molecular neurobiological alterations can affect behavior. *Development and Psychopathology, 9,* 907–929.

Post, R. M., Weiss, R. B., & Leverich, G. S. (1994). Recurrent affective disorder: Roots in developmental neurobiology and illness progression based on changes in gene expression. *Development and Psychopathology, 6,* 781–813.

Powles, W. E. (1992). *Human development and homeostasis.* Madison, CT: International Universities Press.

Price, J. L., Carmichael, S. T., & Drevets, W. C. (1996). Networks related to the orbital and medial prefrontal cortex; a substrate for emotional behavior? *Progress in Brain Research, 107,* 523–536.

Putnam, F. W. (1997). *Dissociation in children and adolescents: A developmental perspective.* New York: Guilford Press.

Raine, A. (2002). Biosocial studies of antisocial and violent behavior in children and adults: a review. *Journal of Abnormal Child Psychology, 30,* 311–326.

Raine, A., Brennan, P., & Mednick, S. A. (1994). Birth complications combined with early maternal rejection at age 1 year predispose to violent crime at age 18 years. *Archives of General Psychiatry, 51,* 984–988.

Raine, A., Lencz, T., Bihrle, S., LaCasse, L., & Colletti, P. (2000). Reduced prefrontal gray matter volume and reduced autonomic activity in antisocial personality disorder. *Archives of General Psychiatry, 57,* 119–127.

Raine, A., Meloy, J. R., Bihrle, S., Stoddard, J., Lacasse, L., & Buchsbaum, M. S. (1998). Reduced prefrontal and increased subcortical brain functioning assessed using positron emission tomography in predatory and affective murderers. *Behavioral Sciences and the Law, 16,* 319–332.

Raine, A., Park, S., Lencz, T., Bihrle, S., LaCasse, L., Widom, C. S., Al-Dayeh, L., & Singh, M. (2001). Reduced right hemisphere activation in severely abused violent offenders during a working memory task: An fMRI study. *Aggressive Behavior, 27,* 111–129.

Raine, A., Reynolds, C., Venables, P. H., Mednick, S. A., & Farrington, D. P. (1998). Fearlessness, stimulation-seeking, and large body size at 3 years as early predispositions to childhood aggression at age 11 years. *Archives of General Psychiatry, 55,* 745–751.

Raine, A., Stoddard, J., Bihrle, S., & Buchsbaum, M. (1998). Prefrontal glucose deficits in murderers lacking psychosocial deprivation. *Neuropsychiatry, Neuropsychology, and Behavioral Neurology, 11,* 1–7.

Raine, A., Venables, P. H., & Mednick, S. A. (1997). Low resting heart rate at age 3 years predisposes to aggression at age 11 years: Evidence from the Mauritius Child Health Project. *Journal of the American Academy of Child and Adolescent Psychiatry, 36,* 1457–1464.

Reiss, A. J., & Roth, J. A. (1993). *Understanding and preventing violence.* Washington, DC: National Academy of Sciences.

Ricciardelli, P., Ro, T., & Driver, J. (2002). A left visual field advantage in perception of gaze direction. *Neuropsychologia, 40,* 769–777.

Rinaman, L., Levitt, P., & Card, J. P. (2000). Progressive postnatal assembly of limbic-autonomic circuits revealed by central transneuronal transport of pseudorabies virus. *Journal of Neuroscience, 20,* 2731–2741.

Rogers, R. D., Eseritt, B. J., Baldacchino, A., Blackshaw, A. J., Swainson, R., Wynne, K., Baker, N. B., Hunter, J., Carthy, T., Booker, E., London, M., Deakin, J. F. W., Sahakian, B. J., & Robbins, T. W. (1999). Dissociable deficits in the decision-making cognition of chronic amphetamine abusers, opiate abusers, patients with focal damage to prefrontal cortex, and tryptophan-depleted normal volunteers: evidence for monoaminergic mechanisms. *Neuropsychopharmacology, 20,* 322–339.

Rolls, E. T. (2000). The orbitofrontal cortex and reward. *Cerebral Cortex, 10,* 284–294.

Rosenblum, L. A., Coplan, J. D., Friedman, S., Basoff, T., Gorman, J. M., & Andrews, M. W. (1994). Adverse early experiences affect noradrenergic and serotonergic functioning in adult primates. *Biological Psychiatry, 35,* 221–227.

Ruby, P., & Decety, J. (2001). Effect of subjective perspective taking during stimulation of action: A PET investigation of agency. *Nature Neuroscience, 4,* 546–550.

Sabban, E. L., & Kvetnansky, R. (2001). Stress-triggered activation of gene expression in catecholaminergic systems: Dynamics of transcriptional events. *Trends in Neuroscience, 24,* 91–98.

Savage, C. R., Deckersbach, T., Heckers, S., Wagner, A. D., Schacter, D. L., Alpert, N. M., Fischman, A. J., & Rauch, S. L. (2001). Prefrontal regions supporting spontaneous and directed application of verbal learning strategies. Evidence from PET. *Brain, 124,* 219–231.

Schaffer, H. R., & Emerson, P. E. (1964). The development of social attachments in infancy. *Monographs of the Society for Research in Child Development, 29* (3, whole No. 94).

Schoenbaum, G., Chiba, A. A., & Gallagher, M. (2000). Changes in functional connectivity in orbitofrontal cortex and basolateral amygdala during learning and reversal training. *Journal of Neuroscience, 20,* 5179–5189.

Schore, A. N. (1994). *Affect regulation and the origin of the self: The neurobiology of emotional development.* Mahwah, NJ: Erlbaum.

Schore, A. N. (1996). The experience-dependent maturation of a regulatory system in the orbital prefrontal cortex and the origin of developmental psychopathology. *Development and Psychopathology, 8,* 59–87.

Schore, A. N. (1997a). Early organization of the nonlinear right brain and development of a predisposition to psychiatric disorders. *Development and Psychopathology, 9,* 595–631.

Schore, A. N. (1997b, October). *The relevance of recent research on the infant brain to clinical psychiatry.* Unpublished Grand Rounds presentation, Department of Psychiatry, Columbia University School of Medicine. New York, NY.

Schore, A. N. (1998a). The experience-dependent maturation of an evaluative system in the cortex. In K. Pribram (Ed.), *Brain and values: Is a biological science of values possible* (pp. 337–358). Mahwah, NJ: Erlbaum.

Schore, A. N. (1998b). Early shame experiences and infant brain development. In P. Gilbert & B. Andrews, (Eds.), *Shame: Interpersonal behavior, psychopathology, and culture* (pp. 57–77). New York: Oxford University Press.

Schore, A. N. (1998c, February). *Early trauma and the development of the right brain.* Unpublished plenary address, Lifespan Conference, "Understanding and Treating Trauma: Developmental and Neurobiological Approaches." UCLA Campus, Los Angeles.

Schore, A. N. (1998d, October). *The relevance of recent research on the infant brain to pediatrics.* Unpublished address, Annual Meeting of the American Academy of Pediatrics, Scientific Section on Developmental and Behavioral Pediatrics, Section Program, Translating neuroscience: Early brain development and pediatric practice. San Francisco.

Schore, A. N. (1998e, October). *The relevance of recent research on the infant brain to clinical psychiatry.* Unpublished keynote address, Royal Australian and New Zealand College of Psychiatrists, Faculty of Child and Adolescent Annual Conference. Sydney, Australia.

Schore, A. N. (1998f, November). *Early trauma and the development of the right brain*. Unpublished keynote address, C. M. Hincks Institute Conference on "Traumatized parents and infants: The long shadow of early childhood trauma." University of Toronto, Toronto, Canada.

Schore, A. N. (1999a, March). *The development of a predisposition to violence: The critical roles of attachment disorders and the maturation of the right brain*. Unpublished invited presentation, Children's Institute International Conference, "Understanding the Roots of Violence: Kids Who Kill." Good Samaritan Hospital, Los Angeles.

Schore, A. N. (1999b, April). *Early trauma and the development of the right brain*. Unpublished invited address, Conference, "Psychological Trauma: Maturational Processes and Therapeutic Interventions." Boston University School of Medicine, Boston.

Schore, A. N. (1999c, October). *The enduring effects of early trauma on the right brain*. Unpublished invited address, Annual Meeting of the American Academy of Child and Adolescent Psychiatry, Symposium, "Attachment, Trauma, and the Developing Mind." Chicago.

Schore, A. N. (1999d, December). *Parent-infant communication and the neurobiology of emotional development*. Unpublished symposium, Zero to Three 14th Annual Training Conference. Los Angeles.

Schore, A. N. (2000a). *Foreword to the reissue of Attachment and loss, Vol. 1: Attachment by John Bowlby*. New York: Basic Books.

Schore, A. N. (2000b). Attachment and the regulation of the right brain. *Attachment & Human Development, 2*, 23–47.

Schore, A. N. (2000c). The self-organization of the right brain and the neurobiology of emotional development. In M. D. Lewis & I. Granic (Eds.), *Emotion, development, and self-organization* (pp. 155–185). New York: Cambridge University Press.

Schore, A. N. (2000d, March). *Early relational trauma and the development of the right brain*. Unpublished invited presentation, Anna Freud Centre. London.

Schore, A. N. (2000e, November). *Healthy childhood and the development of the human brain*. Unpublished keynote address, Healthy Children Foundation Conference, Luxembourg, and World Health Organization (Sponsors). Luxembourg.

Schore, A. N. (2001a). The effects of a secure attachment relationship on right brain development, affect regulation, and infant mental health. *Infant Mental Health Journal, 22*, 7–66.

Schore, A. N. (2001b). The effects of relational trauma on right brain development, affect regulation, and infant mental health. *Infant Mental Health Journal, 22*, 201–269.

Schore, A. N. (2001c). The Seventh John Bowlby Memorial Lecture, "Minds in the making: Attachment, the self-organizing brain, and developmentally-oriented psychoanalytic psychotherapy." *British Journal of Psychotherapy, 17*, 299–328.

Schore, A. N. (2001d). *Plenary Address: Parent-infant emotional communication and the neurobiology of emotional development*. In Proceedings of Head Start's Fifth National Research Conference, Developmental and Contextual Transitions of Children and Families: Implications for Research, Policy, and Practice, pp. 49–73.

Schore, A. N. (2001e, January). *The development of a predisposition to violence: The critical roles of attachment disorders and the maturation of the right brain*. Unpublished plenary address, Caring Foundation and Safe Start Conference. New Orleans, LA.

Schore, A. N. (2001f, March). *Early relational trauma and the development of the right brain*. Unpublished keynote address, Joint Annual Conference, Australian Centre for Posttraumatic Mental Health and The Australasian Society for Traumatic Stress Studies. Canberra, Australia.

Schore, A. N. (2001g, June). *Regulation of the right brain: A fundamental mechanism of attachment, trauma, dissociation, and psychotherapy, Parts 1 & 2*. Unpublished addresses, Conference,

"Attachment, Trauma, and Dissociation: Developmental, Neuropsychological, Clinical, and Forensic Considerations," University College of London Attachment Research Unit and the Clinic for the Study of Dissociative Disorders, Sponsors. London.

Schore, A. N. (2002a). Neurobiology and psychoanalysis: Convergent findings on the subject of projective identification. In J. Edwards (Ed.), *Being alive: building on the work of Anne Alvarez* (pp. 57–74). East Sussex, U.K. Brunner-Routledge.

Schore, A. N. (2002b). Dysregulation of the right brain: a fundamental mechanism of traumatic attachment and the psychopathogenesis of posttraumatic stress disorder. *Australian & New Zealand Journal of Psychiatry, 36,* 9–30.

Schore, A. N. (2002c). Clinical implications of a psychoneurobiological model of projective identification. In S. Alhanati (Ed.), *Primitive mental states: Volume III, Pre- and perinatal influences on personality development* (pp. 1–65). London: Karnac.

Schore, A. N. (2003a). *Affect dysregulation and disorders of the self.* New York: Norton.

Schore, A. N. (2003b). *Affect regulation and the repair of the self.* New York: Norton.

Schuengel, C., Bakermans-Kranenburg, M. J., & Van Ijzendoorn, M. H. (1999). Frightening maternal behavior linking unresolved loss and disorganized infant attachment. *Journal of Consulting and Clinical Psychology, 67,* 54–63.

Segal, M., Korkotian, E., & Murphy., D. D. (2000). Dendritic spine formation and pruning: common cellular mechanisms? *Trends in Neuroscience, 23,* 53–57.

Siegel, A., Roeling, T. A. P., Gregg, T. R., & Kruk, M. R. (1999). Neuropharmacology of brain-stimulation-evoked aggression. *Neuroscience and Biobehavioral Reviews, 23,* 359–389.

Siegel, D. J. (1999). *The developing mind: Toward a neurobiology of interpersonal experience.* New York: Guilford Press.

Siever, L. J., & Trestman, R. L. (1993). The serotonin system and aggressive personality disorders. *Integrative Clinical Psychopharmacology* 8 (Suppl. 2): 33–39.

Sirven, J. I., & Glosser, D. S. (1998). Psychogenic nonepileptic seizures. Theoretic and clinical considerations. *Neuropsychiatry, Neuropsychology, and Behavioral Neurology, 11,* 225–235.

Spangler, G., & Grossman, K. (1999). Individual and physiological correlates of attachment disorganization in infancy. In J. Solomon & C. George (Eds.), *Attachment disorganization* (pp. 95–124). New York: Guilford Press.

Spangler, G., Schieche, M., Ilg, U., & Ackerman, C. (1994). Maternal sensitivity as an organizer for biobehavioral regulation in infancy. *Developmental Psychobiology, 27,* 425–437.

Spear, L. P. (2000). The adolescent brain and age-related behavioral manifestations. *Neuroscience and Biobehavioral Reviews, 24,* 417–463.

Spence, S., Shapiro, D., & Zaidel, E. (1996). The role of the right hemisphere in the physiological and cognitive components of emotional processing. *Psychophysiology, 33,* 112–122.

Spencer, J. P. E., Jenner, A., Aruoma, O. I., Evans, P. J., Kaur, H., Dexter, D. T., Leesa, A. J., Marsden, D. C., & Halliwell, B. (1994). Intense oxidative DNA damage promoted by L-DOPA and its metabolites. Implications for neurodegenerative disease. *Federation of European Biochemical Societies, 353,* 246–250.

Sroufe, L. A. (1996). *Emotional development: The organization of emotional life in the early years.* New York: Cambridge Universty Press.

Starkstein, S. E., & Robinson, R. G. (1997). Mechanism of disinhibition after brain lesions. *Journal of Nervous and Mental Disease, 185,* 108–114.

Stern, D. N. (1983). The early differentiation of self and other. In S. Kaplan & J. D. Lichtenberg (Eds.), *Reflections on self psychology.* Hillsdale, NJ: Analytic Press.

Stern, D. N. (1985). *The interpersonal world of the infant.* New York: Basic Books.

Stoll, M., Hamann, G. F., Mangold, R., Huf, D., & Winterhoff-Spurk, P. (1999). Emotionally evoked changes in cerebral hemodynamics measured by transcranial Doppler sonography. *Journal of Neurology, 246*, 127–133.

Stuss, D. T., & Alexander, M. P. (1999). Affectively burnt in: A proposed role of the right frontal lobe. In E. Tulving (Ed.), *Memory, consciousness, and the brain: The Talin conference* (pp. 215–227). Philadelphia: Psychology Press.

Stuss, D. T., & Levine, B. (2002). Adult clinical neuropsychology: Lessons from studies of the frontal lobes. *Annual Review of Psychology, 53*, 401–433.

Sullivan, R. M., & Gratton, A. (2002). Prefrontal cortical regulation of hypothalamic-pituitary-adrenal function in the rat and implications for psychopathology: Side matters. *Psychoneuroendocrinology, 27*, 99–114.

Sullivan, R. M., & Szechtman, H. (1995). Asymmetrical influence of mesocortical dopamine depletion on stress ulcer development and subcortical dopamine systems in rats: Implications for psychopathology. *Neuroscience, 65*, 757–766.

Szatkowska, I., Grabowska, A., & Szymanska, O. (2001). Evidence for the involvement of the ventromedial prefrontal cortex in a short-term storage of visual images. *NeuroReport, 12*, 1187–1190.

Teicher, M. H., Ito, Y., & Glod, C. A. (1996). Neurophysiological mechanisms of stress response in children. In C. R. Pfeffer (Ed.), *Severe stress and mental disturbances in children* (pp. 59–84). Washington, DC: American Psychiatric Press.

Thompson, R. A. (2000). The legacy of early attachments. *Child Development, 71*, 145–152.

Timms, R. J. (1977). Cortical inhibition and facilitation of defense reaction. *Journal of Physiology, 266*, 98P–99P.

Tranel, D. (1994). "Acquired sociopathy": The development of sociopathic behavior following focal brain damage. In D. C. Fowles, P. Sutker, & S. H. Goodman (Eds.), *Progress in experimental personality and psychopathology research* (Vol. 17, pp. 285–311). New York: Springer-Verlag.

Tremblay, L., & Schultz, W. (1999). Relative reward preference in primate orbitofrontal cortex. *Nature, 398*, 704–708.

Trevarthen, C. (1990). Growth and education of the hemispheres. In C. Trevarthen (Ed.), *Brain circuits and functions of the mind* (pp. 334–363). Cambridge, U.K.: Cambridge University Press.

Trevarthen, C. (1996). Lateral asymmetries in infancy: Implications for the development of the hemispheres. *Neuroscience and Biobehavioral Reviews, 20*, 571–586.

Tronick, E. Z., & Weinberg, M. K. (1997). Depressed mothers and infants: Failure to form dyadic states of consciousness. In L. Murray & P. J. Cooper (Eds.), *Postpartum depression in child development* (pp. 54–81). New York: Guilford Press.

Tucker, D. M. (1992). Developing emotions and cortical networks. In M. R. Gunnar & C. A. Nelson (Eds.), *Minnesota Symposium on Child Psychology. Vol. 24, Developmental Behavioral Neuroscience* (pp. 75–128). Hillsdale, NJ: Erlbaum.

Tulving, E. (1985). Memory and consciousness. *Canadian Psychologist, 26*, 1–12.

Tzourio-Mazoyer, N., de Schonen, S., Crivello, F., Reutter, B., Aujard, Y., & Mazoyer, B. (2002). Neural correlates of women face processing by 2-month-old infants. *Neuroimage, 15*, 454–461.

van der Kolk, B. A. (1987). *Psychological trauma.* Washington, DC: American Psychiatric Press.

van Honk, J., Hermans, E. S., Putman P., Montagne, B., & Schutter, D. J. L. G. (2002). Defective somatic markers in sub-clinical psychopathy. *NeuroReport, 13*, 1025–1027.

van IJzendoorn, M. H., Juffer, F., & Duyvesteyn, M. G. F. (1995). Breaking the inter-generational cycle of insecure attachment: A review of the effects of attachment-based interventions on maternal sensitivity and infant security. *Journal of Child Psychology and Psychiatry, 36*, 225–248.

van IJzendoorn, M. H., Schuengel, C., & Bakermans-Kranenburg, M. J. (1999). Disorganized attachment in early childhood: Meta-analysis of precursors, concomitants, and sequelae. *Development and Psychopathology, 11*, 225–249.

Verny, T. R. (2002). *Tomorrow's baby*. New York: Simon & Schuster.

Vianna, D. M. L., Graeff, F. G., Brandao, M. L., & Landeira-Fernandez, J. (2001). Defensive freezing evoked by electrical stimulation of the periaqueductal gray: Comparison between dorsolateral and ventrolateral regions. *Neuro Report, 12*, 4109–4112.

Virkkunen, M. (1985). Urinary free cortisol secretion in habitually violent offenders. *Acta Psychiatrica Scandinavica, 72*, 40–44.

Voigt, T., Baier, H., & de Lima, A. D. (1997). Synchronization of neuronal activity promotes survival of individual rat neocortical neurons in early development. *European Journal of Neuroscience, 9*, 990–999.

Volavka, J. (1999). The neurobiology of violence: An update. *Journal of Neuropsychiatry and Clinical Neuroscience, 11*, 307–314.

Vuilleumier, P., Armony, J. L., Clarke, K., Husain, M., Driver, J., & Dolan, R. J. (2002). Neural response to emotional faces with and without awareness: Event-related fMRI in a parietal patient with visual extinction and spatial neglect. *Neuropsychologia, 40*, 2156–2166.

Wang, W., Dow, K. E., Fraser, D. D. (2001). Elevated corticotropin releasing hormone/corticotropin releasing hormone-R1 expression in postmortem brain obtained from children with generalized epilepsy. *Annals of Neurology, 50*, 404–409.

Watanabe, S., Miki, K., & Kakigi, R. (2002). Gaze direction affects face perception in humans. *Neuroscience Letters, 325*, 163–166.

Weiss, S. J., Wilson, P., St. Jonn Seed, M., & Paul, S. J. (2001). Early tactile experience of low birth weight children: Links to later mental health and social adaptation. *Infant and Child Development, 10*, 93–115.

Wicker, B., Michel, F., Henaff, M. A., & Decety, J. (1998). Brain regions involved in the perception of gaze: A PET study. *Neuro Image, 8*, 221–227.

Winston, J. S., Strange, B. A., O'Doherty, J., & Dolan, R. J. (2002). Automatic and intentional brain responses during evaluation of trustworthiness of faces. *Nature Neuroscience, 5*, 277–283.

Wittling, W. (1997). The right hemisphere and the human stress response. *Acta Physiologica Scandinavica, 640* (Supp.), 55–59.

Wittling, W., Block, A., Schweiger, E., & Genzel, S. (1998). Hemisphere asymmetry in sympathetic control of the human myocardinm. *Brain and Cognition, 38*, 17–35.

Wittling, W., & Pfluger, M. (1990). Neuroendocrine hemisphere asymmetries: Salivary cortisol secretion during lateralized viewing of emotion-related and neutral films. *Brain and Cognition, 14*, 243–265.

Wright, C. I., Fisher, H., Whalen, P. J., McInerney, S. C., Shin, L. M., & Rauch, S. L. (2001). Differential prefrontal cortex and amygdala habituation to repeatedly presented emotional stimuli. *Neuro Report, 12*, 379–383.

Yoon, B-U., Morillo, C. A., Cechetto, D. F., & Hachinski, V. (1997). Cerebral hemispheric lateralization in cardiac autonomic control. *Archives of Neurology, 54*, 741–744.

Zald, D. H., & Kim, S. W. (1996). Anatomy and function of the orbital frontal cortex, II: Function and relevance to obsessive-compulsive disorder. *Journal of Neuropsychiatry, 8*, 249–261.

Zald, D. H., & Pardo, J. V. (2002). The neural correlates of aversive auditory stimulation. *Neuroimage, 16,* 746–753.

Zanarini, M. C., Williams, A. A., Lewis, R. E., Reich, R. B., Vera, S. C., Marino, M. F., Levin, A., Yong, L., & Frankenburg, F. R. (1997). Reported pathological childhood experiences associated with the development of borderline personality disorder. *American Journal of Psychiatry, 154,* 1101–1106.

Zhang, L-X., Levine, S., Dent, G., Zhan, Y., Xing, G., Okimoto, D., Gordon, M. K., Post, R. M., & Smith, M. A. (2002). Maternal deprivation increases cell death in the infant rat brain. *Developmental Brain Research. 133,* 1–11.

Zelkowitz, P., Paris, J., Guzder, J., & Feldman, R. (2001). Diatheses and stressors in borderline pathology of childhood: The role of neuropsychological risk and trauma. *Journal of the American Academy of Child and Adolescent Psychiatry, 40,* 100–105.

4

Posttraumatic Stress Disorder and The Nature of Trauma

Bessel A. van der Kolk

THE HUMAN RESPONSE to psychological trauma is one of the most important public health problems in the world. Traumatic events such as family and social violence, rapes and assaults, disasters, wars, accidents and predatory violence confront people with such horror and threat that it may temporarily or permanently alter their capacity to cope, their perception of biological threat, and their self-concepts. Traumatized individuals frequently develop posttraumatic stress disorder (PTSD), in which the memory of the traumatic event comes to dominate victims consciousness, depleting their lives of meaning and pleasure (van der Kolk & van der Hart,1991). Trauma does not only affect psychological functioning; for example, a study of almost 10,000 patients in a medical setting (Felitti et al.,1998) reported that persons with histories of being severely maltreated as a child showed a 4 to 12 times greater risk of developing alcoholism, depression, and drug abuse, attempting suicide, a 2 to 4 times greater risk of smoking, having at least 50 sex partners, acquiring sexually transmitted disease, a 1.4 to 1.6 times greater risk for physical inactivity and obesity, and a 1.6 to 2.9 times greater risk for ischemic heart disease, cancer, chronic lung disease, skeletal fractures, hepatitis, stroke, diabetes, and liver disease.

Prevalence

Traumatic events are very common in most societies, though prevalence has been best studied in industrialized societies, particularly in the United States. Kessler and colleagues (1995) found that in the U.S. at least 15% of the population is reported to have been molested, physically attacked, raped, or involved in combat. Men are physically assaulted more often than women (11.1% vs. 10.3%), while women report higher rates of sexual assault (7.3% vs. 1.3%). Half of all victims of violence in the U.S. are under age 25; 29% percent of all forcible rapes occur before the age of eleven. Among U.S. adolescents aged 12–17, 8% are estimated to have been victims of serious sexual assault; 17% to be victims of serious physical assault; and 40% have witnessed serious violence (Kilpatrick et al., 2000). Twenty-two percent of rapes are perpetrated by strangers, whereas husbands and boyfriends are responsible for 19% and other relatives account for 38%. Men sustain twice as many severe injuries than women. For women and children, but not for men, trauma that results from violence within intimate relationships is a much more serious problem than traumatic events inflicted by strangers or accidents. In 1994, 62% of almost 3 million attacks on American women were made by persons whom they knew, while 63% of the almost 4 million assaults on males were perpetrated by strangers. Four of five assaults on children are at the hands of their own parents. Over a third of the victims of domestic assault experience serious injury, compared to a quarter of victims of stranger assault (van der Kolk, 2000). This illustrates that an assault by someone "known" is not less prevalent than assault by a stranger. Domestic and child abuse are closely related; in homes where spousal abuse occurs, children are abused at a rate 1500% higher than the national average (National Victim Center, 1993).

Many people who are traumatized by horrendous events do not seem to develop lasting effects. The most common effects of traumatization are included in the symptom picture described in the diagnosis of PTSD. However, depression, increased aggression against oneself and others, depersonalization, dissociation, compulsive behavioral repetition of traumatic scenarios, as well as a decline in family and occupational functioning, may occur without these victims meeting full-blown criteria for PTSD. The most common causes of PTSD in men are combat and witnessing of death or severe injury, while sexual molestation and rape are the most common causes of PTSD in women. The capacity of these events to produce PTSD varies significantly, ranging from 56% in patients who regain consciousness in the middle of surgical procedures, to 48.4% of female rape victims and 10.7% of men witnessing death or serious injury. Women have twice the risk of developing PTSD following a trauma than men do.

The Symptomatology of the Trauma Response

When people are faced with a life-threatening or other traumatic experience, they primarily focus on survival and self-protection. They experience a mixture of numbness, withdrawal, confusion, shock, and speechless terror. Some victims try to cope by taking action, while others dissociate. Neither response absolutely prevents the subsequent development of PTSD, though problem-focused coping reduces the chance of developing PTSD. Dissociation during a traumatic event is an important predictor of the development of subsequent PTSD (Shalev et al., 1995). The longer the traumatic experience lasts, the more likely the victim is to react with dissociation.

When the traumatic event is the result of an attack by a family member on whom victims depend for economic and other forms of security (as occurs in victims of intrafamilial abuse) victims are prone to respond to assaults with increased dependence and with paralysis in their decision-making processes. Thus, some aspects of how people respond to trauma are quite predictable—but individual, situational and social factors play a major role in the shaping the symptomatology.

Rape victims, children and women abused by male partners often develop long-term reactions which include fear, anxiety, fatigue, sleeping and eating disturbances, intense startle reactions, and physical complaints. They often continue to dissociate in the face of threat, suffer from profound feelings of helplessness, and have difficulty planning effective action. This makes them vulnerable to develop "emotion focused coping," a style in which the goal is to alter one's emotional state, rather than the circumstances which give rise to those emotional states. This emotion-focused coping strategy accounts for these victims' vulnerability with regard to developing problems of alcohol and substance abuse. Between 25% and 50% of all patients who seek substance-abuse treatment also suffer from a comorbid PTSD diagnosis. The relationship between substance abuse and PTSD is reciprocal: drug abuse leads to assault, and assault leads to substance use.

Diagnostic Issues

In 1980, the diagnosis of PTSD was constructed for inclusion in the third edition of the *Diagnostic and Statistical Manual of Mental Disorders* (*DSM III;* American Psychiatric Association, 1980) to capture the psychopathology associated with traumatization in adults. Over the years, numerous studies have demonstrated that the diagnostic construct of PTSD is clinically relevant to individuals who have suffered single incident traumas such as rape, physical assaults torture, and motor vehicle accidents. However, it has also has become clear that in clinical settings most treatment-seeking patients have been exposed to a range of different traumatic events over their lifespan, and suffer from a variety of psychological problems—only some of which are covered in the definition of PTSD. These include affect dysregulation, aggression against self and others, amnesia and dissociation, somatization, depression, distrust, shame, and self-hatred. These other problems can either be conceptualized as co-morbid conditions, or as part of a spectrum of trauma-related problems that occur depending on the age at which the trauma occurred, the relationship to the individual or situation responsible for the trauma, social support received, and the duration of the traumatic experience(s).

The diagnosis of PTSD is characterized by three major elements:

(1) *The repeated reliving of memories of the traumatic experience.* This tends to involve intense sensory and visual memories of the event often accompanied by extreme physiological and psychological distress, and sometimes by a feeling of emotional numbing, during which usually there is no physiological arousal. These intrusive memories may occur spontaneously, or can be triggered by a range of real and symbolic stimuli.

(2) *Avoidance of reminders of the trauma, and the numbing, detachment, and emotional blunting that often coexist with intrusive recollections.* This is associated with an inability to experience joy and pleasure, and with a general withdrawal from engagement with life. Over time, these features may become the dominant symptoms of PTSD.

(3) The third element of PTSD consists of a pattern of increased arousal, expressed by hypervigilance, irritability, memory and concentration problems, sleep disturbances, and an exaggerated startle response. In the more chronic forms of the disorder, this pattern of hyperarousal as well as the avoidance described in number (1), may be the dominant clinical features. Hyperarousal causes traumatized people to become easily distressed by unexpected stimuli. Their tendency to be triggered into reliving traumatic memories illustrates how their perceptions have become excessively focused on the involuntary search the similarities between the present and their traumatic past. As a consequence, many neutral experiences become reinterpreted as being associated with the traumatic past.

Secondary Effects of Developing PTSD

Once people develop PTSD, the recurrent, unbidden reliving of the trauma in visual images, emotional states, or in nightmares produces a constant re-exposure to the terror of the trauma. In contrast to the actual trauma, which had a beginning a middle, and an end, the symptoms of PTSD take on a timeless character. The traumatic intrusions are horrifying; they interfere with dealing with the past, while distracting from being able to attend to the present. This unpredictable exposure to unbidden memories of the trauma usually leads to a variety of (usually maladaptive) avoidance maneuvers, ranging from avoidance of people or actions that remind them of the trauma, to drug and alcohol abuse, to emotional withdrawal from friends or activities that used to provide potential sources of solace. Problems with attention and concentration keep them from being engaged with their surroundings with zest and energy. Uncomplicated activities like reading, conversing with others, and watching television require extra effort. This loss of ability to focus, in turn, often leads to problems with taking one thing at a time and gets in the way of reorganizing one's life to get it back on track.

Disorders of Extreme Stress (DESNOS)

The DSM IV Field trial (van der Kolk et al., 1996) demonstrated that it was not the prevalence of PTSD symptoms themselves, but depression, outbursts of anger, self-destructive behaviors, and feelings of shame, self-blame and distrust that distinguished a treatment-seeking sample from a nontreatment-seeking community sample with PTSD. The majority of people who seek treatment for trauma-related problems have histories of multiple traumas. One recent treatment-seeking sample (van der Kolk, 2000) suffered from a variety of other psychological problems which in most cases were the chief presenting complaints, in addition to their PTSD symptoms: 77% suffered from behavioral impulsivity, affective lability, and aggression against self and others; 84% suffered from depersonalization and other dissociative symptoms; 75% were plagued by chronic feelings of shame, self-blame and being permanently damaged, and 83% complained of being unable to negotiate satisfactory relationships with others. These problems contribute significantly to impairment and disability above and beyond the PTSD symptoms (Green et al., 1992, Davidson et al., 1991, Kulka et al., 1990). Focusing exclusively either on PTSD or on the depression, dissociation and character pathology prevents adequate assessment and treatment of traumatized populations.

As part of the DSM IV field trial, members of the PTSD taskforce delineated a syndrome of psychological problems which have been shown to be frequently associated with histories of prolonged and severe personal abuse. They called this *Complex PTSD*, or *Disorders of Extreme Stress Not Otherwise Specified* (DESNOS) (Herman, 1992, van der Kolk et al., 1996). DESNOS delineated a complex of symptoms associated with early interpersonal trauma:

(1) alterations in the regulation of affective impulses, including difficulty with modulation of anger and being self destructive,

(2) alterations in attention and consciousness, leading to amnesias and dissociative and depersonalization, episodes,

(3) alterations in self perception, such as a chronic sense of guilt and responsibility, and chronically feeling ashamed,

(4) alterations in relationships with others, such as not being able to trust and not being able to feel intimate with people,

(5) somatization the problem: feeling symptoms on a somatic level, when medical explanations can be found, and

(6) alterations in systems of meaning. These now are listed in the DSM under "associated features of PTSD."

The DSM IV Field Trial of PTSD found that DESNOS had a high construct validity (Pelcovitz, 1998). The earlier the onset of the trauma and the longer the duration, the more likely people were to suffer from a high degree of all the symptoms that comprise the DESNOS diagnosis (Roth et al., 1997; van der Kolk et al., 1996, Ford, 1999; Ford & Kidd, 1998). These studies showed that interpersonal trauma, especially childhood abuse, predicts a high risk for developing DESNOS. Patients with DESNOS are high utilizers of crisis psychiatric care (Ford, 1999) and are usually refractory to conventional PTSD treatment (Ford & Kidd, 1998). Recent studies (McDonagh-Coyle & Ford, 1999) showed that these patients may react adversely to current, standard PTSD treatments, and that effective treatment needs to focus on self-regulatory deficits rather than "processing the trauma."

PTSD has become a common diagnosis for people who become patients in psychiatric hospitals. An examination of the records of the 384,000 Medicaid recipients in Massachusetts between 1997 and 1998 (Macy et al., 1998) revealed that PTSD, together with depression, was the most common psychiatric diagnosis. However, patients with a PTSD diagnosis spent 10 times as much time in the hospital than patients with the diagnosis of depression only. It is inconceivable that the 22,800 Medicaid recipients in Massachusetts who were admitted to psychiatric hospitals and diagnosed with PTSD were admitted following a one–time traumatic incident, such as a rape or a motor vehicle accident. Most likely, the patients suffered from a complex constellations of symptoms. However, because the long-term psychiatric impact of chronic, multiple traumas, receives the same diagnosis (PTSD) as the effects of a one-time incident, this diagnosis fails to capture the complexity of both the psychiatric problems resulting from PTSD, and the treatment thereof.

Historical Background

Awareness of the role of psychological trauma as a contributory factor in psychiatric disturbances waxed and waned throughout the previous century. The study of the traumatic origins of emotional distress began during the last decades of the 19th century. At the Hôpital du Salpêtrière in Paris, Charcot (1887) first proposed that the symptoms of what was then called "hysterical" patients had their origins in histories of trauma. In his first four books, Charcot's student Janet described 591 patients, 257 of whom had a traumatic origin of their psychopathology (Crocq & Le Verbizier, 1989). Janet was the first to propose that during traumatic events, people experience "vehement emotions" that interfere with the integration of the overwhelming physical experience. Instead, the traumatic memories (and the actions related to them) are split off (dissociated) from everyday consciousness and from voluntary control: "they are unable to make the recital which we call narrative memory, and yet they remain confronted by (the) difficult situation" (Janet 1919/1925, p. 661). He described how the memories of these traumas tended to return, not as stories of what had happened, but as re-enactments in the form of intense emotional reactions, aggressive behavior, physical pain, and bodily states that could all be understood as the return of elements of the traumatic experience.

Janet first observed that traumatized patients seemed to react to reminders of the trauma with responses that were relevant to the original threat, but that currently had no adaptive value. On exposure to reminders, the trauma was reactivated in the form of images, feelings, and physical sensations related to the trauma (Janet, 1889/1973). He proposed that when patients fail to integrate the traumatic experience into the totality of their personal awareness, they seem to develop problems assimilating new experiences, as well. "It is as if their personalities had definitely stopped at a certain point, and could not enlarge any more by the addition or assimilation of new elements" (Janet 1911, p. 532). And "all [traumatized] patients seem to have had the evolution of their lives checked; they are attached to an insurmountable obstacle" (Janet, 1919/1925, p. 660). Janet proposed that the efforts to keep the fragmented traumatic memories out of conscious awareness eroded the psychological energy of these patients. This, in turn, interfered with the capacity to engage in focused action and to learn from experience. Unless the dissociated elements of the trauma were integrated into personal consciousness, the patient was likely to experience a slow decline in personal and occupational functioning (van der Kolk & van der Hart, 1989).

As a young physician, during the 1880s, Freud did two clinical rotations at the Salpêtrière. Upon return to Vienna, he attached himself to an older internist, Breuer, with whom he started to carefully study the symptoms of "hysterical" patients and the origins of their symptoms, which often were characterized by marked moto and sensory abnormalities. They summarized their first set of findings in a 1893 paper entitled, "On the Physical Mechanisms of Hysterical Phenomena" (Breuer & Freud, 1893–1895/1955). Because their observations were so astute, it is useful to quote part of their account:

> The .. memory of the trauma . . . acts like a foreign body which long after its entry must be regarded as an agent that is still at work.
>
> At first sight it seems extraordinary that events experienced so long ago should continue to operate so intensely—that their recollection should not be liable to the wearing away process to which, after all, we see all our memories succumb. The following considerations may perhaps make this a little more intelligible.
>
> The fading of a memory or the losing of its affect depends on various factors. The most important of these is *whether there has been an energetic reaction to the event that provokes an affect.* By "reaction" we understand the whole class of voluntary and involuntary reflexes . . . in which . . . the affects are discharged. If this reaction takes place to a sufficient amount a large part of the affect disappears as a result. . . If a reaction is suppressed the affect stays attached to the memory. . . . The injured person's reaction to the trauma only exercises a complete "cathartic" effect if it is an adequate reaction—as, for instance, revenge. But language serves as a substitute for action: with its help, an affect can be 'abreacted' almost as effectively. . . . If there is no such reaction, in either deeds or words, any recollection of the event retains its affective tone to begin with.
>
> "Abreaction," however, is not the only method of dealing with the situation that is open to a normal person who has experienced a psychical trauma. A memory of such a trauma, even if it has not been abreacted, enters the great complex of associations, it comes alongside other experiences, which may contradict it, and is subjected to rectification by other ideas. . . . In this way a normal person is able to bring about the disappearance of the accompanying affect through the process of association. . . .
>
> We must, however, mention another remarkable fact . . . namely, that these memories, unlike the memories of the rest of their lives, are not at the patients' disposal. On the contrary, *these experiences are completely absent from the patient's memory when they are in a normal psychical state, or are only present in a highly summary form . . . .*
>
> *It may therefore be said that the ideas which have become pathological have persisted with such freshness and affective strength because they have been denied the normal wearing-away*

processes by means of abreaction and reproduction in states of unhibited association. (1893, pp. 7–11)

Every contemporary study of traumatic memories has essentially corroborated Janet's and Freud's initial observations that traumatic memories persist primarily as implicit, behavioral and somatic memories, and only secondarily as vague, overgeneral, fragmented, incomplete, and disorganized narratives. Previous work by Foa (1995) and ourselves (Hopper & van der Kolk, 2000, this volume) suggest that these memories change as people recover from their PTSD.

Over time, Freud came to disbelieve the reality of his patients' tales of trauma. In his *Autobiographical Study* he wrote "I believed these stories and consequently supposed that I had discovered the roots of the subsequent neurosis. . . . If the reader feels inclined to shake his head at my credulity, I cannot altogether blame him. . . . I was at last obliged to recognize that these scenes of seduction had never taken place, and that they were only fantasies which my patients had made up . . ." (1925/1959 p. 34). However, like Janet before him, Freud kept being fascinated with the issue of patients' apparent compulsion to arrange their lives in such a way that they would repeat their trauma over and over again. Freud (1925/1959) proposed that the compulsion to repeat was a function of repression: because the memory is repressed, the patient "repeats the repressed material as a contemporary experience," rather than locating it in the past.

In "Beyond the Pleasure Principle" (1920/1955) Freud described how patients suffering from traumatic neuroses often experienced a lack of conscious preoccupation with the memories of their accident. He postulated that "perhaps they are more concerned with NOT thinking of it." Yet, it appeared that Freud also was concerned with not thinking about the horrible real life experiences that can destroy people's capacity to function. He did so by focusing on his patients' intrapsychic reality: interest in personal meaning making crowded out interest in the external reality that had given rise to these meaning systems. Psychiatry, as a discipline, came to follow Freud in his explorations of how the normal human psyche functioned: Real-life trauma was ignored in favor of fantasy.

Little attention was paid to further exploration of "traumatic neuroses" until the outbreak of the Second World War, when Kardiner wrote of his experiences treating World War I veterans in "The Traumatic Neuroses of War" (1941). In this book, he emphasized the psychobiological nature of traumatic stress. He noted that sufferers of "traumatic neuroses" develop an enduring vigilance for and a sensitivity to environmental threat, and stated that "the nucleus of the neurosis is a *physioneurosis*. This is present on the battlefield and during the entire process of organization; it outlives every intermediary accommodative device, and persists in the chronic forms. The traumatic syndrome is ever present and unchanged." He described extreme physiological arousal in these patients; they suffered from sensitivity to temperature, pain, and sudden tactile stimuli: "These patients cannot stand being slapped on the back abruptly; they cannot tolerate a misstep or a stumble. From a physiologic point of view there exists a lowering of the threshold of stimulation; and, from a psychological point of view a state of readiness for fright reactions" (p. 95). Central in Kardiner's thinking, as it had been for Janet and Freud, is that fact that: "[t]he subject acts as if the original traumatic situation were still in existence and engages in protective devices which failed on the original occasion. This means in effect that his conception of the outer world and his conception of himself have been permanently altered" (p. 82).

At the end of the Second World War, Kardiner (Kardiner & Spiegel, 1946) lamented that "these conditions [traumatic neuroses] are not subject to continuous study . . . but only to periodic efforts which cannot be characterized as very diligent. Though not true in psychiatry generally, it is a deplorable fact that each investigator who undertakes to study [traumatic neuroses] considers it his sacred obligation to start from scratch and work at the problem as if no one has ever done anything with it before." This proved true for the subsequent 30 years, until the issue of traumatic neuroses was rediscovered in the wake of the Vietnam War and the emergence of the women's movement. When the importance of trauma was rediscovered, starting around 1978, many of the early formulations that had long since been forgotten proved to be remarkably accurate. However, progress in understanding the function of attachment in shaping the individual and rapid developments in the neurosciences gave a new shape to these old insights.

The Psychobiology of Trauma

During the past two decades, important advances have been made in the understanding the nature and treatment of PTSD. Probably the most important progress has been in the area of understanding the neurobiological underpinnings and in the area of treatment. Modern research has come to elucidate the degree to which PTSD is, indeed, a "physioneurosis," a mental disorder based on the persistence of biological emergency responses.

To understand how trauma affects psychobiological activity, it is useful to briefly revisit some basic tenets of neurobiology. McLean (1990) defined the brain as a detecting, amplifying, and analyzing device for maintaining us in our internal and external environment. These functions range from the visceral regulation of oxygen intake and temperature balance to the categorization of incoming information necessary for making complex, long-term decisions affecting both individual and social systems. In the course of evolution, the human brain has developed three interdependent subanalyzers, each with different anatomical and neurochemical substrates:

(1) the brain stem and hypothalamus, which are primarily associated with the regulation of internal homeostasis,
(2) the limbic system, which is charged with maintaining the balance between the internal world and external reality, and
(3) the neocortex, which is responsible for analyzing and interacting with the external world.

It is generally thought that the circuitry of the brain stem and hypothalamus is most innate and stable, that the limbic system contains both innate circuitry and circuitry modifiable by experience, and that the structure of the neocortex is most affected by environmental input (Damasio, 1995). If that is true, trauma would be expected to leave its most profound changes on neocortical functions, and least affect basic regulatory functions. However, while this may be true for the ordinary stress response, trauma—stress that overwhelms the organism—seems to affect people over a wide range of biological functioning, involving a large variety of brain structures and neurotransmitter systems.

The Interrelation Between Regulatory Functions

The brain stem, hypothalamus, limbic system, and the neocortex in concert monitor relations with the outside world and assess what is new, dangerous, or gratifying. To accomplish this assessment, the brain needs to take in new sensory information, categorize its importance, and integrate it with previously stored knowledge. Most importantly, it needs to determine what is significant, and filter out irrelevant information. After the meaning of an incoming signal has been categorized, the brain (usually unconsciously) needs to "formulate" an appropriate plan of action, while attending to both short-term and long-term consequences. This evaluation then needs to lead to the initiation of an appropriate response, which needs to be terminated once the challenge is gone (Panksepp, 1998; Damasio, 1996). Moreover, in order to remain in a state of relative stability, people need to learn to engage in sustained activities without being distracted by irrelevant stimuli.

The organism needs to learn from experience and to be able to entertain a range of alternatives without becoming disorganized, or acting upon them. In order to do this, they need to learn to discriminate relevant from irrelevant stimuli, and to only select what is appropriate for achieving one's goals. Much evolution of the human brain has consisted of developing the capacity to form highly complex mental images and collaborative social relationships that allow complex thought in the context of social systems. For this to be successful, the organism needs to integrate its own immediate self-interest with a capacity to adhere to complex social rules (Donald, 1991). People with PTSD usually have serious problems carrying out a host of these functions. The degree of impairment is determined not only by the severity of their PTSD symptomatology, but also by the age at which the trauma occurred, the length of time that the traumatic event lasted, and the degree of social support that the individual received.

A century ago, James noted that the power of one's intellect is determined by one's perceptual processing style. The ability to comprehend (i.e., grasp, hold together, take hold of—from the Latin *cum-prendere*) depends on stimulus sampling and the formation of schematic representations of reality (Pribram, 1987). There seem to be qualitatively significant differences between the ways people with PTSD sample and categorize experience, and the ways in which non-traumatized people do (van der Kolk & Ducey, 1989, McFarlane et al., 1993). Failure to *com-prehend* the experience (i.e., to dissociate) plays a critical role in making a stressful experience traumatic (van der Kolk, van der Hart, & Marmar, 1996).

The Apparent Uniqueness of Traumatic Memories

A century of study of traumatic memories shows that

(1) they are primarily imprinted in sensory and emotional modes, although a semantic representation of the memory may co-exist with sensory flashbacks (van der Kolk & Fisler, 1995);

(2) these sensory experiences often remain stable over time and unaltered by other life experiences (Janet, 1893; van der Kolk & van der Hart, 1991),

(3) they may return, triggered by reminders, at any time during a person's life, with a vividness as if the subject is having the experience all over again (DSM IV),

(4) these sensory imprints tend to occur in a mental state in which victims may be unable to precisely articulate what they are feeling and thinking (Rivers, 1918; Blank, 1985).

While transformation of memories of day-to-day experiences is the norm, the flashbacks and other sensory reexperiences of PTSD seem not to be updated or attached to other experiences. Triggered by a reminder, the past can be relived with an immediate sensory and emotional intensity that makes victims feel as if the event were occurring all over again. Patients with PTSD seem to remain embedded in their trauma as a contemporary experience and often become "fixated on the trauma" (Kardiner, 1941). While most patients with PTSD construct a narrative of their trauma over time, it is characteristic of PTSD that sensory elements of the trauma itself continue to intrude as flashbacks and nightmares, altered states of consciousness in which the trauma is relived, unintegrated with an overall sense of self. Because traumatic memories are so fragmented, it seems reasonable to postulate that extreme emotional arousal leads to a failure of the central nervous system (CNS) to synthesize the sensations related to the trauma into an integrated whole.

The availability of neuroimaging studies of patients with PTSD has provided an opportunity to determine which brain structures are affected by traumatic experiences and hence, how these structures are mobilized differently in response to traumatic reminders, compared with their response to neutral stimuli. This has facilitated a rapid increase in our understanding of the potential mechanisms of PTSD, and promoted the exploration of new therapeutic techniques.

Psychophysiological Effects of Trauma

One of the principal contributions of the trauma research to psychiatry has been the clarification that the development of a chronic trauma-based disorder is qualitatively different from a simple exaggeration of the normal stress response (Yehuda & McFarlane, 1996). It also has become clear that PTSD is not an issue of simple conditioning: Many people who do not suffer from PTSD, but who have been exposed to an extreme stressor, will again become distressed when they are again confronted with the tragedy. Pitman (Pitman et al., 1993) has pointed out that the critical issue in PTSD is that the stimuli that cause people to overreact may not be conditional enough; a variety of triggers not directly related to the traumatic experience may come to precipitate extreme reactions.

Abnormal psychophysiological reactions in PTSD occur on two very different levels: (1) in response to specific reminders of the trauma, and (2) in response to intense, but neutral stimuli, such as loud noises—signifying a loss of stimulus discrimination.

Conditional Responses to Specific Stimuli

PTSD sufferers experience heightened physiological arousal in response to sounds, images, and thoughts related to specific traumatic incidents. A large number of studies has confirmed that people with PTSD, but not controls who did not develop PTSD, respond to such reminders with significant increases in heart rate, skin conductance, and blood pressure (Dobbs & Wilson, 1960; Blanchard et al., 1986; Pitman et al., 1987). The highly elevated autonomic responses to reminders of traumatic experiences that happened years, and sometimes decades ago, illustrate the intensity and timelessness with which these memories continue to affect current experience (Pitman et al., 1993). Post and colleagues (1992) have demonstrated that life events play a critical role in the first episodes of major affective disorders, but become less pertinent in precipitating subsequent occurrences. This capacity of triggers with diminishing strength to produce the same response over time is termed "kindling."

Medications that decrease autonomic arousal, such a β-adrenergic blockers and benzodiazepines, tend to decrease traumatic intrusions, while drugs that stimulate autonomic arousal may precipitate visual images and affect states associated with prior traumatic experiences in people with PTSD, but not in controls. For example, in patients with PTSD, the injection of drugs such as lactate (Rainey et al., 1987; Jensen, 1998) and yohimbine (Southwick et al., 1993) tend to precipitate panic attacks, flashbacks (exact reliving experiences) of earlier trauma, or both. In our own laboratory, approximately 20% of PTSD subjects responded with a flashback of a traumatic experience when they were presented with acoustic startle stimuli.

Hyperarousal to Intense, but Neutral Stimuli.
Loss of Stimulus Discrimination

Excessive stimulation of the CNS at the time of the trauma may result in permanent neuronal changes that have a negative effect on learning, habituation, and stimulus discrimination. These neuronal changes do not depend on actual exposure to reminders of the trauma for expression. The abnormal startle response (ASR) characteristic of PTSD (American Psychiatric Association, 1993) is one example of this phenomenon. Several studies have demonstrated abnormalities in habituation to the ASR in PTSD (Shalev et al., 1993; Ornitz & Pynoos, 1989). Interestingly, people who previously met criteria for PTSD, but no longer do so, continue to show failure of habituation of the ASR (van der Kolk et al., unpublished data; Pitman et al., unpublished data).

The failure to habituate to acoustic startle suggests that traumatized people have difficulty evaluating sensory stimuli, and mobilizing appropriate levels of physiological arousal (Shalev & Rogel-Fuchs, 1993). Thus, the problems that people with PTSD have with properly integrating memories of the trauma and getting mired in continuously reliving of the past, is mirrored physiologically in the misinterpretation of innocuous stimuli as potential threats. To compensate, these people tend to shut down. However, the price for shutting down is decreased involvement in ordinary, everyday life.

The Hormonal Response in Post Traumatic Stress Disorder

In well-functioning people, stress produces rapid and pronounced hormonal responses. However, chronic and persistent stress inhibits the effectiveness of the stress response and induces desensitization (Axelrod, 1984). PTSD develops following exposure to events that overwhelm the individual's capacity to re-establish homeostasis. Instead of returning to baseline, there is a progressive kindling of the individual's stress response. Initially, only intense stress is accompanied by the release of endogenous, stress-responsive neurohormones such as cortisol, epinephrine, and norepinephrine (NE), vasopressin, oxytocin and endogenous opioids. In PTSD, even minor reminders of the trauma may precipitate a full-blown neuroendocrine stress reaction: It permanently alters how an organism deals with its environment on a day-to-day basis, and it interferes with how it copes with subsequent acute stress.

While acute stress activates the HPA axis and increases glucocorticoid levels, organisms adapt to chronic stress by activating a negative feedback loop. Counterintuitively, people with PTSD have low levels of serum cortisol. In a study by Resnick and colleagues (1998), the investigators collected blood samples from 20 acute rape victims and measured their cortisol response in the emergency room. Three months later, a prior trauma history was taken, and the subjects were evaluated for the presence of PTSD. Victims with a prior history of sexual abuse were significantly more likely to have developed PTSD three months following the rape than rape victims who did not develop PTSD. Cortisol levels shortly after the rape were correlated with histories of prior assaults: the mean initial cortisol level of individuals with a prior assault history was 15 μg/dl, compared to 30 μg/dl in individuals without such a history. These findings can be interpreted to mean either that prior exposure to traumatic events results in a blunted cortisol response to subsequent trauma, or in a quicker return of cortisol to baseline following stress.

These results show that cortisol basically functions as an "anti-stress" hormone: It shuts off the other biological reactions that were initiated by the stress response. Simultaneous activation of catecholamines and glucocorticoids stimulates active coping behaviors, while increased arousal in the presence of low glucocorticoid levels would provoke undifferentiated fight or flight reactions.

Trauma and the Central Nervous System

The Disintegration of Experience

In a series of studies we have demonstrated that traumatic memories initially have few narrative elements: When PTSD patients have their flashbacks, the trauma is relived as isolated sensory, emotional and motoric imprints of the trauma, without a storyline. We have shown this in victims of childhood abuse (van der Kolk & Fisler, 1995), assaults and accidents in adulthood (van der Kolk, Burbridge, & Suzuki, 1997), and in patients who gained awareness during surgical procedures (van der Kolk, Hopper, & Osterman, 2001). These studies support Janet's 1889 observations and confirm the notion that what makes memories traumatic is a failure of the CNS to synthesize the sensations related to the traumatic memory into an integrated semantic memory. Sensory elements of the experience are registered separately and are often retrieved without the patient appreciating the context to which this sensation or emotion refers.

These observations lead to the notion that in PTSD, the brain's natural ability to integrate experience breaks down. A variety of CNS structures have been implicated in these integrative processes:

(1) the parietal lobes are thought to integrate information between different cortical association areas (Damasio, 1989),

(2) the hippocampus is thought to create a cognitive map that allows for the categorization of experience, and its connection with other autobiographical information (O'Keefe & Nadel, 1978),

(3) the corpus callosum allows for the transfer of information from both hemispheres (Joseph, 1988), integrating emotional and cognitive aspects of the experience,

(4) the cingulate gyrus is thought to play a role of both amplifier and filter that help to integrate the emotional and cognitive components of the mind (Devinsky et al., 1995), and

(5) the dorsolateral frontal cortex, which is where sensations and impulses are "held in mind" and compared with previous information to plan appropriate actions.

The frontal lobes, in general, are thought to function as a "supervisory system" for the integration of experience (Shallice, 1988). Recent neuroimaging studies of patients with PTSD have suggested a role for most of these structures in the neurobiology of PTSD.

Neuroimaging Studies in PTSD

As of 1999, there have been seven published studies utilizing neuroimaging of patients with PTSD (Rauch et al., 1996; Gurvits et al., 1998; Bremner et al., 1995, 1999; Stein et al., 1996; Liberson, 1999; Shin et al., 1999). Four studies have used MRI to measure hippocampal volume in individuals with PTSD and three studies have used positron emission tomography (PET) (Rauch et al., 1996; Shin et al., 1999; Bremner, 1999) to measure differential activation of the CNS in response to traumatic and nontraumatic scripts in patients with PTSD.

Hippocampal Volume

Three different studies have shown that people with chronic PTSD have decreased hippocampal volumes, ranging from 8% (Bremner et al., 1995, Stein, 1997) to 26% (Gurvits et al., 1998). The fact that the only prospective study of acutely traumatized individuals, (Shalev, personal communication, 1999) failed to identify correlation between hippocampal volume and PTSD severity, suggesting that this hippocampal shrinkage is a function of chronicity. Recent research suggests that the hippocampal changes may not be irreversible. (McEwen, 1999; Starkman & Cushing, 1999). In animals, decreased hippocampal functioning has been shown to cause behavioral disinhibition (Gray, 1982) and makes animals more likely to define incoming stimuli as emergencies and react with fight or flight responses. If the same is true for humans, this might contribute to the problems of PTSD patients with "taking in" and processing arousing information, and to learn from such experiences. The decreased size of the hippocampus might play a role in the ongoing dissociation and misinterpretation of information in the direction of threat. Their altered biology would make them vulnerable to react to newly arousing stimuli as a threat, and to react with aggression, or withdrawal, depending on their premorbid personality (Ademac et al., 1991).

Symptom Provocation Studies

Rauch, van der Kolk and colleagues conducted a PET scan study in which patients with PTSD were exposed to vivid, detailed narratives of their own traumatic experiences (Rauch et al., 1996). During exposure to the script of their traumatic experiences, these subjects demonstrated heightened activity only in the right hemisphere—specifically, in the areas that are most involved in emotional arousal: the amygdala, the insula, and the medial temporal lobe. During exposure to their traumatic scripts there was a significant decrease in activation of the left inferior frontal lobe: Broca's area, which is thought to be responsible for translating personal experiences into communicable language. A study by Shin and colleagues (1999), utilizing a slightly different paradigm, essentially confirmed these findings in a different trauma population. In another study, Lanius and colleagues (submitted) exposed six subjects with PTSD and six controls to a traumatic script, measuring their responses with MRI scans. This investigator consistently found decreased activation of the thalamus and the dorsolateral prefrontal cortex in PTSD patients during exposure to their trauma scripts.

These early neuroimaging studies of patients with PTSD present us with a range of surprising findings which force us to re-evaluate our previous concepts of the pathophysiology of PTSD. Of the various findings, increased activation of the amygdala in response to traumatic scripts is the least surprising. After all, it has been well established that the amygdala is centrally involved in the interpretation of the emotional valence of incoming information, and that confrontation with feared stimuli activates the amygdala and related structures (LeDoux, 1992). Exposure to traumatic scripts frequently provokes autonomic activation of patients with PTSD (e.g., Pitman et al., 1987; Keane, 1998), and this is likely mediated by activation of the amygdala and related structures. It is well-understood that the information evaluated by the amygdala is passed on to areas in the brain stem that control autonomic and neurohormonal response systems. By way of these connections, the amygdala transforms sensory stimuli into emotional and hormonal signals, thereby initiating and controlling emotional responses.

High level stimulation of the amygdala can also interfere with hippocampal functioning (Ademac, 1991; Squire & Zola-Morgan, 1991). Thus, extreme emotional arousal may prevent the proper evaluation and categorization of experience by interfering with hippocampal functions. It is possible that, when this occurs, sensory imprints of experience are stored in memory; however, because the hippocampus is prevented from fulfilling its integrative function, these various imprints are not combined into a unified whole (van der Kolk, 1994). The experience is laid down, and later retrieved as iso-lated images, bodily sensations, and smells, and sounds that feel alien and separate from other life experiences. Decreased hippocampal functioning is likely to interfere with the localization of incoming information in time and space, and to cause continued fragmentation of experience. The recent find-ings of decreased dorsolateral frontal cortex activation would further provide a neurobiological explanation of why people with PTSD plunge into re-experiencing their trauma with limited consciousness; they are simply remem-bering elements of experiences belonging to the past. In our pilot study, using single-photon emission tomographty (SPECT) as an outcome measure of eye movement desensitization and reprocessing (EMDR) treatment subjects had increased activation of the dorsolateral prefrontal cortex following effective treatment.

Hemispheric Lateralization

The finding of hemispheric lateralization in subjects exposed to their personal-ized trauma scripts indicates that there is differential hemispheric involvement in the processing of traumatic memories. This may have important implica-tions for understanding the nature of PTSD. The right hemisphere, which developmentally comes "on-line" earlier than the left hemisphere, is involved in the expression and comprehension of global non-verbal emotional commu-nication (i.e., tone of voice, facial expression, visual/spatial communication), and allows for a dynamic and holistic integration across sensory modalities (Davidson, 1989). This hemisphere is particularly integrated with the amyg-dala, which assigns emotional significance to incoming stimuli and helps to regulate the autonomic and hormonal responses to that information. While it is exquisitely sensitive to emotional nuances, it has, at best, a rudimentary capacity to think or communicate analytically, to employ syntax, or to reason (Henninger, 1992; Davidson, 1989).

   In contrast, the left hemisphere, which mediates verbal communication and organizes problem-solving tasks into a well-ordered set of operations and pro-cesses information in a sequential fashion (Davidson, 1989), seems to be less active in PTSD. It is in the area of categorization and labeling of internal states that people with PTSD seem to have particular problems (Krystal, 1978; van der Kolk, McFarlane, & Weisaeth, 1996). It is conceivable that failure of left hemi-sphere function during states of extreme arousal is responsible for the derealiza-tion and depersonalization reported in acute PTSD (Marmar et al., 1995; Shalev et al., 1996).

New Directions for Treatment

For over a century it has been understood that traumatic experiences can leave indelible emotional memories. Contemporary studies of how the amygdala is activated by extreme experiences dovetail with the laboratory observation that "emotional memory may be forever" (LeDoux et al., 1991). The accumulated body of research suggests that patients with PTSD suffer from impaired cortical control over subcortical areas responsible for learning, habituation, and stimulus discrimination. The concept of indelible subcortical emotional responses, held in check to varying degrees by cortical and hippocampal activity, has led to the speculation that delayed onset PTSD may be the expression of subcortically mediated emotional responses that escape cortical, and possibly hippocampal, inhibitory control (van der Kolk & van der Hart, 1991; Pitman et al., 1993; Shalev et al., 1992).

The early neuroimaging studies of PTSD showed that, during exposure to a traumatic script, there was decreased Broca's area functioning and increased activation of the right hemisphere. This would imply that it is difficult for traumatized individuals to verbalize precisely what they are experiencing, particularly when they become emotionally aroused. They may experience physiological arousal, and fragments of memories may be activated, but they often seem to be too hyper- or hypo-aroused to be able to "process" and communicate what they are experiencing. A relative decrease in left hemispheric representation provides an explanation of why traumatic memories are experienced as timeless and ego-alien: The part of the brain necessary for generating sequences and for the cognitive analysis of experience is not functioning properly. Our research (Rauch et al., 1996) can be interpreted as showing that during activation of a traumatic memory, the brain is "having" its experience. The person may feel, see, or hear the sensory elements of the traumatic experience, but he or she may be physiologically prevented from being able to translate this experience into communicable language. When they are having their traumatic recall, victims may suffer from speechless terror in which they may be literally "out of touch with their feelings." Physiologically, they may respond as if they are being traumatized again. Particularly when a victims experience depersonalization and derealization they cannot "own" what is happening, and thus cannot take steps to do anything about it.

To help traumatized individuals process their traumatic memories, it is critical that they gain enough distance from their sensory imprints and trauma-related emotions so that they can observe and analyze these sensations and emotions without becoming hyperaroused or engaging in avoidance maneuvers. The selective serotonin reuptake inhibitors (SSRIs) seem to be able to accomplish exactly that. Studies in our laboratory have shown that SSRIs can help PTSD patients gain emotional distance from traumatic stimuli and make sense of their traumatic intrusions (van der Kolk et al., 1995). The apparently relative decrease in left hemisphere activation while re-experiencing the trauma suggests that it is important to help people with PTSD find a language in which they can come to understand and communicate their experiences. It is possible that some of the newer body-oriented therapies, dialectical behavior therapy, or EMDR may yield benefits that traditional insight-oriented therapies may lack.

To make meaning of the traumatic experience usually is not enough. Traumatized individuals need to have experiences that directly contradict the emotional helplessness and physical paralysis that accompany traumatic experiences. In many people with PTSD, such helplessness and paralysis becomes a habitual way of responding to stressful stimuli, further weakening their feelings of control over their destiny. The critical steps in treating PTSD can be summarized as follows (for more details see: van der Kolk, McFarlane, & van der Hart, 1996):

1. *Safety.* When people's own resources are inadequate to deal with threat, they need to rely on others to provide them with safety and care. After having been traumatized, is critical that the victim re-establish contact with his or her natural social support system. If this system is inadequate to ensure the safety of the patient, institutional resources need to be mobilized to help the patient find a place to recover.

2. *Anxiety management.* After the patient's safety has been assured, there may be a need for a variety of psychological interventions. They need to learn to *name* the problems they face, and learn to formulate appropriate solutions. Assault victims must learn to distinguish between the real life threats and the haunting, irrational fears which are part of PTSD. If anxiety dominates, victims need to be helped to strengthen their coping skills. Practical anxiety management skills training may include deep muscle relaxation, breathing control, role-playing, covert modeling, thought stopping, and guided self-dialogue.

3. *Emotional processing.* To put the event(s) in perspective, the victim needs to re-experience the event without feeling helpless. Traditionally, following Freud's notion (Breuer & Freud, 1893–1895/1955) that words can substitute for action to resolve a trauma, this has been done by helping people to talk about the entire experience. They are asked to articulate what they think happened, and what led up to it; their own contributions to what happened; their thoughts and fantasies during the

event; what was the worst part of it; and their reactions to the event in detail, including how it has affected their perceptions of themselves and others. Such exposure therapy is thought to promote symptom reduction by allowing patients to realize that: (a) remembering the trauma is not equivalent to experiencing it again; (b) that the experience had a beginning, a middle, and an end, and that the event now belongs to one's personal history.

In recent years, a variety of new techniques has been developed that have the potential of desensitizing patients with PTSD without fully engaging them in a verbal reliving of the traumatic experience. Of these treatments, EMDR has been best studied (Chemtob et al., 2000). Although traditional exposure therapy can be very helpful in overcoming traumatic intrusions, it needs to be applied with care. Some patients, on recalling their trauma, may become flooded with both the traumatic memories and memories of previously forgotten traumas. Increased activation of traumatic memories may be associated with increased shame, guilt, aggression, and increase in alcohol and drug use.

Conclusions

The rediscovery of trauma as an etiological factor in mental disorders is only about 20 years old. During this time there has been an explosion of knowledge about how experience shapes the CNS and the formation of the self. Developments in the neurosciences have started to make significant contributions to our understanding of how the brain is shaped by experience, and how life itself continues to transform the ways biology is organized. The study of trauma has probably been the single most fertile area within the disciplines of psychiatry and psychology in helping to develop a deeper understanding of the interrelationships among emotional, cognitive, social and biological forces that shape human development. Starting with PTSD in adults, but expanding into early attachment and coping with overwhelming experiences in childhood, our field has discovered how certain experiences can "set" psychological expectations and biological selectivity. Research in these areas has opened up entirely new insights into how extreme experiences throughout the lifecycle can have profound effects on memory, affect regulation, biological stress modulation, and interpersonal relatedions. These findings, in the context of the development of a range of new therapy approaches, are beginning to open up entirely new perspectives on how traumatized individuals can be helped to overcome their past.

References

Adamec, R. E. (1991). Individual differences in temporal lobe processing of threatening stimuli in the cat. *Physiology and Behavior, 49*(1), 455–464.

Ademac, R. E. (1991). The role of the temporal lobe in feline aggression and defense. *Psychological Record, 41*(1), 233–252.

American Psychiatric Association. (1980). *Diagnostic and statistical manual of mental disorders* (3rd edition). Washington, DC: Author.

American Psychiatric Association. (1994). *Diagnostic and statistical manual of mental disorders* (4th edition). Washington, DC: Author.

Axelrod, J., & Reisine, T. D. (1984). Stress hormones, their interaction and regulation. *Science, 224,* 452–459.

Blanchard, E. B., Kolb, L. C., & Gerardi, R. J. (1986). Cardiac response to relevant stimuli as an adjunctive tool for diagnosing post traumatic stress disorder in Vietnam veterans. *Behavior Therapy, 17,* 592–606.

Blank, A. A. (1985). The unconscious flashback to the war in Vietnam veterans: Clinical mystery, legal defense, and community problem. In S. M. Sonnenberg & J. A. Talbot (Eds.), *The trauma of war: Stress and recovery in Vietnam veterans* (pp. 293–308). Washington, DC: American Psychiatric Association.

Bremner, J., Narayan, M., Staib, L. H., Southwick, S. M., McGlashan, T. H., & Charney, D. S. (1999). Neural correlates of memories of childhood sexual abuse in women with and without posttraumatic stress disorder. *American Journal of 156*(11), 1787–1795.

Bremner, J. D., Randall, P., Scott, T. M., Bronen, R. A., Seibyl, J. P., Southwick, S. M., Delaney, R. C., McCarthy, G., Charney, D. S., & Innis, R. B. (1995). MRI-based measured of hippocampal volume in patients with PTSD. *American Journal of Psychiatry, 152,* 973–981.

Breuer, J., & Freud, S. (1955). Studies on hysteria. In J. Strachey (Ed. and Trans.), *The standard edition of the complete psychological works of Sigmund Freud* (Vol. 2, pp. 1–305). London: Hogarth Press. (Original work published 1893–1895)

Brown, G. L., Goodwin, F. K., & Ballenger, J. C., et al. (1979). Aggression in humans correlates with cerebrospinal fluid metabolites. *Psychiatry Resesearch, 1,* 131–139.

Cahill, L. (1997). The neurobiology of emotionally influenced memory: implications for understanding traumatic memory. *Annals of the New York Academy of Sciences, 821,* 238–246.

Charcot, J. M. (1887). *Leçons sur les maladies du système nerveux faites à la Salpetriere* [Lessons on the illnesses of the nervous system held at the Salpêtrière], Tome 3. Paris: Progrès Médical A. Delahaye & E. Lecrosnie.

Chemtob, C., Tolin, D., Pitman, R., & van der Kolk, B. A. (2000). Treatment of PTSD with EMDR. In E. Foa, M. J. Friedman, & T. Keane (Eds.), *Treatment guidelines for post traumatic stress disorder*. New York: Guilford Press.

Coccaro, E. F., Siever, L. J., Klar, H. M., & Maurer, G. (1989). Serotonergic studies in patients with affective and personality disorders. *Archives of General Psychiatry, 46,* 587–598.

Crocq, L., & De Verbizier, J. (1989). Le traumatisme psychologique dans l'oeuvre de Pierre Janet [Psychological trauma in the work of Pierre Janet]. *Annales Médico-Psychologiques, 147*(9), 983–987.

Damasio, A. (1989). Time-locked multiregional retroactivation: A systems-level proposal for the neural substrate of recall and recognition. *Cognition, 33*(1–2), 25–62.

Damasio, A. (1994). *Descartes' error: Emotion, reason, and the human brain*. New York: Grossett/Putnam.

Davidson, J., Smith, R., & Kudler, H. (1989). Familial psychiatric illness in chronic posttraumatic stress disorder. *Comprehensive Psychiatry, 30,* 339–345.

Davidson, J. R. T., Hughes, D., Blazer, D. G., & George, L. K. (1991). Post-traumatic stress disorder in the community: An epidemiological study. *Psychological Medicine, 21*, 713–721.

Davidson, R. J., & Tomarken, A. J. (1989). Laterality and emotion: An electrophsyiological approach. In F. Boller & J. Grafman (Eds.), *Handbook of neuropsychology* (Vol. 3, pp. 419–441). Amsterdam: Elsevier.

Devinsky, O., Morrell, M. J., & Vogt, B. A. (1995). Contributions of anterior cingulate cortex to behavior. *Brain, 118*, 279–306.

Dobbs, D., & Wilson, W. P. (1960). Observations on the persistence of traumatic war neurosis. *Journal Nervous and Mental Diseases, 21*, 40–46.

Donald, M. (1991). *Origins of the modern mind.* Cambridge, MA: Harvard University Press.

Felitti, V. J., Anda, R. F., Nordernberg, D., Willimason, D. F., Spitz, A. M., Edwards, et al. (1998). Relationship of childhood abuse to many of the leading causes of death in adults: The adverse childhood experiences (ACE) study. *American Journal of Preventative Medicine, 14*(4), 245–258.

Foa, E. B., Riggs, D. S., Massie, E. D., & Yarczower, M. (1995). The impact of fear activation and anger on the efficacy of exposure treatment for posttraumatic stress disorder. *Behavior Therapy, 26*(3), 487–499.

Ford, J. D. (1999). Disorders of extreme stress following war-zone military trauma: associated features of posttraumatic stress disorder or comorbid but distinct syndromes. *Journal of Consulting and Clinical Psychology, 67*(1), 3–12.

Ford, J. D., & Kidd, T. P. (1998). Early childhood trauma and disorders of extreme stress as predictors of treatment outcome with chronic posttraumatic stress disorder. *Journal of Traumatic Stress, 11*(4), 743–761.

Freedman, S. A., Brandes, D., Peri, T., & Shalev, A. Y. (1999). Predictors of chronic post-traumatic stress disorder: A prospective study. *British Journal of Psychiatry, 174*, 353–359.

Freud, S. (1955). Beyond the pleasure principle. In J. Strachey (Ed. & Trans.), *The standard edition of the complete psychological works of Sigmund Freud.* (Vol. 18, pp. 7–64). London: Hogarth Press. (Original work published 1920)

Freud, S. (1959). An autobiographical study. In J. Strachey (Ed. & Trans.), *The standard edition of the complete psychological works of Sigmund Freud.* (Vol. 20, pp. 1–74). London: Hogarth Press. (Original work published 1925)

Gray, J. F. (1982). *The neuropsychology of anxiety: An enquiry into the functions of the septo-hippocampal system.* New York: Oxford University Press.

Green, A. H. (1978). Self-destructive behavior in battered children. *American Journal of Psychiatry, 135*, 579–582.

Green, B. L. (1982). Assessing levels of psychological impairment following disaster: consideration of actual and methodological dimensions. *Journal of Nervous and Mental Disease, 170*(9), 544–552.

Gurvits, T., Shenton, M., Hokama, H., Ohta, H., Lasko, N., Gilbertson, M., Orr, S., Kikinis, R., Jolesz, F., McCarley, R., & Pitman, R. (1998). Magnetic resonance imaging (MRI) study of hippocampal volume in chronic combat related posttraumatic stress disorder. *Biological Psychiatry, 40*, 1091–1099.

Henninger, P. (1992). Conditional handedness: Handedness changes in multiple personality disordered subject reflects shift in hemispheric dominance. *Counsciousness and Cognition, 1*, 265–87.

Herman, J. L. (1992). *Trauma and recovery.* New York: Basic Books.

Janet, P. (1893). L'Amnesie continue [Continued amnesia]. *Revue Generale des Sciences, 4*, 167–179.

Janet, P. (1911). *L'état mental des hysteriques* [The mental state of hysterics] (2nd ed.). Paris: Felix Alcan.

Janet, P. (1925). *Psychological Healing* (Vol. 1–2) (C. Paul & E. Paul, Trans.). New York: Macmillan. (Original work published 1919)

Janet, P. (1973). L'automatisme psychologique: Essai de psychologie experimentale sur les formes inferieures de l'activité humaine [Psychological automatism: A test in experimental psychology on the inferior forms of human activity]. Paris: Felix Alcan, (Original work published 1889)

Joseph, R. (1988). Dual mental functioning in a split-brain patient. *Journal of Clinical Psychology, 44*(5), 770–779.

Kardiner, A. (1941). *The traumatic neuroses of war.* New York: Paul B. Hoeber.

Kardiner, A., & Spiegel, H. (1947). *War stress and neurotic illness.* New York: Paul B. Hoeber.

Kessler, R. C., Sonnega, A., Bromet, E. J., Hughes, M., & Nelson, C. B. (1995). Posttraumatic stress disorder in the National Comorbidity Survey. *Archives of General Psychiatry, 52*(12), 1048–1060.

Kilpatrick, D., Acierno, G., Saunders, R., Resnick, B. E., Best, H. S., Connie, L., & Schnurr, P. P. (2000). Risk factors for adolescent substance abuse and dependence: Data from a national sample. *Journal of Consulting and Clinical Psychology, 68*(1), 19–30.

Kosten, T., Mason, J., Giller, E., Ostroff, R., & Harkness, L. (1987). Sustained urinary norepinephrine and epinephrine elevation in posttraumatic stress disorder. *Psychoneuroendocrinology, 12*(1), 13–20.

Krystal, H. (1978). Trauma and affects. *The Psychoanalytic Study of the Child, 33*, 81–116.

Kulka, R. A., Schlenger, W. E., & Fairbank, J. A., et al. (1990). *Trauma and the Vietnam war generation.* New York: Brunner/Mazel.

LeDoux, J. E. (1992). Emotion as memory: Anatomical systems underlying indelible neural traces. In S. A. Christianson (Ed.), *The handbook of emotion and memory* (pp. 269–288). Hillsdale, NJ: Erlbaum.

LeDoux, J. E., Romanski, L., & Xagoraris, A. (1991). Indelibility of subcortical emotional memories. *Journal of Cognitive Neuroscience, 1*, 238–243.

Lewis, D. O. (1992). From abuse to violence: Psychophysiological consequences of maltreatment. *Journal of the American Academy of Child and Adolescent Psychiatry, 31*, 383–391.

Liberzon, I., Abelson, J. L., Flagel, S. B., Raz, J., & Young, E. A. (1999). Neuroendocrine and psychophysiologic responses in PTSD: A symptom provocation study. *Neuropsychopharmacology 21*(1), 40–50.

Macy, R. D. (1998). *Prevalance rates for PTSD and utilization rates of behavioral health services for an adult medicaid population.* (n = 380,000). Unpublished Ph.D. diss.

Mann, J. (1987). Psychobiologic predictors of suicide. *Journal of Clinical Psychiatry, 48*(12), 39–43.

Marmar, C. R., Weiss, D. S., Metzler, T. J., Ronfeldt, H. M., & Foreman, C. (1995). Stress responses of emergency services personnel to the Loma Prieta earthquake Interstate 880 freeway collapse and control traumatic incidents. *Journal of Mental and Nervous Diseases, 183*, 36–42.

McDonagh-Coyle, A., McHugo, G., Ford, J., Mueser, K., Demment, C., & Descamps, M. (1999). Cognitive-behavioral treatment for childhood sexual abuse survivors with PTSD. *Proceedings of the International Society for Traumatic Stress Studies, 15*, 36.

McEwen, B. S. (1999). Stress and hippocampal plasticity. *Annual Review Neuroscience 22*, 105–122

McEwen, B. S., de Leon, M. J., Lupien. S. & Meaney, M. J. (1999). Corticosteroids, the aging brain and cognition. *Trends in Endocrinology and Metabolism, 10*, 92–96.

McFarlane, A. C., Weber, D. L., & Clark, C. R. (1993). Abnormal stimulus processing in PTSD. *Biological Psychiatry, 34*, 311–320.

McLean, P. (1980). *The triune brain.* New York: Oxford Universities Press.

Murburg, M. (ed.), (1994). *Catecholamine function in posttraumatic stress disorder.* Washington, DC: American Psychiatric Press.

National Victim Center. (1993). *Crime and victimization in America: Statistcal overview.* Arlington, VA: Author.

O'Keefe, J., & Nadel, L. (1978). *The hippocampus as a cognitive map.* Oxford: Clarendon Press.

Ornitz, E. M., & Pynoos, R. S. (1989). Startle modulation in children with post-traumatic stress disorder. *American Journal of Psychiatry 147,* 866–870.

Panksepp, J. (1998). *Affective neuroscience.* New York: Oxford Universities Press.

Pelcovitz, D., van der Kolk, B. A., Roth, S. H., Mandel, F. S., Kaplan, S. J., & Resick, P. (1997). Development of a criteria set and a structured interview for disorders of extreme stress (SIDES). *Journal of Traumatic Stress,* 10(1), 3–16.

Perry, B. D., Giller, E. L., & Southwick, S. M. (1987). Altered platelet alpha-adrenergic binding sites in posttraumatic stress disorder. *American Journal of Psychiatry, 144*(11), 1511–1512.

Pibram, Karl H. (1994). *Origins Brain and self organization.* Hillsdale, NJ: Erlbaum.

Pitman, R., Orr, S., & Shalev, A. (1993). Once bitten twice shy: Beyond the conditioning model of PTSD. *Biological Psychiatry, 33,* 145–146.

Pitman, R. K., Orr, S. P., Forgue, D. F., de Jong, J., & Claiborn, J. M. (1987). Psychophysiologic assessment of posttraumatic stress disorder imagery in Vietnam combat veterans. *Archives of General Psychiatry, 44,* 970–975.

Post, R. M. (1992): Transduction of psychosocial stress into the neurobiology of recurrent affective disorder. *American Journal of Psychiatry, 149,* 999–1010.

Post, R. M., Weiss, S. R. B., & George, M. S. (1994, May). *A Sensitization and kinding components of PTSD.* American Psychiatric Association 150 Annual Meeting, Philadelphia.

Rainey, J. M., Aleem, A., Ortiz, A., Yaragani, V., Pohl, R., & Berchow, R. (1987). Laboratory procedure for the inducement of flashbacks. *American Journal of Psychiatry, 144,* 1317–1319.

Rauch, S. L., van der Kolk, B. A., Fisler, R. E., Alpert, N. M., Orr, S. P., Savage, C. R., Fischman, A. J., Jenike, M. A., & Pitman, R. A. (1996). A symptom provocation study of posttraumatic stress disorder using positron emission tomography and script-driven imagery. *Archives of General Psychiatry, 53*(May), 380–387.

Resnick, H. S., Yehuda, R., & Acierno, R. (1997). Acute post-rape plasma cortisol, alcohol use, and PTSD symptom profile among recent rape victims. *Annals of the New York Academy of Sciences, 821,* 433–436.

Rivers, W. H. R. (1918). The repression of war experience. *The Lancet,* 2(Feb.), 173–177.

Roth, S. H., Newman, E., Pelcovitz, D., van der Kolk, B. A., & Mandel, F. S. (1997). Complex PTSD in victims exposed to sexual and physical abuse: Results from the DSM-IV Field Trial for Posttraumatic Stress Disorder. *Journal of Traumatic Stress,* 10(4), 539–555.

Sapolsky, R. M., Krey, L., & McEwen, B. S. (1984). Stress down-regulates corticosterone receptors in a site specific manner in the brain. *Endocrinology, 114,* 287–292.

Shalev, A. Y., Peri, T., Caneti, L., & Screiber, S. (1996). Predictors of PTSD in injured trauma survivors: A prospective study. *American Journal of Psychiatry, 153,* 219–225.

Shalev, A. Y., Orr, S. P., & Pitman, R. K. (1993). Psychophysiologic assessment of traumatic imagery in Israeli civilian patients with posttraumatic stress disorder. *American Journal of Psychiatry, 150,* 620–624.

Shalev, A. Y., & Rogel-Fuchs, Y. (1993). Psychophysiology of PTSD: From sulfur fumes to behavioral genetics. *Journal of Mental and Nervous Diseases, 55*(5), 413–423.

Shalev, A. Y., Orr, S. P., Peri, T., Schreiber, S., & Pitman, R. K. (1992). Physiologic responses to loud tones in Israeli patients with post-traumatic stress disorder. *Archives of General Psychiatry*, *49*, 870–875.

Shallice, T. (1988). *From neuropsychology to mental structure.* New York: Cambridge University Press.

Sheline, Y. I., Sanghavi, M., Mintun, M. A., & Gado, M. H. (1999). Depression duration, but not age predicts hippocampal volume loss in medically healthy women with recurrent major depression. *Journal of Neuroscience 19*, S034–S043.

Shin, L. M., McNally, R. J., Kosslyn, S. M., Thompson, W. L., Rauch, S. L., Alpert, N. M., Metzger, L. J., Lasko, N. B., Orr, S. P., & Pitman, R. K. (1999). Regional cerebral blood flow during script-driven imagery inchildhood sexual abuse-related PTSD: A PET investigation. *American Journal of Psychiatry*, *156*(4), 575–584.

Southwick, S. M., Krystal, J. H., Bremner, J. D., Morgan, C. A., Nicolaou, A. L., Nagy, L. M., Johnson, D. R., Heninger, G. R., & Charney, D. S. (1997). Noradrenergic and serotonergic function in posttraumatic stress disorder. *Archives of General Psychiatry*, *54*(8), 749–758.

Southwick, S. M., Krystal, J. H., Morgan, A., Johnson, D., Nagy, L., Nicolaou, A., Henninger, G. R., & Charney, D. S. (1993). Abnormal noradrenergic function in post traumatic stress disorder. *Archives of General Psychiatry*, *50*, 266–274.

Southwick, S. M., Yehuda, R., & Giller, E. L. (1993). Personality disorders in treatment-seeking combat veterans with post-traumatic stress disorder. *American Journal of Psychiatry*, *150*, 1020–1023.

Squire, L. R., & Zola-Morgan, S. (1991). The medial temporal lobe memory system. *Science, 253*, 1380–86.

Starkman, M. N., Giordani, B., Gerbski, S. S., Berent, S., Schork, M. A., & Schteingart (1999). Decrease in cortisol reverses human hippocampal atrophy following treatment of Cushing's disease. *Biological Psychiatry 46*, 1595–1602.

Stein, M. B., Koverola, C., Hanna, C., Torchia, M. G., & McClarty, B. (1997). Hippocampal volume in women victimized by childhood sexual abuse. *Psychological Medicine 27*(4), 951–959.

Valzelli, L. (1982). Serotonergic inhibitory control of experimental aggression. *Psychopharmacological Research Communications, 12*, 1–13.

van der Kolk, B. A. (2000). The diagnosis and treatment of complex PTSD. In R. Yehuda, (ed.), *Current treatment of PTSD.* Washington, DC: American Psychiatric Press.

van der Kolk, B. A. (1994). The body keeps the score: Memory and the evolving psychobiology of posttraumatic stress. *Harvard Review of Psychiatry, 1*, 253–265.

van der Kolk, B. A., (2000). Adult sequelae of assault. In A. M. Friedman, H. I. Kaplan, & B. J. Sadock (Eds.), *Comprehensive textbook of psychiatry* (pp. 2002–2008). Baltimore: Williams and Wilkins.

van der Kolk, B. A., Bessel, A., Burbridge, J. A., & Suzuki, J. (1997). The psychobiology of traumatic memory: clinical implications of neuroimaging studies. *Annals of the New York Academy of Sciences 821*, 99–113.

van der Kolk, B. A., Dreyfuss, D., Michaels, M., Saxe, G., & Berkowitz, R. (1994). Fluoxetine in posttraumatic stress disorder. *Journal of Clinical Psychiatry, 55*, 517–522.

van der Kolk, B. A. & Ducey, C. P. (1989). The psychological processing of traumatic experience: Rorschach patterns in PTSD. *Journal of Traumatic Stress, 2*, 259–274.

van der Kolk, B. A., & Fisler, R. E. (1995). Dissociation and the fragmentary nature of traumatic memories: overview and exploratory study. *Journal of Traumatic Stress, 8*(4), 505–525.

van der Kolk, B. A., Hopper, J., & Osterman, J. (2001). Exploring the nature of traumatic memory: Combining clinical knowledge with laboratory methods. *Journal of Aggression, Maltreatment, and Trauma, 4*(2), 9–31.

van der Kolk, B. A., McFarlane, A. C., & Weisaeth, L. (Eds.). (1996). *Traumatic stress: the effects of overwhelming experience on mind, body, and society.* New York: Guilford Press.

van der Kolk, B. A., McFarlane, A. C., & van der Hart, O. (1996). A general approach to treatment of posttraumatic stress disorder. In B. A. van der Kolk, A. C. McFarlane & L. Weisaeth (Eds.), *Traumatic stress: the effects of overwhelming experience on mind, body, and society* (pp. 417–440). New York: Guilford Press.

van der Kolk, B. A., Pelcovitz, D., Roth, S., Mandel, F., McFarlane, A. C., & Herman, J. L. (1996). Dissociation, somatization, and affect dysregulation: The complexity of adaptation to trauma. *American Journal of Psychiatry.*

van der Kolk, B. A., Perry, C., & Herman, J. L. (1991). Childhood origins of self-destructive behavior. *American Journal of Psychiatry, 148,* 1665–1671.

van der Kolk, B. A., & van der Hart, O. (1989). Pierre Janet and the breakdown of adaptation in psychological trauma. *American Journal of Psychiatry, 146*(12), 1530–1540.

van der Kolk, B. A., & van der Hart, O. (1991). The intrusive past: The flexibility of memory and the engraving of trauma. *American Imago, 48*(4), 425–454.

van der Kolk, B. A., & van der Hart, O. (1991). The intrusive past: The flexibility of memory and the engraving of trauma. *American Imago: Psychoanalysis Culture, 48,* 425–454.

van der Kolk, B. A., van der Hart, O., & Marmar, C. R. (1996). Dissociation and information processing in posttraumatic stress disorder. In B. A. van der Kolk, A. C. McFarlane & L. Weisaeth (Eds.), *Traumatic stress: The effects of overwhelming experience on mind, body and society* (pp. 303–327). New York: Guilford Press.

Yehuda, R., Giller, E. L., Southwick, S. M., Lowy, M. T., & Mason, J. W. (1991). Hypothalmic-pituitary-adrenal dysfunction in posttraumatic stress disorder. *Biological Psychiatry, 30,* 1031–1048.

Yehuda, R., Keefe, R. S. E., Harvey, P. D., Levengood, R. A., Gerber, D. K., Geni, J., Siever, L. J. (1995). Learning and memory in combat veterans with posttraumatic stress disorder. *American Journal of Psychiatry, 152,*137–139.

Yehuda, R., & McFarlane, A. C. (1995). Conflict between current knowledge about posttraumatic stress disorder and its original conceptual basis. *American Journal of Psychiatry, 152*(12), 1705–13.

Yehuda, R., Southwick, S. M., Mason, J. W., & Giller, E. L. (1990). Interactions of the hypothalamic-pituitary adrenal axis and the catecholaminergic system of the stress disorder. In E. L. Giller (Ed.), *Biological assessment and treatment of PTSD.* Washington, DC: American Psychiatric Press.

5

EMDR and Information Processing in Psychotherapy Treatment: Personal Development and Global Implications*

Francine Shapiro and Louise Maxfield

EYE MOVEMENT desensitization and reprocessing (EMDR) is a treatment approach that has been surrounded by confusion since it was introduced in 1989 (Shapiro, 1989), partly because of its name. I (F.S.) originally called it *eye movement desensitization,* because the eye movements appeared to result in desensitization, and, at the time, I was a behaviorist, thinking in terms of anxiety reduction. However, by 1990, it became apparent that other forms of stimulation in addition to the eye movement were also effective and that the treatment effects extended far beyond desensitization. If the situation presented itself again, I would actually call it *reprocessing therapy.* However, since EMDR is 14 years old, we're keeping the name and the acronym. For the purposes of this chapter on the application of EMDR to personal development, you could probably think of EMDR as "Emotional and Mental Development and Reorganization."

EMDR was originally designed to treat traumatic memories and it has been found efficacious in the treatment of posttraumatic stress disorder (PTSD;

*This paper is based on a talk by the first author presented at Cutting Edge Conference, University of California, San Diego, March, 2001.

Chambless et al., 1998; Chemtob, Tolin, van der Kolk, & Pitman, 2000; Maxfield & Hyer, 2002; Van Etten & Taylor, 1998). More than a dozen controlled studies have found it to be both effective and efficient (e.g., Carlson, Chemtob, Rusnak, Hedlund, & Muraoka, 1998; Ironson, Freund, Strauss, & Williams, 2002; Lee et al., 2002; Marcus, Marquis, & Sakai, 1997; Rothbaum, 1997; Scheck, Schaeffer, & Gillette, 1997; Wilson, Becker, & Tinker, 1997; and Wilson, Tinker, & Becker, 1995), with several studies reporting a 77–90% remission of PTSD in single-trauma victims in as few as 5 hours of treatment. Consequently, it is now commonly used to treat a range of complaints that follow distressing life experiences. EMDR is an integrative approach that brings together the wisdom of all the different orientations, synthesizing elements of psychodynamic, cognitive, behavioral, person-centered, and body-based therapies in structured procedures and protocols (Shapiro, 2001, 2002a). It is applied in eight phases, and works with all past, present, and future aspects of the presenting problem.

The Adaptive Information Processing Model

The adaptive information processing (AIP) model (Shapiro, 2001) was developed to explain and predict EMDR treatment effects. This model states that all memory is associated, and that learning occurs through the creation of new associations. For example, in order to recognize an object in our world, the perceptions of the present have to link into the memory network of past experiences for the object to be identified. If we have never seen a microphone before, we have absolutely no idea what to do with it. However, as someone demonstrates the use of the microphone, this new information is linked with other information stored in memory networks, and we are able to integrate microphones into our worldview. We also begin a memory network incorporating our experiences with microphones which guides our future perceptions and behaviors in this context. If a child's early experiences involved being hit on the head with a microphone, these early effects may be stored and rise unbidden when a microphone is perceived in the present. Unhealed, this earlier experience implicitly sets the groundwork for all future perceptions. However, within all of us there is an information processing system that creates a network of memory associations to allow us to move adaptively through our world. The problems arise when this intrinsic system has not been able to function, resulting in inappropriate memory storage. Consequently, EMDR clinical work rests upon the bedrock of addressing those experiences which are dysfunctionally rather than adaptively stored.

A Natural System

The information processing system is an intrinsic physical system that is geared to take psychological disturbance to mental health. Let us use the example of an argument with someone at work. Our body reacts, our minds chatter, and we feel upset. Then we talk about the incident, think about it, and maybe dream about it. Time passes, and soon the argument does not bother us any longer. We understand what happened in the interaction; we have an idea of what to do; we go back and talk to the person; we do not have that physiological arousal. It can be said that the experience was "adaptively resolved." The useful aspects of the interaction were learned and stored in memory, with appropriate emotion, available to provide future guidance. The useless aspects were discarded; the negative self-talk, the negative arousal, the negative emotions—all of these are gone. This natural, normal information processing takes us adaptively through the world and has a direct effect on not only cognition, but emotion and body sensation. If you notice how your body feels as you first repeat the words *no* (five times) and then *yes* (five times) after you have closed your eyes and allowed yourself to get comfortable, you will see that there is no separation between mind and body. There is clearly a physical resonant to a cognitive process.

Unprocessed Memories

The AIP model (Shapiro, 2001) states that when an incident is not fully processed, the perceptions, thoughts, and emotions that were experienced during the event are generally stored in state-dependent form. This storage may be in an isolated memory network where the information cannot link up with more appropriate information and learning cannot take place. Moreover, because all new experiences link up with memory networks containing similar or reminiscent past events, the memory of the incident is going to adversely influence our current perceptions, reactions, and behaviors. As a new situation arises, a static, generally unchanging, brain state is elicited with the same perceptions, affects, cognitive distortions, and behaviors as those of the initial event. This process is probably involved in the pronounced symptoms of PTSD. The nightmares, the flashbacks, the intrusive thoughts of PTSD appear to be the reactivation of the perceptions of the moment, the thoughts and sounds, the emotions, and physical sensations experienced during the incident. This formulation applies not only to traumatic events, but to experience in general.

The AIP model (Shapiro, 2001, 2002a) defines *trauma* as any negative event that has had a lasting negative effect upon self or psyche. Events such as the Criterion A events for PTSD (APA, 2000) are *large–T traumas*, while other events are *small–T traumas*. Small–T traumas can be apparently minor incidents of humiliation, conflict, and rejection. Deficit experiences (e.g., neglect, attach-ment difficulties) that occur during developmental windows can also function as small-T traumas. With frequent repetition of such events, the memory network becomes predominant, organizing similar experiences in associated channels of information, and precipitating a continued pattern of behavior, cognition, and related identity structures. The memories of unprocessed large–T and small–T traumas are stored in a similar fashion; inherent within them are the emotions of the original incident, and the physical reactivity that was present at that moment in time.

Information Processing during EMDR

EMDR is formulated to expedite the accessing and processing of those dys-functionally stored memories that have not been assimilated into the larger associative network. The goal of EMDR therapy is to forge new connections between the unprocessed memory and more adaptive information that is con-tained in other memory networks. EMDR focuses directly on all the perceptual components of memory (imagery, cognition, affect, body sensations) and main-tains these in a dynamic state while the client simultaneously engages in a dual attention task, eye movements. Research has shown that eye movements de-crease the vividness and emotionality of memories (e.g., Andrade, Kavanagh, & Baddeley, 1997; Kavanaugh, Freese, Andrade, & May, 2001; Sharpley, Montgomery, & Scalzo, 1996; van den Hout, Muris, Salemink, & Kindt, 2001), and it appears that the decreased salience of the targeted memory allows ac-cess to other information. EMDR uses a free association procedure to elicit this material. Associative links are thus created between the targeted memory and adaptive information, allowing the memory to be processed and integrated, in a catalytic learning process (for discussions of active mechanisms and hypothe-ses, see Maxfield, 2002; Rogers & Silver, 2002; Shapiro, 2001, 2002a; Siegel, 2002; Stickgold, 2002; van der Kolk, 2002; for contemporary overviews, see also Perkins & Rouanzoin, 2002; Shapiro 2002b).

The EMDR procedures utilize the inherent healing mechanisms of the infor-mation processing system and typically result in an adaptive resolution. Clients frequently report changes in emotions (elimination of distress and elicitation of positive affects), cognitions (insights, reformulation of beliefs), physiology (elimination of arousal), behavior (increased function), and identity (personal growth, individuation).

Case Study

As we shall review in a subsequent section, at the beginning of trauma pro-cessing, the EMDR client identifies a negative self-referencing belief that is associated with the target memory, as well as a desired positive belief. Julie was an incest survivor. Prior to EMDR she believed the molestation to be her fault and engaged in self-defeating behaviors in numerous life areas. Even though she "knew" that victims were not responsible for being assaulted, this information did not change her feelings about herself and her experience. Her negative sense of self was largely based on having identified with her father's actions while she was being raped. Her negative belief was "I'm a whore," which she explained was due to the fact that she momentarily thought as her father raped her, "Do this! Do this and I'll have you for the rest of my life." In other words, her feelings about one fleeting thought that went through her mind defined her sense of self for the next 20 years. Her desired cognition was "I was an abused child." Although this is clearly not a statement indicating the type of empowerment one would wish for a client, it was as far as she could go in imagining herself as healed.

During the initial treatment session, EMDR processing created associative links between her memories and more adaptive information, so that she no longer felt responsible. Julie was able to recognize fully the negative impact that the experience had upon her development. However, "I was an abused child" was only a transitory step along the way. She experienced a clear differentiation between her father and herself. In psychodynamic terms, a spontaneous reconversion of an introjected perpetrator occurred. At the end of the session in which she made affective and cognitive connections to a sense of spirituality and self-love, she was able to state with confidence, "I'm a strong, resilient woman." Her evolved sense of personal identity emerged as the event took on a different meaning. It now had different memory associations and a different affect load; her perceptions of the event had shifted. EMDR did not erase the memory, but changed its significance. Julie said, "It's still an ugly picture, but it's not ugly because of me." EMDR processing allows an assimilation of what is useful and allows the rest to be discarded.

Small–T Traumas

Now, another experiment. Do you remember being humiliated during grade school? Let's try the following to see if it still has an effect on you. Please read through these instructions and complete the experiment before continuing to the next paragraph. Close your eyes, notice your body, just notice how your body feels, and bring back the memory of being humiliated. Notice what happens to your body and notice the thoughts that emerge as you go back to that time. Then just let it go and open your eyes.

When you brought up the memory, did you find your body twinge a little? Was some of the heat of that childhood emotion there, did the thought that was there at the time come across your consciousness? If so, we would say that the information from that experience has not been processed adequately, and that this recollection has within it some of the perceptions, emotions, and cognitions from the actual event. Some persons find that the tentacles of such childhood experiences are wrapped somewhere in their present life, and are evident as issues with authority, public speaking, or social problems. Because all current experiences link up with related memory networks, if those networks contain unprocessed material, and if those physical sensations are still there, the emotions that arise are not new emotions, per se, but a reactivation of affects stored from the earlier event. The bottom line is that the past is present, the memories are physically stored, and all experiences are connected. If an early experience is still hot, it is going to generate that heat in the present.

Some people find that when they thought of that childhood humiliation, their bodies did not change; the thought that came up was "Boy, he shouldn't have been teaching" or "Boy, I was really something." We would say that the experience has been adequately processed, the person has learned what is necessary, and it guides them appropriately; the experience has been assimilated and personal growth has taken place.

Some may wonder why a humiliation can be considered a small-T trauma, and how the ubiquitous events of humiliation in grade school can have a lasting effect upon self or psyche. It may simply be an evolutionary process, with childhood humiliation the evolutionary equivalent of being cut out of the herd, resulting in anxiety and fear. Although such experiences may appear "small" from an adult vantage point, the child's perspective may be very different. Individuals react differently to different events; some are distressed, others resilient. The child's reaction to the humiliation will be influenced by prior events stored in memory networks; such events may have helped the child to become resilient or vulnerable. There may be a genetic component related to vulnerability in the storage system, just as some have more vulnerability in cardiac or respiratory systems. It might be that there was a window of opportunity right after the event where a good friend came over and put an arm around the child and said "It'll be okay."

Whatever the reason for the individual differences, if a child's information processing system was overwhelmed by the event, the memory of the experience will generally be stored essentially as it was input. The experience can have detrimental effects for years. In treatment, the time since the event need not be a crucial factor, since stored memories can be accessed.

If a memory can be accessed, it can be processed. Regardless of how long ago the event occurred, healing is simply a matter of forging the appropriate linkages between memory networks. In other words, focused information processing asks us to consider our notions about "What is the function of time in therapy?"

EMDR Treatment

Goals

The basic goal of treatment is for the client to achieve the most profound and comprehensive effects possible, in the shortest period of time, while maintaining stability, within a balanced system. This goal is achieved when the distressing memories are processed and integrated within adaptive memory networks, and when all past, present, and future aspects are addressed.

While emotion is often the critical element to be addressed in treatment, clients can be hesitant to work with affect. They may say, "With the way I feel, why would I want to get in touch with my feelings?" These natural tendencies toward "avoidance," particularly in trauma victims, need to be directly addressed by clinicians. Rather than viewing treatment in a monodimensional model which places the onus for compliance solely on the client, clinicians practicing integrative therapies, such as EMDR, recognize that treatment must encompass the full range of human experience—including a fear of the treatment itself. If we address the comprehensive clinical picture, we have to determine and foster those factors that will make it worthwhile for this human being to engage in therapy. Focused procedures that provide evidence on a session-by-session basis to both client and clinician that change has taken place are, we believe, one of the best ways to encourage a sustained engagement.

Although treatment should result in the elimination of the core symptoms, it should not be considered complete with the simple reduction of distress. Certainly, with EMDR there is a rapid alleviation of core symptoms. For instance, three published controlled studies reported that after four to five hours of EMDR treatment, 77% to 90% of single trauma victims no longer met the diagnostic criteria for PTSD (Marcus et al., 1997; Rothbaum, 1997; Wilson et al., 1995, 1997). Clearly, the ability to use focused interventions for rapid change, to maximize the time that we have with clients, to give them incentive to continue, in order to address the entire clinical picture is extremely important. The attainment of subclinical status is not the entire story. When possible, treatment should also address the lifelong ability of the individual to feel joy, to bond, to experience intimacy, and to have a fulfilling life.

The Eight Phases of Treatment

EMDR is a treatment approach designed to enhance information processing. During EMDR, the distressing memory that was originally stored in dysfunctional form, in an isolated network, is targeted and fully activated. It is then linked to more adaptive or appropriate memory networks of information. As the target becomes integrated with the other material, the memory is transformed and adaptively resolved. The client experiences this transformation with shifts in image, thought, affect, and body sensation.

EMDR uses an eight-phase structured approach (for full delineation of procedures, see Shapiro, 2001). The first phase of treatment is history-taking, evaluation, and treatment planning. In addition to the elements of assessment common to most psychotherapies, the EMDR therapist also identifies key life events that are potential targets for EMDR processing. These can be both small-T and large-T traumas. Also identified are the present situations that cause distress and the skill deficits that interfere with adaptive functioning.

The second phase of treatment is preparation. The client is educated about symptoms, offered appropriate levels of expectation about the treatment, and a therapeutic alliance is established. The therapist ensures that the client has adequate stabilization and self-control, and can regulate affect, manage stress, and cope with crisis. Clients with multiple small- and large-T childhood traumas often have impairments in these areas, and substantial treatment time may be devoted to skill and resource development prior to addressing painful traumatic memories. Trauma processing does not proceed until the client shows indicators of readiness and sufficient ability to use the self-control techniques. These techniques are used to close incomplete sessions, and to ensure client stability in between sessions.

The third to sixth phases of treatment are those involved in processing a distressing memory, present trigger, or future template. Each phase is formulated to mobilize the material and facilitate its linkage with other adaptive information. The detailed case study below illustrates this aspect of EMDR.

In the seventh phase, closure, the therapist determines whether the psychological material has been adequately processed and, if not, assists clients with the self-calming interventions developed in phase two. The client is also instructed to use a log to self-monitor responses in between sessions, and to use the self-control techniques. The final phase of EMDR treatment is the reevaluation of the previous work at the beginning of each subsequent session.

The therapist assesses whether the treatment effects have been maintained, identifies current triggers that cause distress, and assists the client in developing resources to cope with future related situations. Various EMDR protocols are utilized to address specific diagnoses and clinical complaints (e.g., Grant, 2002, Shapiro, 2001, 2002; Vogelman-Sine, Sine, Smyth, & Popky, 1998).

Case Study

This case study describes the processing of a large-T trauma, an earthquake that resulted in PTSD. As is typical in EMDR treatment, insights, affects, body sensations, and memories of other events emerged, and were processed in the resolution and integration of the traumatic event.

Lynne was a 30-year-old woman who sought treatment for PTSD at the MRI EMDR Research Center (for detailed transcript see Popky & Levin, 1994; Shapiro, 2002a; Shapiro & Maxfield, 2002). She had developed PTSD two years previously, after a severe earthquake. During the earthquake, she had sheltered in a doorway, expecting to die. Lynne asserted, "Even though my mind says I'm safe, my body doesn't believe my mind. There's an outside force I have not accounted for." Lynne expressed concern that she would not "be able to react quickly enough." In the first phase of EMDR (history-taking, assessment), she also reported two earlier earthquakes. During one of them, she had been in a hypnosis class at the university and the professor had just put her under hypnosis when the earthquake struck. Although this was distressing, she did not develop PTSD until after the third earthquake.

During the second phase of EMDR, client strengths are developed by combining relaxation, imagery, and EMDR in interventions that assist the client in acquiring new skills and resources. Self-calming techniques are an important element of treatment and are used to "close" incomplete sessions, as well as to maintain client stability between and during sessions. Lynne was taught the use of the safe-place visualization as a calming and self-soothing technique.

In the third phase of EMDR, the memory of the distressing event is fully assessed. First, the client is asked to identify an image of the event. Lynne described herself as sheltering in a doorway, expecting to die. Next the client is asked to identify a related negative self-referencing belief and a desired positive belief. For Lynne the negative belief was, "I'm helpless—out of control," and the desired positive belief was "I can handle what comes up." EMDR clients then rate their confidence in the desired positive belief on the Validity of Cognition (VOC) scale (Shapiro, 1989, 2001), where 1 is completely false and 7 is completely true. Lynne gave the positive statement a validity rating of 2. After this, clients are asked to identify the feelings that arise when they focus on the image and the related negative belief, and to rate the level of distress. Lynne reported feeling a high level of anxiety. On the Subjective Units of Distress (SUD) Scale (Wolpe, 1958), where 0 is no disturbance and 10 is the worst possible, Lynne rated her distress at 8. Finally, the EMDR client is asked to identify the body location for these feelings. Lynne stated that her anxiety was located in her solar plexus.

In the fourth phase of EMDR, the client is asked to focus on the image, negative thought, and body sensations, while simultaneously engaging in a dual attention task. The client maintains this internal focus while simultaneously moving the eyes from side to side for 15 or more seconds (depending upon nonverbal cues), following the therapist's fingers as they move across the visual field. Eye movements are the most commonly used dual attention stimuli, although auditory tones and tactile stimulation are also used. After the set of eye movements, the client is told "Blank out (or 'Let go of') the material, and take a deep breath," and then is asked "What do you get now?" The client may say that nothing has changed, or may report an image, thought, sensation, or emotion. This free association elicits information that is related to the target being processed, and indicates a linking of the traumatic memory with the new material. Generally, the clinician then directs the client's attention to the new information, for the next set of eye movements, according to standardized procedures and a set of guiding principles (Shapiro, 2001). This cycle of alternating focused attention and client feedback is repeated many times to ensure that all aspects of the memory network are addressed. It is typically accompanied by shifts in affect, physiological states, and cognitive insights. When processing is not observed, the clinician intervenes with a set of procedures geared to restimulate the processing system.

Lynne started out focusing on the first earthquake, and then moved through a sequence of material. During sequential sets she reported feeling "woozy," feeling tired, memories of the second earthquake, running happily around the house as a child with her brother, and a molestation experience with her brother. She commented about this: "It really shook my sense of reality." She then reported playing with her father, a bad experience with her father, and another negative childhood experience. She commented about this, "I was just thinking what a chaotic place it was to live in and what an unsafe place it was to be." As she continued with processing, childhood themes of lack of safety and chaos were apparent. After each set, more related material emerged, and was processed and integrated. In addition to new insights, affects of fear and sadness were processed along with the initial sense of anxiety. At the end of this phase, Lynne reported no distress related to the original targeted trauma, hiding in the doorway during the earthquake.

Phase five of EMDR focuses on the expression and consolidation of the client's cognitive insights. The original targeted image is paired with the most enhancing positive cognition during sets of eye movements. This could be the desired positive belief identified in phase three, or a more therapeutically beneficial belief that emerged during the fourth phase. The focus is on incorporating and increasing the strength of the positive cognition until strong confidence in the belief is apparent (e.g., VOC of 6 or 7). When Lynne thought of the original image of huddling in the doorway, and paired it with the belief "I can handle what comes up," she gave it a VOC of 6. The ecological validity of this statement is found in the fact that it did not strengthen to a "7" or completely true—since there are definitively circumstances in life where this would not be the case. But the adaptive resolution of the memory, and her sense of self-empowerment, are evident when asked how the memory of the earthquake now felt. She brought it to mind and laughed, saying, "Well, what occurs to me is yeah, that was an earthquake. Yeah, that was an earthquake all right."

The Relevance of Childhood Events

In Lynne's case, we started off with the earthquake, and then went down channels of association, back to childhood and the chaotic environment, which appeared to be the foundation of her distress. When the early memories were processed, the PTSD symptoms were eliminated. This was clearly seen at post-treatment, and at 3-month and 1-year follow-ups where the SUD levels were reported as 0 (from pretreatment 8) and the Impact of Event Scale was 0 (from pretreatment 41). The fear of earthquakes appeared to be related to distress from her childhood instability and chaos, to the "ground shifting under her feet" when she was young.

During EMDR processing, the associations of past and present in the targeted network became clear. These connections, unique for each individual, are fascinating in their own right, as in this instance we see that the figurative sense of her "reality being shaken" in a variety of childhood experiences is connected to the actual physical sensation of shaking during the earthquake. It also opens up intriguing questions regarding the connection of family of origin to adult attachments. On intake Lynne described her father as narcissistic and abandoning—yet during processing she recalls the desire to protect him in an extremely chaotic environment. Interestingly, Lynne's first husband was diagnosed as bipolar, and she described her present husband as emotionally labile, evincing radical shifts between affection and coldness. The parallels of the adult relationships to the childhood ones—and to the earthquake experience of being rocked from side to side—become evident during comprehensive processing of the memory network. EMDR processing eliminated the distress related to both childhood and adult experiences, by creating associative links between the memories and more adaptive information. After EMDR, Lynne no longer had PTSD for the targeted incident, and the positive effects generalized to other memories within the targeted network.

Research has shown that childhood trauma increases vulnerability for developing PTSD (Breslau, Chilcoat, Kessler, & Davis, 1999). The AIP model (Shapiro, 2001) suggests this occurs when the criterion A events necessary to diagnose PTSD link into previously established memory networks which contain similar affects. Each subsequent event adds to the potential for overt symptomology and decreases personal stability as the memory network becomes progressively overloaded with unprocessed material. In the case of Lynne, her childhood traumatizations laid the groundwork for her PTSD symptoms, including the pronounced sense of powerlessness. While the identified stressor was the most recent earthquake, the associative links to her childhood became clear during the EMDR processing. However, recognizable "Criterion A" events are not necessary to cause severe debilitation. Even ubiquitous events (e.g., humiliation, rejection, conflict) can serve as small-T traumas and have lasting negative effects upon the developing psyche.

Given the associative nature of the memory system, EMDR provides an opportunity for comprehensive healing. The information processing system is a body system, and just like other physical systems, it moves toward healing. For example, if the body is cut, the wound will close and heal, unless there is a block or repeated trauma. As you remove the block, the individual begins the healing process. The information processing system works in the same way. An overload at the time of the trauma can block processing, so that healing does not occur. During EMDR, the stored dysfunctional information is accessed, the information processing system is stimulated and then maintained in a dynamic form, allowing the accessed information to proceed to healing. Again, it does not matter whether it is a large-T or small-T trauma; the system works to create new associative links that allow more adaptive responding.

Case Study: Small-T Trauma

Another way to think about EMDR is to say that it catalyzes a learning process and metabolizes the experiential contributors to clinical problems. Small- and large-T traumas contribute to the development of both diagnosable disorders and subclinical distress. This contribution stems from the unprocessed memory elements which can influence the individual's perceptions, reactions, emotions, thoughts, beliefs, and behaviors. The unprocessed memory elements can be directly triggered by environmental or internal stimuli, and can have a pervasive effect on personality, cognitions, and behavior.

The notion that experiential contributors can directly underlie a wide range of disorders can be illustrated by the example of body dysmorphic disorder. The individual feels that there is something wrong with them physically, but their perspective is distorted and, to objective observers, there is nothing wrong. This disorder is responsible for a lot of self-loathing, suicides, and unnecessary surgeries. Traditionally, it has been reported as difficult to treat (Neziroglu, McKay, Todaro, & Yaryura-Tobias, 1996), with variable success rates. However, EMDR has been reported as very successful when applied to this disorder (Brown, McGoldrick, & Buchanan, 1997). For instance, one of seven consecutive cases believed, for 24 years, that she was covered with unsightly hair. Before leaving the house, she spent four to five hours plucking out every visible hair on her body. Where did this disorder originate? The clinician asked the client, "When is the first time you remembered feeling that?" It turned out that it was a disparaging remark that an aunt made about her underarm hair. EMDR was used to process the early memory; after three sessions, all symptoms were eliminated. She was able to go swimming in a bikini and dancing wearing a low-cut dress. The client was symptom-free at one-year follow-up.

There was probably a convergence of family dynamics, early history, and genetic factors that allowed that type of statement to cause such a deleterious and lasting effect. However, the bottom line is that processing the memory resulted in a remediation of the configuration. The characteristics in her personality that had developed around "I'm terrible, I'm ugly" were able to change and shift into more adaptive and positive characteristics.

Trauma, Attachment, and Development

For single-trauma victims, treatment can be simple and rapid. The client has well-developed resources and skills stored in multiple memory networks. Although the trauma memory is in an isolated network, EMDR is able to readily create links with available adaptive information, and positive associations are created. The negative experience is effectively integrated and assimilated into the life history. For multiple-trauma victims whose memory networks do not contain adequate resources, treatment can be lengthy and complex as substantial preparation time may be required (Korn & Leeds, 2002; Shapiro,

2001). Those with childhood histories of trauma, poor attachment, and/or neglect often have deficits in affect regulation, interpersonal skills, and impulse control. Memory networks contain multiple overlapping unprocessed negative experiences, which limit the client in their responses to life events. EMDR treatment results in a generalizing effect so that it is not necessary for each of the associated memories to be processed. However, the developmental deficits caused by the early traumatization must be adequately addressed to allow fully adaptive functioning.

Determining what experiences are required for a child to develop into a healthy, happy adult, capable of intimacy and love, is the frontier of the developmental psychologist. There is still much to be learned about how to assist those with childhood deficits. Within the AIP paradigm, effective treatment for these clients can be conceptualized as building an infrastructure of positive memory networks, and facilitating associative links between networks. This is an integrative challenge, as we seek to synthesize wisdom from different psychotherapeutic approaches to help clients develop resources and skills that can enhance their function and life enjoyment. Although more work needs to be done in this area, there are a number of areas of promising research. Among these is a new EMDR protocol that helps clients have readier access to positive affects (Korn & Leeds, 2002).

In the following section we provide examples of two children with attachment disorders. Treatment was fairly straightforward and rapid for 14-year-old Todd because he had experienced many positive interactions with his family and his development had not been severely impaired. However, for 5-year-old Ashley, treatment was long-term and complex. Her mother had not been able to provide adequate closeness and nurture because of a prior traumatic loss, and the impairment in the attachment relationship resulted in multiple deficits in Ashley's development. This case also illustrates the intergenerational transmission of pain and distress.

Case Study: Classic Attachment Disorder

Todd was a 14-year-old with classic attachment disorder (Shapiro & Forrest, 1997). He disliked being touched, would not make eye contact, and was socially withdrawn and avoidant. EMDR was used to target the anger he felt toward his parents. During the session, he remembered an early incident that had occurred when he was 3 or 4 years old. He had been dropped off at a day care center. For some reason, he became terrified that his parents were never going to return to pick him up, and thought that he had been abandoned. The experience of that day was locked into his system, and he kept people at a distance. EMDR processing was rapid because Todd had many other positive experiences in multiple memory networks; he came from a loving home and there were many counter examples present. As the negative experience was integrated, associative links were made to these other memories. Todd became a loving and affectionate child since there had been minimal developmental derailment.

Case Study: Attachment Disorder and Development Deficits

More complex cases of attachment disorders must involve multifaceted treatment. Intergenerational issues in attachment are demonstrated in the following case study (Lovett, 1999; Shapiro & Forrest, 1997). Ashley was a 5-year-old, brought in by her mother Maura, because she was self-mutilating, beating up her brother, and expressing hatred toward her mother. As the clinician interviewed Maura, it was revealed that Maura had experienced a traumatic loss as a child. When she was 8 years old, her parents adopted a baby, and Maura adored her adopted brother. However, Maura's parents discovered the baby was sick and while Maura was at school they gave the baby back. When Maura returned home, she discovered the baby was gone. Maura shut down emotionally, determined not to let anyone get close to her again. She kept others at a distance for years, and was not emotionally available to her own children. Unable to connect, she treated her children equally; if one needed shoes, both would get shoes. If one had a birthday, they would have to wait to celebrate both together. So they were both treated equally. But the maternal bond was not present.

In working with this family, the clinician decided to treat Maura first, so that, later, when Ashley was ready to bond with her mother, Maura would be able to connect. Maura worked on the pain, grief, and anger elicited by the memory of losing her adopted brother. As that loss was healed, Maura began to reach out to her own children. Then Ashley was treated, not only by processing earlier events, but by actually creating the infrastructures necessary for healthy living. Treatment lasted for about 2 years and consisted of combinations of play therapy, art therapy, and EMDR, in a strong and positive therapeutic relationship. However, a major element in treatment, was the resolution of Maura's pain, and her increased emotional availability to Ashley.

Impact of Mother's Trauma on Attachment

Although there can be many reasons for problems with attachment, this chapter focuses primarily on the deleterious effects that prior trauma experienced by the mother may have upon the attachment process. Traumatized mothers may have difficulty responding to their children with empathy and/or appropriate nurturance (Hesse & Main, 1999, 2000). Instead of caring and closeness, they may distance themselves from the infant and react with anger, anxiety, sadness, fear, or distress. Some mothers, like Maura, are unaware of their own behavior and its roots in prior trauma.

Attachment is achieved through synchrony and coordination between mother and child. The cry of the infant is an automatic, genetically based, evolutionary encoded behavior to elicit closeness and caring from a caregiver, and the child's sense of identity is built in the reciprocal context of this relationship. What happens when the child does not receive an appropriate or consistent response to her cries, or when her natural essential communications are unnaturally ignored or rebuffed? Then the child's development may be derailed by deficits in the dyadic interaction needed to foster her growth. Without the natural actions and reactions that are physiologically and evolutionarily based, the development of primary psychic infrastructures may be impaired. These may include personal identity, ability to trust one's own perceptions, awareness of being in a cause and effect universe, and the sense of being an active agent. Instead, the child becomes disorganized, distressed, and dissociative. If consistent appropriate attention is not part of the interactive process, the consequences for the child are likely to be both physiological and psychological (see also Hesse & Main, 1999, 2000; Perry, 1997; Schore, 1994; Siegel, 1999, 2002; van der Kolk, 2002). Again, there is no separation between mind and body.

Treatment Issues

Because Ashley's relationship with her mother failed to provide the basic elements necessary for the development of primary identity, this had to be built piecemeal in the relationship between Ashley and her therapist. In treatment, Ashley learned to express emotions, to trust, and to know that she was important. The therapeutic relationship was an invaluable component as it provided focused interactive attention. One of the goals of treatment was to teach Ashley that she was in a cause and effect universe, where actions had consequences, where she was a distinct individual and could have an effect. Many of our adult disorganized patients with attachment issues also need to acquire awareness of being an agent in a cause and effect universe, before a real sense of self can emerge. Like a figure/ground relationship, a sense of self can only evolve in the context of relationships with others. Research has shown that neglect is often more damaging to children than abuse alone (Cicchetti & Toth, 1995).

These effects may be related to the lack of opportunity for the neglected child to develop an understanding of their place in the world, of a cause and effect universe where they can influence others and the world around them.

The EMDR treatment of attachment difficulties in families involves treatment of both the child and the caregiver. Caregiving involves automatic implicit responses to the child, such as facial expression, that cannot be produced as a matter of choice or by cortical self-monitoring (see also van der Kolk, 2002). Hence, processing of previous disruptive experiences is strongly recommended, prior to attempts at maternal self-regulation or control. Appropriate EMDR targets for the caregiver include the relationship she had with her own caregivers, any traumas that have affected her ability to engage interpersonally, recent losses or traumas, as well as any experiences which led to the child becoming a source of anxiety, fear, anger, and/or sadness. Thorough processing of these types of events is expected to result in their resolution for the caregiver, with the result that she will then be able to provide appropriate consistent caring and closeness to her infant.

The physiological effects of insufficient interaction between mother and infants has been widely discussed with regard to consequent deficits in cortical structures (see the contributions of Schore and Siegel in this volume). In addition, the effects of impaired relationships between mother and child are evident in some new research on children with asthma (Madrid, Ames, Skolek, & Brown, 2000). A pilot study directed attention at a previously identified correlation between the development of asthma in children, and disruptions of maternal-infant bonding, where grief over significant unresolved loss can be a major contributing factor (Klaus & Kennel, 1976). When the mothers' grief and bonding disruption were successfully treated, the children's asthma improved or was eliminated. The effect on the children was greatest when the mothers' grief was resolved while the children were still young. When treatment was provided later, the child also required treatment. This example also illustrates the concept of resiliency and the ability to recover, and demonstrates how key events can have lasting effects.

Individuation

One more experiment. Close your eyes and think about an early negative memory from childhood. Look at the characteristics of this early memory and notice whether it has within it the characteristics of undue responsibility: "I am wrong or I did something wrong." Or the characteristics of "I'm not safe." Or the characteristics of "I don't have choices; I'm not in control." These seem to be the three major categories of cognitive themes: responsibility, safety, and choices. Now think about the most recent time that you were very upset. This could be with a client, an associate, a spouse, a family member, whatever. Is it in the same cognitive category? Are there similar emotions there? Is this something that might be worth processing?

Responsibility, Safety, Choices

Notice that these themes are critical in the individuation process, and are related to both the ability to separate between self and others, and adaptively define a personal relationship with the outside world. Where should appropriate responsibility be allocated? Am I safe in the world? Do I have an internal locus of control? A great deal of the processing has to be done around those areas to remediate our more debilitated clients. They are often pivotal issues for childhood trauma victims, and EMDR is used to address the full clinical picture, with past, present, and future aspects which include not only building the appropriate psychic infrastructure, but offering education in adaptive social behaviors that were not learned as children.

EMDR has been used effectively in the treatment of sex offenders in the Canadian prison system (Shapiro & Forrest, 1997). Treatment consisted of processing the childhood traumas, and then focusing on their own abusive behavior. The cognitive themes of responsibility-safety-choices, which have often been used to assist victims in placing appropriate responsibility on the perpetrator, were used to help perpetrators break through their own denial, placing responsibility on themselves. This is such an extremely important aspect of treatment, it is worth underscoring conceptually: The stored affects and perceptions skew present awareness, so until their childhood memories are processed the offenders often have internalized responsibility for their own childhood abuse. They are blaming themselves—blaming the recipient, the victim. It is therefore no surprise that as an adult they perceive the world in the same way and also blame their own victims. Until they can place the full responsibility on the one that perpetrated against them, they will be unable to take appropriate responsibility for their own abusive behaviors. *Denial* is not simply the absence of responsibility—it is often the displacement of appropriate responsibility that parallels the childhood perceptions. Processing that allows a thorough working through of the childhood experiences, fostering insight along with adaptive resolution of negative affects, has the potential to aid judicious treatment in ways that surpass mere attempts to self-monitor behaviors driven by unresolved trauma histories.

The EMDR protocol used to treat the Canadian pedophiles processed the earlier etiological memories, the present triggers, and templates for appropriate future action. As noted, in the initial stage of the protocol, first, the offenders learned to place responsibility for their own victimization on those who mistreated them. Once their own earlier disruptions were handled, once their earlier memories were processed, they were able to move into accepting responsibility for their adult behavior. As they focused on issues of safety, they realized that they no longer had to act as they had in the past. They recognized that they had choices regarding their behavior, and they could make the choice, which they often verbalized as "Let me do something that is useful, to expiate." Some began working with the police in prevention programs to make sure that other children were not abused. We often see victims, after trauma resolution, make a decision to, "Let me make it fruitful; Let me be useful; Let me help others." We see exactly the same thing with perpetrators. If we do not work with our perpetrators, we will always be working with victims.

Treatment of Maladaptive Personality Styles

The AIP model (Shapiro, 2001) posits that EMDR can change maladaptive personality traits, not just transient symptoms (see also Manfield & Shapiro, in press). Treatment can be more than the acquisition of self-control techniques and affect management skills used to take us out of the state of anxiety and move us into a positive affect. Maladaptive personality patterns and characteristics are understood to be rooted in dysfunctional memory configurations. Stored within these networks, in an essentially intact form, are the negative affects and distorted perceptions of the traumatic experience. Therefore, regardless of current age, the client may respond from the vantage point of development arrested at the time of the small-T or large-T trauma. When we process dysfunctionally stored negative memories, so that these connect with more adaptive information and take on different affects and meaning, there is a shift in the person's self-concept and their sense of self in the world. The assimilation of these fully processed memories is the basis of healthy personality development, and is apparent in changed attitudes and behaviors.

These changes are beneficial, not only to the individual, but also to society. Much violent behavior is transmitted from one generation to the next; traumatized mothers cannot appropriately attend to their children, who may then develop various disorders. Although there may be other contributors to these disorders, processing related etiological events can be effective in reducing or eliminating the complaints. The effect of healing one person can have a profound influence on family, local community, and society.

In South Africa, during Apartheid, mothers were imprisoned and separated from their children. There is a whole generation of children whose early

attachments were disrupted; many of these individuals are now extremely violent, and apparently incapable of feeling empathy or interpersonally connected
(see also Perry, 1997). But, humans are resilient, and the AIP model maintains
that these neurological deficits can be reversed, using very sensitive therapy, a
close therapeutic relationship, and appropriate processing (Shapiro, 2001).

Goals and Responsibilities

Psychologists take on the responsibility of caring for the psyche of their
clients. What are we doing for the psyche, or soul, of the world? What
are we doing for the under-served populations on this planet? For developing countries? For countries with very little mental health service infrastructure? For countries who have few mental health professionals at all? We are
looking forward to future opportunities to teach paraprofessionals in these
countries to use the most robust integrative protocols under appropriate
supervision.

For example, after a hurricane in Mexico, members of the EMDR Humanitarian Assistance Programs (HAP; www.emdrhap.org) traveled to Mexico to
do pro bono work; one was from Canada, another from the United States.
They found schoolyards of traumatized children, and were invited to work
with the Mexican critical incident group. In order to provide treatment to so
many with such limited resources, a group EMDR protocol was developed,
which included the "butterfly hug" (Jarero, Artigas, Mauer, Alcala, & Lupez,
1999). The children were asked to draw a picture of the hurricane and to rate
their feelings on a scale of 0–10. Monitored by the HAP clinicians, the children looked at their pictures, crossed their arms, and tapped their shoulders.
Then another picture was drawn, and the procedure repeated for a series of
pictures. From one picture to the next, a steady decrease in distress, a decline
in the amount of disturbance, and a change in content was evident. Follow-up
showed that treatment effects were maintained.

After a Nicaraguan disaster, the Mexican team, now trained in EMDR, flew
to Nicaragua to help the victims there; having received the benefits of treatment
in their own country they wanted to share it with others. At one time, they were
working with a group of 25 orphans in a mountain area where a mudslide had
occurred. In additon to the butterfly hug, the clinicians also worked with the
children by patting them rhythmically on their hands. On the day following
the first group treatment, as the children sat around waiting for the second
day's session, they started patting each other as they had been patted the day
before. This desire to help one another is what is often blocked by trauma.

People who are hurting often withdraw or hurt others. Those that are healed want to help. This becomes another goal of the individual work: To foster the ability to reach beyond the trauma to each other, to connect to each other, and as in this case, to reach out to help each other.

The probability that individuals will experience happiness and the opportunity to grow to their full human potential can be dampened, or even extinguished, through the effects of unresolved negative experiences. While the processing of these memories liberates the individual and allows the experiences to be appropriately assimilated, if the memories remain unprocessed, they will be dysfunctionally stored. Then the person's potential is constrained by static brain states, resulting in the activation of stored perceptions, cognitions, and affects, with related maladaptive behaviors. These effects are detrimental, not only to the individual; they can cascade onto others and into the next generation. Whatever the cause—the unhealed traumas of disasters or war, the disruptions born of poverty and violence in the inner cities, separations of parents and children due to natural or manmade disasters, genocide or ethnopolitical violence—people who are hurting are likely to hurt others, whether deliberately or unintentionally. Whether this transmission of pain is caused explicitly or implicitly, this process must be addressed by our profession.

Those that have been healed can open up to life and they can open up to service. Therefore, one of the goals of psychotherapy is undoing, on all levels, the effects of trauma. Large-T trauma events can cause the obvious symptoms of PTSD. These symptoms are generally so disruptive and make life so unmanageable that clients come into therapy and can be healed. Not only are the symptoms of PTSD eradicated in treatment, the underlying configurations that have caused lives of "quiet desperation" are also healed. These are individuals like Lynne who, without awareness, married men who were duplicates of her father.

Victims of small-T traumas may not seek treatment because their symptoms do not appear to interfere with their function. We do not give them a diagnosis; their lives are not unmanageable, and they remain mostly unaware of the deleterious effects of these experiences. These are individuals like Maura, who was unaware of the repercussions of unhealed loss, individuals who reenact their traumas with their children through automatic behaviors, movements, and expressions, and thus transmit their pain to the next generation.

Given all we know about the psychological and physical effects of unhealed trauma, we must help the underserved become aware of how they are affecting each other and the next generation. This knowledge must be presented to the general public, and information should be provided in both education and comprehensive treatment programs. Research is needed to identify precisely what experiences are necessary to foster the development of a healthy, happy adult who is capable of love, joy, and service. Then we can improve our educational programs to encourage these types of interactions and experiences with the natural family setting. We also need to develop procedures to orchestrate this development within a clinical setting when it has not occurred naturally. To this end, we must integrate our many tools and the wisdom of different psychotherapeutic orientations to develop methods to efficiently engender the appropriate developmental stages for these parents and children alike.

It is clear that the healing of trauma victims is of supreme importance and must be multidimensional in scope. Treatment for individuals must comprehensively address cognitive, somatic, and affective elements, to achieve changes in both understanding and implicit reactions. Treatment for traumatized families must address both parents and children. At a societal level, it must address both perpetrators and victims. The multidimensional approach is absolutely essential to ensure that the negative effects and the cycles of interpersonal abuse, regardless of their origin, are ended within one generation. What better goal can we have as a profession than to extend these benefits not only to any one family, such as Maura and Ashley, but to the underserved populations worldwide?

References

American Psychiatric Association. (2000). *Diagnostic and statistical manual of mental disorders* (4th ed., text revision). Washington, DC: Author.

Andrade, J., Kavanagh, D., & Baddeley, A. (1997). Eye-movements and visual imagery: a working memory approach to the treatment of post-traumatic stress disorder. *British Journal of Clinical Psychology, 36,* 209–223.

Breslau, N., Chilcoat, H. D., Kessler, R. C., & Davis, G. C. (1999). Previous exposure to trauma and PTSD effects of subsequent trauma: Results from the Detroit area survey of trauma. *American Journal of Psychiatry, 156,* 902–907.

Brown, K. W., McGoldrick, T., & Buchanan, R. (1997). Body dysmorphic disorder: Seven cases treated with eye movement desensitization and reprocessing. *Behavioural & Cognitive Psychotherapy, 25,* 203–207.

Carlson, J. G., Chemtob, C. M., Rusnak, K., Hedlund, N. L., & Muraoka, M. Y. (1998). Eye movement desensitization and reprocessing for combat-related posttraumatic stress disorder. *Journal of Traumatic Stress, 11,* 3–24.

Chambless, D. L., Baker, M. J., Baucom, D. H., Beutler, L. E., Calhoun, K. S., Crits-Christoph, P., Daiuto, A., DeRubeis, R., Detweiler, J., Haaga, D. A. F., Bennett Johnson, S., McCurry, S., Mueser, K. T., Pope, K. S., Sanderson, W. C., Shoham, V., Stickle, T., Williams, D. A., & Woody, S. R. (1998). Update on empirically validated therapies. *The Clinical Psychologist, 51,* 3–16.

Chemtob, C. M., Tolin, D. F., van der Kolk, B. A., & Pitman, R. K. (2000). Eye movement desensitization and reprocessing. In E. B. Foa, T. M. Keane, & M. J. Friedman (Eds.), *Effective treatments for PTSD: Practice guidelines from the International Society for Traumatic Stress Studies* (pp. 139–155, 333–335). New York: Guilford Press.

Cicchetti, D., & Toth, S. L. (1995). A developmental psychopathology perspective on child abuse and neglect. *Journal of American Academy of Child and Adolescent Psychiatry, 34*(5), 541–565.

Grant, M., & Threlfo, C. (2002). EMDR and the treatment of chronic pain. *Journal of Clinical Psychology, 58,* 1505–1520.

Hesse, E., & Main, M. (1999). Second-generation effects of unresolved trauma in non-maltreating parents: Dissociated, frightened, and threatening parental behavior. In D. Diamond & S. J. Blatt (Eds.), Psychoanalytic theory and attachment research I: Theoretical considerations. *Psychoanalytic Inquiry, 19,* 481–540.

Hesse, E., & Main, M. (2000). Disorganization in infant and adult attachment: Description, correlates, and implications for developmental psychopathology. *Journal of the American Psychoanalytic Association. 48*(4), 1097–1127.

Ironson, G. I., Freund, B., Strauss, J. L., & Williams, J. (2002). Comparison of two treatments for traumatic stress: A community-based study of EMDR and prolonged exposure. *Journal of Clinical Psychology, 58,* 113–128.

Jarero, I., Artigas, L., Mauer, M., Alcala, N., & Lupez, T. (1999, November). *EMDR integrative group treatment protocol and the butterfly hug.* Paper presented at the annual meeting of the International Society for Traumatic Stress Studies, Miami, FL.

Kavanaugh, D. J., Freese, S., Andrade, J., & May, J. (2001). Effects of visuospatial tasks on desensitization to emotive memories. *British Journal of Clinical Psychology, 40,* 267–280.

Klaus, M., & Kennel, J. (1976). *Maternal-infant bonding.* St. Louis: Mosby.

Korn, D. L., & Leeds, A. M. (2002). Preliminary evidence of efficacy for EMDR resource development and installation in the stabilization phase of treatment of complex posttraumatic stress disorder. *Journal of Clinical Psychology, 58,* 1465–1488.

Lee, C., Gavriel, H., Drummond, P., Richards, J., & Greenwald, R. (2002). Treatment of post-traumatic stress disorder: A comparison of stress inoculation training with prolonged exposure and eye movement desensitization and reprocessing. *Journal of Clinical Psychology, 58,* 1071–1089.

Lovett, J. (1999). *Small wonders: Healing childhood trauma with EMDR.* New York: Free Press.

Madrid, A., Ames, R., Skolek, S., & Brown, G. (2000). Does maternal-infant bonding therapy improve breathing in asthmatic children? *Journal of Prenatal and Perinatal Psychology and Health 15,* 90–117.

Manfield, P., & Shapiro, F. (in press). The application of EMDR to the treatment of personality disorders. In J. F. Magnavita (Ed.), *Handbook of personality: Theory and practice.* New York: Wiley.

Marcus, S. V., Marquis, P., & Sakai, C. (1997). Controlled study of treatment of PTSD using EMDR in an HMO setting. *Psychotherapy, 34,* 307–315.

Marks, I. M., Lovell, K., Noshirvani, H., Livanou, M., & Thrasher, S. (1998). Treatment of posttraumatic stress disorder by exposure and/or cognitive restructuring: A controlled study. *Archives of General Psychiatry, 55,* 317–325.

Maxfield, L. (2002). Commonly asked questions about EMDR and suggestions for research parameters. In F. Shapiro (Ed.), *EMDR as an integrative psychotherapy approach: Experts of diverse orientations explore the paradigm prism.* Washington, DC: American Psychological Association Books.

Maxfield, L., & Hyer, L. A. (2002). The relationship between efficacy and methodology in studies investigating EMDR treatment of PTSD. *Journal of Clinical Psychology, 58,* 23–41.

Neziroglu, F., McKay, D., Todaro, J., & Yaryura-Tobias, J. A. (1996). Effect of cognitive behavior therapy on persons with body dsymorphic disorder and comorbid axis II diagnoses. *Behavior Therapy, 27,* 67–77.

Perkins, B., & Rouanzoin, C. (2002). A critical examination of current views regarding eye movement desensitization and reprocessing (EMDR): Clarifying points of confusion. *Journal of Clinical Psychology, 58,* 77–97.

Perry, B. (1997). Incubated in terror: Neurodevelopmental factors in the cycle of violence. In J. Osofsky (Ed.), *Children, youth and violence: Searching for solutions* (pp. 124–149). New York: Guilford Press.

Popky, A. J., & Levin. C. (1994). *Transcript of EMDR treatment session.* Palo Alto, CA: Mental Research Institute EMDR Research Center.

Rogers, S., & Silver, S. M. (2002). Is EMDR an exposure therapy?: A review of trauma protocols. *Journal of Clinical Psychology, 58,* 43–59.

Rothbaum, B. O. (1997). A controlled study of eye movement desensitization and reprocessing for posttraumatic stress disordered sexual assault victims. *Bulletin of the Menninger Clinic, 61,* 317–334.

Scheck, M. M., Schaeffer, J. A., & Gillette, C. S. (1998). Brief psychological intervention with traumatized young women: The efficacy of eye movement desensitization and reprocessing. *Journal of Traumatic Stress, 11,* 25–44.

Schore, A. N. (1994). *Affect regulation and the origin of self: The neurobiology of emotional development.* Hillsdale, NJ: Erlbaum.

Shapiro, F. (1989). Efficacy of the eye movement desensitization procedure in the treatment of traumatic memories. *Journal of Traumatic Stress Studies, 2,* 199–223.

Shapiro, F. (1995). *Eye movement desensitization and reprocessing: Basic principles, protocols and procedures* (1st ed.). New York: Guilford Press.

Shapiro, F. (2001). *Eye movement desensitization and reprocessing: Basic principles, protocols and procedures* (2nd ed.). New York: Guilford Press.

Shapiro, F. (2002a). *EMDR as an integrative psychotherapy approach: Experts of diverse orientations explore the paradigm prism.* Washington, DC: American Psychological Association Books.

Shapiro, F. (2002b). EMDR twelve years after its introduction: Past and future research. *Journal of Clinical Psychology, 58,* 1–22.

Shapiro, F., & Forrest, M. (1997). *EMDR.* New York: Basic Books.

Shapiro, F., & Maxfield, L. (2002). EMDR: An information processing treatment for PTSD. *In Session: Journal of Clinical Psychology. Special Issue: Treatment of PTSD, 58,* 933–946.

Sharpley, C. F., Montgomery, I. M., & Scalzo, L. A. (1996). Comparative efficacy of EMDR and alternative procedures in reducing the vividness of mental images. *Scandinavian Journal of Behaviour Therapy, 25,* 37–42.

Siegel, D. J. (1999). *The developing mind: Toward a neurobiology of interpersonal experience.* New York: Guilford Press.

Siegel, D. J. (2002). The developing mind and the resolution of trauma: Some ideas about information processing and an interpersonal neurobiology of psychotherapy. In F. Shapiro (Ed.), *EMDR as an integrative treatment approach: Experts of diverse orientations explore the paradigm prism* (pp. 85–121). Washington DC: American Psychological Association Books.

Stickgold, R. (2002). EMDR: A putative neurobiological mechanism of action. *Journal of Clinical Psychology, 58,* 61–75.

van den Hout, M., Muris, P., Salemink, E., & Kindt, M. (2001). Autobiographical memories become less vivid and emotional after eye movements. *British Journal of Clinical Psychology, 40,* 121–130.

van der Kolk, B. A. (2002). Beyond the talking cure: Somatic experience and subcortical imprints in the treatment of trauma. In F. Shapiro (Ed.), *EMDR as an integrative treatment approach: Experts of diverse orientations explore the paradigm prism* (pp. 57–83). Washington DC: American Psychological Association Books.

Van Etten, M. L., & Taylor, S. (1998). Comparative efficacy of treatments for posttraumatic stress disorder: A meta-analysis. *Clinical Psychology and Psychotherapy, 5,* 126–144.

Vogelmann-Sine, S., Sine, L. F., Smyth, N. J., & Popky, A. J. (1998). *EMDR chemical dependency treatment manual.* New Hope, PA: EMDR Humanitarian Assistance Programs.

Wilson, S. A., Becker L. A., & Tinker, R. H. (1995). Eye movement desensitization and reprocessing (EMDR) treatment for psychologically traumatized individuals. *Journal of Consulting and Clinical Psychology, 63,* 928–937.

Wilson, S. A., Becker, L. A., & Tinker, R. H. (1997). Fifteen-month follow-up of eye movement desensitization and reprocessing (EMDR) treatment for PTSD and psychological trauma. *Journal of Consulting and Clinical Psychology, 65,* 1047–1056.

Wolpe, J. (1958). *Psychotherapy by reciprocal inhibition.* Stanford, CA: Stanford University Press.

6

Dyadic Regulation and Experiential Work with Emotion and Relatedness in Trauma and Disorganized Attachment

Diana Fosha

Introduction

Mary Main ended her talk (2001) with a plea and a mandate: "Effective interventions effect change. Study and document that process." Precisely. In the unfolding conversation between clinicians and affective neuroscientists, the data of clinical change processes can spur the next wave of progress in neuroscience, namely the elucidation of the psychobiology of plasticity.

Emergent understandings based on advances in *affective neuroscience* (Damasio, 1994, 1999; LeDoux, 1996, 2002; Panksepp, 1998, 2000; Porges, 1997; Schore, 1994; Siegel, 1999), *attachment theory and research* (Ainsworth, Blehar, Waters, & Wall, 1978; Bowlby, 1973, 1980, 1982, 1991; Fonagy, Steele, et al., 1995; Main, 1995), and developmental research *into mother-infant interaction* (Beebe & Lachmann, 1994; Emde, 1988; Jaffe, Beebe, Feldstein, Crown, & Jasnow, 2001; Stern, 1985; Trevarthen, 2000; Tronick, 1989, 1998), are increasingly informing and transforming how we do clinical work (Beebe & Lachmann, 2002; Fosha, 2000b, 2002a; Hughes, in preparation; Lachmann, 2001; Rothschild, 2000; Stern et al., 1998; van der Kolk, 2001). Clinicians can make this a truly two-way conversation by putting forth their privileged understanding of how change occurs, and what change looks like when it occurs. Accompanied by a descriptive phenomenology of the healing process, the data documenting change in psychotherapy can then shape future questions in neuroscientific and developmental research. What clinical experience reveals about the mind can thus contribute to the further unlocking of the secrets of the brain and of the developmental processes by which the brain is molded; such scientific advances can, in turn, only further enhance the effectiveness of therapeutic intervention.

For instance, it appears that (a) the right brain and subcortical structures like the amygdala, the periaqueductal gray, and the brainstem are centrally involved in emotional processing, that (b) the prefrontal cortex plays a major role in affect regulation and secure attachment, and that (c) trauma and emotional neglect—which lead to disorganized attachment—compromise the structure and function of right hemisphere, subcortical structures and the prefrontal cortex. But it also appears that therapeutic interventions that involve emotion, the body, somatosensory activation, and bilateral information-processing mechanisms (see Fosha, 2000b, 2002a; Levine, 1997; Neborsky, this volume; Rothschild, 2000; Shapiro, this volume; Siegel, this volume) are effective in functionally reversing the effects of trauma. How does neuroscience explain such therapeutic results? What mechanisms operate in the brain when life-long patterns of behavior, emotion regulation, and relatedness are rapidly transformed?

The Paradox Between Continuity and Plasticity

Questions such as these reveal a paradox between continuity and plasticity, between structure and state, between vulnerability and resilience, between intransigence and transformation.

CONTINUITY OF PSYCHIC ORGANIZATION OVER THE LIFESPAN AND ITS INTERGENERATIONAL TRANSMISSION

On the side of continuity, we have powerful evidence that affect-regulating experiences with caregivers become immortalized in the psychic organization of the child (Cassidy, 1994; Fonagy et al., 1991; Hesse & Main, 1999, 2000; Main, 1995) and shape the landscape of the brain, particularly the right brain (e.g., Schore, 1996; Siegel, 1999; Trevarthen & Aitken, 1994). For example, neglect and emotional deprivation in the first years of life lead to left hippocampal shrinkage, corpus callosum damage, and dendritic burnout (Schore, this volume; Siegel, this volume; Teicher, 2002). The characteristics of affect-regulating relationships, or lack thereof, are also immortalized through their transmission to future generations (Fonagy, Steele, et al., 1995; Main, 1995). The intergenerational transmission of attachment states of mind is an extraordinarily robust finding, with wide-ranging implications. Witness the continuity of the Adult Attachment Interview (AAI) ratings over time (Main, this volume), and its uncanny capacity to predict the attachment status of babies yet unborn (Fonagy et al., 1991). We have evidence of the stability of attachment classifications over time and their power to predict academic and social functioning, predisposition to pathology, and vulnerability for trauma (see Main, 1995). Such evidence strongly supports the psychoanalytic axiom that early experiences with caregivers determine lifelong patterns (Seligman, 1998), which makes the possibility of effecting change seem quite daunting (Fosha, 2000b, pp. 55–56).

RESPONSIVENESS OF PSYCHIC ORGANIZATION TO CURRENT CONDITIONS
And yet—on the plasticity side of the paradox—we have equally powerful data that document the suppleness of the psyche and its attuned responsiveness to current conditions, especially those favoring self-righting tendencies (Eagle, 1995; Emde, 1981, 1988; Lamb, 1987). As Siegel notes, in children, security or insecurity of attachment is *not* a characteristic of the *individual*, but rather of a *relationship*: it is not uncommon for a child to be securely attached with one parent, and disorganized (or insecurely attached) with the other (Main, 1995). There is evidence that just *one* relationship with a caregiver (and that caregiver does *not* have to be the principal caregiver) who is capable of autobiographical reflection, in other words, a caregiver who possesses a high reflective self function, can enhance the resilience of an individual: Through just one relationship with an understanding other, trauma can be transformed and its effects neutralized or counteracted (Fonagy, Leigh, et al., 1995).[1] Moreover, there is growing evidence that changes in the child's attachment status occur reliably as attachment-focused interventions produce changes in the caregiver (Marvin, Cooper, Hoffman, & Powell, 2002; van den Boom, 1990). For example, changes in the attachment status of toddlers from disorganized to secure are being obtained by means of a 20-session group intervention protocol

---

[1] Disorganized attachment in the child is not a function of trauma or loss suffered by the caregiver; disorganized attachment in the child is the function of *unresolved and unprocessed* trauma or loss in the caregiver, which then interferes with that caregiver's capacity to sustain coherent and integrated autobiographical reflection. The capacity to process trauma is reflected in the capacity for constructing a cohesive and coherent autobiographical narrative (Main, this volume) or, differently expressed, having a high reflective self function (Coates, 1998; Fonagy, 1997; Fonagy & Target, 1998). Parents with a high reflective self function, independent of their own attachment status or trauma histories, tend to have securely attached children (Fonagy, Steele, et al., 1995; Main, 1995).

with their caregivers (Marvin et al., 2002). As parents move from defensive processes to increased empathy for their children, the children's attachment security increases.

Thus, on one side we have the *continuity* of psychic organization over time and the power of early experience to shape mind, brain, psyche, and behavior of both the individual and future generations. On the other side, there is the equally compelling evidence of the psyche's exquisite *responsiveness* to current conditions, especially when these conditions favor the activation of the individual's self-righting, self-healing mechanisms. It is here, on the side of plasticity, that we find these change phenomena in search of a biology. And it is in this rich soil that the affective neuroscience of psychotherapeutic healing can take root and flourish.

The data I contribute have been obtained through the application of Accelerated Experiential-Dynamic Psychotherapy (AEDP), a treatment model with a therapeutics informed by a healing-centered metapsychology (Fosha, 2000b, 2002a, 2002b). AEDP seeks to effect its healing by facilitating the individual's visceral experience of core affective phenomena within an emotionally engaged patient-therapist dyad: *the provision and fostering of new emotional experiences is both AEDP's method and its aim.* In the next section of this chapter I will present AEDP, and show how it is harmonious with the implications of recent advances in affective neuroscience and developmental studies. This is followed by a case study I call "Fright without solution." The title comes from a paper by Hesse and Main (2000) on the role of fear in disorganized attachment. I present clinical work from two consecutive sessions which proved pivotal in fostering a major transformation in the patient. Detailed transcript material is provided and microanalyzed to illustrate AEDP and the actual moment-to-moment tracking of affective experience involved in experiential clinical work. The relationship between the *dyadic regulation of affective states* and *the experience of intense emotion* in therapy, in development, and in psychopathology will be explored throughout.

TOWARD AN EFFECTIVE THERAPY INFORMED BY AFFECTIVE NEUROSCIENCE AND ATTACHMENT STUDIES

Affective Neuroscience

The neurobiological processes involved in the processing of emotion and affect regulation in optimal development, and compromised in trauma, involve the right brain: The right brain, the dominant hemisphere for affect regulation, is early maturing and dominant in the first 3 years of life, indicating the essentially affective nature of mental functioning in the first years of life. Right brain functioning, the quality of the right mind, so to speak, involves processes that are affect-laden, visual/imagistic, sensorimotor, and somatic; the language in which emotional experience is encoded is nonlinear and not linguistically mediated, but, instead, body-focused, and experiential.

Crucial aspects of the development of the brain are shaped in early experiences (Damasio, 1994) between infant and caregiver (Schore, 1996). During the first 2 years of life, the brain is growing at the most rapid rate of the entire lifespan. Dyadic emotional processes between infants and caregivers involving attunement, empathy, affective resonance, gaze sharing, entrained vocal rhythms, and mutually shared pleasure (Beebe & Lachmann, 1994; Jaffe et al., 2001; Panksepp, 2000; Stern, 1985; Trevarthen, 2000; Tronick, 1989, 1998), processes primarily mediated by the right brain, are associated with positive affective states (Schore, 1996; Siegel, 1999). The maintenance of positive affective states associated with dyadic experiences of affective resonance has been suggested to be crucial to optimal neurobiological development. "The baby's brain is not only affected by these interactions, *its growth literally requires brain-brain interactions* and occurs in the context of a positive relationship between mother and infant" (Schore, 1996, p. 62, italics added; see also Trevarthen & Aitken, 1994). The positive affects associated with these moment-to-moment, dyadic, right-brain to right-brain affective experiences are the stuff of secure attachment (Schore, 2000). And secure attachment is at the foundation of optimal mental health and resilience, and operates as a powerful protective factor against the development of trauma.

Disorganized attachment appears to strongly predispose the individual to the development of psychopathology and vulnerability to trauma. Both trauma and the chronic states of dyadic misattunement that become the constituents of disorganized attachment are highly stressful states that compromise development. Trauma is marked by the arousal of the "vehement emotions" (Janet, 1889, in van der Kolk, 2001, p. 3), which are so intense that they interfere with the appraisal and processing of emotional experience and thwart its integration into a coherent narrative. The high levels of arousal that define the vehement emotions interfere with the functioning of areas of the brain, such as the frontal lobe, the prefrontal cortex, and the hippocampus, which are involved in appraisal and executive processes, and lead instead to the automatic and fragmentary nature of sensory and emotional experience characteristic of posttraumatic stress disorder (van der Kolk, 2001).

The sequelae of emotional neglect and deprivation are as stark and damaging as those of overt trauma. Chronic involvement in such states leads to actual dendritic shrinking and atrophy of certain regions of the brain (Schore, this volume; Siegel, 1999; Teicher, 2002). In infancy, aversive dyadic interactions actually have been shown to lead to neuronal cell death in "affective centers" in the limbic system as a result of the high corticosteroid levels generated, as well as to lead to alterations in opiate, dopamine, noradrenaline, and serotonin receptors (LeDoux, 2002; Lyons-Ruth, 2001; Schore, this volume; Siegel, 1999; van der Kolk, 1996).

Frank emotional trauma and the chronically misattuned dyadic interactions characteristic of disorders of attachment (see below), immerse the individual in highly stressful states, involving prolonged exposure to unmetabolized, intense, and intensely negative affects. The evidence suggests that such high stress is damaging. The right hemisphere, certain subcortical structures and neural pathways connecting the orbito-frontal cortex and the right hemisphere, all aspects of brain functioning involved in the processing of emotional experience, are adversely affected. The individual's capacity to process and regulate emotion, fundamental to human relatedness, is substantively affected. The sequelae of trauma and neglect not only become evident in the dramatic disturbances of posttraumatic stress disorder (PTSD), but also make themselves known and felt in the havoc wreaked on social relationships and the devastating ruin of a baseline of well-being.

Attachment Studies: Attachment and the Dyadic Regulation of Affective States

The moment-to-moment dyadic regulation of affect through psychobiological state attunement is the mechanism through which attachments are formed (Fosha, 2001; Schore, 1996). The attachment paradigm (Bowlby, 1973, 1980, 1982), fundamental to understanding human emotional development, is thus intimately linked with emotion regulation and right brain development. Attachment status (secure, organized insecure, or disorganized) reflects the capacity of the dyad to regulate intense affective experience while simultaneously maintaining mutual connection (Fosha, 2000b). Optimally, the processing of emotional experience solidifies, rather than taxes and erodes, the attachment bond.

Evolutionarily, the function of attachment has been to protect the organism from danger. The attachment figure, an older, kinder, stronger, wiser other (Bowlby, 1982), functions as a safe base (Ainsworth et al., 1978), and is a presence that obviates fear and engenders a feeling of safety for the younger organism. The greater the feeling of safety, the wider the range of exploration and the more exuberant the exploratory drive (i.e., the higher the threshold before novelty turns into anxiety and fear). Thus, the fundamental tenet of attachment theory: *security of attachment leads to an expanded range of exploration.* Whereas fear constricts, safety expands the range of exploration. In the absence of dyadically constructed safety, the child has to contend with fear-potentiating aloneness. The child will devote energy to conservative, safety enhancing measures, that is, defense mechanisms, to compensate for what's missing. The focus on maintaining safety and managing fear drains energy from learning and exploration, stunts growth, and distorts personality development.

The qualities of effective caregiving have been elucidated by research into what promotes optimal development and secure attachment. The caregiver's *affective competence* (Fosha, 2000b), reflected in her own internal working models and reflective capacity (Fonagy, Steele, Steele, Higgitt, & Target, 1994; Fonagy, Steele, et al., 1995; Fonagy & Target, 1998; Main, 1995), has been found to promote secure attachment. Conversely, the caregiver's compromised affective competence, that is, her inability to flexibly attune to the child in the process of dyadic affect regulation, makes it necessary for the child to institute *defense mechanisms to compensate for such caregiving lapses*, leading to insecure attachment organizations, or disorganized attachment states of mind, when even defensive efforts fail.

1. *The caregiver's affective competence.* The caregiver qualities that have been empirically demonstrated to be crucial to the child's affective competence— to promote the development of secure attachment in the child, all involve the caregiver's competence in the regulation of emotions, hers and the child's (Ainsworth et al., 1978; Bates, Maslin, & Frankel, 1985; Cassidy, 1994; Emde, 1983; Panksepp, 2000; Schore, 2000; Trevarthen, 2000). A quality I wish to highlight here is the capacity to go "beyond mirroring" (Grossman in Fonagy, Steele, et al., 1995): It involves actively helping the child with stressful and distressing situations, which are beyond their resources to manage. This emotional *lending of a hand*, mostly involving the management of the high-stress categorical emotions, is crucial to dyadic affect regulation. The caregiver's affective competence—informed by an internal working model where affect and relatedness, self and other, and feeling and dealing can all operate in harmony—is at the foundation of the child's sense of security (Fosha, 2000b).

2. *Existing in the heart and mind of the other: the caregiver's reflective self function.* Being able to reflect on emotional experience, one's own and that of the other, is another aspect of affective competence. This has been called the capacity for reflective self function by Fonagy (Fonagy, Steele, et al., 1995), and the capacity for maintaining a coherent and cohesive autobiographical narrative by Main (1995). Most remarkably, this autonoetic capacity (Siegel, 1999) has been shown to interrupt the intergenerational transmission of psychopathology (Main, this volume), and to promote the child's resilience under stress (Fonagy, Steele, et al., 1994).

The caregiver's capacity for reflective self-functioning allows the caregiver to attune to the child and his needs, without her response unduly reflecting the pulls of her own emotional experience. The result of receiving such caregiving is that the child has the experience of *existing in the heart and mind of the other* as himself, and not as an extension of the caregiver.[2] Such experiences become internalized in the individual's own reflective self function that "equips the individual with ballast, a self-righting capacity" (Fonagy et al., 1994, p. 250). The individual develops his own reflective self function which allows him to modulate emotions, coordinate self attunement and other responsiveness, and respond flexibly to new situations.

Thus, the roots of security and resilience are to be found in the sense of being understood by and having the sense of existing in the heart and mind of a loving, caring, attuned and self-possessed other, an other with a mind and heart of her own. In the face of the demonstrated potency of the reflective self function, we can assert, as Fonagy and his colleagues do, that "[t]he biological need to feel understood . . . takes precedence over almost all other goals" (Fonagy, Steele, et al., 1995, pp. 268–269). In one bold move, empathy becomes a central tool for serving the most basic adaptational aims of the human being. And the right-brain to right-brain communication underlying empathy becomes crucial to both the developmental and therapeutic endeavors.

3. *The institution of defense mechanisms to compensate for caregiving lapses: the resulting attachment classification.* The quality of attachment reflects the capacity of the dyad to regulate the intense emotions associated with the vicissitudes of their relationship while maintaining connection. The caregiver assists the child in handling his overwhelming emotions; a large part of the caregiver's affective competence vis-à-vis her child's emotions depends on her ability to regulate her own emotions—triggered by the situation, *and* by the child's emotions—so that they enhance, rather than disrupt, her functioning. The caregiver's own secure internal working model allows her to *feel and deal* while maintaining connection (Fosha, 2000b), and helps her child do the same.

When the caregiver's emotional availability, responsiveness, and reflective capacities are compromised, often as a result of her own trauma and loss, dyadic affective regulation cannot proceed optimally. The more the child's emotions trigger the caregiver's fear, shame, helplessness, or guilt, the more she will disengage emotionally. Desperate to maintain and restore the attachment bond, the child resorts to the *defensive exclusion* of whichever emotions produce

---

[2] I have added the *"heart"* to Fonagy's (1997) beautiful phrase "existing in the mind of the other" in order to highlight the essentially affective nature of the reflection in question.

aversive reactions in the caregiver, regardless of how vital they might be to him (Bowlby, 1980; Main, 1995).

The chronic reliance on defenses against emotional experience instituted to compensate for these lapses in the caregiver's affect-regulatory capacities produces adaptations which are categorized by the attachment classifications, that have been translated into affective functional strategies (Fosha, 2000b). Whereas secure attachment involves the capacity to *feel and deal* without the need to resort to defense mechanisms, the two types of organized insecure attachment are the result of defensive strategies: the strategy of dealing but not feeling in avoidant attachment, and the strategy of feeling *(and reeling)*, *but not dealing* in resistant/ambivalent attachment. However, when even defensive efforts are overwhelmed by the disruptive emotions resulting from unreliable caregiving, we are in the realm of disorganized attachment (Main, 1995, 1999): The only way both self and relationship can be maintained is through momentary immobility—the individual can neither *feel* (dissociation) nor *deal* (paralysis).

Characteristics of a Therapy Informed by Affective Neuroscience and Attachment Studies

What are the implications for a therapy, informed by this wealth of insight into the nature of processes underlying optimal development, attachment psychopathology, and trauma (see also Main, this volume; Schore, this volume; Siegel, this volume; van der Kolk, this volume)? I discuss four of its features below. Note that the therapist's empathy and *affective competence* (Fosha, 2000b) are indispensable and underlie all four:

1. To access emotion and harness its profoundly adaptive and healing resources in therapy, it is important to be able to engage the relevant neurobiological processes. Emotional experience is not processed through language and logic; as the right hemisphere speaks a language of images, sensations, impressions, and urges toward action, therapeutic discourse must be conducted in a language that the right hemisphere speaks. Therapies dealing with disorders that are fundamentally emotional in nature need to be able to reliably access sensory, motoric, and somatic experiences to engage them in a dyadic process of affect regulation and eventual transformation. This requires the bottom-up processing approach of experiential therapies, rather than the top-down approach of most cognitive and insight-focused therapies (Greenberg, Rice, & Elliott, 1993; van der Kolk, 2001). There is a premium on

activating right-brain mediated emotional processes through techniques that focus on sensory, somatic, and motoric experience, and
that involve reliving and picturing, rather than narrating, interpreting,
and analyzing.

2. By definition, dyadic affect regulation takes two to tango. Applying the
central dictum of attachment theory, that safety promotes an expanded
range of exploration, therapist activities that promote the patient's sense
of safety are essential and underlie otherwise frightening emotional
explorations. The therapist's emotional engagement, willingness to go
"beyond mirroring" and actively share in the hard emotional work,
and willingness to make use of her emotional experience are essential
constituents of the therapeutic process. So is the striving to help the
patient feel that he exists "in the heart and mind" of the therapist.

3. Given the centrality of defense in the attachment-based understandings
of psychopathology, a treatment model must also be adept at working
with defenses and getting past them, so as to gain direct experiential
access to feared-to-be-unbearable emotional experiences.

4. Once the patient feels safe, and the impact of defenses has been reversed, bottom-up processing will result in bringing the vehement emotions to the fore. A therapy must have techniques not only for accessing,
but also for processing such intense, usually highly negative and toxic,
emotions. Techniques need to help the individual metabolize these intense emotions so that their activation is not only *not* traumatic (i.e.,
the individual is not retraumatized through the emotional exposure) but
eventually therapeutic; when emotions are adequately processed, the
adaptive benefits of emotional experience can be reached. Thus, emotions and the invaluable information they contain need no longer be
excluded and can be integrated within the individual's autobiographical
narrative, making it increasingly coherent and cohesive.

Accelerated Experiential-Dynamic Psychotherapy (AEDP)

Accelerated experiential-dynamic psychotherapy (AEDP) puts into practice
these fundamental elements. AEDP is characterized by an empathic, affirming,
and emotionally engaged stance and its experiential, dyadic, affect-centered
techniques. *The visceral experience of core affective phenomena within an emotionally engaged
dyad is considered to be the key mutative agent* (Fosha, 2000b, 2001, 2002a). AEDP is
described at length in my book, *The Transforming Power of Affect* (2000b); here,
I will focus on four of its distinguishing features, crucial in the context of

this chapter:

1. AEDP therapeutic stance and techniques aim to facilitate the patient's access to deep, experiential, emotion-centered, body-focused, somato-sensory-motor experiencing. Once affective experience is thus viscerally accessed, regulated, and worked through, AEDP aims to harness reflective processes in order to metabolize and integrate experience, alternating waves of experience and reflection.

2. The therapist's emotional engagement and use of her affect in the therapeutic process define AEDP's therapeutic stance. AEDP aims to (a) foster the establishment of an emotionally engaged, empathy-based patient-therapist bond within which affect regulation of previously disruptive emotional experiences can be processed; and (b) bring about a deep, body-focused, affective-somato-sensory way of being both *in* the patient, as well as *between* patient and therapist. AEDP seeks to entrain dyadic affective processes involving attunement, empathy, and repair following miscoordination: face to face, eyes to eyes, affect to affect, these are essential to creating psychobiological state attunement and fostering a process of right-brain to right-brain communication within the patient-therapist dyad.

3. Restructuring and bypassing defenses so as to arrive at core affect informs all AEDP therapeutic stance and techniques, an aspect of AEDP deeply informed by the experiential STDP (Short-Term Dynamic Psychotherapy) tradition (Davanloo, 1990; McCullough Vaillant, 1997; Neborsky, this volume; Solomon et al., 2001). As both AEDP and attachment theory emphasize the centrality of defensive processes in the development of psychopathology, AEDP techniques for minimizing the impact of defenses are central in this endeavor.

4. AEDP uses a diverse array of techniques derived from both the experiential STDPs (Davanloo, 1990; McCullough Vaillant, 1997; Solomon et al., 2001) and experiential therapies (Gendlin, 1996; Greenberg & Paivio, 1997; Greenberg et al., 1993; Kurtz, 1990) to both access and work with the "vehement emotions" that are aroused in traumatic situations, and dyadically regulate them until their adaptive action tendencies (see below) can come to the fore.

Thus, AEDP has a two-factor theory of therapeutic change: It involves affect and relatedness. Empathy, attunement, and the establishment of security and safety are essential, but not sufficient. The bond that gets created as a result of dyadic processes, the adult therapeutic equivalent of secure attachment, serves as a matrix, a holding environment in which deep emotional processes, the kind mediated by limbic system and right brain, can be experientially accessed, processed, and worked through, so that they can eventually be integrated within the individual's autobiographical narrative.

The visceral, embodied experiencing and full processing of affective phenomena activates adaptive *affective change processes* involving categorical emotion, relatedness, the body, and the self (Fosha, 2002a). The benefits of these affective change processes (see below) can be reaped through their embeddedness in a relational matrix that makes use of the emotions of both partners.

AEDP's therapeutics are rooted in a change-based metapsychology rather than a psychopathology-based metapsychology. The patient's visceral *experience of change* is key: "There is a distinct physical sensation of change, which you recognize once you experienced it. . . . When people have this even once, they no longer helplessly wonder for years whether they are changing or not. Now they can be their own judges of that" (Gendlin, 1981, p. 7).

Affective Change Processes

Optimal Development

Affective change processes are naturally occurring phenomena: They reflect how we are wired. Their transformational effects operate not only in therapy (Fosha, 2002a, 2002b), but in development (Beebe & Lachmann, 1994; Tronick, 1989), in romance (Person, 1988), in religious experiences (James, 1902), in life-changing conversions (e.g., Martin Luther, Gandhi; see Cooper, 1992), in authentic contact and communication (Buber, 1965), and in transforming experiences at trauma conferences! Affective change processes are at work whenever profound changes happen rapidly and one's self is simultaneously deeply engaged, challenged, and supported (Buber, 1965; Stern et al., 1998).

The dyadic regulation of affective states, the experience and expression of categorical emotion, the empathic reflection of self, somatic focusing, and *focusing on the experience of transformation itself* (and affirming the transformation of the self) are the five affective change processes that AEDP focuses on (Fosha, 2002a). These change processes operate moment-to-moment, have clear-cut affective markers, and operate through transformations of state, in other words, in quantum leaps rather than in a slow, gradual, and cumulative fashion, in which the new state is characterized by greater access to emotional resources.

The hallmark of each process is a characteristic *core affective experience*, associated with a transformation of state specific to its mode of action. The experience, expression, and communication of these core affective phenomena, *in the context of a secure, emotionally facilitating dyadic relationship,* culminate in the activation of yet another state, the *core state,* in which maximally effective, transformational therapeutic work takes place. The manifestations of both core affect and core state phenomena associated with each affective change process are summarized in Table 6.1.

Therapeutic work with the affective change processes is a three-stage process (see Figure 6.1), involving three states (defense, core affect, and core state) and two state transformations (from defense to core affect, and from core affect to core state):

The full visceral experience of a specific core affective phenomenon constitutes the first state transformation. When interventions aimed at counteracting defenses, anxiety, helplessness, and shame are effective, *core affective experience* is accessed. The state in which the individual experiences core affect is experientially and psychodynamically discontinuous with the defense-dominated state that precedes it: Characteristic processing is right-brain mediated, that is, it is largely sensorimotor, image-dominated, visceral, nonlinear. There is also much greater access to previously unconscious material, a phenomenon referred to in the experiential STDP[3] literature as "unlocking the unconscious" (Davanloo, 1990): It is as if a door opens to previously unavailable (dissociated, unconscious, split off, neglected, forgotten, ignored) perceptions, memories, and fantasies, organized around that core affective experience. Also unlocked are highly adaptive emotional resources which were previously unavailable to the individual; the enormous healing potential residing within them is released.

The shift from core affect to core state represents the second state transformation. This shift is invariably accompanied by positive affects. The full experience of core affect, unhampered by defense, culminates in the activation of another state, the *core state,* in which there is also no anxiety or defensiveness. The body is not rocked by any particular emotion. There is vitality, relaxation, ease, and clarity. Core state refers to an altered state of openness and contact, where the individual is deeply in touch with essential aspects of his own experience. In this state, experience is intense, deeply felt, unequivocal, and declarative; sensation is heightened, imagery is vivid, pressure of speech is absent, and the material moves easily. Effortless focus and concentration also are features of the core

---

[3] Existing within a tradition devoted to enhancing the effectiveness and efficacy of psychotherapy, the *experiential STDPs* (e.g., Davanloo, 1990; Fosha, 2000b; McCullough Valiant, 1997; Solomon et al., 2001) are models of treatment that have pioneered techniques designed to shorten the length of psychodynamic treatment without losing any of its depth through a systematic focus on the patient's visceral experience of emotion (see Fosha, 2000b, appendix).

TABLE 6.1
The Phenomenology of Affective Change Processess

PROCESS	STATE TRANSFORMATIONS		CONSEQUENCES
AFFECTIVE CHANGE PROCESS	CORE AFFECTIVE PHENOMENA	CORE STATE PHENOMENA	ADAPTIVE CONSEQUENCES
Experience and Expression of Core Emotion	core emotions: anger, sadness, joy, fear, disgust	adaptive action tendencies associated with each emotion; core state experiencing	emotional resources associated with each adaptive action tendency; unlocking unconscious material; new cycle of transformation activated
Dyadic Regulation of Affective States attunement, disruption, and repair	core relational experiences; affective resonance, "in sync" feelings in response to attunement; reparative tendencies in response to disconnection	feelings of intimacy and closeness; trust; core state experiencing	secure attachment; resilience; capacity to move easily between self-attunement and other-receptivity; unlocking unconscious material; new cycle of transformation activated
Empathic Reflection of the Self empathy, validation, "going beyond mirroring"	receptive affective experiences of feeling known, seen and under-stood; having the sense of "existing in the heart and mind of the other"	"true self" experiences of feelings "alive," "real," "like myself"; core state experiencing	secure attachment; resilience; reflective capacity; self-esteem; consolidation of the self; empathy and self-empathy; unlocking unconscious material; new cycle of transformation activated
Somatic Focusing shifting from in-the-head thinking to in-the-body sensing and feeling	*the felt sense;* embodied experiencing	*the body shift;* bodily states of relaxation, openness and being in touch; core state experiencing	activation of self-righting tendencies; ease, calm, flow, energy, vitality, *joie de vivre;* unlocking unconscious material; new cycle of transformation activated
Focus on the Experience of Transformation the activation of the meta-therapeutic processes: mastery; mourning the self; and affirming the self and its transformation	transformational affects: joy and pride; emotional pain; the healing affects of (a) feeling moved and emotional within oneself; (b) love, gratitude, and tenderness toward the other	adaptive action tendencies associated with each emotion; core state experiencing	self-confidence and exploratory zest; clarity, perspective, acceptance; empathy and self-empathy; unlocking unconscious material; new cycle of transformation activated

FIGURE 6.1
THE THREE STATES AND TWO STATE TRANSFORMATIONS OF AEDP

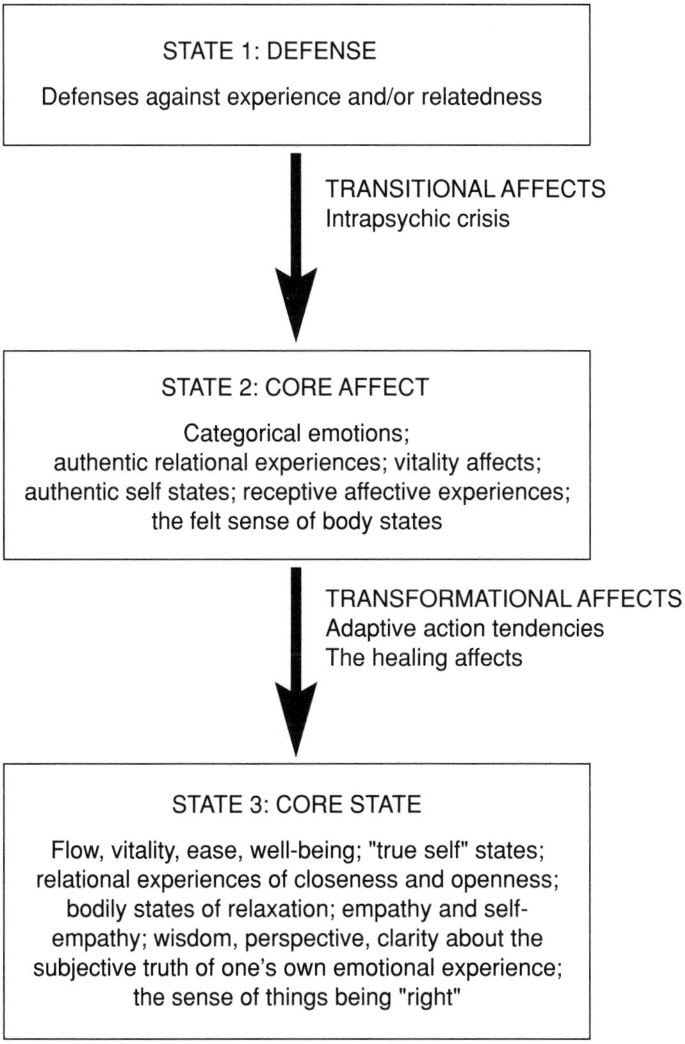

STATE 1: DEFENSE

Defenses against experience and/or relatedness

TRANSITIONAL AFFECTS
Intrapsychic crisis

STATE 2: CORE AFFECT

Categorical emotions;
authentic relational experiences; vitality affects;
authentic self states; receptive affective experiences;
the felt sense of body states

TRANSFORMATIONAL AFFECTS
Adaptive action tendencies
The healing affects

STATE 3: CORE STATE

Flow, vitality, ease, well-being; "true self" states;
relational experiences of closeness and openness;
bodily states of relaxation; empathy and self-
empathy; wisdom, perspective, clarity about the
subjective truth of one's own emotional experience;
the sense of things being "right"

state. Relating is deep and clear, as self-attunement and other-receptivity easily coexist. *Core state phenomena* include but are not limited to (1) the sense of strength, clarity, and resourcefulness associated with the release of *adaptive action tendencies;* (2) *core relational experiences* of love, tenderness, compassion, generosity, and gratitude, relational experiences emergent from a state of *self*-possession; (3) *core self experiences* of what individuals subjectively consider to be their "true self"; (4) *core bodily states* of relaxation, openness, and vitality that emerge in the wake of the *body shift;* and (5) *states of clear and authentic knowing and communication* about one's subjective "truth." Through such complete processing of affective experience, the experiencer of the emotions gets to a new place, fostering what Person described as the "flux in personality, the possibility for change, and the impetus to begin new phases of life and undertake new endeavors" (1988, p. 23). The core state which follows the experience of core affect is optimally suited for the therapeutic integration and consolidation that translate in-session changes into lasting therapeutic results. *It is in the core state that the reflective self function can operate at its fullest potency.*

I will focus on two of the affective change processes—*the dyadic regulation of affective states* and *the experience and expression of the categorical emotions*—as they figure prominently in the case to be presented (see Fosha, 2002a, for a discussion of each affective change process). They involve the regulation of two types of core affective experience, the *vitality affects* and the *categorical emotions,* respectively.

The vitality affects (Stern, 1985; Siegel, 1999) are the micro-affects through which fluctuations in attunement are expressed. They refer to subtle, ongoing, moment-to-moment, qualitative shifts in arousal, energy, feeling, and rhythm (Siegel, 1999; Stern, 1985). Their "elusive qualities are better captured by dynamic, kinetic terms, such as "surging," "fading away," "fleeting," "explosive," "crescendo," "decrescendo," "bursting," "drawn out," and so on.... [The vitality affects] are experienced as dynamic shifts or patterned changes within ourselves" (Stern, 1985, pp. 54–57).[4]

By contrast, *the categorical emotions* (Darwin, 1872)—fear, anger, joy, sadness, disgust—macro-emotions initially processed subcortically (Damasio, 1999, 2000), are big, distinct emotional experiences. Each categorical emotion has its own universal physiological signature (Ekman, 1983; Zajonc, 1985), as well as its own set of characteristic dynamics (Darwin, 1872; Lazarus, 1991; Tomkins, 1962, 1963). Unlike the fleeting, shifting nature of the vitality affects, the distinct bodily correlates of the categorical emotions are highly salient and an integral aspect of how we experience them.

---

[4] The *vitality affects,* as discussed here, significantly overlap with what Damasio (1999) refers to as the *background emotions.*

Now the focus is on how the experience and expression of these two types of *core affective experience* become transformational vehicles for the individual.

THE DYADIC REGULATION OF AFFECTIVE STATES THROUGH THE VITALITY AFFECTS

All affective change processes are dyadically regulated—in development and therapy—until the dyad's regulatory strategies become internalized in the procedural repertoire of the individual. In four of the affective change processes (2–5 in Table 6.1), dyadic regulation operates in the experiential background; however, in the first affective change process, the dyadic process itself is in the experiential foreground.

The dyadic regulation of affective states through fluctuations in voice, gaze, rhythm, touch, and timing is a fundamental aspect of interpersonal interaction throughout the lifespan. In infancy, however, emotional communication *is* communication. It is all there is. And vitality affects are to emotional communication what words are to verbal communication.

The research of the clinical developmentalists into the characteristics of moment-to-moment caregiver-infant emotional communication (Beebe & Lachmann, 1994; Emde, 1988; Gianino & Tronick, 1988; Trevarthen, 1993, 2000; Trevarthen & Aiken, 1994; Tronick, 1989; Tronick & Weinberg, 1997) reveals three phases in the psychobiological process of coregulating affective states: *attunement* (the coordination of affective states), *disruption* (the lapse of mutual coordination), and *repair* (the reestablishment of coordination under new conditions). For example, attuned mutual coordination occurs when the infant's squeal of delight is matched by the mother's excited clapping and sparkling eyes. Now somewhat overstimulated, the baby arches his back and looks away from the mother, down-regulating through lowering arousal. A disruption has occurred and there is miscoordination: the mother, still excited, is leaning forward, while the baby, now serious-faced, pulls away. However, the mother picks up the cue, and begins the repair: she stops laughing and, with a little sigh, quiets down. The baby comes back and makes eye contact, a soft relaxation on his face. Mother and baby gently smile. They are back in sync, the new coordination now occurring around a different affective state than the one that prevailed few seconds before. In striving to reach and maintain mutual coordination, both partners regulate their own affect through interacting with the other.

The coordinated state has positive affective markers and motivational properties; both partners experience pleasure on achieving coordination, strive to maintain it, and work hard to restore it when it is disrupted. The disruption of coordination has negative affective markers and also has powerful motivational properties; in healthy dyads, it activates reparative tendencies aimed at restoring affective coordination and a positive affective state.[5] Even when the affects being coordinated are negative affects, the achievement of mutual coordination is associated with positive affect! This process is at work in the clinical situation when the therapist empathizes with the patient: as therapist and patient resonate with the patient's experience of negative affect, positive relational affects, even if fleeting, often come to the fore.

Mutually shared affective interactions, achieved through psychobiological state attunement, result in the amplification of positive affective states and the reduction of negative ones. Such experiences, which can "crescendo higher and higher," leading to "peak experiences of resonance, exhilaration, awe and being on the same wavelength with the partner" (Beebe & Lachmann, 1994, p. 157), deepen relatedness and security of attachment (Fosha, 2000b, p. 63).

The process of moment-to-moment mutual coordination and affect regulation is considered to be the fundamental mechanism by which attachment is established (Schore, 2000). Countless repetitions of the sequence of attunement, disruption, and repair lead to an affective competence, as the individual internalizes the affect-managing strategies of the dyad (Fosha, 2000b, 2001, 2002a). The experience of being able to repair the stress of disrupted relatedness (i.e., transform negative affects into positive affects and disconnection into reconnection), leads to the individual's confidence in his own abilities, and trust in the capacity of others to respond (Tronick, 1989). Success with efforts to repair dyadic disruptions leads to a certain emotional stick-to-itiveness in the face of adversity which is at the heart of *resilience* (Fonagy et al., 1994).

Thus, the transformation that occurs as the result of the optimal dyadic regulation of affective states is twofold: (a) It leads to the establishment of increasingly secure attachment, which promotes optimal development and fosters maximal learning through the expansion of the range of exploration. (b) Furthermore, the maintenance of positive affective states associated with dyadic experiences of affective resonance has been shown to be crucial to optimal neurobiological development (Schore, 1996, p. 62). However, note that the amplification of the positive affects achieved is through the *repair* of disruption following miscoordination, and *not* through the exclusion of negative states. Disruption and its negative affects is as natural a phase of optimal functioning as is attunement. It is also as vitally important, as we will see below.

---

[5] In dyads where pathological processes are dominant, the negative affect motivates more than momentary disengagement, leading to the establishment of pathological affect-regulating strategies. For instance, the babies of depressed mothers favor withdrawal into the self as an affect-regulating strategy (Tronick & Weinberg, 1997).

This has uncannily precise parallels in treatment (Fosha, 2000b, 2001). Research shows that the therapist's attunement to the patient's affective state and the patient's experience of feeling safe, understood, and affectively resonated with are probably the most powerful contributors to the achievement of positive therapeutic outcome (see also Bohart & Tallman, 1999; Rogers, 1957; Rosenzweig, 1936; Safran & Muran, 2000). When both partners feel in sync and engage around their respective experiences, the individual feels deeply understood, the core state is activated, and mutative therapeutic work can take place.

THE REGULATION OF CATEGORICAL EMOTIONS: THEIR EXPERIENCE AND EXPRESSION
Fear, anger, sadness, joy, and disgust, the categorical emotions that appear on everyone's list, are biological forces to be reckoned with. Darwin (1872/1965) was the first to describe their phenomenology and dynamics and fully appreciate their importance in human adaptation. The categorical emotions are processes of appraisal (Lazarus, 1991); they amplify and make salient that in the environment which is most important to the individual, and thus they heighten motivation (Tomkins, 1962, 1963). Through them, we are able to communicate to ourselves and to others that which is of importance (Bowlby, 1991). For Darwin (1872/1965), as for Bowlby (1991), the most important function of emotional expression is communication among individuals.

There is something particularly powerful about the transformation inherent in the full visceral experience of the categorical emotions. As William James wrote "Emotional occasions . . . are extremely potent in precipitating mental rearrangements. The sudden and explosive ways in which love, jealousy, guilt, fear, remorse, or anger can seize upon one are known to everybody. Hope, happiness, security, resolve . . . can be equally explosive. And emotions that come in this explosive way seldom leave things as they found them" (1902/1985, p. 198).

The full visceral experience of the categorical emotions leads to two kinds of transformations, both highly therapeutic: (1) Through the experience of the specific emotion, the individual gains access to the previously unconscious network of feelings, thoughts, memories, and fantasies associated with the emotion. This is what allows the deep working through of dynamic material related to the roots of the patient's pathology. In that way, core affect is *the royal road to the unconscious* (Fosha, 2000b). (2) Each categorical emotion is associated with an *adaptive action tendency* that " . . . offers a distinctive readiness to act; each points us in a direction that has worked well to handle the recurrent challenges of human life" (Goleman, 1995, p. 4). With the release of the adaptive action tendencies, the individual accesses deep emotional resources, renewed energy, and an expanded repertoire of adaptive behaviors. For example, the adaptive action tendencies released by fully experienced anger often include a sense of strength, assertiveness, and power, which lead to the rediscovery of psychic strength, self-worth, and affective competence.

THE INTEGRATION OF THE DYADIC REGULATION OF VITALITY AFFECTS AND CATEGORICAL EMOTIONS WITHIN THE THREE-PHASE MODEL OF ATTUNEMENT, DISRUPTION, AND REPAIR

Discussions of the centrality of affect regulation in the establishment of attachment have focused on the vitality affects (Schore, 2000; Siegel, 1999; Sroufe, 1995). However, fundamentally, attachment is an evolutionary solution that counters the disorganizing effects of the categorical emotion of fear in the face of danger. Furthermore, the attachment classification system is based on whether the individual is able to manage the big categorical macro-emotions (e.g., fear, grief, anger, joy), associated with the vicissitudes of attachment (e.g., separation, loss, and reunion) or whether defensive strategies need to be instituted when the regulation of such categorical emotions is beyond the emotional resources of the individual. Any psychological model informed by attachment theory must include the regulation of the categorical emotions. The three phases of the dyadic affect regulatory process—attunement, disruption, and repair—provide a model for how change processes reflected in vitality affects and categorical emotions can be coherently integrated into the treatment of the sequelae of trauma and disorganized attachment.

The vitality affects are the affects of attunement: they both express it and are vehicles for its achievement. As a function of their ephemeral and fluid nature, they are well suited to dyadic coordination and mutual affective sharing. However, as discussed above, the categorical emotions are highly individual experiences. By their very nature, the categorical emotions belong to the second phase of the process of dyadic affect regulation, the disruption phase. A burst of tears, an explosion of anger, a paroxysm of laughter, disrupt the smooth surface of dyadic coordination. Take an ordinary interaction: Mother and baby are happily playing. Energized by the crescendo of affectively resonant states shared between them, with a big grin of delight, the baby enthusiastically yanks the mother's hair; the mother grimaces and, for a split second, shows a face of anger. The baby wails in fear and despair. Ordinary, but disruption *par excellence.*

If the dyad can contain and work with the affect storm, whether big or small, momentary or longer-lasting, then it will be possible to regain mutual coordination in a way that does not make the exclusion and curtailment of the categorical emotion necessary. If the dyad can process the categorical emotion, defenses against the emotion may not be necessary. The coordination that emerges upon the success of repair gives rise to a new coordinated state, which is more complex and more inclusive as it contains within it the initially divergent information of each partner's experience: through the dyadic processing of affective disruptions, an expanded state of consciousness emerges, which is how growth and learning take place for both partners (Tronick, 1998). Three transformational processes are activated: (1) adaptive action tendencies associated with the categorical emotion, (2) bond-strengthening and learning-promoting brain states resulting from positive resonant shared affects, and (3) the dyadic expansion of consciousness of each partner toward greater complexity.[6]

The Development of Psychopathology

In optimal development, affective change processes naturally unfold and the individual can reap their adaptive benefits. In pathogenic environments, affective change processes, instead of bringing psychic gains, bring aversive results as the experience and expression of core affective phenomena meet with disruptive, nonfacilitating responses from the primary attachment figure. For instance, the expression of distress meets with the other's anxiety; desire for contact elicits the other's withdrawal; the offering of love is met with indifference; authentic self-expression evokes angry rejection. The caregiver is unable to maintain coordination in the face of the child's spontaneous emotional experience; some aspect of the child's emotional being triggers profound discomfort in the caregiver, who responds either inadequately, with *errors of omission* (e.g., withdrawal, distancing, neglect, denial), or attackingly, with *errors of commission* (e.g., blaming, shaming, punishing, attacking). The disruption in mutual coordination caused by core affect cannot be dyadically repaired.

---

[6] A technical note: The vitality affects are the surface manifestations of categorical emotions when these latter are not at their most intense. Stopping the action and focusing on the individual's experience at any point of the emotion-laden dyadic process can lead to the unfolding of a categorical emotion. It is a clinical judgment call as to which source of therapeutic healing will most benefit the patient at any given moment: that which comes as a result of reparation and restoration of attunement and its positive affects, a dyadic process, or that which comes as a result of accessing the adaptive action tendencies associated with each categorical emotion and the emotional resources it unlocks, a deeply intrapsychic process. Of course, it is in those therapeutic moments, when both of these processes are optimally engaged, that a deep transformation, on the order of a paradigm shift of procedural strategies, happens for the patient. It is that which we strive for and that which occurs over the course of the 2 sessions I will present later in this chapter.

These disruptive reactions on the part of the attachment figure (i.e., the errors of commission or omission) elicit a second wave of emotional reactions. The individual has to contend not only with the initial emotion-stimulating event; now he also has to contend with a second emotion-stimulating event, namely, the negative reaction of the figure of attachment. Fear and shame, *the pathogenic affects* (Fosha, 2002a), arise when the response of the attachment figure to the individual's core affective experience is disturbing and disruptive. When shame and fear[7] are elicited by disruptive experiences with attachment figures *and* cannot be dyadically repaired, individuals find themselves alone, emotionally overwhelmed, unable to be real and unable to count on the safety of the emotional environment. Highly aversive, the hallmark of *the pathogenic affects* is that they are experienced by an individual who is alone, as the affect-regulating attachment relationship has collapsed.

The combination of (1) interrupted core affective experiences, (2) compromised self-integrity and disrupted attachment ties, and (3) the overwhelming experience of the pathogenic affects in the context of unwilled and unwanted aloneness leads to *unbearable emotional states:* these include experiences of helplessness, hopelessness, loneliness, confusion, fragmentation, emptiness, and despair, the "black hole" (van der Kolk, 2001) of human emotional experience, where the individual is at his most depleted, with no safety and no access to emotional resources. The attempt to escape the excruciating experience of these unbearable emotional states becomes the seed for defensive strategies that, when chronically relied on, culminate in the development of psychopathological conditions (see top half of Figure 6.2).

The patient comes to rely upon defenses, denying, avoiding, numbing, or disavowing the affectively laden experiences that wreaked such havoc in the past and are expected to do so again. Psychic survival becomes possible only through the *defensive exclusion* (Bowlby, 1980) of the very processes

---

[7] There is a crucial distinction to be made between fear and shame as core affective experiences (core affects, for short) and fear and shame as pathogenic affects. As core affect, fear provides important adaptive information about the dangerous aspects of the situation that elicits it and triggers the adaptive action tendencies associated with it—i.e., flight, immobility, but also notably, attachment-seeking behaviors. A child who is afraid of a dog or of a stranger runs to the caregiver for assistance. Similarly, shame as a core affect arising in response to a specific event or behavior is an essential tool for social learning. That kind of shame can be metabolized in the context of an affect-facilitating environment (Hughes, 1998; Schore, 1996), as the attuned caregiver repairs and reestablishes the feeling of connection. Fear and shame become problematic only when they are elicited by the attachment relationship itself and their disruptive effects cannot be dyadically repaired. It is then that they function as pathogenic affects. Fear about the very person who is supposed to be the safe base disrupts the attachment relationship and its essential protective function (Hesse & Main, 1999, 2000). Shame which is not about a specific behavior but which, instead, is about the essential nature of the self disrupts the very integrity of self experience and of the individual's ongoing sense of being (Hughes, 1998; Schore, 1996).

FIGURE 6.2

AFFECT REGULATORY DIFFICULTIES AND THE DEVELOPMENT OF PSYCHOPATHOLOGY

CORE AFFECTIVE PHENOMENA	→	FAILURES OF DYADIC REGULATION	→	THE PATHOGENIC AFFECTS	→	UNBEARABLE STATES OF ALONENESS	→	CONSEQUENCES
core emotions; core relational experiences; reparative tendencies in response to disconnection; "true self" experiences; spontaneous bodily states; the realization of emotional truth; the healing affects		misattunement and the failure to repair *errors of omission* (withdrawal, avoidance, denial, neglect) *errors of commission* (criticism, humiliation, punishment, ridicule)		fear shame		loneliness, despair, helplessness and hopelessness, emptiness, sense of self as "bad" "defective," "worthless"; fragmentation, loss of control, falling apart, confusion, panic		the institution of defenses against experiencing and/or relatedness

THE REVISED TRIANGLE OF CONFLICT

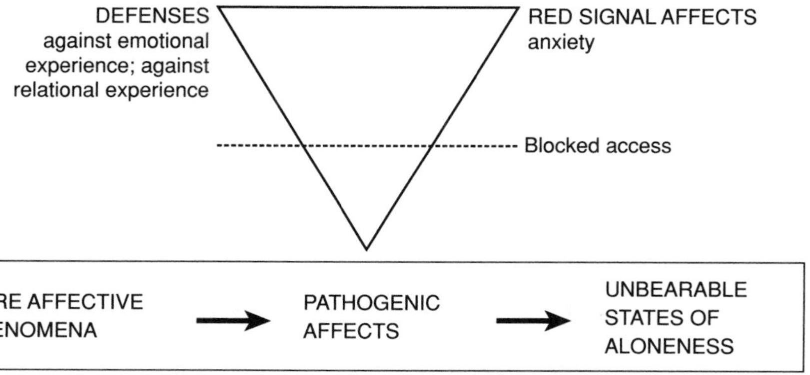

RED SIGNAL AFFECTS
anxiety

------ Blocked access

DEFENSES
against emotional
experience; against
relational experience

CORE AFFECTIVE PHENOMENA	→	PATHOGENIC AFFECTS	→	UNBEARABLE STATES OF ALONENESS

that constitute optimal psychic health. Core affective experiences and their adaptive consequences are preempted, leaving the individual with terribly reduced resources to face the challenges of the world. The expanded triangle of conflict[8] schematically represents how emotional experience comes to be structured (see bottom half of Figure 6.2).

Returning to the paradox between continuity and change and between vulnerability and resilience: All emotional experiences occur in a relational context. Precisely how experience is structured depends on that emotional environment. Any triangle of conflict is embedded within a particular self-other-emotion configuration (see Figure 6.3), which is AEDP's version of an internal working model (Bowlby, 1982), where *emotion* is prominently structured in. Different self-other-emotion configurations give rise to different kinds of functioning. By changing one element of the self-other-emotion configuration, the individual's experience can dramatically change and emotion can be processed quite differently (as represented by different versions of the triangle of conflict).

Regardless of the severity of psychopathology, each individual's functioning occurs on a continuum, with self-at-best functioning and self-at-worst functioning representing the opposite ends of the continuum. The structure of the self-at-best functioning, which arises in emotional environments experienced as affect-facilitating, is represented by one version of the triangle of conflict (see Figure 6.4A). The other version of the triangle of conflict represents the structure of the self-at-worst functioning characteristic of psychopathology, the most severe version of which arises in emotional environments experienced as affect-aversive (see Figure 6.4B).[9] The individual's experience continues to be responsive to the emotional environment throughout the life cycle, which is why how we are with our patients deeply matters.

As all individuals have available to them higher or lower states of functioning, the goal in AEDP is (a) to create a psychotherapeutic environment that

---

[8] The inclusion of the pathogenic affects and the unbearable emotional states at the bottom of this schema differentiates the triangle of conflict AEDP relies upon in its moment-to-moment tracking of the patient's experience from the triangle of conflict usually relied upon in the other experiential STDPs. The representation of these types of experiences at the bottom of the triangle of conflict signals the importance AEDP accords to their full experiential exploration. That these types of experiences are experientially explored in AEDP and not bypassed as rapidly as possible on the way to the exploration of the categorical emotions is one of the differences between AEDP and the other experiential STDPs.

[9] It is beyond the scope of this chapter to discuss how the respective emotional environments conducive to either self-at-best and self-at-worst functioning are in fact co-constructed. (Interested readers are referred to Fosha [2000b], where such issues are discussed in depth.) Suffice it to say here that how the individual experiences the emotional environment plays an important role in which self configuration is activated, as does the nature of the environment.

FIGURE 6.3
THE SELF-OTHER-EMOTION TRIANGLE

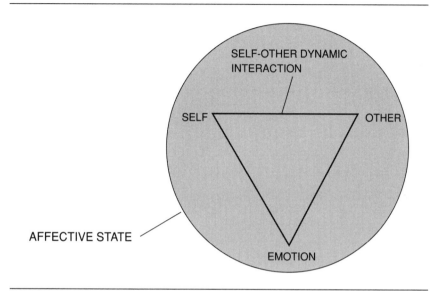

has the highest likelihood of facilitating the highest state of functioning where the patients' access to their resources is maximized and (b) to proceed to do the very difficult work of dealing with the trauma from such a position.

Treatment

In AEDP, the goal is *to lead with* (Fosha, 2000b) a corrective emotional experience (Alexander & French, 1946). The therapist seeks to create a safe and affect-friendly environment from the get-go, and to activate a patient-therapist relationship in which it is clear that the patient is deeply valued and will not be alone with emotional experiences. If this is accomplished, the patient will feel sufficiently safe to take the risks involved in doing deep and intensive emotional work (Fosha & Slowiaczek, 1997). We want to be able to explore self-at-worst functioning from within a self-at-best structuring of emotional experience activated by the here-and-now patient therapist relationship. (See the case later in this chapter, for an illustration of this principle at work.)

Trauma therapy in essence involves undoing the individual's aloneness in the face of overwhelming emotions. More specifically, the first phase of therapeutic

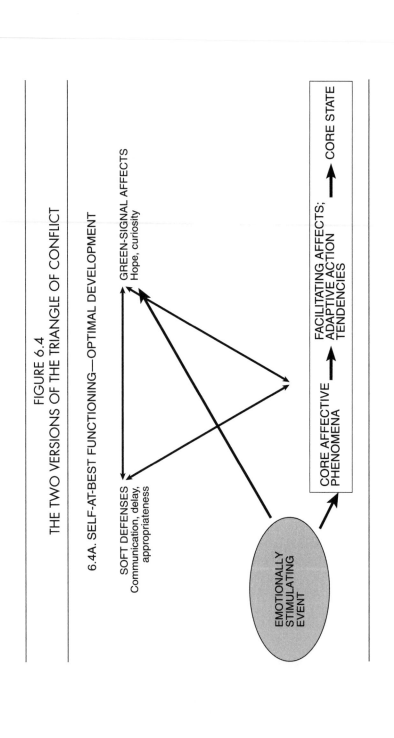

FIGURE 6.4
THE TWO VERSIONS OF THE TRIANGLE OF CONFLICT

6.4A. SELF-AT-BEST FUNCTIONING—OPTIMAL DEVELOPMENT

SOFT DEFENSES
Communication, delay,
appropriateness

GREEN-SIGNAL AFFECTS
Hope, curiosity

EMOTIONALLY
STIMULATING
EVENT

CORE AFFECTIVE
PHENOMENA → FACILITATING AFFECTS;
ADAPTIVE ACTION
TENDENCIES → CORE STATE

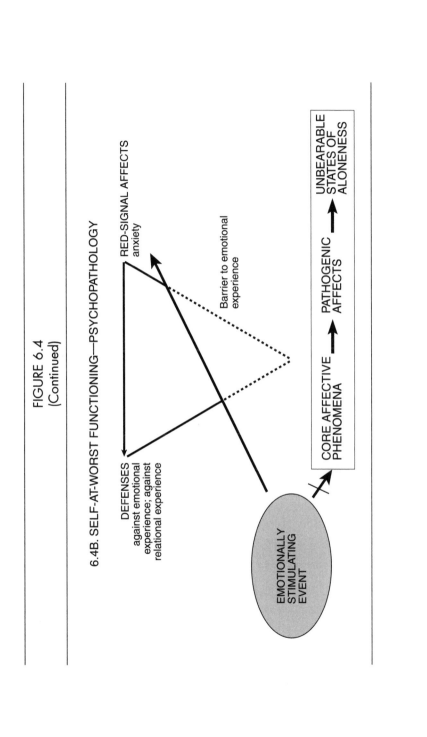

FIGURE 6.4
(Continued)

6.4B. SELF-AT-WORST FUNCTIONING—PSYCHOPATHOLOGY

DEFENSES
against emotional
experience; against
relational experience

RED-SIGNAL AFFECTS
anxiety

Barrier to emotional
experience

EMOTIONALLY
STIMULATING
EVENT

CORE AFFECTIVE
PHENOMENA

PATHOGENIC
AFFECTS

UNBEARABLE
STATES OF
ALONENESS

work involves processing and dealing with all aspects of experience that are the result of either (a) *defenses*, such as dissociation, against emotional experiences, (b) *pathogenic affects*, such as fear and shame, and/or (c) *unbearable emotional states*, such as helplessness, loneliness, and despair (see bottom half of Figure 6.2). Once (a) defenses are bypassed, (b) the destructive impact to the pathogenic affects is counteracted in the therapeutic dyad, and (c) the aloneness of the unbearable emotional states is transformed through the emotional sharing of the patient-therapist relationship, a *state transformation* occurs and the second phase of therapeutic work is ushered in: the individual can then access core affective experiences unhampered by either defense or pathogenic affects (see Fosha, 2002a, for a more detailed discussion of this). With the proper emotional support, fully accessing and dyadically processing the categorical emotions and other core affective experiences is not retraumatizing but actually has the potential for being deeply restorative, *if carried to completion*. Like Gendlin wrote: "Nothing that feels bad is ever the last step" (1981, pp. 25–26).

The mourning process is a perfect example of flawless dyadic regulation of categorical emotions: The individual's immersion in the full experience of grief (core affect) is contingent upon the availability of a support system. Others demonstrate caring through assisting the mourner, validating the importance of grief work, and allowing him to become immersed in grief and ritual; those in the support system take over the responsibilities of daily life until the individual is ready to resume them. Aloneness in the face of overwhelming grief is traumatic and leads to pathological mourning or melancholia (Volkan, 1981). On the other hand, support allows the mourning process to move toward completion and healing: Immersion in the grief and other affects involved in the processing of loss often leads to clarity and the ability to place the loss in the perspective of an entire life, allowing the eventual reengagement in life activities. Eventually, the individual can emerge with a new perspective, new clarity, deeper wisdom, and a revitalized capacity to embrace and affirm life.

The three-phase process of attunement, disruption, and repair is fundamental to AEDP's mode of therapeutic action: It constitutes an integrated model in which both categorical emotions and vitality affects play a crucial role in the exploration of both affective and relational experience, and where disruption is part and parcel of the process of reaching a higher level of mutual coordination. Attachment involves moment-to-moment attunement, but also the capacity to integrate disruptive experiences, in other words, the macro-affects associated with attachment vicissitudes, into a coherent and cohesive narrative. Thus, therapeutic work of necessity involves both attunement to vitality affects and help in processing the categorical emotions until they can be integrated and their disruption contained, metabolized, and repaired. The reintegration of the categorical emotions within the ongoing flow of dyadic interaction is at the heart of the treatment of trauma.

Attunement is maintained through vitality affects, the ripples of affect on the surface of ongoing interaction and affective communication. It is a going-on-being that just keeps moving forward. And then something happens. There is a disruption. Ordinary or extraordinary. The disruption is not just another ripple on the surface of the lake. The categorical emotions are on the scene— big emotions, big reactions. Nothing subtle. Fear. Anger. Joy. Excitement. Passion. Disgust. All of a sudden something happens and the flowing, going-on-being nature of things is disrupted. *And the disruption is registered in the categorical emotions.* We go from the dimension of ongoing horizontal, to the dimension of the vertical: from flowing along the surface of ongoing relatedness, we are in the depths of big experience. The texture of shared-ness is replaced by the experience of vehement subjectivity and emotion.

Janet characterized the emotions of trauma as being "vehement." They demand attention and they are deeply personal. If these emotions—categorical, vehement, highly personal—are processed, something profoundly transformative happens. All of a sudden, we have more than glimpses into the soul of the individual; rather, a panorama opens before us. The unconscious is unlocked and the deep secrets of the soul, secrets organized around specific emotions, come to the fore. In their being fully processed—their somatic, cognitive, fantasy, and motoric aspects are closely tracked, dyadically regulated, and experientially explored—the opportunity exists to take advantage of their adaptive gifts. Fully feeling our fear, we can protect ourselves. Under the aegis of categorical anger, we can go to battle on behalf of the interests of our territorial selves. These are deep resources we want to access. And once there is the opportunity to experience and express these emotions, not only is the individual enriched by benefiting from the resources released by their adaptive action tendencies, but the wave of emotion, now spent, can now be reintegrated into the ongoing interaction. Through their dyadic regulation in coordination with a supportive other, the vehemence of the categorical emotions, born of disruption, becomes transformed into suppleness and grace, a modulated quality which allows them to be once again the nourishment for the vitality affects, around which the dyad can coordinate. Furthermore, the relationship becomes more structured by how disruptions are repaired.

Important insights about trauma work in therapy emerge from a model that integrates both vitality affects and categorical emotions within the phasic cycling through attunement, disruption, and repair. In the affective sharing process, the individual is not alone with frightening and intense feelings. The process of emotional engagement can simultaneously foster the authenticity of self and the deep sense of connection with another. And authenticity and connection, in turn, enhance the capacity to process intense emotion. In the realm of core affective experience, the difference between aloneness and the sense of being integrated in the mainstream of relational existence is created by the act of affective communication with one other person, who is open, attuned, sincere (see Ferenczi, 1931, p. 138) and willing to remain emotionally engaged through thick and thin.

In both trauma and disorganized attachment, the caregiver's absorption in and disorganization by her own unprocessed and unresolved emotional experience leaves the child frightfully alone with three overwhelming emotional challenges: (i) his own emotional experience that he needs help regulating (and which, instead of being met with empathy and help, disorganizes the caregiver); (ii) the disrupted attachment bond; and (iii) the second wave of intense and disturbing feelings in reaction to the direness of the situation in which he finds himself. As discussed earlier, this nightmarish combination produces the unbearable emotional states, the "black hole" of trauma and disorganized attachment, and it is precisely in this turmoiled setting that defenses against emotional experience are instituted.

Affect-regulatory difficulties in the caregiver compromise the child's functioning. Unreliable caregiving necessitates chronic reliance on the defensive exclusion of emotional experience (insecure, but organized, attachment), or leads to the even more disruptive inability to maintain organization and coherence in the face of intense emotions, and with the individual becoming disorganized and nonfunctional (disorganized attachment). This is precisely the process by which autobiographical narratives come to lack cohesion and coherence, with gaps where the thread of integrated emotional experience is broken (Hughes, in preparation). The individual survives, the attachment bond hobbles along. The price for this Faustian compromise, the defensive exclusion of adaptive emotion, eventually leads to the huge problems in living that produce the crises and suffering that bring people to seek our assistance.

In the next part of this chapter, the ideas sketched out above encounter the reality of the clinical situation. The work involves the first and second affective change processes, *the dyadic regulation of affective states* and *the experience and expression of core emotion*. More specifically, the work shows patient and therapist tackling the problem of how the intense emotion of fear can be dyadically regulated and processed. It is an illustration of AEDP in action, albeit in the chaotic, complex, nonlinear fashion of real-life, day-to-day clinical work.

FRIGHT WITHOUT SOLUTION: ITS (RE)SOLUTION IN EXPERIENTIAL-DYNAMIC THERAPEUTIC WORK

The journey that you are about to witness involves the grappling of the therapeutic dyad with vehement, overwhelming fear, the fundamental emotion in disorganized attachment. The case provides an opportunity to examine and discuss: (1) the role of fear in disorganized attachment (Hesse & Main, 1999, 2000); (2) the patient/therapist moment-to-moment dyadic negotiation of the process of attunement, disruption, and repair (Fosha, 2001; Tronick, 1989, 1998); (3) differential strategies of intervention for dealing with categorical emotions vs. pathogenic affects (Fosha, 2002a); (4) the use of the therapist's affect in experiential psychotherapeutic work (Fosha, 2000a, 2001); and (5) the qualitatively different organizations that characterize functioning dominated by defense, core affect, and core state (Fosha, 2002a, 20002b).

What we first witness are patterns reflecting the intransigence side of the paradox, that is, procedures established during childhood and repeated over a lifetime: a patient's maladaptive attachment strategies, and her concomitant inability to experience adaptive anger, come into view. These become transformed in the course of one session and its aftermath, through therapeutic work that seeks to dyadically help the patient experience and process the fear that paralyzes her capacity to experience anger. Defensive exclusion of intense emotion no longer necessary, the patient's narrative becomes not only coherent and cohesive, but flowing and resilient.

The patient in this case, a 50-year-old woman, exhibited the functioning characteristics of the preoccupied state of mind with respect to attachment *in relationship to her husband*.[10] She used *denial* to avoid seeing her marriage for what it was, and relied on a variety of other defense mechanisms (e.g., *dissociation, somatization, avoidance*) to ward off intense feelings of anger, pain, and grief.[11] Reliance on these strategies allowed her to maintain her highly problematic marriage. The price of these strategies included psychosomatic symptoms,

---

[10] I emphasize this because in other important relationships in her current life the patient exhibited functioning more indicative of secure attachment.

[11] As attachment theorists make clear (Main, 1995), the insecure attachment phenotype is the result of defensive strategies. These strategies represent best efforts to protect against unbearably painful feelings of fear and loss, rendered all the more unbearable by the attachment figure's inability to *feel and deal, and* maintain affectionate connection (Fosha, 2000b). A secondary sense of safety is achieved through the application of these defensive strategies (Main, 1995). The attachment bond survives, but the cost of the defensive exclusion of adaptive emotion required to maintain it is high; it takes a toll on the individual.

anxiety, depression, and a compromised ability to mother her children. It also prevented the patient from effectively dealing with the marriage, thus unwittingly contributing to its disintegration.

At the time of the session, the patient, whom I shall call Emily, and her husband, whom I shall call Clay, had been separated for some months. The question pending was whether the separation was a prelude to getting back together, or to divorce. The fate of the marriage in the balance, despite major changes in other areas of her life, in relation to Clay, Emily was still prone to resort to preoccupied attachment strategies: though considerably weakened by treatment, the tendency to sacrifice the self at the altar of the relationship, and to avoid disruptive emotions, was nonetheless alive and kicking.

Crisis disrupts defenses; in this case, the crisis unraveled the organization of the preoccupied state only to reveal the underlying tendencies toward attachment disorganization. But *because* it disrupts defenses, crisis can be a major transformational opportunity (Lindemann, 1944), if the individual is supported through it.[12] The crisis this session deals with was in fact precipitated by the patient's exercise of her *newly found capacities*—unprecedented clarity, assertiveness, and autonomy in response to her husband. This leap forward terrifies her. Within minutes of having taken a stand, she undoes her assertiveness, and reverts to hyperfocusing on the other at the expense of the self. The "problem" is that this strategy no longer works; her inability to tolerate her own assertiveness is now painful for Emily. She arrives at the session distressed, anxious, and confused.

It rapidly becomes clear that the problem is anger. We witness *in vivo* a pathognomonic pattern: When defenses are bypassed and the patient is on the brink of fully experiencing anger, she backs off, dissociates, and becomes confused. Exploring what stands between the patient and her experience of anger, we uncover the experience of pathogenic fear.

Some experiential STDPs, notably Davanloo's model (1990), use highly confrontational techniques to rapidly break through defenses. AEDP's conceptualization of pathogenic affects leads to a different clinical strategy: Instead of pushing past the fear so as to gain access to anger as rapidly as possible, here, the experiential focus of the session switches to fear itself. The *visceral* experience of fear unlocks the door to the past: encapsulated in it is a history of trauma—abuse, helplessness, and terror.

---

[12] The profoundly therapeutic transformational potential of crisis through its making entrenched defenses much more fluid was clearly recognized by Davanloo, who made the iatrogenic creation of "an intrapsychic crisis" the hallmark of his technique (1990).

On Fear

Like all categorical emotion, the full visceral experience of fear releases adaptive action tendencies which give the organism an evolutionary edge. Two adaptive action tendencies are released by fear: one is to flee from the danger situation; the other is to seek protection of the attachment figure. Both adaptive, the prototype of these tendencies coming together is a little child running *away from* a fierce dog and *into* the arms of his mother.

However, deep problems arise when the figure of safety and the source of the danger are one and the same: When the primary caregiver is also the source of danger, as is the case with an abusive caregiver, the child is placed in an irresolvable dilemma, what Hesse and Main (2000) called "fright without solution." It is impossible to simultaneously *run toward and flee from* the same figure. To flee from the source of the danger means to abandon the attachment relationship and be exposed to loss and the fear of utter aloneness. To flee into the arms of the caregiver means to rush headlong into the tidal wave of abuse, which threatens the self with annihilation. This is the paradigmatic emotional situation which underlies disorganized attachment and which predisposes people to reliance on dissociative mechanisms (Liotti, 1999), and it is the essential experience revealed in the session. As the first layer of defenses/coping strategies ebbs, what comes to the fore is the phenomenology of disorganized attachment, with confusion and paralysis as its two experiential hallmarks, and with dissociation as a dominant defense mechanism.

FEAR AND THE PROCESS OF ATTUNEMENT, DISRUPTION, AND REPAIR

Dyadic affective processing involves countless cycles of attunement, disruption, and repair. The therapist's emotions are used throughout to empathize, to affirm and support, but also to challenge. Early in the session, defense work is accomplished through attunement and affective coordination: through vocal and rhythmic entraining, and through affective mirroring and resonance, defenses naturally fade and the patient has increasingly greater access to authentic emotional experience: her language becomes increasingly vivid, imagistic, and somatic. Right-brain mediated processing is in ascendance.

However, while attunement is necessary, it is not sufficient to fully render defenses vestigial: with deepening affect, and the heralding of angry feelings on the experiential horizon, dissociative defenses re-assert themselves. The therapist ups the ante: Continuing to make use of her own emotions, here anger on the patient's behalf, she begins a more direct challenge to the patient's defenses. By definition, head-on defense work is disruptive. During the challenge to the defenses, patient and therapist are definitely not on the same page. Feeling safe in the relationship with the therapist allows the patient to not withdraw from difficult emotional experience, but to remain emotionally engaged and keep struggling. The challenge to the patient's defenses eventuates in the visceral breakthrough that "unlocks" the unconscious: the patient relives her fear of her husband and of her mother, triggered by vivid memories of being subjected to the uncontrollable rages of both. What happens next provides the opportunity to reflect on the nature of *disruption* in the psychotherapeutic process.

On Disruption

As there are two dyadic partners, there are at least two sources of disruption: disruptions of mutual coordination initiated by the patient and therapist-initiated disruptions, which can be either deliberate or inadvertent. In this case, the disruptions of mutual coordination initiated by the patient, that is, her shifts of states, are seamlessly repaired. Therapist-initiated disruptions that are the outcome of technique are part-and-parcel of strategic intervention. However, not all disruption is the result of willed and mindful clinical risk-taking. Disruption also occurs as a result of the therapist's lapses, such as not understanding or being on a different page than the patient. The session presented here has examples of all three types of *disruptions: patient-initiated, therapist-initiated/deliberate,* and *therapist-initiated/ inadvertent.* The disruption just described, that of the therapist's use of her own emotion of anger on the patient's behalf to do defense work, is an example of a deliberate disruption.

The next round of the work involves an inadvertent disruption, but one that eventually turns out to be productive once it is repaired and coordination is restored. Having gotten the breakthrough, the therapist is working to facilitate the emergence of the adaptive action tendencies of the fear. But it is precisely at the point that another wave of defenses comes to the fore. This happens several times: with each cycle, the visceral experience of the emotion deepens, but leads to defense, rather than to the release of adaptive action tendencies. The problem is that the therapist is mistakenly assuming that the patient's fear is functioning as a core affect. In fact, Emily's fear is operating as a pathogenic affect: it triggers contradictory adaptive action tendencies, thus the patient's paralysis, confusion, and dissociative deflating. It is an *in vivo* instance of how defenses arise to compensate for caregiving lapses—in this case, of the therapist's. Sufficient iterations of this "stuck" sequence occur; the therapist realizes that the reparative experience must take place within the therapeutic relationship before further progress can be made. Once again making use of her own self, the therapist removes pressure from the patient to act in any particular way, thus affirming, through action, a stance of unconditional support for the patient, regardless of whatever particular choice she might make. The disruption repaired, the restored mutual coordination and the ushering in of core state are heralded by the appearance of the affect of relief.

The *irreparable* disruption that intense emotions invariably caused in the patient's *past* relationships does not occur within the patient-therapist relationship. Liberated from its being embedded in a *pathogenic* self-other-emotion configuration (patient–mother/husband–fear) through being part of an *adaptive* self-other-emotion configuration (patient–therapist–fear), the patient's fear as a pathogenic affect is transformed and its emotion-inhibiting effects are no longer in operation. There is a dyadically expanded state of consciousness (Tronick, 1998). In the new state, the patient is able to include previously disowned aspects of her affective experience. Instead of *defensive exclusion* (Bowlby, 1980), we see *affective inclusion* (Fosha, 2000b) and thus, expanded and enriched functioning. But, as this is a dyadic process, the therapist is also changed by the experience: From this struggle emerges a deeper understanding of the different technical strategies to work with core affect as opposed to pathogenic affect an understanding that informs this chapter.

In the material that follows, text in parentheses describes the nonverbal aspects of the patient's communication, while the text in brackets reflects the author's micro analysis of the ongoing interaction.

The First Session: An Investigation of the 5-Minute Gap

Setting Up the Focus of the Work

In experiential work, we always want to work with concrete situations and specific details, so as to maximize emotional immediacy. As the patient comes in with a ready-made specific example, we are off and running. This is how the session begins:

Pt: I am really confused.

Th: Hmm.

Pt: I'll tell you what I'm confused about. Clay called me this morning and he said, "How would you like to go to the museum Saturday afternoon for a couple of hours?" And, umm, it was like . . . where is that coming from?! (*rapid speech, shallow breathing*) And, I said, "Oh!" And he said, "I thought it would be nice." And I said, "Actually, I have plans." So he said, "Oh. OK." So I said, "Well, it's a nice thought. Maybe we can do it another time." And he said, "Well, I'll have to think about what the other time might be." And I said, "OK." And he said, "Good-bye." And I said, "Good-bye," and I hung up the phone.

(Big sigh). . . . I'm really upset about all this. What I'm really upset about is Clay and how I really . . . I just don't understand. I mean, I said "No"! *I said 'No'!* I said, "I'm sorry. I have other plans." And 5 minutes later *(exasperated)* I had to call him up and tell him I changed my plans and that I could meet with him.

The patient sets up the problem here most explicitly: having asserted herself with her husband and said a clear, declarative "No," she is unable to tolerate the resulting anxiety: five minutes later she has to undo it. The session becomes devoted to investigating what happened in the 5-minute gap between the saying of the "No," and its withdrawal.

Pt: I don't know why I did that! I don't know why I didn't leave it alone. [I didn't leave it alone] because I knew Clay was sort of . . . I felt like he would be angry at me. He *was* angry with me. *(As patient engages in self-dialogue, her speech becomes quite pressured.)* So, what if he's angry at me?! . . . I don't want him to be angry with me . . . I don't understand why I had to take it back. But I did. I don't know. I don't know why I didn't ask him anything. . . . I don't know. *(Starts sounding and looking quite upset here, as if she's fighting back the tears.)* [Note the back and forth between the two sides of the dissociation: knowing and not knowing, caring and not caring.]

Th: What's sooo upsetting to you right now? *[Therapist focuses on the most immediate and intensely upsetting feeling in the here-and-now: setting up the experiential immediacy of the work.]*

Pt: There's no way that Clay is ready to do whatever he thinks he's going to do on Saturday night because he isn't ready to be in a relationship with me. He's just not ready. And, I don't want to be with him. I don't want to disappoint him, I guess. I don't want to hear about how I didn't do or say right, or I didn't do this right. I don't want to . . . be disappointed by him. I don't want to feel isolated. I don't want to sit there in the museum with him sitting over here and me sitting over here *(makes the motion of a huge distance between them)*. . . . I don't want to be at the museum with us the way we are. I don't want to have a drink with him. I don't want to have a glass of wine with him. . . . I don't know anymore.

The patient speaks of her awareness of her husband's anger. "I felt like he would be angry at me. He *was* angry with me. So, what if he's angry at me?! . . . I don't want him to be angry with me." The patient's focus on her husband's anger might suggest the operation of projective mechanisms for dealing with her own anger. From within AEDP's adaptation-centered perspective, however, the therapist hears the patient's concerns about her husband's anger as evidence of the patient's experience of the other. While the two are not contradictory, when there is a choice to be made, the therapist goes with the more experience-near alternative.

The moment-to-moment tracking of the patient's emotional experience leads to an in-session enactment of the presenting problem of assertiveness and its immediate undoing: As Emily builds to an affective crescendo and is poised on the brink of a breakthrough of *her* angry feelings, she deflates, undoing her good work with an "I don't know anymore." Confusion replaces the clarity and decisiveness she experienced only seconds before. This sequence occurs a few more times in material not included here.

Identification and Clarification of Defenses Against Affective Experience

Th: Wait!

Pt: What? (*laughs nervously*).

Th: Wait! Because it seems to me that you know a lot about how you feel. *[Feedback about strengths and adaptive capacities.]* But there's something about putting it together and staying with it, that's difficult for you. *[Identification of defense against affective experience.]* . . . I mean, when you talk about how Clay is always disappointed by you, what does that feel like for you? What do you feel like *inside* when he makes you feel like you're not doing the right thing, or you're saying the wrong thing, or you're saying it the wrong way. . . . He's always telling you you're shutting him down, you're putting him down. . . . What's that like for you??? (*impassioned rhythm*). *[The therapist makes use here of a crescendo of affective intensity after identification of defense to prime the affective pump.]*

Pt: It feels crappy. . . . It's depressing. It makes me feel sad. You know, on some levels, it makes me feel bad about myself. I end up doubting myself. I end up not feeling good about myself. And I don't seem to be able to get pissed at him. I end up feeling bad about myself when what I should be is pissed at him. And I was starting to get pissed about it when I finally left the house and I thought . . . "What the fuck do I need that for?!" Why do I need to be . . . With most everyone else, I can say pretty much what I want to say. . . . and with Clay I pretty much have to bite my tongue all the time. I feel like whatever I do or say is the wrong thing. Now, feeling that way, why would I want to go out with him Saturday night?

Affective contagion and the dyadic process of entraining vocal rhythms and coordinating affective states are powerful tools of affective transformation and can often be successfully used to bypass defenses against affect (Fosha, 2001), as happens here. Affect (the therapist's) begets affect (the patient's). The patient gets into a deeper state where she is emotionally in touch with the self-thwarting consequences of her defenses, as well as with the core affect, that is anger, that she is defending against. "And I was starting to get pissed about it when I finally left the house and I thought . . . 'What the fuck do I need that for?!' " Articulating her reasons for not wishing to get together with her husband, Emily declares that she feels angry. Awareness of the negative consequences of her defensive strategies, such as bad feelings about herself and the inability to speak in her own voice, heightens the patient's motivation to do the difficult work ahead. The stage is set for the wave of experiential work, the goal of which is, at this moment, to help the patient get visceral access to her anger.

Deepening Affect and Bypassing Defenses Through Dyadic Affective Engagement and Somatic Focusing

Th: So let's look at what happened in the 5 minutes between your saying "I have plans Saturday and . . . (*Pt. interrupts*)

Pt: I got nervous.

Th: What did you get nervous about?

Pt: Well . . . that Clay was gonna think that maybe everything is *not* OK. Because somehow I led Clay to believe that if he could find himself, I would be there for him. That's what I led Clay to believe. That when he's ready to come back to me, I'm ready for him. [*Patient spontaneously describes in greater detail her strategies of appeasement and denial.*]

Th: So what scares you about his entertaining the possibility for one second that maybe that's not the only thing that's going on with you? [*Continuing to challenge.*]

Pt: Because I feel like I'll lose the opportunity to reconnect with him in the future if, in fact, he's able to turn himself into a giving human being (*highly resigned, matter-of-fact tone of voice.*)

The psychodynamic formulation of the problem in the terms of the triangle of conflict is complete: The patient is afraid (inhibiting anxiety) that if she allows herself to feel angry (core affect), she will lose her husband (aversive consequences of affective experience); thus, she denies her feelings and appeases him (defense). Authentic emotional experience is relinquished to preserve the bond and avoid the loss of her husband. As Emily says this, the tone of matter-of-fact resignation in her voice is striking. Given the powerful therapeutic alliance in operation with this patient, the therapist opts for a high-risk intervention: *affective self-disclosure* to bypass defenses, and heighten affective experiencing. Such high-risk strategies represent in-the-moment disruptions in dyadic coordination: Patient and therapist are not on the same wavelength, as the therapist's aim is to help the patient experience the very emotion she most wants to avoid. The intervention elicits painful affect, with which the therapist empathizes. The patient's feeling deepens. This disruption now repaired, a new coordination comes into being. We witness a state transformation, the emergence of core state phenomena and the beginning of mutative work.

The Use of the Therapist's Affect to Challenge Defenses: A Therapeutic Disruption in the Service of a More Inclusive Coordination

Th: I want to tell you a reaction I'm having because if I don't say it, I think I'll try to spend too much energy trying to suppress it and that's no good for our work (*impassioned tone*). This is soooo upsetting to me. Like, I think that this is about abuse of some sort. [*This is telegraphic for saying "I think your inability to stand by your 'no' can only be explained by your prior experiences of abuse."*] There's this terror that takes you over and I can't stand watching it. It's very difficult. It makes me mad. It makes me mad on your behalf. [*Affective self-disclosure of the therapist's experience.*]

Pt: Well, what is he doing?

Th: It doesn't make me mad at Clay. It makes me mad at you. It makes me mad that you're doing this to yourself.

Pt: And, I'm really reaalllly upset (*starts to cry here, and holds her open hand over her chest as though she's holding something in*)! Because I can't understand. I can't understand what hold he has over me. I can't understand why I can't let go. I just . . . I can't . . . I cannot figure out. I cannot understand what motivates me to hang onto something that doesn't *feeeel* good. I cannot explain it. I have explained sooo many things . . . [*Emergence of painful affect, as patient articulates her distress about her own impotence, paralysis, and confusion.*]

Th: (*in empathic tone, the therapist mirroring patient's gesture of putting her hand over her chest*) What's inside, Emily? What's inside? [*Empathy in response to emergence of painful affect; repair and restoration of attunement; beginning of experiential somatic focusing.*]

Pt: (*clutching her chest, poignant voice*) There's something soooo . . . It feels soooo *wrong*. But I cannot figure out why I can't let go of this fantasy of this life that we're gonna have together. [*The defense of denial is becoming deeply ego-dystonic to the patient.*]

Th: What's inside right now? What's in your chest? What are you holding in with your hand? [*Experiential somatic focusing; inviting the right brain to speak.*]

Pt: It just . . . it's like a giant. . . . It's not a knot, it's just like a great . . .

Th: What?

Pt: (*with deep engagement and very intense emphasis, more declarative tone*) It feels like a piece of phlegm or something. It's just something... it just feels heavy. It's just like all this suppressed reaction is creating this giant mass and I feel like I'm choking on it right now. And I don't understand why I can't get it out. I don't understand why I can't... [*Note how, as the affective experience is deepening, and the patient's language is changing, it is becoming more graphic, more image-laden, more experiential; the right brain is speaking back.*]

Th: Focus in on what's in your chest. Focus in on how you're feeling. What's in your body?

Pt: I feel like I'm gonna choke. I feel like I'm choking on something. I swear. I feel like I'm choking on... (*dramatic shift: sits up tall; speaks in clear, strong voice, very emphatic*)... I mean, so I said "No!" Why did I have to call him up and say "Yes"?! Because you know what? As much as I've been honest with you, and as much as I've been honest with everybody, I've been completely dishonest with Clay (*assertive, strong, declarative tone; slightly incantational quality*). [*Core state: reflective self function in operation.*]

Th: Yes, you have (*echoing slight incantational quality of patient's speech*). [*Therapist matches patient's vitality affects; reestablishment of coordination.*]

Pt: *Completely* dishonest with Clay! I have led him to believe that he is still the only person in the world for me. And that I will be ready for him. Because I really thought I would be... [*Full dyadically expanded state includes awareness of, and responsibility for, defenses.*]

Th: What's in your chest? What are you choking on? What are you choking on and what are you afraid of? [*Refocusing on somatic and affective experience.*]

Pt: (*continues in straightforward, clear, strong voice with slight incantational quality*) I had this dream of my life. I liked the illusion of my life. I liked the way my husband looked. I liked the way my husband sounded. I liked that my husband was successful. I liked the trappings of my life. I liked the way it looked. Even though everyone knows that it was an illusion, so it's no longer what it looked like to everybody else because I've been extremely honest about how it was an illusion.... I'm still in love with the illusion of this life. I still... [*Patient strongly articulates the denial at the foundation of her entire existence.*]

Th: So, what's in the phlegm? What's in the mass of phlegm that's in your throat? [*Speaking a somatic language; keeping affective pressure on.*]

Pt: I'm very, very... I'm really pissed at Clay (*angry tone of voice, almost with something of a hissing quality*). I'm really pissed off at him! [*Beginning of affective breakthrough of anger.*]

The combination of the therapist's affective self-disclosure, empathy, affective matching, somatic focusing, and keeping a tight focus on the patient's affective experience leads to the first mini-breakthrough: In the here-and-now, in the present tense, the patient declares that she *is* angry and sounds it: "I'm very, very . . . I'm really pissed at Clay (*angry tone of voice, almost with something of a hissing quality*). I'm really pissed off at him!"

In the experiential STDPs, this is not an endpoint, but the beginning of the next phase. Now the aim is to facilitate full visceral access and deepen this experience of anger through exploring its somatic correlates and accompanying fantasies. This is done through using the technique of *portrayal*, that is, asking the patient to imagine what she would do, and what she would feel like if, in thought and fantasy, she were to let go of her inhibitions and fully allow herself to go where full satisfaction of her anger and rage would take her.

Experiential Work to Deepen the Visceral Experience of the Categorical Emotion of Anger: The Emergence of Fear

Th: (*emphatic tone of voice*) If you get rid of this heavy thing that's oppressing you, what's the anger inside you like? What is it like? What are you clutching inside? (*in response to the patient pressing her hand against her chest and clutching her shirt*) [*The therapist takes the newly expanded coordination as a green light to continue to press toward greater experiential focusing; emphatic tone, somatic language.*]

Pt: (*very dramatic tone*) It feels like bile. Like green bile. Like something really, really venomous. It's like . . . (*pronounced shift of tone, posture, and direction of gaze*) I don't know (*patient deflates, spaces out*) . . . [*After somatic, charged, highly experiential, primary process account of venomous anger inside her chest, as she is on the verge of exploring the full expression of her anger, i.e., what happens if the bile comes out, patient dissociates the affect in the very moment and deflates.*]

Th: What's the matter? (*concerned tone, soft*) [*Recoordination through tone matching.*]

Pt: I don't know. I just . . . I really can't . . . (*shift, back in contact*) I can't really meet with Clay.

Th: What happened, Emily? What's coming up when you say you can't meet with Clay? [*Therapist is closely tracking the moment-to-moment shifts in patient's vitality affects.*]

Pt: (*return of emphatic tone of voice*) Every time I get together with Clay I completely forget everything. I forget who I am. I'll give you a perfect example (*gives example of her relinquishing her own desires and acceding to his wishes*). How did he engineer that?! How did that happen? And how did I let that happen?

Th: It's not how did *he* engineer it. Let's look at what *you're* doing because you can't tolerate displeasing him for 5 minutes! *[Matching patient's returning determination, the therapist ups the ante and continues challenge.]*

Pt: No *(she says in agreement)*. I don't want him not to like *me (ironic tone; contemptuous toward her own defenses)*. And he doesn't like me anyway *(laughs)*. It's pretty stupid. I think that's the part that really gets me *(angry tone of voice)*. That I have tried to be as flexible and agreeable, and as accommodating as I can and he still sits there and tells me . . . (makes big dismissive gesture)

Th: *(mirroring patient's dismissive gesture)* What's *that? [Affective resonance around rising anger; matching vitality affects.]*

Pt: He tells me that he can't talk to me. You know, that I shut down the conversation. That I don't . . .

Th: Everything that you do is wrong *(long pause)*. I mean, why don't you just give up on yourself altogether?! *(said provocatively)* Why don't you go to the museum . . . and sit there . . . and take crumbs?! *(Long heavy pause)*. *[Increase of pressure through paradoxical siding with defenses and their consequences as patient's visceral experience of anger seems closer to the surface again; therapist-initiated disruption.]*

Pt: *(momentarily deflates)* I can't imagine. I mean, the only thing that could happen was that he was in therapy yesterday. That's the only thing that happened. *[Dissociation of affect.]*

Th: But look! You're saying "what happened?", "what happened?," "what happened?" . . . *[Another high risk, high affect intervention: therapist continues to be contemptuous of patient's defenses, while tracking very closely the patient's response to her interventions; maintaining disruption of coordination.]* HOW DID YOU FEEL?! What happened to this venomous bile?! What happens if it comes out instead of sitting inside you choking you?! I mean, what happens if this fire in your eyes—if you give it permission . . . *[Pressuring toward expression of the anger.]*

Pt: *(voice becoming stronger)* I don't know. You know, I have let it out in every other way. I'm telling you, I really, really . . . But when it comes to Clay I'm like—*[Repair of disruption in progress.]*

Th: . . . You do not exist. You are annihilated *(again said softly, deliberately, yet gravely)*. You're pleasant. You hide your feelings. You can't tolerate displeasing him. God forbid that he should spend 3 minutes feeling insecure *(said in a provocatively sweet tone of voice)*. WHAT HAPPENS if this bile comes out? I mean, you have a choice. Or, let's put it this way. You ARE making a choice. . . . *You are* choking on your own bile. WHAT are you gonna do about it??!! . . . What happened in these 5 minutes that you couldn't tolerate— what happens if Clay sees what you really feel? *(long pause)* *[Application of pressure through challenging defenses and graphically spelling out their operation and consequences.]*

Pt: *(clear, declarative, deliberate, no-nonsense tone of voice)* I guess my whole life is gonna change. Even though my whole life has changed, it hasn't completely changed. It's like I have a lot of privacy now and I can do what I want. And, I'm gonna have to start dealing with Clay big time.... And I'm really afraid of Clay. I really am afraid of him. *[Reestablishment of coordination through direct declaration of emotional experience: core state.]*

The toxic labeling of defenses and the application of challenge and pressure in the context of dyadic relatedness, AEDP's modification of classic ISTDP technique (Fosha, 2001, 2002a), succeeds in getting past defenses (initially denial, then dissociation) and anxiety and gets the breakthrough. Interestingly, what breaks through is not core affect but rather *core state*. The patient sits up and, with unhampered access to reflective functioning, can clearly declare her subjective emotional truth. From core state, there is a breakthrough of core affect. But it is not anger that breaks through. Another emotion comes to the fore: fear.

The Breakthrough of Fear

Pt: I really am afraid of him.

Th: Ummmmh.

Pt: And, I'm not afraid of Arnie. And I don't even know Arnie. I'm really not afraid... I really... I trust Arnie more that I trust Clay, and I've known Arnie for 10 days! *(long pause).*

Th: That's a huge...

Pt: *(continues in declarative tone of core state; gathers momentum as she goes)* Maybe I don't want to mess with Clay. I don't want to start with Clay. He can be a very nasty guy. I mean, he turned that venom on Robin. He's a... He's very smart. He can twist things around. He can twist you up in a knot. And he has so much... He can be very venomous. There's a lot of hate inside of him. You know, he's got a lot of—whew! *(shift from core state to core affect: patient's eyes widen, her face is pale, her breathing is fast and shallow)* I think I don't want to be on the receiving end of that. And maybe that's changed, but...

Th: *(with feeling)* That's very scary! *[Empathic elaboration of affective experience; maintaining attunement.]*

Pt: *(nods in agreement)* I'm really afraid to get Clay going *(looks frightened).*

Th: What's the fear like? What happens inside of you when...

Pt: *(winces, closes her eyes, and puts her hand over her eyes, frightened, sobbing, gasping)* I just thought of my mother. *[Unlocking of unconscious material; associative link between husband and mother.]*

Th: (*soothing tone*) Mmmm. You're scared... [*Maintaining empathic contact while patient is in the deep experience of core affect.*]

Pt: (*sobbing*) Yes.

Th: (*empathic tone*) You're really scared. [*Maintaining empathic contact.*]

Pt: (*continuing to sob*) I really am.

Th: She hurt you. [*Empathic elaboration.*]

Pt: They both have this same quality to their anger. It's very irrational. And it's very, very venomous. There's an enormous quality of... of venom. It's venomous. It's venomous.

Th: (*soothing tone*) Mmmm.

Pt: It's very, very intense. It's very mean spirited—and it's very nasty.

Th: What came up about your mother?

Pt: I just had this image of my mother being very angry at me. [*Right-hemisphere mediated experiencing.*]

Th: What do you see?

Pt: I don't know. It's just she... All of a sudden she came up in my mind. This feeling of being terrified.

Th: Just terrified. What's the little girl feeling?

Pt: Well, you know, I told you that the way I could... just not making any waves was the way to avoid it or to keep it from getting any worse. So, I guess I don't want to make any waves with Clay. [*In previous sessions, the patient has used the metaphor of a tidal wave to capture the quality of her mother's irrational anger, and the metaphor of not making waves to describe her coping strategies.*]

Th: What happens if you let yourself, if you keep looking at your mother? It's scary. I know it's scary [*Encouraging further exploration while maintaining empathic support.*]

Pt: I don't... I mean I can't really come up... I don't... [*Reemergence of dissociative defense.*]

Th: You let it go.

Pt: (*defensive laugh*) Yes!

Th: You had it. It's not that you can't come up with it. You came up with it and were terrified and you let it go. [*Identification of operation of dissociative defense.*]

Pt: I just can't put a place to it. I can't.... I was thinking of Clay and his anger and I just... All of a sudden I just remembered my mother. And I'm not remembering a specific time. I'm really not.

Th: I understand. I understand (*pause*).

The patient goes back and forth between husband and mother, between past and present, without marking the shifts; in the unconscious material that core emotion unlocks, accessing material mediated by the right hemisphere. Connections are affective. The patient's mother and husband are affectively linked through the similarity of their terrorizing anger and its impact on the patient.

Pt: I was just thinking about being in the museum with Clay.... *(long pause)* I have done nothing, nothing!— I've done nothing to cross Clay.... You know, if I told him that I was gonna change the lock on the door... *(her eyes widen with fear)* whewww ... Someone said, "Just have your husband announced when he comes into the building. You should tell the doorman that if your husband comes to the apartment he needs to be announced. At least you would know if he's coming up at any point." I said, "Oh, I couldn't do that." *[Patient self-regulates during the pause; comes back organized; back on track.]*

Th: So we're talking about terror. *[Affective resonance, and amplification.]*

Pt: Yeah, because ...

Th: We're talking about terror. We're talking about ... how utterly terrorized and frightened you are. And then this picture of your mother came into your mind and you let go of that. It's like you can't let yourself know what a state of siege you have lived under. What a Holocaust of destruction—of annihilation.[13] *[Earlier in session patient brought up material related to the Holocaust, spontaneously making a link with her experience with Clay.]* *(Long pause.)*

Pt: I don't know what I'm gonna do about Saturday night. *[Clashing adaptive tendencies, lead to confusion and the patient resorts to "I don't know."]*

Th: Stop for a second. *[Therapist-initiated disruption, inadvertent; having gotten the breakthrough, the therapist expects further unfolding and/or the release of adaptive action tendencies, and is taken aback by the resurgence of defense.]*

---

[13] Earlier in the session, the following interaction occurred:

Th: What touched you about the Holocaust museum?

Pt: Well, there were all these pictures of all these people that died in the Holocaust, like a yearbook, but all the pictures were of these people, but *before* the Holocaust. Before Hitler came into power. So, they were all smiling and dressed in their Sunday best. And looking very fresh, and very young and very happy. Filled with promise. But, it was actually a catalog of death. And of disappointment. And of despair. But it was before they realized how their life was going to end up. And the image of all these ... *(starts getting choked up)* ... shining, happy faces *(puts her hand over her eyes to hide her tears)* ... filled with all this promise. And when you realize the reality of what happened to them.... Soooo many pictures! It just goes on and on and on. It's sooo sad ... that I just started to cry. It's just ... very powerful. It's more powerful than looking at emaciated bodies with tattoos on. It's much more powerful because these seem like people that you can identify with. But, you can identify with people who, page after page, that ended up annihilated *(long pause)*. Oh God! You know, this is something that I have not been able to really ... what happens between Clay and me is not right. And I know it. And I haven't been able to help it.

Pt: *(laughs nervously)* OK.

Th: This is part of what you do. You dissociate. *(Long pause.)*

Pt: I don't know *(voice starts to crack and tremble)* . . . I don't know if you're ever had anyone . . . so furious at you, making no sense whatsoever *(big gulp; starts to sob)*. There's absolutely no way . . . to turn that person away from the assault that follows because it isn't based on anything that you've really done. It's all imaginary. If somebody . . . If somebody goes on the attack and it doesn't matter what it is, it's immaterial what the reason is . . . *[Another wave of affective breakthrough; the patient repairs the disconnection by deepening her communication, and, in the process, deepening her own self experience.]*

Th: Mmmm. *[expressing sorrow, compassion.]*

Pt: *[Continuation of affective breakthrough]* It's not about what you've done. It's about this anger. It's about their letting off and just directing it at you. And because it's irrational, you don't really know where it's gonna go. You don't really know when it's gonna be spent. You don't really know . . . It's so . . . The intensity. It's like being near a fire. It's a feeling of—that you're gonna get burnt if you're not careful. It doesn't help that it's not about you because you're there. And it's being directed at you. And it felt that way with my mother. And it always felt that way with Clay when he got angry.

Th: *(calm voice)* I mean, you've been living under a reign of terror and you still are. Right? That's what you're telling me. And you are telling me, you know, that it's bullshit about the idyllic life. It's not the idyllic life. It's fear. It's utter and total fear. That's why you don't get angry. That why you don't make waves. That's why you cannot tolerate 5 minutes. There's an enormous, enormous, enormous fear. *(Long pause.)*

Pt: *(declarative tone)* When I told Clay that I couldn't meet him—that I had plans—I knew that that upset him. Because I said "Can we do it another day?" and he said, "Well, I'll try." You know? And I knew that he was angry—whatever. . . . Uhhh. I don't know. *[Clashing adaptive tendencies; the return of the "I don't know."]*

Th: You know, in my experience, we go back and forth and we sort of like elaborate, and there's momentum and it makes more and more sense, and there are deeper and deeper feelings. And I feel I understand you better and better. And we're getting to a deeper place. And then there's that moment when you pull it together, which is, "Oh my God! You've been living under a reign of terror. No wonder you're utterly paralyzed and in total fear." And . . . that's when you space out. After you make link after link after link between Clay's rage and your mother's rage, after this utterly poignant heartbreaking way in which you describe being at the mercy of this utterly irrational attack and venom, and you're terrified, but then there's a little way in which you disconnect. [*Articulation of alternation between deep affective experience and dissociative defenses.*]

Pt: But that's how I get through the anger. [*Elaboration of reason for defenses.*]

Th: That's how you survived. [*Empathic affirmation.*]

Pt: That's how I deal with anger like that.

Th: Whose anger?

Pt: My mother's anger. Clay's anger. That's the way I deal with that anger. I have to—I just zone out. I can't take it anymore.

Th: Because . . . what happens if you let yourself know . . . what happens if you let yourself *really* know—everything we've done tonight. What happens?

Pt: What happens if I acknowledge it?

Th: Yeah.

Pt: *(big sigh)* I guess I would want to keep myself away from it. Or I would want to get angry back. I don't know *(laughs nervously)*. [*Again, articulation of anger followed by backing away through "I don't know."*]

Th: All I know is that you step away. Because what you've articulated to me is that if you dare, dare take this on, you will be annihilated.

Pt: Oh, it's dangerous! [*Confirms interpretation.*]

Th: Utterly. Utterly. Utterly dangerous. [*Affective mirroring, echoing.*]

Pt: I tell you when I start to turn away from Clay it's gonna be really, really nasty. . . . And I haven't really been able to find the strength to do that.

Th: Right.

Pt: It's really been too much of . . . *(laughs nervously)*

Th: Of . . . ???

Pt: The pain that I've suffered in my life. I want to get away from that. I don't want to move toward it. And I guess everything I've done is to avoid having to experience anymore of that anger and venom. [*Articulation of the unbearable emotional states that have made defensive strategies seem like the only solution.*]

Th: Right.

Pt: And that's why I keep the peace with Clay.

Th: Right.

Pt: Because I don't want to have a conversation with him about when I change the locks. *(shudders)* I don't want to be around that kind of reaction.

Th: Right.

Pt: 'Cause it's just been sooo devastating every time in my life that I've had to deal with that reaction. I don't want to go there again. I don't want to revisit it.

Th: How are you feeling? Tell me what you're feeling right now.

Pt: I'm just frightened (*laughs nervously*). Well . . . I really am frightened. I mean, the strongest feeling I have right now is in acknowledging how frightened the feeling of being frightened is. . . . And I'm afraid to tell Clay that I really don't want to go on Saturday night. *[Patient is finally able to articulate which action tendency she favors and the reason why she can't do it.]*

The long sequence above demonstrates how, with each wave of the visceral experience of fear, there is a further elaboration of the patient's experience and the unconscious links between her abusive mother and Clay. However, while there is an unlocking of previously unconscious material, there is no resolution: There is no transformation from core affect to core state, there is no release of adaptive action tendencies. With every new round of work, the deeper affect brings to life more trauma and invariably leads to another round of "I don't know"s. Nevertheless, it is important to note how patient and therapist strive toward repair: It is as if they both know that the patient needs something from the therapist, and that as soon as it is provided, the calm of reestablished coordination will ensue. It is only in retrospect that I, the therapist, realize that the patient's visceral experience of fear is activating clashing adaptive action tendencies, and that what she is experiencing is *a fright that feels without solution* (Hesse & Main, 2000). A corrective experience has to occur in the here-and-now patient-therapist dyad. In the next sequence, the therapist offers unconditional support, the patient feels relief, the vicious cycle of affect (fear) and dissociation ("I don't know") is broken, and the patient can leave the session.

Corrective Experience: Affirming the Patient and Taking Off the Pressure

Th: Emily, what you did with me tonight is so brave. It takes a lot of courage to know that you're afraid. It's very important. . . .

Pt: (*nods*)

Th: This is what I have to say to you. Live with this session . . . for tonight. Just live with it. Sleep on it. Don't put any pressure on yourself to decide or not decide. Or do. Or not do. No pressure. Live with this session. And let's see where it goes. You don't have to know right this second about what you're gonna do Saturday. Give yourself time to live with it. I think feeling the fear, and knowing it, and knowing what you're afraid of, and knowing how deep it is, and how lifelong it is, and how it has shaped your life, you know, as I said, it's taken enormous courage—to be here. It's OK. You don't have to decide anything this moment. *[Empathy for where patient is; validation of the patient; taking off the pressure for action.]*

Pt: *(big sigh)* Good *(nervous laugh)*.

Th: You don't have to do anything. You do not have to do one single thing— except give yourself credit for what you have done—and make room—for things going where they need to go. That's all.

Pt: *(relaxes, direct, declarative tone)* That feels right.

Th: OK?

Pt: Yeah. Yeah. Yeah, that feels very right. *[Affective marker of state transformation.]*

The therapist affirms the patient's courage and lends a helping hand through taking the pressure to act off the patient. In the context of the therapeutic relationship, the feeling of safety is reestablished: Fear can function as a core affect and its adaptive benefits can be adaptively reaped. Unfortunately, because of time constraints, the session did not allow what would have been optimal: another round of the experiential exploration of "that feels very right." On its own, it would not be overwhelming evidence of the state transformation. However, the next session provides ample evidence of transformational processes having been, in fact, fully engaged.

The Next Session

The session above documents how work that seeks to access sensory, somatic, motoric right-brain mediated experience can access the emotional experiences at the core of traumatic and attachment disorders. Vignettes from the next session, included and microanalyzed below, document the phenomena of the process of change and its result—*core state. Core state* is an affective state marked by genuineness, balance, perspective, and truth-telling. In core state throughout the session, Emily has access to her experience and the benefit of a fully operant reflective self function. We hear about the aftermath and consequences of the affective/experiential work of the previous session, and we also hear the patient's experience of the therapeutic process and her reflections on the process of change.

The next vignette is of the opening moments of the second session. Emily looks different: Her face is animated, her eyes are bright and there is liveliness, engagement, and lightness in her manner. There is a relaxed, happy smile on her face. It is the first exchange between the patient and therapist since last session.

The Subsiding of the Fear, the Operation of the Reflective Self Function, and the Accessing of Emotional Resources

Pt: Last Thursday was *really* amazing! It was amazing, because it made an amazing difference. An *amazing* difference!

Th: Hmm.

Pt: And, I thought it's interesting because I was like *desperate* to find out *what* to do. I needed to know what to do about Saturday night. And your advice was ... so good. "Just ... forget it! Throw the question out! Don't think about it. Just stick with how you feel." So, since I clearly didn't have an answer, I did just what you said. And I kept thinking about how I felt. And about our conversation about being afraid of Clay, and then that triggering me back to being afraid of my mother and my father. *[Note that not a word had been said about the patient's father in the previous session; but clearly a lot of processing went on, both conscious and unconscious, between the sessions.]*

Th: Yes.

Pt: And that intense feeling of fear. And I just kept thinking about it and thinking about it. And it was ringing truer and truer. And ... I just stayed with it. And the next morning I woke up. So, it was Friday. And it was getting close to having to decide what to do. And then I thought, you know what, I'm just gonna go. I'll go. And, it's very possible that ... And I'll see what happens ... I mean, I wasn't feeling frantic anymore. And, I wasn't really feeling frightened anymore. *[The patient's state transformation is marked by a resolution of the fear, the accessing of emotional resources, e.g., self-confidence, resilience, and the calm of core state.]*

Th: Hmmm.

Pt: And, ummm ... I thought, I'll go. And maybe I can go and I can be real. Maybe if I'm not afraid ... Maybe, if, in fact, you take this fear out, and you examine it in the light of day and you say, "Well, exactly what are you afraid of? What are the things you're afraid of? So, you're afraid that you won't be married anymore? You're not! You're afraid that he'll leave you? He did! You're afraid that he'll be angry at you? He is! Are you afraid that he's gonna hit you? No! Did he ever hit you? No. So, he's not gonna do bodily harm. And, if anything, the anger that he's had in the past, he doesn't even have now. So ... what are you afraid of exactly? *[An extraordinary example of the affective processing of the reflective self function at work.]*

Th: Hmmm.

Pt: So, what you're afraid to do is to say how you feel. So ... *(laughs ruefully)* ... do it! See if you can just do it since there's nothing to be afraid of.

In clear language, the patient documents that the fear is gone. With its resolution, the patient gains access to emotional resources which allow her to put the situation in perspective, differentiating between the past and the current reality, which the patient feels amply able to face. After the frightened paralysis and immobility of the last session, it is quite an experience to hear the patient say to herself, "So, what you're afraid to do is to say how you feel. So, see if you can just do it since there's nothing to be afraid of." The unconditional acceptance of the patient's emotional reality in the previous session enables Emily to reframe the issue of fear as having been afraid to be real, to be her real self.

The Undoing of Dissociation: Adaptive Access to Anger

In the next vignette, the patient relates how her meeting with her husband actually went. She describes a process where she is able to be emotionally present and authentic, and has access to her emotions in an adaptive and appropriate manner. Patient and husband engage in genuine conversation. Gone are the tactics of appeasement and the strategies of denial. The patient is honest and comes clean, taking responsibility for her own contribution to the marital difficulties.

Pt: And I really told him about this discovery that I had made. And how I felt about it. And I started to explain to him, not our history, but our recent past in the last year. How I had not really been honest with him.

Th: Uh huh.

Pt: And that I always knew how I felt *before* I saw him and I knew how I felt *after* I saw him. But I never seemed to be in touch with how I felt while I was *with* him. And that I was so desperate to keep from losing him that I . . . chose not to really be real. And that a lot of it was a sham, really. And that I, you know . . . *[Patient acknowledges how defenses prevented her from being authentic in the couple's interactions.]*

Th: Hmmm.

Pt: And that, I never told him that I didn't want him to pick up my phone. And that it bothered me that he called me on the cell phone and so, I told him inadvertently. The thing with, you know, the lock on the door . . . And just coming to the apartment. And I said, "I know you may think that I told you how I felt . . . but I never really got angry about it. But I was very angry about it. But, somehow, in front of you, I lost it. I lost my real feelings about what was happening." And I just told him about it. I just shared it with him. *[No longer* *afraid, the patient is able to be assertive and direct about her feelings with her husband.] (Both patient and therapist sigh deeply.)*

The Do-Over

Clay asks Emily to go out with him the following Saturday night, in an uncanny real-life version of a controlled experiment, giving us a chance to compare before and after. This time, Emily is direct and she declines. Self assertion and adaptive action tendencies are smoothly in operation; she faces her husband's anger without missing a beat.

Pt: . . . And he said, "OK. I'm not angry about it." And I said, "I don't give a shit whether you're angry about it or not!" I said, "It has nothing to do with how you think or feel about it. It has to do with the fact that I don't want to do it. And you know what? If I lose you because I don't want to do it, I already lost you" *(laughs)*. It's like, what am I losing here?!

The Patient's Supervision of the Therapist: Reflections on the Mutative Aspects of the Therapeutic Process

By exploring the patient's experience of therapeutic process in detail, we have a tremendous opportunity to learn what makes a difference and how interventions are received. Here, the patient spontaneously offers her take on, and response to, the therapist's affective self-disclosure the previous session, when in response to patient's self-sabotage, the therapist tells the patient that the patient's abandoning of her own self makes her (the therapist) angry.

Pt: This process is *incredible!* It's just *incredible.* This whole thing about why . . . I thought it was really interesting . . . when you said to me, "You know what? I have to stop *(puts her hands out in front of her to accentuate stop)*. Maybe this is not professional. And maybe this is not what I should be doing. But if I don't, we won't be able to finish this session." . . . And then you said, "You know what? I used to be mad at Clay. I'm not mad at Clay anymore. I'm mad at you!" And I thought, ooooohhh! *(laughs nervously)*.
Th: So, how did you feel about that?
Pt: Then I thought, "Yeah! Right on Diana! *(laughs loudly)*. Now you got it!" Really! . . . The interesting thing is I felt that some of your anger at Clay has been misplaced. But, I didn't want to divert it. . . . because I was happy somebody was feeling it . . . Because I couldn't get angry at Clay, I was so glad that at least you could get angry at Clay. In some respects, I felt like you were my surrogate.

Th: Uh huh.

Pt: I also felt that you were trying to say, "Look! This is how you do it. You wanna know how to do it?" . . . I was never really sure how angry you were. But, the truth of the matter is, that's exactly the truth . . . . People just have the power you give them. You say, "I'm sorry, but you don't have that power anymore." It's like, "Ahhhhhh!" *(makes motion of someone being strangled).* They don't have it anymore. They can't do it. *[Spontaneous undoing of projective mechanisms.]*

Th: Right.

Pt: They cease to be a threat. They cease to be the enemy. They cease to be important. I mean, they can still be the problem. But, who cares?! *(She's talking fluidly, directly, and purposefully here). [Projection undone.]*

Pt: So, it was very interesting . . . But this fear! And then being able to sit there and talk about Clay and then have the feeling go back to its source.

Th: Yes.

Pt: It really seems to be if it doesn't go back to its source, it doesn't really get understood or resolved. *[Patient's spontaneous reflections on the healing mechanisms of the therapeutic process.]* And I'm telling you when I . . . It took me a while for everything to settle. And that great advice . . . "Just stay with it."

Th: Uh huh.

Pt: "You don't have to do anything else." And I trust you, so I said, "OK. I'm not doing anything else but staying with this." And when I woke up in the morning it was like this *giant* cloud had been lifted. *[Subjective experience of state transformation and the emergence of core state.]*

From within core state, the patient reflects on her experiences of the past session, and addresses three issues: her experience of the therapist's use of affective self-disclosure of anger; her clear awareness that, in the abusive relationships in adulthood, it takes two to tango; and her subjective experience of the state transformation marking the arrival of core state. An excellent example of working on the *self-at-worst* state from the perspective of *self-at-best* functioning, this is the therapeutic equivalent of a cohesive and coherent autobiographical narrative: In a calm, related fashion, the patient articulates her perspective of the vehement affective experiences of the previous session.

The Emergence of the True and Real Self: The Realness Is Very Desirable

Pt: And, you know what Clay said to me *(laughs proudly and with ironic awareness)* which is really funny? He said, "I see so many changes in you, and they are sooo appealing."

Th: Hmm.

Pt: So, here it's like . . . all my life I wanted this guy to be crazy about me *(laughs ruefully)*. And um . . . And forget about this guy, but life in general. Now that I am myself, I can have what I want. I have to decide what I want. But, I can have what I want. I can make things happen because in being myself, I'm . . . it's very desirable. *[In touch with her deep and genuine sense of self, she has access to the emotional resources required to make decisions and live a full life, which only gives rise to greater confidence and ease and relaxation.]*

Th: Uh huh.

Pt: The realness is very desirable.

Outcome

The patient's assertiveness and capacity to make constructive use of her anger continued to unfold. These gains were maintained, bolstered by a few sessions of intensive experiential work with the core emotion of anger and rage. But the mutative work occurred in the sessions presented above. The visceral unfolding and exploration of the fear, and the undoing of its pathogenic status through a corrective experience within the therapeutic relationship, were at the core of the transformation of a lifelong pattern, where a lifelong inability to experience and express anger was reversed within one session and its aftermath.

Conclusion

Throughout both sessions, moment-to-moment tracking of the patient's affective experience, reflected in ever-shifting vitality affects, underlies the therapeutic work. Together, the two sessions illustrate the three states and two state transformations characteristic of AEDP work:

1. *Defense.* In the early part of the session, the patient's core experience can barely be glimpsed through the haze of defenses and anxiety.
2. *Core affect.* Then, the first state transformation occurs. Rather than experiencing defensive contortions, there is a breakthrough of core affect. Eventually, dyadic conditions are co-constructed that allow a solution to the fright that previously had no solution. Adaptive action tendencies can come to the fore and inform the patient's experience.
3. *Core state.* The deep experience of core affect and the consequent activation of the patient's adaptive action tendencies lead to the second

state transformation: a move into core state. Core state—with its characteristic embodied and mindful experiencing—comes online and the patient's experience is suffused with a sense of efficacy, agency, clarity, and calm. The patient comes into her own.

To pick up the theme of continuity vs. plasticity articulated in the introduction: The *continuity* of pathogenic patterns in the psyche, set early in life, is evident as soon as the session begins: The patient reacts to a seemingly innocuous present-day incident with an intensity befitting the child faced with her mother's out-of-control rages; the patient reacts virtually as though her mother were present and she (the patient) were a small child. The patient's affective experiences come forward with a vehemence unmodulated by time, experience, and reality (Siegel, 1999; van der Kolk, 2001).

But then, the evidence of therapeutic impact reveals a major degree of *plasticity* in the psyche: A sudden and deep transformation reverses a life-long pattern; emotions that were till then vehement become graceful and supple, and are able to inform reflective self functioning. Defensive exclusion is dyadically undone, making way for a much more inclusive and differentiated coordination: Motivated gaps in the autobiographical narrative of the individual can be filled in, dramatically improving narrative coherence (Hughes, in preparation; Main, this volume). Unlike in disorganized attachment where, at crucial moments, the individual can neither feel nor deal, after the work, the patient can now both feel and deal. And, as she adds, she therefore feels real, present, and very much herself in the process.

While the vehement aspect of trauma is most dramatic—the flashbacks, the dissociative phenomena—the greatest cost of trauma comes from how it rents the fabric of relatedness, creating isolation, alienation, and despair (van der Kolk, 2001). The goal of this chapter has been to show how the vehement emotions can be dyadically regulated, so that the individual can benefit from the *adaptive* transformational power of the categorical emotions. AEDP engages a dialectical process where the transformational potential of both categorical emotions *and* of empathy-based, affect-regulating, attuned relatedness (monitored through vitality affect shifts) can be therapeutically harnessed and applied to therapeutic purpose through experiential work. In therapy, these right-brain mediated processes—processes involved throughout development in attachment and emotion regulation—are entrained and brought to the experiential fore. Thus, they become a *felt* part of the individual's experience, forces that the patient can feel at work in body and mind. The experiential, imagistic, sensorimotor, and somatic aspects of the present approach are central to its effectiveness: Their importance cannot be sufficiently emphasized.

That which is *first felt* can *then* be *reflected upon* and known; it is out of such lived knowledge that a coherent and cohesive autobiography can be constructed from the ground (of experience) on up, so to speak.

Our understanding of the neurobiology of attachment and trauma is unfolding with increasing pace. Now, our understanding of the neurobiology of healing has to catch up so that the therapeutic interventions by which the suffering of trauma and disorganized attachment are relieved can continue to grow in precision and effectiveness.

References

Ainsworth, M. D. S., Blehar, M. C., Waters, E., & Wall, S. (1978). *Patterns of attachment: A psychological study of the strange situation.* Hillsdale, NJ: Erlbaum.

Alexander, F., & French, T. M. (1946). *Psychoanalytic therapy: Principles and application.* New York: Ronald Press. Reprint. Lincoln: University of Nebraska Press, 1980.

Allen, J. G. (2001). *Traumatic relationships and serious mental disorders.* New York: Wiley.

Anchin, J., & Fosha, D. (in preparation). *An experiential method for psychoanalysis.* Manuscript.

Bates, J. E., Maslin, C. A., & Frankel, K. A. (1985). Attachment security, mother-child interaction, and temperament as predictors of behavior-problem ratings at age three years. In I. Bretherton & E. Waters (Eds.), *Growing points of attachment theory and research. Monographs of the Society for Research in Child Development, 50* (Serial No. 209), 167–193.

Beebe, B., & Lachmann, F. M. (1994). Representation and internalization in infancy: Three principles of salience. *Psychoanalytic Psychology, 11*(2), 127–165.

Beebe, B., & Lachmann, F. M. (2002). *Infant research and adult treatment: Co-constructing interactions.* Hillsdale, NJ: Analytic Press.

Bohart, A. C., & Tallman, K. (1999). *How clients make therapy work: The process of active self-healing.* Washington, DC: American Psychological Association.

Bowlby, J. (1973). *Attachment and loss: Vol. 2. Separation.* New York: Basic Books.

Bowlby, J. (1980). *Attachment and loss: Vol. 3. Loss, sadness, and depression.* New York: Basic Books.

Bowlby, J. (1982). *Attachment and loss: Vol. 1. Attachment* (2d ed.). New York: Basic Books.

Bowlby, J. (1991). Post-script. In C. M. Parkes, J. Stevenson-Hinde, & P. Marris (Eds.), *Attachment across the life cycle* (pp. 293–297). London: Routledge.

Buber, M. (1965). *The knowledge of man: Selected essays.* New York: Harper Torchbooks.

Cassidy, J. (1994). Emotion regulation: Influence of attachment relationships. *Monographs of the Society for Research in Child Development, 69*(Serial No. 240), 228–249.

Coates, S. W. (1998). Having a mind of one's own and holding the other in mind: Commentary on paper by Peter Fonagy and Mary Target. *Psychoanalytic Dialogues, 8,* 115–148.

Cooper, A. M. (1992). Psychic change: Development in the theory of psychoanalytic techniques. *International Journal of Psychoanalysis, 73,* 245–250.

Damasio, A. R. (1994). *Descartes' error: Emotion, reason and the human brain.* New York: Grosset/Putnam.

Damasio, A. R. (1999). *The feeling of what happens: Body and emotion in the making of consciousness.* New York: Harcourt Brace.

Darwin, C. (1965). *The expression of emotion in man and animals.* Chicago: University of Chicago Press. (Original work published 1872)

Davanloo, H. (1990). *Unlocking the unconscious: Selected papers of Habib Davanloo.* New York: Wiley.

Eagle, M. N. (1995). The developmental perspectives of attachment and psychoanalytic theory. In S. Goldberg, R. Muir, & J. Kerr (Eds.), *Attachment theory: Social, developmental and clinical perspectives* (pp. 407–472). Hillsdale, NJ: Analytic Press.

Ekman, P. (1983). Autonomic nervous system activity distinguishes among emotions. *Science, 221,* 1208–1210.

Emde, R. N. (1981). Changing models of infancy and the nature of early development: Remodeling the foundation. *Journal of the American Psychoanalytic Association, 29,* 179–219.

Emde, R. N. (1983). The pre-representational self and its affective core. *Psychoanalytic Study of the Child, 38,* 165–192.

Emde, R. N. (1988). Development terminable and interminable. *International Journal of Psycho-Analysis, 69,* 23–42.

Ferenczi, S. (1931/1980). Child analysis in the analysis of adults. In M. Balint (Ed.), E. Mosbacher (Trans.), *Final contributions to the problems and methods of psychoanalysis* (pp. 126–142). New York: Brunner/Mazel.

Fonagy, P. (1997). Multiple voices vs. meta-cognition: An attachment theory perspective. *Journal of Psychotherapy Integration, 7,* 181–194.

Fonagy, P., Leigh, T., Kennedy, R., Matoon, G., Steele, H., Target, M., Steele, M., & Higgitt, A. (1995). Attachment, borderline states and the representation of emotions and cognitions in self and other. In D. Cicchetti, S. L. Toth, et al. (Eds.), *Emotion, cognition, and representation* (pp. 371–414). Rochester, NY: University of Rochester Press.

Fonagy, P., Steele, M., Steele, H., Higgitt, A., & Target, M. (1994). The theory and practice of resilience. *Journal of Child Psychology and Psychiatry, 35,* 231–257.

Fonagy, P., Steele, M., Steele, H., Leigh, T., Kennedy, R., Matoon, G., & Target, M. (1995). Attachment, the reflective self, and borderline states. In S. Goldberg, R. Muir, & J. Kerr (Eds.), *Attachment theory: Social, developmental, and clinical perspectives* (pp. 233–278). Hillsdale, NJ: Analytic Press.

Fonagy, P., Steele, M., Steele, H., Moran, G. S., & Higgitt, A. (1991). The capacity for understanding mental states: The reflective self in parent and child and its significance for security of attachment. *Infant Mental Health Journal, 12,* 201–218.

Fonagy, P., & Target, M. (1998). Mentalization and the changing aims of child psychoanalysis. *Psychoanalytic Dialogues, 8,* 87–114.

Fosha, D. (2000a). Meta-therapeutic processes and the affects of transformation: Affirmation and the healing affects. *Journal of Psychotherapy Integration, 10,* 71–97.

Fosha, D. (2000b). *The transforming power of affect: A model of accelerated change.* New York: Basic Books.

Fosha, D. (2001). The dyadic regulation of affect. *Journal of Clinical Psychology/In Session,* 2001, 57 (2), 227–242.

Fosha, D. (2002a). The activation of affective change processes in AEDP (Accelerated Experiential-Dynamic Psychotherapy). In J. J. Magnavita (Ed.), *Comprehensive handbook of psychotherapy. Vol. 1: Psychodynamic and object relations psychotherapies.* New York: Wiley.

Fosha, D. (2002b). *True self, true other and core state: Toward a clinical theory of affective change process.* Paper presented at the Los Angeles Psychoanalytic Society and Institute, Los Angeles, California.

Fosha, D., & Greenberg, L. S. (2002). *Toward a clinical phenomenology of affect and emotion.* Presented at the conference on Attachment and Integration of the Society for the Exploration of Psychotherapy Integration (SEPI), San Francisco.

Fosha, D., & Slowiaczek, M. L. (1997). Techniques for accelerating dynamic psychotherapy. *American Journal of Psychotherapy, 51,* 229–251.

Gendlin, E. T. (1981). *Focusing.* New York: Bantam New Age Paperbacks.

Gendlin, E. T. (1996). *Focusing-oriented psychotherapy: A manual of the experiential method.* New York: Guilford Press.

Gianino, A., & Tronick, E. Z. (1988). The mutual regulation model: The infant's self and interactive regulation. Coping and defense capacities. In T. Field, P. McCabe, & N. Schneiderman (Eds.), *Stress and coping* (pp. 47–68). Hillsdale, NJ: Erlbaum.

Goleman, D. (1995). *Emotional intelligence: Why it can matter more than IQ.* New York: Bantam Books.

Greenberg, L. S., & Paivio, S. C. (1997). *Working with emotions in psychotherapy.* New York: Guilford Press.

Greenberg, L. S., Rice, L. N., & Elliott, R. (1993). *Facilitating emotional change: The moment-by-moment process.* New York: Guilford Press.

Hesse, E., & Main, M. (1999). Second-generation effects of unresolved trauma in nonmaltreating parents: dissociated, frightened, and threatening parental behavior. *Psychoanalytic Inquiry, 19*(4), 481–540.

Hesse, E., & Main, M. (2000). Disorganized infant, child, and adult attachment: Collapse in behavioral and attentional strategies. *Journal of the American Psychoanalytic Association, 48*(4), 1097–1127.

Hughes, D. A. (1998). *Building the bonds of attachment: Awakening love in deeply troubled children.* Northvale, NJ: Aronson.

Hughes, D. A. (in preparation). The psychological treatment of childhood PTSD and attachment disorganization: Integrative dyadic psychotherapy. Manuscript.

Jaffe, J., Beebe, B., Feldstein, S., Crown, C., & Jasnow, M. (2001). Rhythms of dialogue in infancy: coordinated timing in development. *Monographs of the Society for Research in Child Development, 66* (Serial No. 265).

James, W. (1985). *The varieties of religious experience: A study in human nature.* New York: Penguin Books. (Original work published 1902)

Kurtz, R. (1990). *Body-centered psychotherapy: The Hakomi method.* Mendocino, CA: LifeRhythm.

Lachmann, F. M. (2001). Some contributions of empirical infant research to adult psychoanalysis: What have we learned? How can we apply it? *Psychoanalytic Dialogues, 11*(2), 167–185.

Lamb, M. E. (1987). Predictive implications of individual differences in attachment. *Journal of Consulting and Clinical Psychology, 55,* 817–824.

Lazarus, R. S. (1991). *Emotion and adaptation.* New York: Oxford University Press.

LeDoux, J. (1996). *The emotional brain: The mysterious underpinnings of emotional life.* New York: Simon & Schuster.

LeDoux, J. (2002). *Synaptic self: How our brains become who we are.* New York: Viking.

Levine, P. (1997). *Waking the tiger: Healing trauma.* Berkeley, CA: North Atlantic Books.

Lindemann, E. (1944). Symptomatology and management of acute grief. *American Journal of Psychiatry, 101,* 141–148.

Liotti, G. (1999). Disorganization of attachment as a model for understanding dissociative psychopathology. In J. Solomon & C. George (Eds.), *Attachment disorganization* (pp. 291–317). New York: Guilford Press.

Lyons-Ruth, K. (1998). Implicit relational knowing: Its role in development and psychoanalytic treatment. *Infant Mental Health Journal, 19*(3), 282–289.

Lyons-Ruth, K. (2001). The two-person construction of defenses: Disorganized attachment strategies, unintegrated mental states and hostile/helpless relational processes. *Psychologist/Psychoanalyst, XXI* (1), 40–45.

Main, M. (1995). Recent studies in attachment: Overview with selected implications for clinical work. In S. Goldberg, R. Muir, & J. Kerr (Eds.), *Attachment theory: Social, developmental and clinical perspectives* (pp. 407–472). Hillsdale, NJ: Analytic Press.

Main, M. (1999). Epilogue. Attachment theory: Eighteen points with suggestions for future studies. In J. Cassidy & P. R. Shaver (Eds.), *Handbook of attachment: Theory, research, and clinical applications* (pp. 845–888). New York: Guilford Press.

Main, M. (2001). *Attachment disturbances and the development of psychopathology.* Paper presented at conference on *Healing Trauma: Attachment, trauma, the brain, and the mind.* University of California at San Diego School of Medicine, San Diego.

Marvin, R., Cooper, G., Hoffman, K., & Powell, B. (2002). The circle of security project: Attachment-based intervention with caregiver-preschool child dyads. *Attachment and Human Development, 4*(1): 1–31.

McCullough Vaillant, L. (1997). *Changing character: Short-term anxiety-regulating psychotherapy for restructuring defenses, affects, and attachment.* New York: Basic Books.

Nahum, J. P. (1998). Case illustration: moving along . . . and, is change gradual or sudden? *Infant Mental Health Journal, 19*(3), 315–319.

Neborsky, R. This volume.

Panksepp, J. (1998). *Affective neuroscience: The foundations of human and animal emotions.* New York: Oxford University Press.

Panksepp, J. (2000). The long-term psychobiological consequences of infant emotions. *Infant Mental Health Journal, 22,* 132–173.

Person, E. S. (1988). *Dreams of love and fateful encounters: The power of romantic passion.* New York: Norton.

Porges, S. (1997). Emotion: An evolutionary by-product of the neural regulation of the autonomic nervous system. In C. S. Carter, B. Kirkpatrick, & I. I. Lenderhendler (Eds.), *The integrative neurobiology of affiliation. Annals of the New York Academy of Sciences,* Vol. 807. New York: The New York Academy of Sciences.

Rogers, C. R. (1957). The necessary and sufficient conditions of therapeutic personality change. *Journal of Consulting Psychology, 21,* 95–103.

Rosenzweig, S. (1936). Some implicit common factors in diverse methods of psychotherapy. *American Journal of Orthopsychiatry, 6,* 412–415.

Rothschild, B. (2000). *The body remembers: The psychophysiology of trauma and trauma treatment.* New York: W. W. Norton.

Safran, J. D., & Muran, J. C. (2000). *Negotiating the therapeutic alliance: A relational treatment guide.* New York: Guilford Press.

Schore, A. N. (1994). *Affect regulation and the origin of the self: The neurobiology of emotional development.* Hillsdale, NJ: Erlbaum.

Schore, A. N. (1996). The experience-dependent maturation of a regulatory system in the orbital prefrontal cortex and the origins of developmental psychopathology. *Development and Psychopathology, 8,* 59–87.

Schore, A. N. (2000). Effects of a secure attachment relationship on right brain development, affect regulation, and infant mental health. *Infant Mental Health Journal, 22,* 7–66.

Seligman, S. (1998). Child psychoanalysis, adult psychoanalysis, and developmental psychology: An introduction. *Psychoanalytic Dialogues, 8,* 79–86.

Shapiro, F. (1995). *Eye movement, desensitization and reprocessing: Basic principles, protocols, and procedures.* New York: Guilford Press.

Siegel, D. (1999). *The developing mind: Toward a neurobiology of interpersonal experience.* New York: Guilford Press.

Solomon, M. F., Neborsky, R. J., McCullough, L., Alpert, M., Shapiro, F., & Malan, D. H. (2001). *Short-term therapy for long-term change.* New York: Norton.

Sroufe, L. A. (1995). *Emotional development: The organization of emotional life in the early years.* Cambridge, U.K.: Cambridge University Press.

Stern, D. N. (1985). *The interpersonal world of the infant: A view from psychoanalysis and developmental psychology.* New York: Basic Books.

Stern, D. N., Sander, L. W., Nahum, J. P., Harrison, A. M., Lyons-Ruth, K., Morgan, A. C., Bruschweiler-Stern, N., & Tronick, E. Z. (1998). Non-interpretive mechanisms in psychoanalytic psychotherapy: The "something more" than interpretation. *International Journal of Psychoanalysis, 79,* 903–921.

Teicher, M. (2002). Scars that won't heal: the neurobiology of child abuse. *Scientific American 286,* 3: 68–75.

Tomkins, S. S. (1962). *Affect, imagery, and consciousness: Vol. 1. The positive affects.* New York: Springer.

Tomkins, S. S. (1963). *Affect, imagery, and consciousness: Vol. 2. The negative affects.* New York: Springer.

Trevarthen, C. (1993). The self born in intersubjectivity: an infant communicating. In U. Neisser (Ed.), *The perceived self: Ecological and interpersonal sources of self-knowledge* (pp. 121–173). New York: Cambridge University Press.

Trevarthen, C. (2000). Intrinsic motives for companionship in understanding: their origin, development, and significance for infant mental health. *Infant Mental Health Journal, 22,* 95–131.

Trevarthen, C., & Aitken, K. J. (1994). Brain development, infant communication, and empathy disorders: Intrinsic factors in child mental health. *Development and Psychopathology, 6,* 597–633.

Tronick, E. Z. (1989). Emotions and emotional communication in infants. *American Psychologist, 44*(2), 112–119.

Tronick, E. Z. (1998). Dyadically expanded states of consciousness and the process of therapeutic change. *Infant Mental Health Journal, 19*(3), 290–299.

Tronick, E. Z., & Weinberg, K. (1997). Depressed mothers and infants: The failure to form dyadic states of consciousness. In L. Murray & P. Cooper (Eds.), *Post-partum depression and child development* (pp. 54–85). New York: Guilford Press.

van den Boom, D. (1990). Preventive intervention and the quality of mother-infant interaction and infant exploration in irritable infants. In W. Koops (Ed.), *Developmental psychology behind the dykes* (pp. 249–270). Amsterdam: Eburon.

van der Kolk, B. A. (1996). The body keeps the score: approaches to the psychobiology of posttraumatic stress disorder. In B. A. van der Kolk, A. C. McFarlane, & L. Weisaeth (Eds.), *Traumatic stress: The effects of overwhelming experience on mind, body and society* (pp. 214–241). New York: Guilford Press.

van der Kolk, B. A. (2001). Beyond the talking cure: Somatic experience, subcortical imprints and the treatment of trauma. In F. Shapiro (Ed.). *EMDR: Toward a paradigm shift*. New York: APA Press.

Volkan, V. (1981). *Linking objects and linking phenomena: A study of the forms, symptoms, metapsychology and therapy of complicated mourning*. New York: International Universities Press.

Zajonc, R. B. (1985). Emotion and facial efference: A theory reclaimed. *Science, 228*, 15–22.

7

A Clinical Model for the Comprehensive Treatment of Trauma Using an Affect Experiencing–Attachment Theory Approach

Robert J. Neborsky

IN THESE TROUBLED times, post–September 11, 2001, this chapter is particularly timely. On that day all of us were exposed in one way or another to the devastating effects of what Shapiro refers to as "large-T trauma." A large percentage of the nation's population suffered from the signs and symptoms of acute trauma exposure. These symptoms are well known to us and they include anxiety, lowered mood, obsessive thoughts, anger, grief, flashbacks of the events, sleep disorders, and nightmares. As time went on, many of us resolved these symptoms. However, a small percentage of people developed clinical anxiety disorders (PTSD) or depression, and required professional intervention.

Who makes up this small percentage? In his longitudinal studies of trauma-exposed individuals, Bowman (2001) stated that one factor stands out in the prediction of who will develop pathology posttrauma exposure—neuroticism. She defines this trait as measured on different personality scales as the "tendency to experience negative affects when exposed to a new event." Apparently this trait is stable across the lifespan from infancy to senescence. It is a very powerful predictor and in fact accounts for twice the variance the actual stressor accounts for. This epidemiological research finding is consistent with clinical observation and attachment research. I hope to offer a new approach to the comprehensive treatment of trauma victims that includes intervention at the level of *neuroticism*. It is my central thesis that within each of us there is an unconscious negative affect processing system that protects us from developing anxiety and/or depression. The system responsible for this function is called the attachment system. What must a healthy attachment system do when exposed to trauma in order to preserve mental health?[1]

1. All of the negative emotion that the event created *and activated* must be "metabolized."[2]
2. The event must be framed in a way that is consistent with the patients' core belief system. Their core belief system is the working model of how the world works. This exists on a continuum from the random universe theory to a perfect order theory (a higher power decides what happens). Their psychologic process must address and formulate beliefs about: (a) where the focus of control resides; (b) the sources of danger and what exposure to danger means; and (c) the meaning of life.

In this chapter I will demonstrate why I believe both of those tasks are a function of a healthy, integrated attachment system. By way of a preview, I will first outline how trauma is processed with an integrated attachment system. Next I will examine how and why chronic disorders of stress happen. And finally, I will address effective treatment vis-a-vis technique and then illustrative clinical case examples.

A Model for Understanding the Effects of Trauma on Our Brains and Minds

Acute trauma by definition exposes the individual to an extraordinary event wherein his or her sense of control is violated. When that occurs, there is a discharge of extreme intense emotion: grief, anger, or fear. This then activates latent unconscious mechanisms for self-repair which, since the time of Freud, have been called defense mechanisms. The purpose of defense mechanisms is

---

[1] I am using Siegel's functional definition of mental health as "adaptability, flexibility and stability of the nervous system over time."
[2] Closely related to Shapiro's concept that negative affects must be "digested."

to restore homeostasis as soon as possible to preserve adaptive capacity. Schore has outlined the stress response circuitry of the infant, showing how essential it is for the child to decrease arousal to preserve neural growth. This innate mechanism for self-preservation also exists in trauma. A person is trapped in a burning building. Everything indicates he is going to die a horrible death. There is no escape. Arousal is off the scales, fear is pumping, and suddenly a remarkable calm takes over. The person is calm, time seems to slow down, there is no pain, and a comforting acceptance of his fate occurs.[3] In this hypo-thetical example, the mechanisms of dissociation and emotional detachment have intervened and prevented panic. If the person is miraculously saved, he will receive care and begin to go about his life. He will talk about his near miss, have dreams about fire, dreams about being trapped and rescued, and will process that event subconsciously until all the implicit memory of the event is detoxified. He will seek and find comfort in his relationships and sup-port institutions that may or may not include counseling. After six months the emotion associated with the event is largely gone—fires in fireplaces do not trigger arousal or flashbacks, and the person has explained to himself why the event occurred and why he survived along the aforementioned philosophical continuums.

Now let's take that same person and imagine he was abused as a toddler—let's say age 2 to 3—he was held down by his caregiver and punished for misbehavior with burning cigarettes. He dealt with the abuse the best he could, but suffers from mild anxiety, depression, and negative thinking. The memory is so painful that he has blocked it and all negative emotions related to the event from consciousness. In the acute situation, the person's response to the fire is the same. After the rescue he begins to suffer from panic attacks that stop his functioning. Not only does he have bad dreams, but also horrible nightmares of torture and butchery. He is flooded with self-destructive impulses and may even attempt suicide. Finally, he seeks professional help and requires medications and extensive psychotherapy. Why? The acute traumatic event unlocked a hidden file in his implicit memory system for which there is no language, only image and feeling.

Understanding this process is crucial to successful work with trauma victims, so let me restate it clearly. The emotions associated with childhood trauma (relational failure, abuse, or neglect) are either repressed or dissociated in an unconscious file. Two things can access and activate the negative emotional consequences of this hidden file: (1) experience of adult trauma, or (2) most

---

[3] Probably mediated by discharge of endogenous opiates.

TABLE 7.1
The Two Responses to Acute Trauma of "Secures" versus "Insecures"

NO TRAUMATIC ATTACHMENT IN UNCONSCIOUS	TRAUMATIC ATTACHMENT IN UNCONSCIOUS
Overwhelming emotion	Overwhelming emotion
No hidden files to activate	Activation of hidden files of emotion
Temporary defense	Temporary and permanent defense
Residual anxiety, acute disorder of stress	Chronic anxiety, acute and chronic disorder of stress
Stress processing (attachment system intact)	Defective stress processing (insecure)
Cognitive reframing of event	Unsuccessful reframing
Return to normal baseline in 6 months	No return to premorbid baseline

common and surprising, by an intimate relationship. I will discuss this second activating dynamic later in this chapter.

When the file is activated by adult trauma, it is like a dam breaking (or Pandora's infamous box) and the affects can create anxiety, depression, somatic conversion symptoms, psycho physiologic disorder, and/or self-abuse. With relational activation, it's more like a slow leak in which paradigms of abuse and neglect enter the person's life, and psychiatric symptoms appear as well. Unlike the first hypothetical person who was in the fire, this person's attachment system is overwhelmed by the unconscious affects stimulated by the trauma, and a disorder of stress develops. A further complication of unresolved trauma is narrative reenactment of the trauma wherein the victim unconsciously recreates the traumatic event over and over again. Literally, they can jump from the frying pan into the fire and back again (Erikson, 1963; Davanloo, 1987; van der Kolk, 1989). Table 7.1 compares the two theoretical trauma responses described above.

A Model for Healing from Trauma

Attachment relationship information is recorded in an unconscious state, which is stored in implicit memory. It is, in effect, our stress-processing mechanism. Securely attached people metabolize life stresses well; insecurely attached individuals metabolize them less efficiently. Life difficulties and intimate relational conflicts mobilize the unconscious attachment system, and symptoms and narrative reenactments occur. Ultimately, the more severe attachment disruptions lead to the kinds of neuropsychological deficits described by Fonagy, Gergely, Jurist, and Target (2002). Because the attachment system is not "localized," but exists as parts of all aspects of emotional experience as reflected in mind-body states, the effects of attachment are *always* present in both gross and subtle ways.

This thesis is central to this chapter as well as to my research goal, which is to establish a comprehensive psychotherapy that alters malfunctioning attachment relationships. So let me outline here what I think happens normally to help trauma victims recover, and then what psychotherapy must do in order to facilitate that process. Our brains have in them inherent trauma processing systems. These are a function of secure attachment. If a child is disturbed by an environmental event, he or she returns to the attachment figure for comfort. Comfort takes many forms, both overt and covert. On the overt level, mothers pick up their children, hold them, distract them, etc. On covert levels, processes like mirroring affect or containment behavior with vocal and tonal synchronization are elicited until the child is restored to calmness and play or exploratory behavior resumes. It is clear (Main, Kaplan, & Cassidy, 1985) that this process becomes internalized and becomes autonomous (i.e., operates without mother or father present) and works at both a conscious and unconscious level. Our biorhythms are intimately involved with stress-trauma management on a day-to-day basis. Our REM[4] sleep in 90-minute bursts, in a 24-hour cycle "digests" trauma that is experienced on a daily basis. In dreaming, the brain compares the trauma with early memory traces of similar experience, and files the memories of the day's events according to an affect-based associative system for further use and potential survival value. Comforting figures may appear in the dream to give care, advice, counsel, and relief, if necessary. The nightly dream process helps the dreamer receive positive resolution of his or her experience, and the dreamer moves on to the next day's activities restored, refreshed, and prepared for survival-based action.

The insecurely attached dreamer may or may not receive comfort for the day's stresses since the caregiver may have been the source of early stress or threat. It is highly likely that the dream will not achieve successful resolution, and hidden files (dissociated or repressed memories and affects) will be activated. The insecurely attached person must constantly recruit other sources

---

[4] In REM (rapid eye movement) sleep information passes bihemispherically from the right hemisphere to the left and then back again. Perhaps, this is how EMDR helps with adaptive information processing.

of comfort within and/or outside of self for comfort. These are in the form of defenses or addictions (see Table 7.2). The person's impaired capacity to metabolize stress will eventually lead to instability, an inability to adapt, or some form of rigid, fixed response pattern. Illness of one kind or another results from defective core unconscious attachments.

I will now present two illustrative cases of insecure attachment, one with mixed therapeutic results, and the other with complete symptom removal and characterologic change following acute trauma. Both patients had cold,

---

TABLE 7.2
Cascade of Possible Maladaptive Defenses Following Trauma

COGNITIVE
Intellectualization
Rationalization
Shortened attention (distraction)
Denial
Repression
Vagueness
Compartmentalization

AFFECTIVE
Dissociation
Introjection
Projection
Somatization
Splitting
Displacement
Turning against self

BEHAVIORAL
Avoidance
Withdrawl
Regression
Compulsion[a]
Dependency

COMBINATION
Isolation of Affect
Impulsivity
Detachment

Note: [a] This includes all possible addictive strategies: alcohol, drugs, love, sex, eating disorders, work, religion, and even psychotherapy. See later discussion on the self-regulatory function of compulsion.

controlling, and dismissive mothers. In the first case, the patient's father died when the patient was 2 years old; in the second case, the patient's father died when the patient was 40 years old.

Clinical History 1: Insecure Attachment: Poorly Resolved Large-T Trauma, Partial Treatment Response—Mixed Outcome

Carol was a beautiful, teenager. Undoubtedly, she could have been a professional model. I saw her at age 15 on an emergency evaluation. Her mother told me that she was found wandering the streets of our village in a disoriented state. Six months earlier, she had been brutally gang raped by a wandering band of migrant workers who had illegally crossed the border from Mexico. She had been seeing a psychologist twice each week and had been rapidly deteriorating. She had begun drinking and abusing marijuana, but her evaluation showed primarily a dissociative fugue state. I hospitalized her and treated her as an inpatient. While Carol was in the hospital, I discovered that her biologic father died of a melanoma of the eye when she was nearly 3. In all inpatient treatment modalities, she adamantly refused to discuss the rape. Upon discharge, Carol had reintegrated from her psychosis to a narcissistic personality. She was haughty, arrogant, dismissive, and drove everyone, peer or adult, away from being close to her. She continued to be highly anxious and showed school problems, truancy, and many phobias. Eventually she bonded with a nice, but very passive, underachieving boyfriend, and moved out of her home and in with him and his family. One day during outpatient therapy, she revealed the awful things that had happened to her. She cried, but the full ranges of emotions were never explored. Soon thereafter she stopped seeing me. A few years later she called me in an emergency. She was terrified. She had been working as a barmaid and told me the following story.

She went to Las Vegas with a man and married him on an impulse. It turned out that he was a member of the Mexican Mafia and was wanted by multiple law enforcement agencies as a violent offender. She had tried to leave him but he threatened to kill her. Eventually she left him and was under police protection. A few days earlier, he had come to her house, kidnapped her, and taken her to the woods (near the original rape), tied her up and sodomized her. She now was under extreme police protection—a witness protection program—and was going to testify against him and have him brought to justice. A detective took a liking to her and acted as a father figure, looking after her. Nevertheless, she was flooded with panic symptoms as well as flashbacks of her original rape. Finally, she dealt with the terror, shame, and self-loathing from years ago. She returned to therapy and this time resolved the trauma, focusing on the loss of her father at age 3, including her irrational guilt and self-blame over his death. Her perpetrator received life imprisonment. After this incident, she left the local area and became a flight attendant, met a supportive, loving Eastern European immigrant businessman and married. On follow up two years later, she returned with no obvious psychiatric problems, but was on complete medical disability for a neurological disorder of unclear origin. She was taking heavy doses of painkillers. Conversion disorder, malingering or addictive disease could not be ruled out.

Clinical History 2. Insecure Attachment, Completely Resolved Large-T and Small-T Trauma

Cheryl, a therapist, had seen me for intensive short-term therapy to resolve problems with intimacy. It seems she had married two men who had little or no capacity for intimacy. Both marriages ended in divorce. We worked through underlying dynamics surrounding her anger at a cold, controlling, and self-centered mother and anger at her father for his dependency and inability to stand up to his wife. The therapy seemed successful and Cheryl terminated. Two years later she called for an emergency appointment. She was suffering from acute PTSD. On the first visit she told me what had happened. Her father, a successful businessman, had started to decline from early dementia, and was getting depressed from his loss of function. Cheryl took him to a doctor, who diagnosed his problem. When she returned home and shared the information with her mother, she became angry and told her husband he was no good to her for anything any longer. Cheryl herself was shocked and angry, but before she could comfort her father, he went to the bedroom. She heard the door lock and immediately thought her father might try to kill himself. In the next instant, she heard a loud noise. She rammed down the door and found him shot in the face. She called the paramedics and then tried to stop the bleeding. He lived until he got to the emergency room, where he died of cardiac arrest. Cheryl witnessed horrors that are usually reserved for a battle scene. She had the entire classic symptoms of PTSD; hyperarousal, sleep disorder, flashbacks—all complicated by acute bereavement. I instituted immediate therapeutic intervention, and after acknowledging her loss, focused on her anger. The deep anger, which was addressed in our earlier work, had returned in spades. It now was further complicated by actual guilt and self-blame for not protecting her father from her mother's rage, and actual guilt for not anticipating her father's lethal action. She was furious with her mother, and that anger experience became the immediate focus. I was able to cleave the anxiety from the anger and her hyperarousal diminished. The next intervention dealt with her anger at her father for his subservience to her mother and, in fact, the proximate event prior to his suicide was her mother's self centered attack on her father. Eventually she was able to forgive her father for his character flaw and, in so doing, freed herself from her compulsive dependency on cold and distant men. With resolution of her anger at her father, she herself dealt more effectively with her mother and told her mother about her anger for her mother's actions, both immediate and long term. The mother herself decided to enter psychotherapy, and their relationship survived and even improved. Six months after termination, Cheryl sent me a wedding announcement with a note that she was ready to accept real love from a man whom she described as warm, caring, supportive, and compassionate.

The Way Faulty Attachment is Transmitted from Generation to Generation

Modern attachment theory focuses on the process of attunement, which is largely a nonverbal, right hemispheric mode of communication between care-giver and child (Schore,1997). Affect regulation through psychic and somatic mechanisms is of critical importance in healthy development. When the child and his environment are out of balance, and *no repair takes place*, small-T trauma occurs, resulting in anger and eventually, defenses. What leads to a trauma-tized state of mind? The key ingredient seems to be a state of helplessness in the face of actual (or perceived) danger (Freud, 1926/1959c). Attunement failures between parent and child always are, by definition, small-T traumas. If they are repetitive, fixed, and rigid, there is no way to process the negative emotion that the trauma creates, and the effects become cumulative (Kahn, 1963). Ideally, small- and even large-T traumatizing experiences are processed in the parent-child dyad. However, when there is *impairment of parental empathy*, these affects are not processed interpersonally, they are stored. In an attempt to define trauma Jones explained, "a traumatized state occurs when a person is unable to respond appropriately to a situation; in turn, this inability to respond is signaled by anxiety-panic" (1995, p. 116). Depending on (a) the child's tem-perament, (b) the degree of the trauma, and (c) the capacity of the caregivers to respond, an insecure attachment may form. I have coined the term "primitive aggressive self-organization (PASO)" to describe the unconscious anatomy of insecure attachments as reflected in clinical practice. I will have more to say about this term later in the chapter. In the optimal parent-child dyad, in Shapiro's metaphor, the negative affects may be "digested" and no pathology results. Table 7.3 categorizes the types of traumas that patients bring with them to therapists in clinical practices.

TABLE 7.3
The Spectrum of Trauma: *Conceptualization of Trauma:*
Small-T as well as Large-T

PARENTING
- Faulty attunement by either or both caregivers
- Faulty empathy by either or both caregivers
- Role reversal by either or both caregivers
- Faulty application of boundaries from caregivers
- Favoritism; sibling rivalry
- Neglect

EXPLOITATIVE
- Sexual abuse
- Physical abuse
- Power abuse: children as pawns (triangulation)

LOSS
- Death of parent or sibling
- Injury of person or body part
- Divorce
- Disasters: natural or manmade

SOCIAL INJUSTICE
- Race
- Sex
- Cultural

I have chosen to present a patient whose core areas of conflict demonstrate how small-T trauma can have major pathogenic effects on the development of mood and behavioral disorders. When preparing for this chapter, I considered presenting a patient with large-T trauma—one whose mother was psychotic and brutally beat both her and her sibling. This patient subsequently developed a life-threatening eating disorder. Ironically, this less traumatic case that I will present below also resulted in a severe eating disorder. Again, Shapiro's terminology, "large-T trauma," refers to the kind of experiences in *DSM-IV* that cause posttraumatic stress disorder: catastrophic experiences outside the realm of ordinary experience. Small-T trauma are those events in childhood that produce a sense of helpless, anxiety, shame, humiliation, and/or abandonment for which there has been no satisfactory repair from any caregiver. Much of this small-T trauma is split off from consciousness and stored in largely inaccessible (nonlinguistic) form in the right hemisphere (Siegel, 1995, 1999). As I stressed earlier, large-T trauma inevitably activates dormant small-T trauma.

It is my proposition that patients who are exposed to small-T trauma (cumulative trauma; Kahn, 1963; Main & Morgan, 1996; Main, & Hesse, 1990;

Main & Solomon, 1986, 1990) develop an insecure attachment underling their mood and behavioral disorders. I believe that effective psychotherapeutic treatment can only occur when the patient faces the complex feelings that are "inside the insecure attachment." The resolution of successful psychotherapy means that the patient and therapist have created an "earned secure attachment" (Pearson, 1994). The secure attachment phenomenon is undoubtedly mediated by complex interactions of neural networks mediated by neurotransmitters in the limbic system. These are primarily serotonin, norepinephrine, and dopamine.[5] It is my opinion that much of psychopharmacology actually manipulates this system. Serotonin reuptake inhibitors ameliorate anxiety, decrease aggression, and induce secure attachment phenomenon. In theory this is a wonderful thing; however, the effect may be largely "state dependent" and new learning often doesn't take place and unfortunately the patient remains dependent on the drug for freedom from depression and anxiety. On the other hand, many psychotherapies with these patients fail as well because the therapists lack either the technical or theoretical skill to overcome the patient's resistance to experiencing the feelings that exist inside the unconscious part of the insecure attachment. Many therapies either do not address resistance or purport to address resistance but in fact do not overcome the barrier to genuine feeling. I frequently see patients who have had years of psychoanalysis and the core attachment pathology has not yielded even to this prolonged technique.

In *Short-Term Therapy for Long Term Change*, I introduced the term *primitive-aggressive self organization* (PASO) as a shorthand to describe the complex mixture of feelings and defenses that exist inside the insecure attachment. It is important to emphasize that these feelings are not conscious. They are highly conflicted and are either repressed or dissociated. It is my belief that all successful therapies restore the patient to a state of secure attachment. Thus, therapy enhances their ability to experience contentment, to have joyful intimate relationships, and to exert healthy self-assertion stability increases and they become resilient to stress-laden situations. Davanloo (1995c) first described the PASO—without using the term—in his pioneering efforts to develop a short-term psychotherapy. Clinicians like myself who trained with Davanloo have developed our own spin-off therapies that rely on his original discoveries. The foundation of the short-term dynamic psychotherapies lies in the belief that the patient must experience his or her *genuine feelings from the past in the present*. The transcript of a consultative interview with a patient with longstanding anxiety, depression, and compulsive overeating will show how this is accomplished. In my work,

---

[5] Acetylcholine is an important cortical neurotransmitter involved with affect regulation as well. It may mediate major defensive operation as well as shame, guilt, and despair (Janowsky & Neborsky, 1980).

I have added an important component to the goal of *genuine feelings from the past in the present*: I want the patient to leave the initial interview with a coherent narrative of the origin of his or her psychopathology. By a coherent narrative, I mean an understanding of the origins of the difficulties that includes the unconscious perspective. The patient will understand the dynamic origin of his or her anxiety, and will understand the role of anger, guilt and/or shame, in depression or self-abuse.

Patients also will understand unconscious anger and its relationship to their other affects. These insights and understandings will be experiential as opposed to intellectual. In some cases, but not all, the intergenerational transmission of the trauma will become clear; however, all comprehensive treatments will trace the origin of their difficulties back to the grandparents. In fact, patients receiving this treatment are freed from the unconscious transmission of the trauma to their children. Currently I am working on a series of cases where I have video-recorded "unlockings of the unconscious"[6] of parents and their adult neurotic children (Lifespan Learning Institute: Hysteria Conference, Los Angeles October 2000). The intergenerational transmission of unconscious trauma is startlingly apparent.

Now let's take a closer look at the PASO and see how it operates and then how I believe small-T trauma is transferred from one generation to the next.[7]

1. At the center of the PASO (insecure attachment) lies *the capacity for secure attachment.* When this is present, the individual has the capacity for contentment. Relationships are intimate and empathy for the feeling processes of others is intact.
2. Next lies the emotion of *pain.* Classically, pain is not considered an emotion against which people defend. In our system it is. Herein we record the emotion of pain, and call it *pain of trauma.*
3. Closely allied to pain is *sadness.* This is the sadness of loss of the closeness with the attachment figure.
4. In this level, the *retaliatory rage* that is repressed in the unconscious can be found. This rage is frequently left unnoticed in traditional therapy. In Bowlby's (1973) model, the existence of this rage for an extended period of time leads to despair.
5. *Anxiety* is found at this ring of the PASO that surrounds the sadness and/or the rage.

---

[6] A term invented by Davanloo (1995a) to describe the process that I will demonstrate in the transcript.
[7] I want to thank Solomon (co-author of *Short-Term Therapy for Long Term Change*) for her illustration of the PASO and the idea of using Russian dolls (see Figure 7.1).

FIGURE 7.1
THE "PASO"

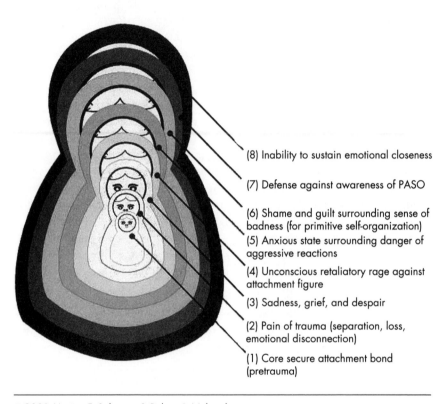

(8) Inability to sustain emotional closeness

(7) Defense against awareness of PASO

(6) Shame and guilt surrounding sense of badness (for primitive self-organization)

(5) Anxious state surrounding danger of aggressive reactions

(4) Unconscious retaliatory rage against attachment figure

(3) Sadness, grief, and despair

(2) Pain of trauma (separation, loss, emotional disconnection)

(1) Core secure attachment bond (pretrauma)

©2001 Marion F. Solomon & Robert J. Neborsky

6. This level contains the *crippling inhibitory affects* of shame or guilt.
7. Overlaying the aforementioned affects are the defenses. There are several layers of *defenses: the tactical, the dynamic, or classical and the characterologic*.
8. Layer 8 is seen only in more highly resistant cases: we call this the *defense against emotional closeness*. This is a defensive position in which detachment from all relatedness pervades the person's psyche.

Although I haven't schematized it, grief is also frequently encountered between the defenses and the guilt-shame layer. This sadness is a function of the lost time and opportunities the patient has suffered from the existence of his or her defenses. Sexual feeling is located between layers 4 and 5. Sexuality and aggressive feeling can be commingled when certain types of abuse and empathic failures occur.

Short-term dynamic psychotherapy explores this structure in each and every psychotherapy session. The way this is done varies with different styles of short-term therapy. But all short-term therapies focus on the patient's resistance (defenses), and techniques are used to overcome those defenses. It is the defenses that interfere with the patient's ability to process painful affects and restore a healthy operative self. Shapiro has demonstrated beyond any doubt that experience of affect is more essential to cure than is interpretation. In her (1995; Solomon, et al., 2001) model of therapy, the therapist's job is to give the brain the opportunity to process affective-laden information in a safe atmosphere. She emphasizes the neutrality of the therapist and stresses the brain's inherent ability to process traumatic information and to develop a positive solution. EMDR allows dissociated and repressed affects to become conscious and to be "re-processed." Short-term dynamic psychotherapy operates in much the same way. The cure is promoted by the patient's ability to access the emotions described in the PASO—layers 1 through 6.

I want to focus on two particular aspects of the unconscious for the purposes of this volume. One is the intergenerational transmission of trauma (Ainsworth & Eichberg, 1991), and the other is compulsive behavior. Main (Main & Hesse, 1990; Main, 1993; Main & Goldwyn, 1998) has discussed data that show that psychopathology can be predicted in children of mothers with an incoherent narrative found on the adult attachment interview. The incoherent narrative is thought to reflect unresolved trauma in the mother. Mothers with unresolved trauma defend against the affects that are mobilized in that area of trauma. However, that trauma which is not processed is repeated in behavior. The mothers in effect treat their children the same way they themselves were treated.

In this presentation, the patient was overly controlled by her mother, as was her mother by her grandmother. The sad loss was the loss of mutuality of joyful interchange between mother and child. Further compounding the problem in this particular case, the patient was made to feel responsible (role reversal) for the mother's illness and heart condition. The child began to feel angry with the mother, and neither mother nor grandmother could tolerate the child's anger. The child's anger developed in intensity and power. The intensity of the anger became associated with death wishes toward the mother. The mother's real illness compounded the fear (anxiety) over the death wishes. The patient loved her mother and began to feel guilty not only over her angry feelings toward mother but also over the "perceived" damage her existence caused her mother (high blood pressure, heart attack, stress). Next, the mother, who in some way found her child to be a burden, became embroiled in a power struggle with the daughter over food intake. (This most likely represents a reenactment of a power struggle with mother's mother.) Food soon became a weapon with which the patient could express negative autonomy, and a way in which the child could passive-aggressively express anger against mother and also relieve guilt through punishment of self.

Over time, the patient naturally begins to grow, develop, separate, and individuate in her march toward autonomy. However, the damage was already done (Stroufe, Egeland, & Krentger, 1990). Her self-regulatory processes are disordered. Her attachment has turned from potentially secure to insecure preoccupied with a fully developed PASO. (This is a clinical assumption in the patient was not given a formal adult attachment interview.) Another way of thinking about this issue is that she has failed to separate and individuate in a positive frame. Instead, she is always with the mother, who suppressed her joyful side, and she is full of unconscious anger directed now not outwardly against mother, but against herself. The guilt over the rage against mother is continuously undone by self-abuse. The more she can destroy her health, the less guilty and the less anxious she feels.

What, one might ask, drives this process over years and years, and why doesn't the patient just learn new behaviors? The answer is, she can't. First the information she needs to unlearn is split off into nonverbal right-hemisphere memory. The process is driven by the propensity for transference, projection, and projective identification with authority figures in her life. It is eerie and hard to acknowledge, but there is a powerful unconscious force in trauma patients called narrative reenactment (van der Kolk, 1989, 1991). Freud (1918/1959b) recognized it, as did Erikson (1963) and Davanloo (1988, personal communication). So the patient is driven to attach herself to figures that resemble her mother and grandmother so she can reenact the original trauma. The reasons behind this are controversial. Davanloo believes that the compulsion to repeat is a superego phenomenon to punish the self over and over again for the unconscious anger at the offending relative. Earlier theorists like Freud (1911/1959a, 1926/1959c) and Erikson (1963) saw it as an attempt to master the trauma. It is probably a combination of both, particularly in patients who present for therapy.

In my opinion, the compulsive behavior serves another function as well. Since there is no internal, stable, secure attachment, the patient has to rely on external sources for stability. Her feelings themselves are not a secure place. Compulsion is predictable, stable, and reliable—albeit rigid, and maladaptive. It is also self-destructive in that overeating and bulimia can result in an actual death of the self. Therefore, the compulsive behavior compensates for the missing capacity to support and soothe oneself in the face of adversity.

The Technique of Treating Attachment Trauma

The therapeutic approach that I have adopted is modeled after the use of the Central Dynamic Sequence (see Table 7.4) (Davanloo, 1989a, 1989b, 1999a, 1999b, 1999c).

The term Central Dynamic Sequence was coined by collaboration between Malan and Davanloo in the 1960s and 1970s. They studied a large population of 600 patients with a broad spectrum of psychoneurotic and characterologic difficulties. The techniques within this system were developed from a combination of creative inspiration and simple trial and error—evaluated with videotape for effectiveness. The results of that impressive research effort were never formally published, but anecdotally 80% of the patients showed dramatic improvement.

Davanloo's research suggests that the healing process is facilitated if the patient can experience the feelings "underneath" the anxiety or depression with which the patient presents. The therapeutic process starts with a survey of the patient's areas of disturbance: symptoms and relational problems. After this information is gathered, the patient and the therapist begin to explore a single incident wherein the patient experienced anxiety: This can be in their current life or in the transference in the here and now. I then proceed with psycho-education about what Malan and Davanloo called the *Triangle of Conflict* (Malan, 1979; Davanloo, 1990). The goal is to get the patient to recognize the presence of unconscious affect present in the room, and how that affect is creating problems. Furthermore, the patient is educated about the defense mechanisms, which he or she is using to contain these affects. Next, the patient is shown how these defenses, albeit useful at one time, are now harmful, and must be relinquished in order for the treatment to work. The goal then becomes the experience of unconscious emotion, free of anxiety and free of defense. In order to accomplish this, the patient must ally with the therapist and create what Davanloo has called an unconscious therapeutic alliance.

Usually there is an encounter with raw, un-neutralized aggression, deep grief, guilt, and/or shame. The process then opens the unhealed wounds of past trauma for direct inspection by the patient, and the therapist. The underlying feelings of the original trauma are made conscious, and through the therapist's attunement and empathy, the therapeutic repair occurs. The emotions are worked through with the utilization of visualization and trance, which offers

TABLE 7.4
The Central Dynamic Sequence

PHASE	TASK
1 Inquiry	Gathering areas of disturbance; exploring the difficulties; initial ability to respond
2 Pressuring toward feeling	Leads to resistance in the form of defenses; rapid identification of the character defenses; clarification and challenge to the defenses; psychodiagnosis
3 Challenging resistances	Challenge combined with a lack of respect for resistances; crystallization of the character resistances; application of partial head-on collision to show resistance has paralyzed his functioning and turn patient against his resistance
4 Transference resistances	Mounting challenge to transference resistance; intensify rise in transference feelings; mobilize the therapeutic alliance against the resistance; loosen the psychic system
5 Direct access to the unconscious	Intrapsychic crisis; breakthrough of complex transference feelings; direct view of the psychopathologic forces responsible for the patient's symptom and character disturbance
6 Analysis of the transference	Summarize the I/F-A-D-character system just experienced in the transference in order to resolve residual resistance
7 Dynamic exploration into the unconscious	Now the unconscious therapeutic alliance is in control of the process; patient spontaneously introduces traumatic events; repeated breakthroughs of guilt and grief-laden feelings; consolidation, recapitulation, and psychotherapeutic plan

Data from Davanloo, 1995b.

possibilities for repair. (There is no formal trance induction, but the state of mind of "dreaming while awake" has a trance like quality.) Self-destructive behavior patterns dissipate, and the patient develops self-directed compassion, and empathy for others, including the offending parental figure. The patient and therapist terminate the relationship when the working through is complete, and presenting symptoms and/or character disturbances are gone. Table 7.5 summarizes the progression of the interview from an unconscious traumatized state to either partial or complete resolution.

TABLE 7.5
Techniques Used in Short-Term Dynamic Psychotherapy

---

1. Maintaining a focus

2. Pressure toward feeling

3. Clarifying the experience of feeling, defense, and anxiety

4. Challenging the use of defenses as self-harming

5. Confrontation with the consequences of maintaining defense or characterologic habits to avoid feeling

6. Body experiencing of the core emotions

7. Visualization of the action tendency of each felt emotion in the now

8. Linking of the emotions with events or important figures from the past

9. Affective repair through closeness with the emotions of the therapist

---

Edited Transcript of 6 Hours of Attachment-Based Psychotherapy

Clinical Case 3: Insecure Attachment, Preoccupied: No Large-T Trauma, Complete Resolution of Small-T Trauma in Six Hours of Psychotherapy

The patient is a 45-year-old married woman who works as an assistant for a insurance executive. She has a long history of eating disorders, including bulimia. Her therapist, Sharon, referred her to Dr. Neborsky for a consultation to assist with her ongoing therapy. Dr. Neborsky begins this first session by asking the patient to define her areas of disturbance.

P: I've battled weight most of my life. I have a history of bulimia. Um, I haven't purged in years now . . . and I seem to be stuck with getting to whatever it is that is having me hold on to the weight.

T: Uh-huh.

P: You know, whatever it is that I'm using that for, um, I've had some definite positive shifts with Sharon. I'm a lot less willing to make myself uncomfortable with food in the time I'm eating. But the thing that I'm really aware of is that I'm uncomfortable on a daily basis. You know, sitting in this chair right now, I'm really . . . everything feels in the way. It's hard to sit in a way that my back doesn't hurt. So I can't pretend that I'm not bothered by my weight . . . .

T: Uh-huh.

P: And yet, I seem to keep eating in a way that is keeping me fat.

T: What do you do?

P: I don't diet. Um, I kind of struggle . . . with, um, I'm about to cry . . . I think I've struggled with the fear that to start dieting again will lead to bulimia again.

T: Hum, so there's a painful memory of the days when you had bulimia?

P: Yeah, and I think that I'm afraid that if I can't use the discipline that it sometimes takes to lose the weight that I will start caring too much again . . . (cries).

T: Umm.

P: And that, uh . . . .

T: So you're actually keeping yourself detached from part of your feelings . . . in order to not care.

P: Yeah, yeah, you're right.

T: Now, let's get off the weight topic for just a moment—are there any other areas that you're aware of where there are problems, uh, that we should focus our attention on while we're together here?

P: Um, I have a feeling that if I'm not perfect, I won't be loved.

T: Hum.

P: And I've become aware of that, and can kind of talk myself through that a lot, but, um, its still kind of in that phase of I'm aware of it as its happening and I'm able to say, "No, this is your old stuff." You know, this is not real . . . this is your projection, but, uh . . . .

T: Wait. You're describing fear, aren't you? . . . there's a considerable amount of fear . . . there's two sides of it.

P: (crying) Yeah . . . yeah, I never thought of it as fear, but that's exactly what it feels like.

T: Now, any other areas? Let's keep on going down the inventory of things, you know, that you're concerned about, or anything you'd like.

P: Um . . . (long pause) Hm . . . I don't know where . . . what I'm supposed to . . . .

T: Well, we've talked about, you know, not modifying or modulating your diet because of fear.

P: Uh-huh.

T: We talked about this way you have of trying to stay out of fear by trying to be perfect in order to ensure love . . . anything else? Any depression? Any . . . .

P: Um, yeah, depression.

T: Tell me about that, the history . . . .

P: Um, I'm think when it started . . . I think I was depressed as a teenager and my mother had had a heart attack when I was in the 6th grade. And so I kind of grew up with the stress of, um, thinking that if I did something wrong that she'd die . . . because if she'd get upset, it would raise her blood pressure. This is a conversation my father had, that I shouldn't argue with my mother because if she got really upset and her blood pressure got high, she might have another heart attack and die. (*laughs*) After years of therapy, I can see the humor in that . . .

T: Uh-huh.

P: And how I couldn't make her die.

T: But that would put fear in you, wouldn't it?

P: Oh, definitely (*cries*).

T: You know, every time I mention fear, you start to cry . . .

P: Yeah, I do!

T: What's that about? I mean, what do you experience?

P: I think it's the first time that I've ever thought of the word "fear."

T: In all the therapy?

P: Well, but it's the first time that I've ever thought about it as a big issue.

T: Uh-huh.

P: And I think I'm just getting that it really is a big issue. Just talking about it, I live a lot of my life afraid.

T: Uh-huh.

P: I'm just remembering what it was like to have a mother who's always sick . . . that I was always afraid was going to die . . . (*cries*).

T: Would you share that memory with me?

P: I can remember like coming home from school and feeling anxious about whether or not she was going to be okay when I walked in, you know, and had to be really careful when I had friends over . . . to make sure they're not going to tell her things that I thought might make her upset.

T: Uh-huh.

P: I'm thinking about a memory of being in the 4th grade and making a B+ in math. My parents both taught algebra.

T: Uh-huh.

P: And my mother yelled at me for 45 minutes, just raged about it. I felt really shamed and uncomfortable and abused. (*laughs*) And, uh, I don't know, I just associate that a lot to . . . it's not like I made a B+ in math on purpose, you know. I mean, I was supposed to make all A's . . . .

T: I'm not sure what you're telling me here. It's important. You see, it's coming in in a little bit of a jumble. Are you telling me a story about a way you were being abused? Is that the story?

P: I think that's the story, but also why it became so important to be perfect, and why I became so fearful . . . (*cries*) . . . of trying things . . . of failing . . . .

T: Fear of failure—because you would be abused if you didn't achieve perfection?

P: I think that love is more the word that . . . .

T: Well, you were scolded, I mean, that's pretty severe . . . 30 minutes of rage.

P: Yeah, yeah.

T: Was this before or after your mother had the heart attack?

P: Before (*cries*).

T: You're crying . . . you're expressing something . . . what's going on?

P: Oh, sadness, I think.

T: I think so, too. Sadness related to what?

P: (*sighs*)

T: The relationship related to your mom?

P: Yeah . . . and being treated that way. You know . . . .

T: What was your emotional reaction? You had mentioned shame.

P: Anger . . . I was really angry. I just remember going up to my room and crying on my bed for a few hours.

T: So you wept in the face of anger?

P: Yeah (*sighs*).

T: What was that sigh about?

P: (*laughs*) It just felt good. It's like a deep breath . . . .

T: Can you remember, as you sit here, your anger specifically? Do you have a specific memory of it? How it felt?

P: Yeah. I remember one incident . . . I mean . . . (*punches arms in air*) I feel it here; like shoulders (*touches shoulders*), and punching kinds of feelings . . .

T: Uh-huh. But you didn't do that?

P: No, no.

T: You wept instead.

P: Uh-huh.

(*The patient describes how, in a session with her therapist, Sharon, she fantasized killing her mother by severing her head.*)

T: So the weakness was in being abandoned on the one hand, but it was also a defense against the more angry part of the feeling.

T: A question comes to mind, of course, when you did that, what were your feelings? What was your reaction?

P: I felt really calm . . . it felt really good. It felt like a real release . . . .

T: I'm confused about something—I don't understand why when you really did have the opportunity to kill your mother, you acted so fearful.

P: I don't understand—what do you mean?

T: Well, didn't you tell me after your mom had a heart attack . . . .

P: Oh, right . . . .

T: That your dad told you that if you did anything to upset her, she'd die?

P: Uh-huh.

T: What stopped you from . . .

P: I didn't want her to die.

T: Well, tell me about that. What's that all about?

P: Uh . . . (long pause).

T: See, in the murder fantasy, there was a part of you that wanted her to die . . .

P: Right, but that was like as an adult, like in the last year, that thing that I did with Sharon. I didn't do that as a child.

T: So you didn't have the same feelings when you were a child?

P: I probably did, but I . . . well, I don't know . . . I don't know if I just censored them. You know, I mean, you aren't supposed to kill people, you know? I was raised in a Presbyterian church and went to Sunday school every Sunday, and you weren't supposed to kill people and weren't supposed to wish people were dead.

T: What did that make you, if you did?

P: You'd go to hell . . . (laughs) . . . nothing to be afraid of with that one, just burn there for the rest of eternity . . . I mean, I don't believe in that stuff anymore, but . . . (laughs).

T: But, wouldn't there be a reason for going to hell?

P: Well, yeah, for the sin of wanting your mother to be dead. I don't know. I keep waiting for you to say something. I'm not sure . . . it seems so clear to me.

T: It seems clear to me, too, but it also doesn't seem to me that you're putting 2 + 2 together.

P: I don't know what you mean.

T: Well, the feelings of wanting your mother to be dead, according to you, is a sin and according to you, the way you're taught, you should go to hell and burn.

P: Uh-huh.

T: So you committed a sin, right?

P: Uh-huh.

T: So what's the punishment for the sin, for wanting her dead?

P: I don't know if I wanted her dead then. I think . . . .

T: When did she yell at you?

P: When I was in the 4th grade. I'm not following you . . . .

T: Didn't you just show me all the anger? You know, I'm putting this all together for you, what you've done with Sharon, right? In other words, you said you had all of these murder feelings with your mom and they came out in therapy with Sharon. You knocked your mom's block off and after you knocked her block off, you stomped on her head.

P: Uh-huh.

T: There's no doubt. She's dead.

P: Right.

T: The only question here is when those feelings began.

P: Oh, I see . . . (pause) . . . Well, they probably began before that, but that's the first, like memory, I'm attaching it to.

T: Okay, so . . . what's the punishment?

P: The punishment? To me?

T: Yeah, to you. (long pause) It seems pretty clear and simple to me . . . it's true and simple . . . to live in perpetual fear.

P: Oh, (laughs) it wasn't clear to me at all.

T: It's easy (laughs). I'm sitting here in this chair, and you're sitting there . . . .

P: Yeah . . . Wow . . . (cries). Yeah, that's interesting . . . because there's been so many things like that. I have this fear about me causing other people to suffer. And I have a fear when I'm driving, I mean not a paralyzing fear, but, you know (sighs), I've had the thought is the clearest way to put it, that how horrible it would be if you accidentally ran over somebody with an automobile. You know, how would you live with yourself if you knew you caused another person's death? Wow . . . .

T: Like?

P: Like, if I had done that to my mother . . . (cries). Wow . . . even to the point of just hurting somebody's feelings inadvertently. Just saying something that you don't mean to hurt another person's feelings, and you realize that you have or, I mean, I'll worry about something I said to somebody, and think, gee, you know, I'll almost obsess over, oh, I hope they don't think I meant this . . . .

T: Trying to undo the deed, spending your time undoing it, which you may or may not have done?

P: Yeah, yeah, exactly . . . and working with Sharon, I've come out of projecting a lot of that, but I'm now seeing that that's the same thing.

T: So what feelings are you now relating to? What emotions are you describing?

P: Well, I think fear....

T: Well, it's a combination ... I think there's some guilt.

P: Oh, and guilt.

T: Yeah....

P: Yeah, guilt. (laughs) Oh, I finally get it, it's like, oh, duh, guilt!

T: Yeah, but it's important. Actually, you've been very quick. But I think, like you've been saying—organization—I don't think you're putting together all of the pieces of the psychological puzzle into a coherent whole ... so that you can see that you've had all of these murderous feelings toward your mom as a child, and you lived in a tremendous amount of fear that those murderous feelings would come true, and you feel guilty about having those murderous feelings ... right?

P: (cries) Yeah!

T: And the punishment is to, you know, live in one of the outer rings of hell, which is perpetual fear.

P: (cries) Wow.

T: You know, fear, paralysis ... and really in the sense, almost paralyzed to take positive action on your own behalf.

P: Yeah, absolutely ... fear about my parents who had me when they were 45, and they had not planned to have a third child. And so, um, I knew that, oh boy (laughs), I knew that they had not planned to have a third child and that's when my mother's health problems started, with her pregnancy, and that's when she started having high blood pressure, and they actually wanted to give her an abortion ... and that was 45 years ago when they just didn't do that ... it would have been a medical abortion because of the blood pressure and her kidneys and things like that.

T: What did you say ... "wow"?

P: Because I got this ... went even back that far ... the guilt about causing ... the fear ... causing her to die ... that was already out there before I was even born. The whole thought of ... of, it's like before I was even born, I was causing her to die. Wow, that's pretty big! (sniffs) I'm surprised ... (pause) I'm surprised I'm not 700 pounds! (laughs)

T: That was an amazing connection, wasn't it?

P: Yeah. (laughs)

T: What was the connection?

P: Just the whole thing that I've grown up with all the pressure and guilt and self-punishment. It's amazing that, you know, that I haven't created an even more uncomfortable body . . . .

T: . . . in which to torture yourself, make yourself uncomfortable . . . .

P: Yeah . . . the outer ring of hell.

T: Uh-huh, and guilt over your, um, destroying your mother just based on your own life, your own creation. Nothing that you did or didn't do . . . just your own struggle to survive.

P: Yeah (nods).

T: See, so you use food as a weapon, really, to destroy yourself.

P: Yep. Wow. I know that intellectually, and then get it, and it's . . . .

T: Get it emotionally. Tell me, what's that like? What happens if you let that sink in?

P: (long pause) It's to make the conscious choice of . . . it feels like . . . it feels like there's the option of a conscious choice not to do that. To make, to realize that you don't really need to do this to yourself (long pause). I'm feeling like I could do it, like I could quit doing this . . . and that feels good.

T: Uh-huh, see can you understand now in a deeper fashion the relationship between dieting and bulimia. See, it seems to me that if you're not using one weapon—food—to kill yourself, then you have to substitute and use the bulimia as your secret weapon to hurt yourself.

P: Yeah, because I've never really believed that I deserved to be on the planet. It's like I know it in my mind, but not on a gut level. (cries) Because it was like I grew up believing that I was this big, horrible inconvenience to my parents, and that my mother almost died because of me.

T: Do you have any memory at all of any time blaming yourself for your mother's heart attack?

P: (cries, nods yes) The night she had the heart attack was the night of our band banquet and she wasn't feeling well. I was in the band and I had been nominated as the most outstanding band student that year. And we were having a banquet that night and awards were going to be given out, and she didn't feel well and didn't want to go and I kind of pushed and pushed, until she went. And she actually had her heart attack at the band banquet. (cries) And we went straight to our family doctor's house from the banquet and he called an ambulance and took her to the hospital. She'd had a very serious heart attack.

T: Okay, talk, talk the emotions. What you're feeling, tell me about that . . . .

P: Guilty! (cries) Wow! And at some point later, she told me I had caused her heart attack.

T: So she confirmed it!

P: Yeah.

T: It really seems to me that in part you've taken on this struggle, and you truthfully are trying to induce an illness in yourself. In other words, if you get a heart attack, then it seems to me the debt is, in part, repaid.

P: Wow! (cries) Yeah. I have a good life . . . after ruining hers.

T: So it seems to me that if we really get down to the bottom of the issue, guilt is the major engine of your difficulties, creating this kind of like dilemma you're in where you have to sabotage your efforts to stay healthy. I mean, you see that you're between a rock and a hard place?

P: Yes, I really do, and that's the perfect way to describe how it's felt for a while. It's like on this one hand, wanting to do it but on this other hand, not being able to do it. You know, I've been conscious about resistance about doing that. It's not even like . . . I can't pretend even to myself. It's like, oh, I really want to do it and I'm really trying my best . . . I know I'm not. You know, I know, I've been conscious that I've actually resisted doing . . . .

T: So it's sabotage . . . .

P: Yeah.

T: You see what I mean?

P: Yeah, I totally do.

T: With your help.

P: Uh-huh. And, in fact, when people would notice that I'm losing weight, and I always thought this was because I got so tired of being noticed for losing weight.

T: Well, the mind can work in tricky ways . . . I mean, you may be right, who knows, I wasn't there. But I can give you another spin on it . . . that life was going too good, and you were getting too much glory, and too much recognition, and too much admiration, and then the forces of self-sabotage began to undermine your own thinking, right? And made that the problem! Rather than the unconscious guilt of having a good life after all this stuff with your mom, both the guilt of your very birth, your very creation, you know, causing her harm, and then secondarily, this controlling part of your mom that would suppress your natural instincts. She would just sort of push down the joyous part of you, right? And that makes you very shameful and very angry.

P: (nods, cries)

T: And then you would wish harm to her, and then harm happens to her, and then you're dead in the water. And then you have this guilt that you carry with you for the rest of your life. It's huge. Much bigger than your weight problem.

(The patient recalls an incident in which she was angry at her boss, Roger. She admits to having "pushed down" her anger and asks the therapist if there is a "right way" of expressing it. Dr. Neborsky answers that it's necessary, first, to experience the anger and asks, "How did your anger feel?")

P: My ears were ringing and, um, I felt nauseous . . . my heart was racing.

T: I'm just pointing out to you again . . . you know . . . I'm not blaming you for this, I'm just describing so that you can learn. You're turning your anger against your own body, aren't you?

P: Yeah.

T: Ringing ears, nausea, you're turning the anger against you.

P: Wow, so that's not how most people feel? I mean . . . I just thought that that was . . . wow!

T: That's how people feel anger that's turned inward. Ringing ears and nausea . . .

P: So you can have anger and not those feelings? I don't think I've ever had it (*cries*). It never even occurred to me that you could have anger and not have those feelings.

T: That's anger turned inward, right?

P: I get it.

T: Do you remember the muscular-skeletal part of the anger?

P: Yeah, I was very tense. I was gripping and all that stuff . . . .

T: Uh-huh, so you were having an impulse.

P: Uh, oh, I get it, yeah. I was holding back an impulse to go punch his brains out.

T: That was it?

P: Yeah, that's it, I wasn't having an impulse, I was holding it back.

T: I know.

P: Wow.

T: Can you capture the impulse you were holding back? (*pause*) When you think it through carefully, what's the impulse?

P: Just scream at him . . . .

T: Lash out verbally. Okay.

P: Uh-huh.

T: Okay, but remember, see that's to leave the stressful situation. The impulse is in your arms. That simple. Impulse isn't so much verbal as it is physical. Physical rises when the heart is beating, blood is rushing through your body, right? Because of the rapid heartbeat, that's the anger response. You cut that anger off by turning it out against yourself (*pause*) with the nausea and ringing in the ears. So keep your mind's eye focused on the body, on your body.

P: Uh-huh.

T: Expressing the impulse . . . what would it look like? If you lost control, and you know that I know you never will, but if you did lose control in that room . . . .

P: Oh, I would then jump up to my feet and run toward him, and put my hands around his neck and start shaking him. I would have slapped his face. I would have pulled out his hair implants, and I would have picked him up and swung him around by his hair, and just slammed him against the mirrors, and slammed him against the stereo, and slammed him against the floor . . . in front of everybody. And just slammed him around the room and then, just, just, um . . . (*pause*) thrown him on the floor and jumped on him . . . just jumped up and down with both feet (*pause*).

T: Would he survive . . . that kind of assault? (*long silence*) If you looked at his eyes, what would you see in his eyes?

P: Fear . . . shock . . . um . . . .

T: Pain?

P: Yeah (*nods*).

T: And what would you like him to be thinking?

P: I better stop this behavior (*pause*). I was wrong (*pause*) . . . .

T: To use force and coercion and shame . . . against you . . . .

P: Uh-huh, uh-huh.

T: Would he survive? That was my question.

P: Yeah, he would survive. I would want him to survive. I don't know if he'd survive if I was jumping up and down on him, I mean, its indescribable what I'd do to him.

T: See the conflict? The anger is so strong that he wouldn't survive, but the heart—the love wants him to survive.

P: Wow (*nods*).

T: So tell me, in the scenario where he doesn't survive, with the anger so big that he doesn't survive the assault?

P: Where in the scenario?

T: If you were jumping on his chest, causing him to die . . . .

P: Oh, I get it, it would be breaking limbs and puncturing lungs . . . .

T: Okay, we know that stuff, but what would your reaction be, how would you respond when you came to your senses?

P: (*pause*) I would be really sad.

T: What would you do?

P: Try to save him.

T: How?

P: I'd call 911. I'd start CPR. I'd try to stop . . . try to control the bleeding . . . .

T: And when you realized it was to no avail?

P: Well, I'd probably kill myself! (*long pause*) (*nods*) Wow. (*long pause*) Yeah (*shakes head*), I'd feel so guilty, I wouldn't be able to live with that.

T: So killing yourself would be your way of undoing the crime of killing Roger?

P: Uh-huh. (*long pause*) Hum.

T: Hum, what?

P: Its just amazing to see all this—just amazing—so clearly right now and just see this thing that just goes throughout . . . the anger, that leads to the guilt, that leads to the fear, that leads to the self-destruction, that leads to . . . the self-destruction! (*laughs*) That's pretty much where it stops.

(*The patient returns the next day and says she has never considered her emotions to be genuine experiences. Dr. Neborsky asks the patient to make it a priority not to shut down her emotions, no matter how intense they may become.*)

P: I don't know if I know how.

T: I think you're aware that this is called the helpless position. You're taking helpless positions, and don't know how not to shut down . . . where will that get us?

P: Nowhere.

T: That's the self-sabotage. The first time in the session that self-sabotage is starting to show its head, so to speak, you nod "uh-huh." See the compliance? See, you're showing compliance, aren't you, but it's really pseudo-compliance because nothing's really happening. Why are you smiling?

P: I'm trying so hard to understand (*touches head*), but I know that's not what we're trying to do.

T: But I think you do understand . . . you see, it's not about understanding, it's about action. You shut down in the face of anxiety. Anxiety rises inside your whole being . . . .

P: Uh-huh.

T: Your mouth gets dry . . . .

P: Uh-huh . . . it feels like I've got butterflies in my stomach.

T: That's pure anxiety, isn't it?

P: Uh-huh.

T: No question about it, and your habit has been that when you get anxious, to shut down feelings and to go to intellect. And you understand that doing the same thing with me, you know, is silly because it's going to give you the same result. When you leave, see, that's what I mean by self-sabotage. If you go to your habits when you're here in the therapy session with me, all you do is reinforce the habits. So that sabotages new learning, doesn't it?

P: Yeah, it does (*nods*).

T: I mean when you leave here, it doesn't feel like you've gotten anything out of this session. You won't feel. You won't feel as though you've gotten as much out of the session, perhaps, as you felt you did yesterday.

P: Uh-huh.

T: And I don't want that to happen.

P: Right (*nods*).

T: But I've got to get you to recognize what your habits are. Instead of nodding like the compliant child, to take some action against the habit, to get in new habits. Because you just nod and go through these motions of pleasing me and you get nowhere.

P: (*nods, pause*)

T: So what are you going to do about that wall that shuts down against those feelings that scare you? Because that's what anxiety is, a form of internalized fear. So your feelings are scaring you. They're creating anxiety. You are shutting down and you're going into your people-pleasing mode . . . with me. But that doesn't work. You see that?

P: Uh-huh.

T: So what are you going to do? (*silence*) . . . about the shutting down, about the helplessness, about the people-pleasing façade?

P: (*nods*)

T: Now, you're doing it again!

P: (*smiles, nods*) Right.

T: You smiled, though, and that indicates that you're covering the feeling or something. You're having a reaction, or you wouldn't be smiling if you weren't.

P: It's because I keep switching to here (*touches head*). I'm nodding at, okay, I'm in touch with what you're saying, you know.

T: But you see, that gets you nowhere . . . .

P: I know.

T: And that's not going to cut the mustard, is it?

P: But I don't know what to do.

T: You see, see how it's entrenched? You see, now you're becoming helpless . . . .

P: (laughs)

T: Look at you. You're nodding when I tell you you're helpless. You see there's no action against these defenses, which are the source of your difficulties, which are what's keeping you stuck . . . obviously, which are three defenses . . . .

P: The defenses being?

T: Helplessness, shutting down, right? And being a people-pleaser. We've got like these three core defenses.

P: (softly) Being a people-pleaser . . . shutting down . . . and helplessness.

T: In the face of this anxiety, right?

P: Uh-huh.

T: Those are defenses against anxiety.

P: (nods) Uh-huh.

T: You're doing it again . . . you're nodding at me, but nothing's happening. You're not taking action against your defenses. So what are you going to do?

P: (sighs deeply)

T: You're shutting down . . . did you see the rise of anxiety in your body? (imitates sigh) You start getting anxious and that's the shutting down response, isn't it?

P: I think of that as a getting in touch thing . . . .

T: I don't understand, what do you mean?

P: It's just like, okay, clear your mind and be quiet a second and feel . . .

T: Okay, well that could be really positive . . . .

P: Uh-huh.

T: But what I was also seeing is ignoring a rise in your anxiety. You're nodding . . . because I would hope that you would recognize that you're becoming more anxious. Did you recognize it?

P: Uh-uh (shakes head no).

T: Yes, see, I have the sense that what you're doing is self-hypnosis or self-relaxation . . . in the face of anxiety.

P: I've never thought of that.

T: It's a bona fide technique, okay?

P: Uh-huh.

T: Okay, but I think I can perhaps offer you a better way . . . .

P: Okay, good.

T: But you'll have to endure the anxiety.

P: (*nods*)

T: Do you follow me? You'd have to identify it for what it is.

P: You mean the physical feelings that I'm feeling?

T: Absolutely.

P: Well, I feel like I can't breathe as well... My palms are feeling real sweaty and my throat feels tight (*touches throat*). I have feelings in here (*rubs stomach*), lots of little butterfly feelings in here... a little nauseous. Shoulders feel tight (*touches shoulders*). My neck feels tight (*touches neck*).

T: That's an exquisite description of anxiety. Now, just stay in touch with that experience without defending against it. (*pause*)

P: What if I throw up? (*cries*) I think I'm crying because of the fear.

T: I'm not sure; I wouldn't jump to any conclusions about that. It can be very confusing, I mean you could be having a breakthrough of sadness.

P: (*cries*) This whole feeling of throwing up is about bulimia, you know, it's like...

T: I hear what you're saying, but be careful, okay, let's not make more into sadness than what it is. Nausea can be a symptom of anxiety. It can just be a symptom. I'm sure you have a memory bank about associations of throwing up.

P: Oh, no, I'm just saying that this sadness makes me think about the bulimia.

T: Okay, good, but I think that that's a deflection that the sadness is the issue—that is the feeling that wants to come up... if you look at it like I do.

P: Yeah, right... (*sobs long time*)

T: And truly, feeling this sadness is the cure for the anxiety.

P: (*nods, sobs*)

T: There's waves of it, isn't there? It's like a wave.

P: (*nods, sobs*)

T: Another wave coming?

P: (*nods, sobs*)

T: Is there any thought with this sad feeling... just anything that comes into your thoughts?

P: My mother did... why couldn't I have had parents who were healthy... and loving... and that stuff, you know?

T: How, I mean, does that come into your thoughts?

P: It just flashed, it just flashed.

T: Uh-huh, so these are longings... for a very close relationship.

P: (*nods, cries*)

T: It's really painful . . . the longing for the closeness . . . .

P: (*nods, cries*)

T: Let it come into . . . come into your mind as to what it was that you would have liked.

P: For her to like me.

T: And what would that entail in your imagination? Can you remember?

P: Um, she would not have squelched the things I loved to do . . . she would have encouraged me to do the things that I was good at and loved to do . . . she wouldn't have done the raging that she did . . . she wouldn't have blamed me for her health problems . . . (*long pause*) that's the only stuff that's coming out . . . .

T: Uh-huh.

P: She would have wanted me to be born.

(*The patient recalls her maternal grandmother, a strict, critical woman. The patient felt that in her relationship with her grandmother she was "always walking on eggshells." Dr. Neborsky asks if there was ever any tenderness between the two of them.*)

P: (*shakes head*) I don't remember love and affection (*long pause*) . . . (*shakes head*).

T: What?

P: My eyes just felt dry. It was like all of a sudden, I was just going to fall asleep. (*laughs*)

T: Why?

P: I don't know.

T: Wouldn't that be cutting off feelings?

P: Probably. (*nods, cries*) (*long pause*) Oh, I hated going there . . . I was always afraid of her . . . (*deep breaths*). But I feel sad because a grandmother is supposed to love you . . . and bake you cookies . . . and give you milk, and . . . instead of . . . .

T: Instead of what?

P: Instead of being mean to you and not wanting you around or making you feel that way . . . like a burden.

T: Hum, and your grandmother?

P: . . . it's so sad . . . (*cries*).

T: It's terribly sad, of course it is . . . your grandmother was dismissive as well as controlling toward your mother.

P: (*nods*) Yeah. (*cries*) I was sad for my mother, too, growing up with her . . . (*cries*) (*pause*)

T: Could you just elaborate on that some?

P: Well, she was the victim (?), too. And it makes me angry that she grew up with her, so how could she do that to me?

T: That's the way I see it (*pause*). In other words, if we could just summarize what you just said, your grandmother made your mother feel as though she was a burden, and your mother had some similar issues inside of her and she then transferred those issues to you.

P: Un-huh. (*nods*)

T: Making you feel as though your birth was a burden . . . .

P: (*nods*)

T: And that raising you was a burden . . . just like her mom made her feel.

P: Yeah. (*nods*)

T: So it's kind of a three-generational disturbance.

P: Yeah, and I think that's one of the reasons I decided not to have children myself (*cries*).

T: Go on, tell me about that.

P: I was just afraid that I'd be like them . . . .

T: Even in spite of all your fear therapy?

P: (*cries, nods*)

T: Tell me about that, I would like to understand . . . .

P: Well, I'm not sure that's the only reason I decided not to have kids, but I just . . . because of the anxiety that I feel . . . and all the people-pleasing, and the anxiety . . . like when I have a warped-out (?) mind or something like that. I just have a feeling that I would be short and not give my children what they needed.

T: Well, I can understand . . . that was a very loving act.

P: (*cries, sobs*) (*long pause*)

T: It was love for your unborn child. In a sense, you didn't want to pass the abuse down to the next generation.[8]

(*Dr. Neborsky connects the intergenerational abuse to the patient's self-abuse.*)

T: I hope that if anything happens out of this interview, that you're real clear on self-abuse and what is self-abuse.

P: Yeah, I think I know (*nods*).

---

[8] Main remarked that she felt the patient harbored the unconscious fear of being killed by her child (*if ever conceived*).

T: You're not rationalizing it or intellectualizing it? Not shaming yourself, of course.

P: No, observing it.

T: Yeah, and remember the truth. Do you want to treat yourself the way your grandmother treated you? Do you want to treat yourself the way your mother treated you? Do you want to do that?

P: No.

T: See, call a spade a spade, okay? How would you like me to be of assistance? Is there anything you want from me here in your future? Is there anything you want me to do?

P: I don't know. Um . . . I think, really, that I might want to come back.

T: Okay.

P: (*long pause*) I think I want to look more at the issue . . . have an autonomy without being self-destructive.

T: Okay.

P: That's all that's coming up right now.

T: That's huge! (*both laugh*)

The patient showed a remarkable response to the 6-hour therapy. She rededicated herself to her health, diet, and exercise program. Her self-esteem improved, depression and anxiety lifted, and her relationship with her husband became more loving and intimate.

Discussion and Final Comments

Main has described in this volume how trauma is transmitted from parent to child. But she has also left us with the incredibly optimistic notion that insecurely attached infants can be changed through life's experience. Psychotherapy can be categorized as a life experience. My role in this chapter is to begin to suggest ways to facilitate that process.

I want to underscore what Schore mentioned in his chapter. He stated that any serious remedial therapy must be directed toward the unconscious. This book offers compelling evidence that the disturbances in affect regulation are largely right hemisphere or lower brain stem phenomena. They are by definition nonverbal. As van der Kolk (2001) correctly pointed out, many verbally based talk therapies are destined to fail because they are ineffective in restoring normative affect regulation. Therefore, we must learn to use noninterpretive therapeutic approaches to help our patients move from insecure states to earned secure states. Siegel (1995, 1999) has suggested that the brain and mind can be seen as complex systems that self-organize as they tend to move toward states of maximizing complexity. He has proposed that the principles of complexity theory might be useful in understanding mental well being. Self-organizing brain states that move toward complexity travel a trajectory between chaos on the one hand and rigidity on the other. As states move toward complexity, they are said to achieve the most stable, flexible, and adaptive states. Siegel has also suggested that this may be a useful model for a healthy system and that dynamic therapy may be seen as helping the system to achieve such a flow toward complexity and thus mental well being.

The methodology that I have presented was learned under a mentorship with Davanloo. From him I learned systematic techniques to gain rapid access to unconscious affects in the initial therapeutic contact with patients. What I have done is merge this technique with the recent discoveries of attachment theory and self-regulation. Through the use of these noninterpretive techniques, access to dissociated feeling states can be rapidly experienced, processed, and integrated. These methodologies along with EMDR are the two most powerful therapies that I've witnessed that can bring about *both* rapid and long-lasting change.

All of the authors of this book share a common interest. We are interested in the process of change. No matter what our orientation, we are in the business of helping people change the way they feel, the way they behave, or the way they think. Over my career I've had the privilege of interacting with some great minds that have dedicated themselves to addressing the *most efficient* ways to accomplish that task. Some of those very best minds are represented in this volume.

Now, in truth, the applied science of psychotherapy is a remarkably young science. Psychotherapy itself is only 150 years old. The application of the scientific method to the process of psychotherapy is perhaps only 75 years old. The purpose of my chapter is to highlight the application of 50 years of intensive research in the process of psychotherapy to the clinical situation. I want to suggest that dynamic psychotherapy holds enormous untapped potential to help our patients change in dramatic ways that may be underestimated by large sectors of the professional community.

The backbone of short-term dynamic treatment is the clinician's ability to recognize the patient's dilemma. The patients come for treatment because they are suffering and want help, but they are truly unable, as van der Kolk (2001) pointed out, to do what is required to overcome their difficulties. What is required of them is to *feel* the emotions in the therapeutic dyad, which were not safe for them to feel at an earlier time and an earlier place. They have learned to defend against these experiences and are hence locked in a painful place from which there seems to be no escape. Their inability to feel, despite their willingness to do so, is called resistance.

Now I want to return to Main's (2001) wonderful image of Darwin throwing the tortoise into the ocean and him swimming back to home base. The instinctual force in that turtle exists in all of us. That force is attachment. Davanloo recognized that the therapist could use that force itself, as a tool to get these patients to feel. He called that tool the unconscious therapeutic alliance. You see, the patients want to receive help, want care; they want closeness, comfort, and connection. The therapist needs to communicate to the patient that they can have it, *but to do so they have to swim to shore.* They have to overcome the resistance that sits between you and them. You have to make it clear to them that that's their responsibility—that you're not going to magically and omnipotently do it for them. No, they're going to have to do it themselves. Naturally, they are going to become anxious because they're in a conflict. The patient wants to maintain their resistance, *but they also want to get to shore.* This creates an approach/avoidance conflict which progresses to an intra-psychic crisis. (Ten Have-de Labije, 2001). Or, better stated, we're into "the unconscious space." Entry into "the unconscious space" allows for the resolution of either hypo-arousal states wherein all emotion is shut down, or hyper-arousal states, where the patient is agitated or anxious from affect flooding. The curative factor, different from EMDR, is attachment based where the patient experiences *containment* of the affect through the interpersonal presence of the therapist. Containment, mirroring, and attunement are remarkably soothing to adults as well as children. (These processes are only therapeutically transformations *after* the defenses have been sucessfully overcome. These interventions are ineffective or counter productive when used with defensive affects.) The crucial variable is lowering the anxiety enough so that the patient can contact the core emotional state that heretofore frightened them. Davanloo's method uses an implosion model: feeling dystonic emotion looses anxiety. Others like Shapiro, Mc Cullough and Fosha use anxiety regulating techniques. This covers point one of healing trauma outlined in the introduction. What about the second point, putting trauma into a spiritual/philosophical continuum? Patients undergoing this therapy occasionally compare it to the *transcendent* religious experiences. Frequently they discover a continuous panoramic vision of life, and see that the trauma they have suffered has in some fashion given them the opportunity to explore places in themselves that would have otherwise been locked shut. They report that their brains are opened up to new realities and ways of experiencing themselves, their emotions, and others. They report the fact that they are more tuned in to their loving, empathic capacity than before the trauma. They become capable of living in the "now." This, in and of itself, gives some meaning to their suffering.

In closing, before affect regulation theory our clinical predecessors relied on less sophisticated models to understand and explore the unconscious. Today we have the clinical tools to repair deeply embedded and disrupted neural networks. We are living in an age in which an interpersonal neurobiology is becoming a reality. It's an exciting time for the practice of psychotherapy.

References

Ainsworth, M. D. S., & Eichberg, C. (1991). Effects on infant-mother attachment of mother's unresolved loss of an attachment figure, or other traumatic experience. In C. M. Parkes, J. Stevenson-Hinde, & P. Marris (Eds.), *Attachment across the life cycle* (pp. 160–186). London: Routledge.

Bowlby, J. (1988). *A secure base: Parent-child attachment and healthy human development.* New York: Basic Books.

Bowman, M. (1997). *Individual differences in posttraumatic stress response.* Hillsdale, NJ: Erlbaum.

Davanloo, H. (1987). Clinical manifestations of superego pathology. *International Journal of Short-Term Psychotherapy,* 3(4): 225–254.

Davanloo, H. (1988). Clinical manifestations of superego pathology. Part II. The resistance of the superego and the liberation of the paralyzed ego. *International Journal of Short-Term Psychotherapy,* 3, 1–24.

Davanloo, H. (1989a). Central dynamic sequence in the unlocking of the unconscious and comprehensive trial therapy. Part I. Major unlocking. *International Journal of Short-Term Psychotherapy,* 4(1), 1–33.

Davanloo, H. (1989b). Central dynamic sequence in the major unlocking of the unconscious and comprehensive trial therapy. Part II. The course of trial therapy after the initial breakthrough. *International Journal of Short-Term Psychotherapy,* 4(1), 35–66.

Davanloo, H. (1990). *Unlocking the unconscious.* Chichester, UK: Wiley.

Davanloo, H. (1995a). Intensive short-term dynamic psychotherapy: spectrum of psycho-neurotic disorders. *International Journal of Short-Term Psychotherapy,* 10(3,4), 121–155.

Davanloo, H. (1995b). Intensive short-term dynamic psychotherapy: technique of partial and major unlocking of the unconscious with a highly resistant patient. Part I. Partial unlocking of the unconscious. *International Journal of Short-Term Psychotherapy,* 10(3,4), 157–181.

Davanloo, H. (1995c). Intensive short-term dynamic psychotherapy: major unlocking of the unconscious. Part II. The course of the trial therapy after partial unlocking. *International Journal of Short-Term Psychotherapy,* 10(3,4), 183–230.

Davanloo, H. (1996a). Management of tactical defenses in intensive short-term dynamic psychotherapy. Part I. Overview, tactical defenses of cover words and indirect speech. *International Journal of Short-Term Psychotherapy,* 11(3), 129–152.

Davanloo, H. (1996b). Management of tactical defenses in intensive short-term dynamic psychotherapy. Part II. Spectrum of tactical defenses. *International Journal of Short-Term Psychotherapy,* 11(3), 153–199.

Davanloo, H. (1999a). Intensive short-term dynamic psychotherapy—central dynamic sequence: Phase of pressure. *International Journal of Short-Term Psychotherapy,* 13(4), 211–233.

Davanloo, H. (1999b). Intensive short-term dynamic psychotherapy—central dynamic sequence: Phase of challenge. *International Journal of Short-Term Psychotherapy,* 13(4), 237–260.

Davanloo, H. (1999c). Intensive short-term dynamic psychotherapy—central dynamic sequence: Head-on collision with resistance. *International Journal of Short-Term Psychotherapy, 13*(4), 263–280.

Erikson, E. H. (1963). *Childhood and society.* 2nd ed. New York: Norton.

Fonagy, P., Gergely, G., Jurist, E. L., & Target, M. (2002). *Affect regulation, mentalization, and the development of the self.* New York: Other Press.

Freud, A. (1967). Comment on trauma. In S. S. Furst (Ed.), *Psychic trauma* (pp. 235–245). New York: Basic Books.

Freud, S. (1959a). Remembering, repeating, and working through. In J. Strachey (Ed. & Trans.), *Standard edition of the complete psychological works of Sigmund Freud,* (Vol. 12, p. 150). London: Hogarth Press. (Original work published 1911)

Freud, S. (1959b). Introduction to psychoanalysis and the war neurosis. In J. Strachey (Ed. & Trans.), *Standard edition of the complete psychological works of Sigmund Freud,* (Vol. 17, pp. 207–210). London: Hogarth Press. (Original work published 1918)

Freud, S. (1959c). Inhibitions, symptoms, and anxiety. In J. Strachey (Ed. & Trans.), *Standard edition of the complete psychological works of Sigmund Freud,* (Vol. 20, pp. 75–175). London: Hogarth Press. (Original work published 1926)

Janowsky, D., & Neborsky, R. J. (1980). Hypothesized common mechanisms in the psychopharmacologic and psychotherapeutic treatment of depression. *Psychiatric Annals 10*(9), 356–361.

Jones, J. M. (1995). *Affects as process.* Hillsdale, NJ: Analytic Press.

Kahn, M. (1963). The concept of cumulative trauma. *The Psychoanalytic Study of the Child, 18*, 286–306.

Main, M. (1993). Discourse, prediction, and recent studies in attachment: Implications for psychoanalysis. *Journal of the American Psychoanalytic Association, 41*, 209–244.

Main, M. (1995). Attachment: Overview, with implications for clinical work. In S. Goldberg, R. Muir, & J. Kerr (Eds.), *Attachment theory: Social, developmental and clinical perspectives* (pp. 407–474). Hillsdale, NJ: Analytic Press.

Main, M. (1996). Introduction to the special section on attachment and psychopathology: 2. Overview of the field of attachment. *Journal of Consulting and Clinical Psychology, 64*, 237–243.

Main, M. (2001, March). *Attachment disturbances and the development of psychopathology.* Paper presented at the University of California, San Diego, Cutting Edge Confernce, La Jolla, CA.

Main, M., & Goldwyn, R. (1998). *Adult attachment scoring and classification systems* (Version 6.3). Unpublished manuscript, University of California at Berkeley.

Main, M., & Hesse, E. (1990). Parent's unresolved traumatic experiences are related to infant disorganized status: Is frightened and/or frightening parental behavior the linking mechanism? In M. T. Greenberg, D. Cicchetti, & E. M. Cummings (Eds.), *Attachment in the preschool years: Theory, research, and intervention* (pp. 161–182). Chicago: University of Chicago Press.

Main, M., Kaplan, N., & Cassidy, J. (1985). Security in infancy, childhood, and adulthood: A move to the level of representation. In I. Bretherton & E. Waters (Eds.), *Growing points of attachment theory and research* (pp. 66–104). *Monographs of the Society for Research in Child Development, 50* (2–3, Serial No. 209).

Main, M., & Morgan, H. (1996). Disorganization and disorientation in infant Strange Situation behavior: Phenotypic resemblance to dissociative states. In L. K. Michelson & W. J. Ray (Eds.), *Handbook of dissociation: Theoretical, empirical, and clinical perspectives* (pp. 121–160). Chicago: University of Chicago Press.

Main, M., & Solomon, J. (1986). Discovery of an insecure-disorganized/disoriented attachment pattern. In T. B. Brazelton & M. Yogman (Eds.), *Affective development in infancy* (pp. 95–124). Norwood, NJ: Ablex.

Main, M., & Solomon, J. (1990). Procedures for identifying infants as disorganized/disoriented during the Ainsworth Strange Situation. In M. T. Greenberg, D. Cicchetti, & E. M. Cummngs (Eds.), *Attachment in the preschool years: Theory research, and intervention* (pp. 121–160.) Chicago: University of Chicago Press.

Malan, D. M. (1979). *Individual psychotheraphy and the science of psychodynamics.* London. Butterworth.

Neborsky, R. J. (1998). *A new metapsychology of the unconscious.* Paper presented at University of California, San Diego, Cutting Edge Conference. La Jolla, CA.

Neborsky, R. J. (2000, November). *A study in hysteria.* One-day symposium. Lifespan Learning Institute. Los Angeles.

Pearson, J. L., Cohn, D. A., Cowan, P. A., & Cowan, C. P. (1994). Earned and continuous security in adult attachment. Relation to depressive symptomatology and poverty style. *Development and psychopathology, 6,* 259–373.

Schore, A. N. (1996). The experience-dependent maturation of a regulatory system in the orbital prefrontal cortex and the origin of developmental psychopathology. *Development and Psychopathology, 8,* 59–87.

Schore, A. N. (1997). Early organization of the nonlinear right brain and development of a predisposition to psychiatric disorders. *Development and Psychopathology, 9,* 595–631.

Schore, A. N. (1998). The experience-dependent maturation of an evaluative system in the cortex. In K. H. Pribram & J. King (Eds.), *Brain and values: Is a biological science of values possible?* (pp. 337–358). Mahwah, NJ: Erlbaum.

Shapiro, F. (1995). *Eye movement desensitization and reprocessing: Basic principles, protocols and procedures.* New York: Guilford Press.

Siegel, D. J. (1995). Memory, trauma, and psychotherapy: A cognitive science view. *Journal of Psychotherapy Practice and Research, 4,* 93–122.

Siegel, D. J. (1999). *The developing mind.* New York: Guilford Press.

Solomon, M. F., Neborsky, R. J., McCullough, L., Alpert, M., Shapiro, F., & Malan, D. M. (2001). *Short-term therapy for long-term change.* New York: Norton.

Stroufe, L. A., Egeland, B., & Krentger, T. (1990). The fate of early experience following developmental change: Longitudinal approaches to individual adaptation in childhood. *Child Development, 54,* 1615–1627.

Ten Have-de Labije, J.(Ed.) (2001). *The working alliance in ISTDP: Whose intrapsychic crisis?* Amsterdaum: VKDP.

van der Kolk, B. (1989). The compulsion to repeat the trauma. *Psychiatric Clinics of North America, 12*(2), 658–659.

van der Kolk, B. (1991). Childhood origins of self-destructive behavior. *American Journal of Psychiatry, 148,* 1665–1671.

van der Kolk, B. (2001, March). *Trauma, therapy, and the brain: Latest research findings.* Paper presented at the University of California, San Diego, Cutting Edge Conference, La Jolla. CA.

8

Connection, Disruption, Repair: Treating the Effects of Attachment Trauma on Intimate Relationships

Marion F. Solomon

MANY COUPLES HAVING relationship difficulties enter therapy with vague presenting problems such as "We don't communicate," or "We no longer do things together, we live separate lives." The partners typically cannot articulate what precisely is wrong, but they know something leaves them unsatisfied. Upon entering therapy, they feel unhappy, but are uncertain about why. Or their ideas about what is wrong are driven by anger at each other, and they are therefore unable to work toward any type of resolution. Marital disagreement may constitute a "surface narrative" used to explain unresolved, deeply painful attachment yearnings and defensive emotional disengagement that leads to anger and despair.

This chapter focuses on a model of therapy for couples in which the relationship is affected by a history of what Shapiro (2001) calls "small t" traumatic attachments. Based on the discussions in other chapters of this book, the approach outlined here includes a psychodynamic and neurobiological understanding of trauma (Schore, Chapter 3 Siegel, Chapter 1 van der Kolk, Chapter 4), various defensive response in insecure and disorganized attachments (Main and Hesse, Chapter 2), attuning to underlying needs and emotions in the healing process, (Neborsky, Chapter 7; Neborsky & Solomon, 2001), and formation of a therapeutic alliance with both partners in couples' therapy (Solomon, 1992; Johnson, 1996).

Those who come to couples' therapy generally present a combination of reality conflicts and attachment failures. The basic assumption of an intimate relationship is trust that the partner will be there when it is important to health or welfare. When there is a history of trauma, even small stress levels affect the security of the attachment bonds and can magnify into relationship-threatening events.

To be in any relationship where one feels unrecognized, disconnected, and helpless to change things is deflating, and is the most salient feature of unhappy marriages (Solomon, 1994). A defining factor in relationships that last is the ability to reconnect emotionally after an argument (Gottman & Silver, 1999). When there is a history of attachment traumas, the partners often use protective defenses that lead to disengagement and isolation. This occurs when the very person who is sought out for comfort is the perpetuator of the painful experience. The sense of helplessness and chaos can become unbearable. The result may be a breakdown of the adaptive processes leading to the maintenance of an integrated sense of self (Liotti, 1999). The working model of relationships develops with an inability to trust self or other, and with balance between the yearning for connection and the fear of the contact. People may choose intimate partners with an unconscious wish to repair earlier damage. Often, the sad result is that the forms of engagement of each cause a proneness to recreate the original traumatic experience (Sroufe, 1996). Painful encounters are played out as a preordained script.

If one of the partners is in distress and there is no response (it may be because no clear message is sent), trust of the other is frayed. When disappointing events occur repeatedly, it can feel devastating to an already vulnerable person. The result is a retraumatization, engendering a sense of helplessness and uncertainty. Past and current events merge. Arousal of emotion, without a corresponding memory of the original trauma, results in almost instantaneous anxiety and defense. The reactions may not make sense to the mate. A partner's misunderstanding of the cause may induce feelings of anger, guilt, and shame.

It is the internal model of attachment of each that largely determines the nature and form of the defensive structures reenacted. The greater the intimacy with another person, the more likely that emotions, even archaic ones, will emerge, along with primitive defenses. A therapeutic approach in such situations must help partners acknowledge their sense of vulnerability, discover its roots, tolerate waves of emotion, and find ways to address the underlying pain.

Treatment of Trauma

Various therapeutic models are used to retrieve the affective memory of the trauma through desensitization, reduction of shame, and increased tolerance of affect, in order to maintain the ability to think while experiencing emotion, to achieve symptom mastery, to experience a personal sense of empowerment and self-cohesion, and to develop a capacity for trust and intimacy (Harvey, 1996; Van der Kolk, this volume; Shapiro, this volume; Herman, 1992; Courtois, 1988; McCann & Pearlman, 1990; Johnson, 2002).

Van der Kolk (1996) emphasized the importance of the interpersonal process, noting that successful treatment of trauma victims changes the survivor's relationships with others. To achieve these results in individual or couples' therapy requires (a) the provision of a safe milieu to contain internal emotional outbursts, (b) an opportunity to preserve cognitive awareness in the face of intense feelings, (c) enhancement of the capacity to connect to one's core, and (d) the challenge to face the fear of true closeness with others.

Helping partners to achieve these goals when attachment patterns are permeated with defenses against terror, pain, confusion, rage, guilt, and shame, can present a dilemma to the marital therapist. Traditional modes of systemic and cognitive/behavioral treatment are designed to improve communications, modify dysfunctional behavioral patterns, and enhance positive aspects of the relationship. These methods seem to work for a time, but when there is a history of trauma or traumatic attachment failures, therapeutic efforts often are destined to fail. This is caused by the regressive pull toward old, familiar interactional dynamics. Often, the very elements once considered the basis for love become the principal source of perceived injury. A mate once admired as strong and solidly based is accused of being rigid and unchanging. A partner who was initially seen as passionate and full of energy and excitement is later put down for being overly emotional and chaotic.

When there are long ingrained defenses against traumatic attachment failures, anything can become a source of stress and pain. A look not given, a message not understood, a yearning for closeness not met, become magnified into a recreation of emotions around early trauma. Feelings related to dependency needs and deep unfulfilled yearnings are replaced by rageful feelings and blaming attacks. Defenses reemerge to protect both the vulnerable core self and the object of one's multifaceted loving and hateful feelings. In the treatment setting, when emotion suddenly intensifies, it is a signal that the partners are dealing with an unacknowledged wound in the here-and-now of the session.

The reason it is necessary to focus on here-and-now affect is that the great fear of many people is that their feelings are wrong, or even dangerous. "If you see the effect of my disappointment in you, my crying, clinging tightly, protesting, raging, or showing despair or depression, you will be disgusted and withdraw from me completely." Conversely, with overwhelming emotions, "I can drown you out, so I will not be hurt." Such reactions are not unusual for adults who have experienced early attachment traumas. These negative emotional responses, if not attended to and restructured, will undermine any chance of repair of a couple's relationship. Emotions are vital in organizing key responses to significant others and operate as an internal compass that helps to focus people on their primary needs and goals. Many emotional states emerge in conjoint sessions with couples. Often they are expressed not in words, but in body reactions and facial expressions. Partners may need help in accessing and acknowledging them as they are experienced in the conjoint session. In the process of containing and exploring together such emotions, the therapist can help to clarify internal schemas about the nature of self and other, and cocreate new narratives, thus beginning the process of change.

Techniques of Attachment-Oriented Couples Therapy

Conjoint therapy is designed to help each partner to reconnect with his or her own and each other's needs and emotions. The treatment includes a differential diagnosis of the unique history of trauma and patterns of attachment that each partner brings to the relationship.

Whatever went wrong in the childhood of each partner will be tested in an intimate relationship that includes not only the partner, but in-laws, children, and other family members. If the early childhood trauma was significant, then the individual will frequently invoke defenses to alleviate the relationship difficulty, and then the normative growth of intimacy, empathy, understanding, healthy dependency, and connection that occurs over time will not unfold. Instead, stalemate and stagnation prevail, and conflict and alienation dominate the partners' life together.

Because early painful encounters are frequently preverbal and are followed by defenses designed to protect the vulnerable self of the developing child, clear memory of traumatic events is lost through repression or dissociation, or never having been visually or verbally represented. What remains are the emotional reactions to the painful moment, the unconscious repressed or unrepresented emotion, and later, a faulty or incomplete narrative designed to explain the surges of pain that suddenly arise in relationships. As Freud (1911/1959) noted, we are destined to repeat that which we do not remember. Inevitably, the repressed or unrepresented affect around painful events and defenses designed to protect the wounded self is reenacted in the intimate relationship. "Rather than a continuous coherent narrative, we observe a precise narrative reenactment" (Neborsky & Solomon, 2001). In the worst cases, husbands and wives can become each other's worst nightmare through projective and introjective identification (Dicks, 1967; Scharff & Scharff, 1987). The relationship deteriorates into patterns of attack and defense, becoming a collusive jumble in which they cannot live, but from which they cannot extricate themselves.

Listening to the way that the partners present their issues, what is reported of the history of each, who begins, how each reacts to the other's report of the relationship, what physical and emotional responses are demonstrated, helps the therapist determine whether this is a relationship permeated by traumatic attachments, and suggests various ways to approach the pain. Repair of disrupted attachments is more easily accomplished when a severe traumatic incident was not foreshadowed by a history of earlier "small-T" traumas, such as repeated humiliations of a child who has been made a scapegoat in the family or among peers at school (Shapiro, 2001). When large-T traumas such as rape, violence, and natural disasters have been preceded by this more insidious kind of small-t trauma, states of high alert to danger and rigid patterns of interaction are imprinted in the circuits of the brain (See individual chapters in this volume by Schore, Siegel, & van der Kolk). The temperament of the child, the degree of the trauma, and the capacity of the caregivers to respond, determine the self-organization that forms.

Once a relational pattern is imprinted it becomes part of implicit memory, "the effects become cumulative" (Kahn, 1963). Repetitive attunement failures become fixed, making change more difficult. Moreover, prolonged failure of response can result in development of a primitive aggressive schematic pattern with defensive responses that can follow the person throughout a lifetime of relationships (Neborsky & Solomon, 2001). Hopeful anticipation is often followed by disappointment, defense against further painful encounters, and the pain of a deadlocked relationship.

Therapists often find themselves stymied when working with such deadlocked relationships. They should be viewed as possible diagnostic indicators of early trauma in which fight, flight, or freeze responses were evoked. In such cases, the persistent expectation of impending danger results in a constant need for reassurance, which, if not met, is translated into a sign of betrayal. In a deadly cycle, the initial breach spirals into a battlefield characterized by hyper-alertness for further signs of betrayal, which becomes the norm for the relationship (Johnson, 2001). To vulnerable participants, the relationship always feels tentative, and there is a tendency to test the love to alleviate the constant doubts, even when things are going well. At the same time, any sign that needs might be ignored or denied is met with avoidance, numbness, and criticism, often along with self-doubt and self-blame. The internal message, "I am defective, destructive, and unlovable," is repeatedly confirmed.

In addition, early trauma causes deficits in perceiving and processing ability that may include the capacity to categorize experience, connect to autobiographical narratives of experience, or develop a capacity for empathic attunement toward others. Later, this inability to perceive the emotional states of others, a kind of psychic dyslexia in ability to read facial expressions, leads to a misinterpretation of the communication of others and coincides with negative expectations of others' intentions. There is a failure in contingent communication[1] (Siegel, 1999) which interferes with resolution of problems. In his book *What Predicts Divorce*, Gottman (1994) discussed the complex causes of marital failure.

Gottman's research (1994, 1999) indicated that it is not the number of arguments that partners have, nor the method of dealing with angry feelings, nor even whether they successfully resolve disagreements, that make a difference in defining success or failure in a relationship. The important defining factor is the ability to sustain emotional engagement and to reconnect to each other following arguments.

It is the proneness to overreact to differences, the inability to accept another's views, and inability to reengage after disrupted interactions that are so harmful to intimate relationships. Such failure seems to follow people who have experienced trauma and traumatic attachments. From their early experience, they have learned that it is not safe to depend on others, and when disagreements erupt, they become defensive. In stressful situations they utilize various coping strategies, including walling themselves off from another to avoid emotional engagement, hiding a true self while showing a façade that seems more acceptable, or acting out angrily when they experience disruptions with significant others. These are methods of self-protection developed over time during repeated painful encounters with important figures in their lives.

These protective defenses should not be viewed simply as indications of pathological development, but as the best possible course at the time when an intolerable attachment failure left them no other course. Although it was useful at an earlier time, it has become an impediment in current relationships. To understand the way we learn to attach and protect a vulnerable self in traumatic situations, it is necessary to turn to those who have researched attachment

---

[1] *Contingent communication* describes our ability to send and respond to each other's messages. As adults, we need not only to be cared about and understood, but to have another person simultaneously experience a state of mind similar to our own. With this shared *contingent communication* life can be filled with an integrating sense of connection and meaning.

(Bowlby, 1998; Ainsworth, Blehar, Waters, & Wall, 1978; Main, 1999; Tronick, 1989 Sroufe, 1996; Siegel, 1999). The different defensive maneuvers that are likely to effect intimate relationships throughout the lifespan are reenactments of protective measures developed in early life painful encounters.

Assessing Degree of Relational Disruption

All couples encounter problems at times. Differential diagnosis of the core relational issue and the degree of early trauma is a priority. While secure attachment provides a base of trust in relationships with others, and a sense of efficacy in coping with the environment, those who have experienced traumatic attachments develop coping methods that are likely to put a wall between themselves and intimate others.

Anxious/preoccupied attachment patterns manifest in push-pull relationships in which the message is "Don't come close—don't go away." Avoidant/dismissive relationships are the result of early experiences leading to an expectation that others will not be available. The effect is likely to be development of habitual styles of interacting that avoid stressful or disturbing emotional engagement with significant others. There is an avoidance of eye contact when entering into dialogue about unresolved issues.

Disorganized attachment patterns are usually the most disturbing for the individuals and create the greatest distress in adult relationships which are usually chaotic, alternating between disruption and reconnection. They often originate when trauma follows trauma, and there is no way to overcome the pain, terror, or danger.

It is important to differentiate those who are likely to respond to marital therapy from those whose pathological defenses make the likelihood of change problematic. Because of unconscious processes that the partners have no way of understanding, the choice of a loved one includes the probability of recreating earlier traumatic experience. This occurs because, through repetition, a response is shaped in which the internal working model of each partner can trigger the other's most painful and repressed emotional reactions (Neborsky & Solomon, 2001). This produces a counter-reaction in the mate and eventually shapes each other's responses such that their behavior becomes a reminder of the original wounds. The question is, "Can the imprints of intimate relationships be changed?" If so, what can the marital therapist offer?

An earlier work presented a diagnostic schema for understanding the kinds of imprinted patterns of relating, including a range of disturbances and defenses that are seen in couples' therapy (Solomon et al., 2001 pp. 138–140). The range includes people who have developed the capacity for secure attachments and are in the high functional-adaptive range (Solomon et al., 2001, p. 140). While they may have relationship problems, the issues are not due to unconscious acting out, the outgrowth of old family traumas, or painful attachments. These people have a resilient self and call on a variety of resources when they are in stressful situations. In therapy, such people participate actively in the treatment, communicate needs and distress, and are able to attune to the feelings communicated by a partner.

They make meaningful links between their current partner and figures from the past. They are open to the help offered by the therapists. A variety of treatments can be used to help people with relatively secure attachments. When such people enter therapy, and they do occasionally, they are gratifying to work with.

Current research has found that a marriage in which one of the partners has a secure attachment, an insecurely attached partner may, develop an "earned secure attachment" (Main, 2002; Davila, Burge, & Hammen, 1997; Kirkpatrick & Davis, 1994; Hazan & Shaver, 1987, 1994).

People who have what Kohut (1984) called "self disorders" seem to overlap with the feelings of avoidant, ambivalent, or disorganized insecure attachment. They often begin therapy with high levels of anxiety because of their fear that unconscious emotions will break through and interfere even more in their life problems. In treatment, they demonstrate moderately high resistance, psychic isolation of the self, and fantasies about destruction of self and others. They protect a vulnerable self with defenses such as aggressive distancing, emotional disconnection, repression, projective and introjective identification, and explosive discharge of affect. They have a proneness to emptiness and depression when the loved one separates, even momentarily, and need others to shore up a fragile sense of self, bind others to themselves through dependency and/or fear, and often set up rejection by others through unconscious aggressive acts. In their relationships there is a constant battle for control, and sometimes there is a tendency toward compulsive caretaking to compensate for inordinate feelings of dependency and neediness.

When the stress of their lives together brings such partners into couples' therapy, one or both may demonstrate resistance to the treatment. They may activate repressive defenses immediately, denying that there is any problem, or project problems onto one another, or find that a busy schedule requires them to cancel sessions. In the sessions, they may demonstrate regressive defenses, mood disorders, acting out and externalization of problems. Symptoms arise that may cause significant personal distress, and the functioning of relationships may be severely impaired. In fact, it may be so sufficiently severe that it sabotages the therapy until the deep pain caused by the imminent relational destruction motivates the partners to change.

Sometimes partners find that they must choose between getting well or staying married. Alternately, the willingness of one partner to leave the relationship may be the only factor that motivates the spouse to act differently. In either of these instances, genuine changes can be accomplished only through a therapeutic reworking of unconscious early attachment trauma. This may require individual treatment in addition to the conjoint sessions.

Where partners' personality style falls into the most disturbed end of the spectrum, identified as borderline-narcissistic patterns, (Solomon, 2001), we are likely to find collusive relationships with others who have complementary defenses. Partners form unconscious love bonds that help them ward off painful or frightening emotions and may draw other family members into dysfunctional dynamics. They may have a variety of presenting issues, but the underlying dynamics are similar. These include faulty boundaries, intense separation anxiety, and stormy encounters with others. Relationships are marked by impaired attunement, and often physical and/or emotional abuse. In treatment of such people, we find a history of early attachment trauma, primitive dissociation, high somatization, a fragile self, and high resistance to change.

When pathological disorders caused by very early attachment trauma of both partners are being played out in the couples' relationship, the result can be a destructive deadlock. Change in one partner may mean the end of the marriage. The fear of separation and divorce may result in an attempt to undermine the emotional growth of the partner who has changed. Conjoint therapy rarely succeeds in changing the unconscious interactional pattern of such people. Their defenses are designed to protect the vulnerable selves of both. Therefore, unless methods are found to inspire couples' movement past their resistance to confront the emotional demons, treatment efforts will be futile.

Generally, two people with a history of avoidant modes of relating are unlikely to maintain lasting bonds. Partners who find the behavior intolerable often decide to leave those with entrenched defenses, thus adding to relational distrust. Some very successful people who put their energy into business success to compensate for lack of relational success, maintain relationships in which both partners are unhappy, but choose not to terminate for reasons other than lack of emotional intimacy. The couples that are most likely to try to resolve and improve their emotional and sexual relationship are a combination of an avoidant and an ambivalent partnership. An example of this will be found in the case discussed later in this chapter.

The Effect of Reparative Experiences

New evidence (Main, 2002) indicates that reparative adult experiences enable those with attachment traumas to increase their ability to cope with stress and restore a sense of security. Healing through new relationships occurs frequently, and makes a person who has experienced trauma increase the ability to cope with stress and negative affect. Religious or 12-step experiences, therapeutic experiences, and intimate relationships all offer possibilities for repair.

Among promising new therapeutic models, Neborsky's "Accelerated Analysis" (Personal communication) focuses on accessing unconscious emotions in the here-and-now between patient and therapist; then connecting with defensive maneuvers with attachment figures in the past. Fosha's treatment model is based on a psychotherapist's ability to resonate empathically with a patient's body states and to empathically attune on an intuitive, nonverbal level. The goal is to bypass defenses and process core emotions (Fosha, 2000).

Schore (in press) indicates that a successful therapeutic relationship can function in an interactive affect-regulating context that optimizes the growth of two minds. The brain is mutable throughout our lifespan, forming new synaptic connections and new neural and vascular circuitry with every new incidence of learning and experience (Siegel, this volume; Neborsky, this volume). Increases in complexity in both the patient's and the therapist's continually developing "unconscious right minds" is seen as a major healing factor (Schore, 2001). Moreover, recent studies confirm that insecurely attached people who are married to securely attached partners can, within a period of 5 years' time, modify an insecure attachment pattern (Main, 2002).

This chapter is suggesting a method of "interactive repair" in a conjoint therapeutic experience. The therapist can, through empathic modeling and promotion of direct emotional communication, encourage creation of a growth-facilitating environment that can complete the interrupted developmental process of each. Under such conditions it is possible to help partners affect a transformative experience in which each reconnects with dissociated or repressed emotions, and develops the capacity to empathically attune to each other.

Healing experiences may include suggestions for at-home practice for enhancement of emotional, physical, and sexual intimacy. Mutually satisfying sexual contact, with its opportunities for warmth and holding, eye contact, smell, and taste can play a significant role in reattuning partners to a novel sense of personal well-being. This can occur if the partners have a history of secure attachments, or if they are helped in therapy to overcome the residual effects of trauma in their early attachment experiences.

The Ongoing Process of Treatment

The goal of ongoing treatment is to find ways to help the partners overcome the defensive maneuvers imprinted in their early attachment experiences, break the cycle of mutual hurt, and begin to create the bonding events that distinguish successful couples.

After allowing sufficient time for the partners to present their view of the problems, the therapist shares observations that help each partner understand the pattern of their interactions. It is then possible to focus on normal attachment needs and the lifelong yearning for physical and emotional contact. Then the couple can learn to understand how early wounds and protective defenses have developed into a unique interactional repertoire, which is replayed in all subsequent relationships. Depending on the ability to retain the information without resorting to defenses, treatment may focus on what one partner believed he or she had found in the other to induce relational commitment. The therapist clarifies that with the existence of earlier wounds, people often choose their most intimate relationships with an unconscious wish to heal the past. If the couple has difficulty with these ideas, it is important to see this not as a sign of their resistance alone, but also perhaps as the therapist's failure to convey the message in a way that can be receptively incorporated. If the message elicits shame and it is not repaired, it leads to humiliation, self-blame, and/or strategies to defend a vulnerable core.

If the couple responds by utilizing and giving examples of the ways that their past has played out in their current relationship, it becomes possible to accelerate the healing process. We shall see in the case below how the therapist is able to help partners communicate primary needs and yearnings, and encourage discussion of internal beliefs and attitudes about self and other. In this process, shameful feelings and negative emotional responses are attended to and reframed as a positive path to the emergence of core affect (Fosha, this volume). This allows expressions of vulnerability and hurt feelings to be discussed in the sessions. The therapist's role is to redefine intense emotionality as important expressions of attachment failure, to be carefully observed, and hopefully healed in the current relationship.

From Disruption to Repair

In this task the therapist uses the relationship as a healing milieu. He or she helps partners utilize the power of their emotions and needs to understand what went wrong, and how to organize methods of interactional change.

The therapist encourages the partners to narrate how they came together, what made them choose each other, and what they are yearning for now. There is an exploration of the similarities and differences in their memories and view of the relationship. Further probing helps them to consider how the current relationship is reminiscent of their historical interactions. In the process, the couple can gain clarity in how the reenactment of their early traumatic events has, in fact, been part of their striving toward a reparative experience. Reinforcing their ability to take in and utilize this information, the therapist explains that each partner's growth-seeking role seeks in selecting a partner an intimate connection with someone who resembles significant parental figures. It is normal for people who have been traumatized to select a mate for his or her reenactment qualities in the hope of a reparative experience (Hendrix, 1989). The wish is that, "This time, someone will understand me, accept me, and love me enough, to heal the wounds of the past."

Partners can be helped to understand their own unresolved yearnings, and their wishes for reparenting by the other. Interdependency in intimate relationships is the process by which each takes turns as the benign caretaker, particularly in stressful life conditions (Solomon, 1994). An unhappy marriage is one in which only one partner is allowed to regress, have needs taken care of, feel emotions, and demand attention. Heinz Kohut noted in *How Does Analysis Cure*, that "A good marriage is one in which only one partner is crazy at any given time" (1984, p. 220).

The therapist helps each partner to acknowledge unresolved attachment needs, and process emotions *with each other present*. In the process, partners become more exactly aware of what occurs when needs feel unmet and how defenses emerge in a millisecond to protect the self from unresolved pain. By helping in the process of holding the painful emotion instead of moving into numbing or acting out defenses, there is a building of tolerance for core affect. At that juncture, the defenses that keep them avoiding emotion and each other can begin to diminish. The couple begins to clarify similar and complementary needs, with the therapist helping each to recognize and then empathize with the other's internal experience.

Once the partners understand the active pattern of vulnerability and defense, the therapist can begin to focus on restructuring interactions. Intervention may include a challenge to explore the here-and-now physiological and emotional reactions of each mate and what these responses represent. After reinforcing the idea that their very attempts to protect themselves keep them locked in a distressed pattern, the partners can see that, rather than creating a nonthreatening relationship, the opposite has occurred and is generating increasing alienation. Treatment then can strengthen the emotional ties by suggestions that help the partners to explore the experience of emotional engagement.

At this point the partners may be able to access the unacknowledged feelings that underlie their interactions. With the therapist, they begin to reframe their presenting problems in new terms. The therapeutic alliance helps to provide a secure base from which hidden needs and shameful feelings can emerge and be acknowledged. This secure milieu offers a holding environment in which frightening emotions, once experienced as too dangerous to tolerate, are contained and detoxified. Modeling and identification with the therapist enhances the process of feeling, dealing, and healing (Fosha, this volume).

The following case demonstrates an avoidant, disengaged husband and a wife whose history indicated an ambivalent attachment manifested by alternation between pursuit and disconnection.

Case Example

Beth and Phil are a couple in their late 50s whose two daughters recently left home to attend college in other states. The couple sought marital therapy after Beth, who had always seen herself as an ideal homemaker and caretaker, was feeling very depressed and sought individual treatment. After a year of psychotherapy and a series of unsuccessful attempts to get Phil to listen and understand her needs, she decided that divorce may be the answer to her long-standing unhappiness. This motivated Phil to seek out marital therapy.

Phil had been a highly successful businessman and entrepreneur until the stock market took a dive and he experienced a decrease in the number of deals he could put together. He was therefore in semi-retirement, but not of his own choosing. They sold their large home and purchased a smaller one, saying that they needed less room now that their daughters were grown. They owned a summer condo for many years in a southern California resort area.

When their youngest daughter left for college two years earlier, Beth decided to use her extensive experience as a volunteer and museum docent to open an art gallery. She was quite successful in her first endeavor, and opened a second gallery in the resort community where their second home was located. After a time, she found the business frustrating and was unhappy at the amount of time that they were spending alone together in their condo. Phil, on the other hand, wanted to go to the condo every weekend because he was not comfortable in their new home.

The stress of their new situation, including their reduced role as parents, diminished financial resources, and move to a new neighborhood, all added up to marital frustration and unhappiness. Beth complained that Phil paid little attention to her needs and concerns. Phil, used to being taken care of by a nurturing, available wife, did not understand what was wrong. He tried to advise her when she had difficulties in staffing her businesses, but she did not seem to want his help. He did what he had always done when Beth seemed upset—he withdrew and waited for her to feel better.

When they came to couples' therapy Beth was very upset with Phil and expressed her unhappiness repeatedly. When Phil asked what she wanted him to do, however, her response was, "I told you what is wrong; now you have to figure out what to do." Her upset was evident as she related her feelings, but Phil seemed mystified about what, if anything, to do about those feelings. His pattern of withdrawal was evident.

We began with a relational history; how they met, when and how they decided to marry, what each wanted, expected, and experienced at first. It is important to get a sense of how the partners' particular cycle, of which they are both creators and victims, evolved.

Using a modified genogram, we discovered that each was the youngest child in a family that had escaped from Europe shortly before the Holocaust. When Phil related his family history, his marital pattern of avoidant attachment seemed firmly entrenched by the time the family moved to Chicago when he was 3 years old. Phil was the youngest of four and the only child born in the United States.

Phil's father, a physician in his home country, did not have the energy or the language skills to pass the medical boards in America, and he worked at menial jobs for the rest of his life. Attachment in his family-of-origin meant never letting anyone out of mothers sight for long. Phil's withdrawal was the defensive response to his parents' expectation that everyone was supposed to stay very closely attached. Phil was uncertain as to whether this enmeshment was a generational one that came from his European culture, or a response to the family's trauma. His family did not discuss topics related to emotional hurt. His parents did not talk much. Although Phil was easy going and didn't openly question or challenge his parents, he escaped into books and a very strong work ethic. This was both pleasing to his parents and a path to freedom from an overly enmeshed family. A series of scholarships and job offers allowed him to distance from his family without openly challenging them. Hard work and a quick mind helped him to succeed financially. When he married he moved to California, 3,000 miles from the rest of his family. The other three children still live within the borders of the small town in which they all grew up. Phil helped them all financially, but his visits were rare.

Beth's family had moved from Europe to South America in the mid-1930s, avoiding the direct trauma of the Holocaust, but they suffered through the intermittent reports of trapped relatives. They took action, helping more than a dozen family members escape, and formed a small commune in the South American city in which they lived.

Beth met Phil when she was on vacation in the United States. They both described it as one of the great love affairs. Beth did not return to her family until after she and Phil married, and every year she visited twice, for 3 weeks. When their children were growing up, they sometimes spent their summer vacation with Beth's family. Beth described her parents as wonderful people, but with a great sadness. She saw it as her job growing up to make everyone feel good. It was clear that her self-concept was defined by how successful she was in keeping her family together, and happy. What appeared on the surface as altruistic was in fact, self serving, a process that has been described by others as "the parentified child" (Miller, 1981). Her family reinforced her façad of being always cheerful, helpful, and busy with projects. She learned early that feelings of sadness or anger disrupted the attachment bonds she yearned for.

Phil's self-definition revolved around his ability to maintain boundaries and avoid the pull on his time and attention that his close-knit family demanded of all its members, forcing him to develop rigid boundaries in order to maintain his autonomy. To get involved with the family's emotions felt dangerous. He described them as wonderful people, but always anxious, and he found it difficult to tolerate their anxiety and unhappiness.

Beth and Phil fit well together: the nurturing he needed, while he maintained his autonomy, she was inclined to do; what she needed, the creation of a successful, close-knit family, he provided.

From their history, it was possible to draw some preliminary hypotheses regarding the insecurities and vulnerabilities underlying the position each partner took in the relationship. As long as their life together worked well, the traumas they carried from their family background, their thwarted early attachment needs to develop a self of their own, and the resentments about past and current unmet needs did not emerge. It was not until the family dynamics changed, their financial situation declined, and new pressures were added, that underlying vulnerabilities began to modify the balance of the relationship.

In the sessions both attempted to protect themselves against the terror of revealing a vulnerable self. Each blamed the other for a kind of unhappiness that they were not used to. Because their relationship had many strengths, they had been able to provide for the things that each needed, but it was no longer working. Beth was negative about every suggestion that Phil made. She wanted to express her unhappiness without telling him what he could do to make her feel better. Her emotional states which she wanted him to understand was like an alien language to Phil, who had blocked out feelings for most of his life.

When working with such a distressed couple, it is important to encourage one partner, often the one who appears more unavailable, to describe their experience, while staying connected with the other. When Beth began to talk about her feelings, it was possible to identify how Phil averted his face and his body from his wife. Beth's need for connection when she was most upset reflected the importance to her of his emotional presence. He experienced it as a reflection of his personal inadequacies or insensitivity, and in his own pain, he withdrew when he saw her sadness. This made her angry. It was recreating for her an early experienced attachment dilemma to hurt people she loved or hide her true feelings and hurt herself.

The following is an excerpt from a 1½-hour session early in the couples' therapy. A variety of interventions were used to form an alliance with the therapist, to accelerate their ability to connect to their feelings, and when relevant, to connect their current relationship to past experiences. If there was trauma in early life attachments, there is an ongoing attempt to explore attachment needs, traumatic attachment experiences, underlying emotions and recognition of protective defenses that are being played out in the current relationship. The goal is to recognize patterns that each brings from the past as they are unfolding in the therapy sessions and to repair disruptions in the present of the relationship.

Beth: Are you happy?

Phil: Yes, I am happy.

Beth: Well then there is nothing to talk about.

Therapist: What are you feeling right now Phil? *[Inquiry-Pressure to feel]*

Phil: I'm frustrated. Nothing I do seems to help.

Therapist: What do you tell yourself about you and your abilities?

Phil: This problem I can't solve. I can't even figure out what's wrong. (*Holding back tears when he said this.*)

Therapist: You look so very sad when you say that, Phil. Are there other feelings that go with your look? *[Pressure to connect to feelings]*

Phil: (Beginning to cry), It's not sadness, it's hurt and anger. Everything I do is wrong. So I try not to do anything, and that's wrong too. Beth says she wants me to be close. But she really doesn't. She wants something amorphous—I don't understand it. I just want a nice life. I worked hard all my life.

Beth: You just want to do what you want. You don't go where I want or do the things I am interested in.

Phil: Everything you want to do is here in town. You know I want to get away to the beach house.

Beth: You just sit there all weekend waiting for me to entertain you. I spent my life doing that. I am tired and depressed.

Phil: I just want to get away and have some peace. I don't need you to be there to entertain me.

Beth: If you think that I'm just talking about entertaining you, than you don't understand anything I'm saying to you about what I need.

Phil: What are you saying to me about what you need?

Beth: I've been telling you how I feel. You have to figure out what to do. I can't do that for you. I've been doing my best, but if you cannot do it, well maybe this relationship is not for me for the rest of my life. I have to think about what I want, with or without you.

Phil: (*winced and began to turn away*)

This was a time for a *connecting intervention* from the therapist. Beth did not want to end the relationship, but felt that she could not live with someone with no sense of how unhappy and depressed she felt. She did not recognize that the cause of her depression was not only Phil's emotional unavailability, but also that she carried a lifetime of sadness, her parents' and her own, with no resolution for herself. She had learned early on how to attune to and take care of others when they were distressed, but she had a deep well of tears that had never had an outlet. She was the happy, cheerful, can-do child. Her husband was a can-do partner in many areas, but not in the realm of emotion. He had left behind emotions when he left his family of origin.

Both Phil and Beth had recreated the issues that dominated their families of origin, in which sadness, loss, and grief were supposed to be handled by children who do their best. Beth spent a lifetime as a caretaker, while Phil tried to pull his family out of poverty and despair by getting away and making enough money to help everyone. Beth had learned in her family that when someone is emotional, she could "make it better," but now she was feeling a lot of negative emotion and wanted Phil to "make it better" by reaching out and holding her, instead of pulling away.

When Beth tried to express her emotions, Phil thought she was asking him to read her mind. He did not know how to do this nor did he truly understand her needs. His entire self-image involved taking on a difficult task and overcoming the odds, and it was frustrating to feel that he had failed. Although he was afraid of anger, his own or another's, his anger came to the surface more easily now than in the past.

In situations where early attachment injury resurfaces, threatening what remains of the relational bond, the therapist helps them stay in touch with the emotions related to injured feelings, and helps in the articulation of the impact of the present attachment issues. Additional emotions may spontaneously emerge at this point.

Therapist: Beth, when you relate your needs and they are not understood, what happens inside you? [*Inquiry into physical manifestations of feeling states*]

Beth: I think that I will have to spend the rest of my life feeling alone. And it makes me angry.

As she expressed anger, I asked her to look at Phil and tell him directly that what she wanted from him is that he reach out to her when she told him of her pain. [*Modeling new behavior*]

Therapist: And when he turns away, you get angry at him for leaving you alone with your feelings. [*Interpretation of anger at abandonment*]

Beth: (*turns to Phil and taking both of his hands*) I need you to put your arms around me and hold me and let me cry for as long as I want to cry.

Phil said that it is hard to stay with her when she is telling him how sad he makes her.

Beth: Do you think that I am blaming you for my sadness?

Phil: Well, you are always telling me that I am doing it wrong. So I know I am making you sad. I don't know what to do to fix it, so I feel terrible.

Beth: You think my sadness is about you. . . . No . . . No . . .

Phil: (*puts his arm on her shoulder tentatively*)

Therapist: You look almost afraid to reach out fully and take Beth in your arms. Phil, do you think she will turn away or push you away? [*Interpretation of fear with implied possibility of new behavior*]

Phil: I don't know why I am afraid, but I am.

Phil: (*putting both arms around Beth and pulling her close as she cries deeply*)

Therapist: You look like you are holding back tears yourself, Phil.

Phil: (*cries softly as they hold each other*)

By normalizing what is said as common unconscious feelings, both Phil and Beth had a chance to explore the impasses of their relationship. The venture is successful if the partnership can avoid the cycle of shame and blame, look at the underlying feelings, and choose them as an alternative to defending against painful feelings. No longer does he have to live with dissociated memories of his father's passive distancing and withholding from his mother. No longer does she have to live with dissociated memories of her mother's unresolvable grief over the significant loss of relatives and friends. Further, they can utilize imagery to explore angry impulses or destructive reactions, and to "reframe the pictures" of what has been and what can be.

Anger and tears of sadness may be the surface reactions, but the genuine feelings are hurt, helplessness, fear, shame, and guilt. This session with Beth and Phil freed some of the emotions and begin to make the expression of feelings acceptable between them. Further work then began as we examined the significance of their internal working models to present negative cycles in the relationship.

As partners are able to talk about hidden feelings and impulses without the fear of being judged, new insights are realized and communicated. The therapist, curious about which failures at these moments caused these regressive feelings to arise, has an opportunity to help each of the partners translate feelings like anger and fear into deeper underlying needs that have been thwarted. If emotions are allowed to emerge freely, and are explored in terms of the way the current situation recreates painful experiences of the past, it is possible to consider defenses as the optimal toddler-response, but no longer effective for the adult.

There is often an extraordinary sense of relief in knowing that these feelings are transference from past figures and not a direct response to the relationship. (*Current-past connection decreases* anxiety)

At this point, one or both of the partners may become curious enough about themselves to accept a needed referral to individual therapy. Beth's psychotherapy precipitated Phil's call for marital therapy. As they were finishing conjoint therapy, Phil asked for a referral to individual psychotherapy for himself.

(Important Technical Points to) Change the Patterns in an Intimate Relationship

It is often helpful to utilize an educational component in the couple's therapy. The therapist first delineates the conflictual pattern and negative interaction. Then, it is necessary to examine the unconscious reflex to protect against perceived and experienced wounds. When the couples learn that each constructed an insufficient image of how intimate attachments can work, it opens the way for coconstruction of a new narrative that will work for both in their relationship.

Depending upon the ability of the partners to understand simple descriptions of current developmental and brain research, the therapist considers with them what early experiential failures may now be impacting their current relationship. Pointing out that traumatic experience is often processed in the nonverbal right hemisphere, the early trauma is, in fact, always present, but out of awareness. This is now denying them access to an integrated biographical narrative, and is instead part of their current unsatisfying narrative reenactment. The therapist helps the couple with self-reflection through a series of inquiries into their narrative, adding gentle pressure to explore feelings by query and by noting physical responses and facial expressions.

There is a continuous reframing of the partners' interactions to guide attention toward the current unconscious process. It is done with a series of inquiries, without blame or shame, in an educative way, crystallizing and destigmatizing. In this way the therapist helps to lead the couple to self-reflection about anxiety and defenses that have kept core feelings out of awareness. By reconnecting to the feelings that have kept them cut off from themselves, and cut off from each other, partners can restart their own growth process and reengage with each other. Constantly teaching them what internal elements of their behavior and emotions are hurting the other partner in the relationship reminds the partners that there is unfinished work that needs to be addressed. This process provides opportunities to repair the structures of the self of each.

Over a relatively short period of time of conjoint treatment, feelings that were previously experienced as intolerable, overwhelming, or dangerous are held and contained in the therapeutic milieu. Partners increase the ability to tolerate the intolerable, and develop the courage to face what was once believed to be too unbearable to experience. As they learn to respond behaviorally to one another in ways that are different from past encounters, they experience a new empowerment and increased self-awareness. Self-esteem is bolstered by the journey into the abyss and the courageous encounter with inner sadness, fear, rage, shame, and guilt.

Ultimately, it becomes safe for each partner to permit mutual dependency in the relationship. Couples reparent each other as each partner learns the importance of taking care of each other's regressive needs and emotions. The relationship can take on the quality of Alexander's (Alexander & French, 1946) "corrective emotional experience," the repair of disrupted or traumatic relationships with new people. Partners learn to provide for each other the empathic capacity that the parent could not give the child. Kohut (1984) described this as the normal human need for self objects throughout life to enhance the self in times of stress. While Kohut was describing what occurs in a therapeutic relationship, his descriptions of the process, a very rapid idealization of the other, the desire for mirroring, the yearning for twinship, are similar to what can happen in intimate relationships. In *Narcissism and Intimacy* (1992),

I described the disappointment, disillusionment, and defenses that occur when a partner fails to offer need-responses (self-object). This process shows how problems between couples develop and become reciprocal. It also shows how treatment provides opportunities to repair affect-regulating structures. The result of the therapy can be what Main calls "earned secure attachment." When partners' stances toward attachment and defensive system are reorganized and they have the opportunity to expand their intimate relating, the ability to feel anger, grief, fear, and pain unleashes the ability to feel love, joy, courage, and pleasure. Repair of frayed attachment bonds opens new pathways to autonomy and self-expression of each.

Conclusion

This chapter has considered techniques that help partners connect, facilitate self-regulation functions, and enhance affective experiences. Utilizing verbal and nonverbal methods, the treatment is designed to expand each mate's capacity for contingent communication (Siegel, 1999) and interactive repair. A key to this therapeutic approach is demonstration of interest in each person's method of handling his or her sadness, anger, and emotional pain.

The bonds of love in adults represent an accumulation of the loving attachments developed early in life. When there is interference in the early connections with the object of a child's love, the frustration and pain are diminished through emotional defense mechanisms. Once such defenses are imprinted, they become firmly entrenched modes of relating.

With awareness of one's own and a partner's relational imprints, and with willingness to tolerate the difficulties inherent in breaking the old patterns, relationships can be helped to change. Partnerships can avoid the cycle of shame and blame, can look at the underlying feelings and choose an alternative to acting defensively. To this end, do we focus on specific complaints raised by partners regarding their current or past relationships, or do we focus on how they feel and on how they deal with those feelings?

Although both are necessary, therapeutic work must, to be effective, concentrate on the latter, or therapy will be an endless process. Focusing too much on childhood traumas can reinforce externalization, and cause projection and a sense of victimization. An adult may have been victimized as a child, but the way the person deals with his or her feelings about these issues in the here-and-now is their responsibility. The therapist's principal responsibility, in either individual or couples therapy, is to help patients bear their own feelings so they can express them fully and completely, and therefore appropriately, thus reinforcing healthy boundaries.

Healing occurs in moments of secure attachment, at first provided by the holding environment of the therapeutic millieu. In a series of experiences of attachment injury disruption and repair, the partners strengthen internal coping abilities.

The goal of treatment is to explore the possibility of resurrecting in an adult love relationship the pretraumatized capacity to feel love, joy, and compassion. The therapeutic process is consequently directed toward building the level of responsiveness associated with the emotional accessibility and emotional engagement of a secure attachment. Partners are helped to understand their dependence on one another in order to meet normal attachment needs and are encouraged to express emotions when the needs are thwarted. When they begin to establish a stable, more secure attachment bond in this relationship, the structures of the core self are strengthened. There is paradoxically less need to rely on the other as an external source of stability as autonomy and self expression follow.

We know that these efforts have been successful when partners not only re-discover each other, but also discover for the first time the needs and longings that brought them together in the first place. The goal of successful treatment of those who experienced trauma in their relationships is to recreate a narrative in which the person is not a victim, but the author of a new narrative, in which he or she is in control of events in life. Ultimately, the goal is to restore the normative growth of intimacy, empathy, understanding, healthy dependency, and connection. When this occurs, partners achieve a state of secure attachment with an ability to experience contentment, joyful intimacy, healthy self assertion, and resilliance to stressful situations.

References

Ainsworth, M. D. S., Blehar, M. C., Waters, E., & Wall, S. (1978). *Patterns of attachment: A psychological study of the strange situation*. Hillsdale, NJ: Erlbaum.

Alexander, F., & French, T. M. (1946). *Psychoanaltic therapy: Principles and application*. New York: Ronald Press. Reprint. Lincoln, University of Nebraska Press, 1980.

Bowlby, J. (1998). *A secure base: Parent-child attachment and healthy human development*. New York: Basic Books.

Cassedy, J., & Shaver P. (1999). *Hangbook of attachment*. New York: Guilford Press.

Courtois, C. (1988). *Healing the incest wound: Adult survivors in therapy*. New York: Norton.

Davila, J., Burge, D., & Hammen, C. (1997). Why does attachment style change? *Journal of Personality and Social Psychology, 73,* 826–838.

Dicks, H. V. (1967). *Marital tensions: Clinical studies towards a psychological theory of interaction*. London: Routledge.

Fosha, D. (2000). *The transforming power of affect: A model for accelerated change*. New York: Basic Books.

Freud, S. (1959). Remembering, repeating, and working through. In J. Strachey (Ed. & Trans.), *The standard edition of the complete psychological works of Sigmund Freud* (Vol. 12, p. 150). London: Hogarth Press. (Original work published 1911)

Gottman, J. M., & Hillsdale, M. J. (1994). *The relationship between marital processes and marital outcomes.* New York: Basic Books.

Gottman, J. M., & Silver, N. (1999). *The seven principles for making marriage work.* New York: Guilford Press.

Guidano, V. F., & Liotti, G. (1999). *Cognitive processes and emotional disorders.* New York: Guilford Press.

Harvey, M. (1996). An ecological view of psychological trauma and trauma recovery. *Journal of Traumatic Stress, 9,* 3–23.

Hazan, C., & Shaver, P. (1994). Attachment in and organizational framework for research on close relationships: Target article. *Psychological Inquiry, 5,* 1–22.

Hazan, C., & Shaver, P. (1987). Romantic love conceptualized as an attachment process. *Journal of Personality and Social Psychology, 52,* 511–524.

Hendrix, H. (1989). *Getting the love you want: A guide for couples.* New York: Random House.

Herman, J. L. (1992). *Trauma and recovery.* New York: Basic Books.

Johnsons, S. (1996). *Emotionally focused couple therapy with trauma survivors: Strengthening attachment bonds.* New York: Guilford Press.

Johnson, S. M. (2001). *Creating connection: The practice of emotionally focused marital therapy.* New York: Brunner/Mazel.

Johnson, S. M. (2002). *Emotionally focused therapy with trauma survivors: Strengthening attachment bonds.* New York: Guilford Press.

Kahn, M. (1963). Cumulative trauma. *Psychoanalytic Study of the Child, 18,* 286–306.

Kirkpatrick, L. E., & Davis, K. E. (1994). Attachment style, gender and relationship stability: A longitudinal analysis. *Journal of Personality and Social Psychology, 66,* 502–512.

Kohut, H. (1984). *How does analysis cure?* Chicago: University of Chicago Press.

Liotti, G. (1999). Disorgantization of Attachment as a Model for Understanding dissociatve Psychopathology. In J. Solomon & C. George (eds.), *Attachment disorganization,* (291–317). New York: Guilford Press.

Main, M. (2002, March). *The history of attachment.* Paper presented at "Attachment: from Early Childhood Through the Lifespan." Los Angeles.

Main, M., & Hesse, E. (1990). Parent's unresolved traumatic experiences are related to infant disorganized status: Is frightened and/or frightening parental behavior the linking mechanism? In M. T. Greenburg, D. Cicchetti, & E. M. Cummings (Eds.), *Attachment in the preschool years: Theory, research, and intervention* (pp. 161–182). Chicago: University of Chicago Press.

McCann, I. L., & Pearlman, L. (1990). *Psychological trauma and the adult survivor.* New York: Brunner/Mazel.

Miller, A. (1981). *Prisoners of childhood.* New York: Basic Books.

Neborsky, R., & Solomon, M. (2001). Attachment bonds and intimacy in Solomon, M., Neborsky, R. *Can the primary imprint of love change? Short-term therapy for long-term change?* New York: Norton.

Scharff, D., & Scharff, J. (1987). *Object relations family therapy.* Hillsdale, NJ: Jason Aronson.

Schore, A. N. (1994). *Affect regulation and the origin of the self: The neurobiology of emotional development.* Hillsdale, NJ: Erlbaum.

Schore, A. N. (1998). The experience-dependent maturation of an evaluative system in the cortex. In K. H. Pribram & J. King (Eds.), *Brain and values: Is a biological science of values possible?* (pp. 337–358). Mahwah, NJ: Erlbaum.

Schore, A. N. (in press). Clinical implications of a neurobiological model of projective identification. In S. Alhanati (Ed.), *Primitive mental states, Vol III. Pre- and peri-natal influneces on personality development.* New York: ESF Publishers.

Shapiro, F. (1999) *EMDR: The breakthrough therapy for overcoming anxiety, stress, and trauma.* New York: Basic Books.

Shapiro, F. (2001). *Eye movement desensitization and reprocessing: Basic principles, protocols, and procedures.* New York: Guilford Press.

Siegel, D. J. (1995). Memory, trauma, and psychotherapy: A cognitive science view. *Journal of Psychotherapy Practice and Research, 44,* 93–122.

Siegel, D. J. (1999). *The developing mind.* New York: Guilford Press.

Solomon, M. F. (1992). *Narcissism and intimacy: Love and marriage in an age of confusion.* New York: Norton.

Solomon, M. F. (1994). *Lean on me: The power of positive dependence in intimate relationships.* New York: Simon & Schuster.

Solomon, M. F. (2001). Breaking the deadlock of marital collusion in marital collusion. In M. F. Solomon, R. J. Neborsky, M. Alpert, F. Schapiro, & D. Malin (Eds.), *Short-term therapy for long-term change* (130–154). New York: Norton.

Solomon, M. F., Neborsky, R. J., McCullough, L., Alpert, M., Shapiro, F., & Malin, D. (2001). *Short term-therapy for long-term change.* New York: Norton.

Sroufe, A. (1996). *Emotional development: The organization of emotional life in the early years.* Cambridge, U.K.: Cambridge University Press.

Tronick, E. Z. (1989). Emotions and emotional communication in infants. *American Psychologist, 44,* 112–119.

Index

347